William Lill
The Last Magic

Astrologer and Adept

William Lilly: The Last Magician Astrologer and Adept

Being his autobiography and an anthology

Edited and introduced by
Peter Stockinger
and
Sue Ward

Foreword by David Conway

Mandrake

First Edition

Also published by Mandrake
A German Stargazer's Book of Astrology (*Astronomia Teutsch Astronomei 1545*)
Peter Stockinger (Translator & Editor); Sue Ward (Foreword)

Contents

Foreword

Many years ago when working in London I regularly took the tube from Aldwych station in The Strand to Temple station on the Thames Embank ment. (A shuttle service, little used and expensive to run, it was suspended in 1994.) One day as we waited at Aldwych for the lift to convey us to the platform, a colleague asked if I was familiar with the history of the place. Now, I knew there was a Roman bath nearby, one sightseers today can visit free of charge, but this wasn't what he had in mind. No, he continued, on this spot three hundred years earlier had stood the home of William Lilly, once the foremost astrologer in England. Indeed, Lilly had plied his trade there - at half-a-crown a time. Half-a-crown was a tidy sum in those days.

This last detail I came across because my informant, knowing I was Welsh, had gone on to add that a compatriot of mine, a clergyman named John Evans, had been Lilly's first mentor. It made me curious to learn more about them both.

In the event I learned very little about Mr Evans and that only what his pupil disclosed in his autobiography the *Life of William Lilly*. There he recounts how Evans once conducted a seance at his home in Gunpowder Alley, part of what's now known as the City, for two well-to-do clients, Lord Bothewell and Sir Kenelm Digby, only to find himself carried off *in media res* by mischievous spirits and dumped in a field over the river in Battersea. His misadventure neatly anticipates what happened in 1871 to a medium named Mrs. Guppy, her stoutness matched by her dishonesty, who was whisked away from her bedroom in Highgate, clad only in her shift, and dumped on a table around which a number of people were conducting a seance. This was in Lamb's Conduit Street, Holborn, a good seven miles from Mrs. Guppy's house in Highgate. William Lilly, one suspects, would never have allowed the spirits to manhandle him in such an undignified way.

He was far too clever for that. Deprived of a place in Cambridge because of his father's indigence, he set off on foot from Diseworth in Leicestershire to London, becoming a kind of factotum to Gilbert Wright, Master of a Livery Company and owner of the house in the Strand. When Wright died in 1627 Lilly married his widow

a few months later. And that was how the property came to be his. It was, as I've explained, how I got to hear of him on my way home from the office.
What became clear when I discovered more about Lilly - Mr. Evans soon dropped out of the picture - was that for him astrology had to do with the real world, the world each of us inhabits. As such its workings are in a sense "natural" rather than "supernatural", even if, by their very character, they remain exempt from normal scientific investigation. After reading this book you will better understand why.

Nowadays it is fashionable to dismiss astrology as an outmoded superstition, a pseudo-science discredited by those who are committed to the real thing. As its opponents disdainfully point out, even the celestial events it describes - and presumes to interpret - have no connection with what's going on in the sky, let alone with us and the busy world we live in.

At this point William Lilly would probably put down his quill pen and ask what do we mean by "reality"? Have we, he might persist, any way of defining it? And, being ourselves part of it, what equips us even to try?

For to him and others like him, manifested reality was both One and Many. Or, rather, it is One expressing itself through the Many that comprise it. That we routinely overlook this implicit oneness, while aware of its myriad components, happens because our perception is limited to what our senses equip us to discover. As Plato famously put it, we perceive the shadows within the cave we occupy, but not the figures walking past the entrance that are the cause of them. And if Plato - or astrologers like Lilly for that matter - strike you as somewhat dated, then think instead of the growing acceptance within quantum physics of an "absolute" reality, composed of abstract symmetries and dwelling outside space and time. It is in this underlying "oneness" that astrology finds its justification.

In that "oneness" and, no less important, in the interconnectedness of its constituent parts. To understand this, we need to remind ourselves that the things which make up the world about us, though subject to change and causality, remain integrated within a single Whole. It was, I think, Heraclitus who summed it up as "all things are in all", a statement echoed by the Neoplatonists, most notably Plotinus (who, as it happens, was a critic of the astrology popular in his day). Plotinus famously declared that "the whole is in All, as well as in every part", a notion embraced by German philosophers of the 19th Century and by Hegel in particular. The latter described the Absolute as the ultimate form of Unity, one whose parts have no meaning other than their Unity, while that Unity has no meaning other than its parts. Astrologers had worked that out long before he did.

And this antiquity is what inclines me to believe that traditional astrology, the type described in this book and involving only seven planets, is more dependable (and thus more useful) than its modern equivalent. The latter takes into account not just the original five planets, as well as the sun and the moon, but also relative newcomers like Uranus (1781) and Pluto (1930), not to mention a johnny-come-lately like Chiron (1970). Also in the queue, indeed already gaining acceptance, are the so-called "dwarf" planets such as Charon (one of Pluto's moons), Ceres, Eris, Haumea and Makemake, the last few inhabiting what's known as the Kuyper Belt. No, in astrology, as in oenology, it's safe to say that new wine in old bottles is less reliable than vintage.

And reliable our old friend Lilly and others like him must have been. After all, their livelihood, as much as their reputation, depended on it. And whereas many contemporary astrologers, not least those keen to welcome Chiron, Ceres, Eris *et al* into the fold, tend to favour what I call a "psychological" approach to their craft, striving to analyse in depth the character or motivation of their subjects, more traditional astrologers - the term Neo-Renaissance might describe them - concern themselves with more immediate problems and more practical concerns, albeit - and this cannot be stressed enough - without losing sight of the psychological elements that inform our behaviour, as well as that of others connected to us or to the situation we find ourselves in.

The merit of this book is that it provides the reader, believer and sceptic alike, with all the information he or she needs to understand and, better still, practise the subject it covers. It does so without fuss and without exaggeration. I am confident my friend William Lilly would have liked it.
I hope you do too.

David Conway
Machynlleth
Wales
July 2014

William Lilly: Astrologer & Adept

> Stand fast, oh Man! To thy God and assured principles, then consider thy own nobleness, how all created things both present and to come, were for thy sake created; nay for thy sake God became Man: thou art that Creature, who being conversant with Christ, livest and raignest above the heavens, and sits above all power and authority.

William Lilly wrote these lines in a letter, entitled "To the Student in Astrology" prefacing his astrological textbook *Christian Astrology*. At the time of its publication in 1647 the English Civil War was in its fifth year, and Lilly was established politically as a Parliamentarian. Whilst the Civil War is often pictured as a religious war divided between the Protestant Parliamentarians and the Roman Catholic Royalists, it was not always as simple as that. Elias Ashmole, for example, eventually to become one of Lilly's closest friends and allies, was of the Church of England, but was also a committed Royalist who was an officer in Charles I's army. Lilly, too, was a Protestant who had been brought up to and educated in that religion. He remained a devout and ardent Christian throughout his life. This fact is made clear in the above quotation and in all of his writings and in his numerous acts of generosity. Yet, there are commentators in our time who look askance at Lilly's obvious devotion to his faith, cynically suggesting that his declarations were hollow and self-serving, hypocritical even. Elias Ashmole provides addenda to Lilly's *Life and Times* which clearly show Lilly's generosity both to the Parish of Walton on Thames and to those needing his medical services. Indeed, as an astrologer, too, his fees were gauged according to the means of his clients. If we accept that Lilly was truly devout, or even just suspend disbelief, many questions are answered for us relating to his astrological practise and his attitude towards the occult arts.

We can only speculate about his first encounters with folk magic during his early years spent in the countryside, but it seems reasonable to assume that he would have been exposed to the practices and superstitions common to most rural communities. What is certainly clear is that the urge to investigate these matters further occurred only after he had moved to London. He had arrived there in 1620 to be employed by the merchant Gilbert Wright, largely to compensate for Wright's illiteracy, but his tasks were varied and often menial. Lilly writes in his autobiography that Wright's wife, Marjory, was "very curious to know of such as wear then called Cunning or Wise men whether she should bury her husband? Shee frequently visited such persons, and this occasion begot in mee a little desire to learn something that way, but wanting money to buy books, I layd aside those notions, …" Marjory died in 1624, so we can place Lilly's nascent interest in the occult to between 1620 and 1624. He goes on to relate the stories she had told him about her encounters with magic and its practitioners, in particular, she was a frequent client of Simon Forman, the noted astrologer, physician and magician of the early 17th century. She details various talismans and amulets made by Forman, some of which were found and given to Lilly after her death. Her interest, quite naturally, was for personal ends, but Lilly's later interest was profound and, along with Ashmole, took it upon himself to collect and preserve Forman's papers.

Simon Forman was born on 30 December 1552. The *ODNB* entry concerning his life, (written by Stanley Lee), claims that Lilly's statement that Forman was the son of a chandler, and was born in Westminster, is untrue. Lee states that Forman was born in Quidhampton and that his father, William, served as page to Lady Willoughby. After his father's death, Simon was left destitute and in 1573 made his way to Oxford and entered Magdalen College as a poor scholar. He left Oxford in 1574 and continued to travel until he finally set up residence in London in 1583 where he remained until his death in 1611. There he established himself as a doctor and astrologer. The authorities did not approve of his methods of making a living and, as a consequence, he found himself imprisoned several times. Nonetheless he managed to build up a lucrative practice. In 1588 he began to publicly practise necromancy and to call angels and spirits. A few years later he was summoned by the College of Physicians, interdicted from the practice of medicine and fined five pounds, but he continued his work undeterred. In 1594 he began alchemical experiments and published a book on magic. Although the authorities tried repeatedly to stop Forman from practising and imprisoned him several times, he continued his work supported by influential friends. It is said that Forman was particularly skilled in tracking thieves and finding stolen goods, but he was also famous for his ability to produce magic philters and love potions as well as astrological talismans. It is also known that Forman had an insatiable sexual appetite and therefore he engaged in affairs with nearly all the women he met through his astrological or medical practise. In his autobiography, Lilly dedicates a chapter to Forman, writing about him that he was "judicious" and "fortunate" in horary questions and that sickness (decumbitures) "was his masterpiece". He also had good success in marriage questions but in other questions he was "very moderate".

Clearly, the writings of such a successful practitioner would be of interest to Lilly and it would be quite reasonable to assume that he studied them closely and applied them.

It is clear that Lilly's Christian faith provided no barrier to his deep and abiding interest in the supernatural in all its forms and he was no less a Christian for that interest. It was not only his study and practise of astrology which needed to be squared with his religious beliefs, but also his practise of magic. We argue that there was no struggle for him, indeed for him magic and astrology were natural complements to his more orthodox spirituality. We make this point not only for its own sake and to cast light on Lilly's lesser known activities, but also for the modern practitioner who might believe Christianity and the occult to be mutually exclusive. Indeed, when to be a member of the Church was essential and expected, it might appear to the modern student impossible to marry the two. However, Lilly was not the only one to take this view: numerous educated and socially elevated men and clergymen were just as interested and applied themselves with just as much enthusiasm. None found any paradox or difficulty in this, there was no hypocrisy. Lilly argued this point for his entire life adhering to the view that astrology was "natural" and "rational".

We might usefully consider how he achieved this mystical combination and found neither contradiction nor heresy. We believe that during his time in Hersham, Lilly began to discover and appreciate the writings of Abbot Trithemius. Many years later, in 1647, he published his own translation of Trithemius' *De Septem Secundeis* as part of his pamphlet *The World's Catastrophe.* It seems reasonable to deduce that his study of Trithemius led him to the embrace the Neoplatonist as well as the hermetic thought complex of Christian occultists like Marsilio Ficino or Heinrich Cornelius Agrippa of Nettesheim. The article *William Lilly and the Soul of the World*, included in this anthology, explores the worldview of the Renaissance Platonist shared by Lilly. Ficino, who took many of his ideas from the *prisca theologia* tradition, tried to stretch the boundaries of orthodox Christian practice by introducing seemingly heterodox rituals. He particularly dealt with this subject in the third part of his *De Vita*, and we can assume that Lilly agreed with his views because he included it in *Christian Astrology's* bibliography. Ficino's first important translation was the *Corpus Hermeticum*, and many of the ideas he discovered therein found their way into *De Vita*. Dame Frances Yates observes in her *Giordano Bruno and the Hermetic Tradition* that the third part of *De Vita* was not a commentary on Plotinus, but rather an extensive exegesis of Hermes as found in the *Asclepius*. What we also have to bear in mind here is the fact that throughout his entire life Ficino, who was ordained a priest at the age of 40 years, attempted to merge Christianity and Platonism. In his major work the *Theologia Platonica*, he tried to show how his version of Christianity could be discovered in the Platonist's theories.

This leads us to another very important facet of Lilly's philosophy. Most of the astrologers of the 16th and 17th centuries subscribed to the theory of astral determinism; in other words they believed in an unchangeable fate predicted by the stars. That this notion brought them into constant conflict with the church fathers is well-known and contributes to the notion that the Church, Christianity and the occult were incompatible. Lilly's ideas on the subject were of a different nature, which can be seen in the frontispiece of *Christian Astrology*. Here Lilly is depicted holding a piece of parchment showing an empty square chart inscribed with the words *Non Cogunt*, which stands for *agunt, non cogunt*, "[the stars] incline, they do not compel". This philosophy is straight out of Ficino who wrote in the second volume of his *Theologia Platonica* that the decrees of the intelligences are shown through the stars, *per signa potius quam per causas* ("through signs rather than causes"). Lilly provides us with a wonderful quotation in his pamphlet *Annus Tenebrosus* expressing his fondness for Marsilio Ficino and reiterating his belief in free will:

> And Ficinus, that excellent learned Priest, saith … Many accidents are signified or foreseen by the Stars, which are not done in Heaven. And again … Many things are foretold by means of the Heavenly bodies, as it were by signe, not by causes. … The opinion of this man I esteem more than of a thousand of our own Priests, who blame Astrology because it's above their capacity. (p23)

Remembering Frances Yates' comment regarding Ficino and Plotinus, mentioned above, we find Lilly's agreement expressed in his first published almanac *Angelicus Merlin Junior* from 1644. Here Lilly writes: *I have ever loathed fatall necessity, supposed by* Plotinus *to be maintained by* Ptolomy;... In this regard, Lilly makes a very interesting remark in *Christian Astrology* wherein he explains his point of view very simply.

> ... or for those who would carefully in a natural way prevent those casualties their natures or inclinations would run them into. (p.143)

Determinism is found in the nature of the individual and in the events caused by their reaction to circumstances, but such situations can be avoided and thus changed by the individual. So, the apparent predestiny of life lies within the character of each person; with effort that predestiny can be, at least, flexible. We see that for Lilly free will and determinism were not mutually exclusive, just as the Greeks suggested through their differentiation between *ananke* (inevitable fate) and *heimarmene* (negotiable fate). Embracing this philosophy, Lilly shows that he is adhering to the hermetic as well as Neoplatonic notion of betterment through work on the self leading to increased spiritual awareness. In Lilly's view, fate does not have to be inevitable and can be negotiated which, of course, would have a deep impact on both his astrological method as it would on his magical operations. For him, fate exists solely within the nature of the individual human being, and the apparent fixity of the birth chart becomes wholly fluid and malleable, conditional only on the exertion of effort by the individual.

Lilly's main occupation as an astrologer can also be seen as the mundane expression of his beliefs. As we have already seen, Renaissance Neoplatonism, which drew heavily on hermeticism, and especially Ficino's cosmology, agree entirely with the first principles of astrology. In traditional thought, the cosmos was a hierarchy with God at the top, and often described as a chain. Every entity or being had its own assigned place; descending from the highest and the highest degree of perfection, were angels, planets and elementals, followed by various species of animals, plants and minerals. Here Ficino re-introduced the Platonic concept of the *World Soul* into this static system, always with diminishing levels of perfection in the descending order. As part of his new model, Ficino suggested that all the elements of the chain were connected by active forces of an all-penetrating spirit, the Anima Mundi.

Ficino also taught that astrology was an essential part of this natural system of mutual influences. The practical use of this model can be found in numerous lists of correspondences which have been relied upon by occultists ever since.

His shift from the folk magic of his early life to the more complex practises of Forman and his like, and then further still into the deeply mystical philosophy of his later life which had informed his astrological work for so long, might be explained through his being on the crest of the wave of the occult revival of the period. This revival which drew to it the educated practitioner and is referred to as 'learned magic', far removed from the folk magic of Lilly's childhood.

Since a reliable biography has never been written[1], we must rely on Lilly's own memoirs and other writings in order to garner an accurate image of the man. Certainly, in terms of his magical activities and prowess, we have meagre resources. In this anthology, we attempt to demonstrate Lilly's Hermetic inclinations and practises. The evidence is scant and speculation and opinion are invoked in order to form a conclusion, but in order to reach this point there has been much close reading of Lilly's lesser works, most notably his annual publications which seem rarely to have been examined in any detail. What we deduce from the information available is that, over the years, Lilly's magical thinking matured and deepened so that he became a leading practitioner. We take this view partly based on his social position, in that he was held in high regard by his peers and superiors alike. The respect which was shown to him by all classes of people, but particularly the educated classes, speaks of someone in a leadership position. This position may well have been within a relatively small group, although not solely astrologers. From the way in which the contention caused by John Gadbury unfolded and resolved, we can clearly see a group of people drawing closely around Lilly. ...

The year of 1632 seems to represent a turning point or milestone in Lilly's career as astrologer and magician, but such situations do not come out of nowhere and we must seek the ground upon which the seed was sown. Lilly

---

[1]For a detailed analysis of the available publications, see our investigation, *Monster of Ingratitude*.

had clearly made a good impression on the Wrights given the trust they placed in him and, following his wife's death, Wright awarded an annual allowance of twenty shillings to Lilly which remained in place at least until Lilly wrote his *Life and Times.* His life became more comfortable and in 1625 his responsibilities increased when his employer left London to escape the plague, but this also left him with more time to indulge his own interests in play and in music. Wright had remarried and in 1627 Lilly had married Wright's widow, kept secret for three years because of the anticipated opposition of her family. This turned out to be a well-founded suspicion because several law suits by the family followed.

Lilly was married for only six years before he himself was widowed and during that time he had paid close attention to his much older wife. He seems to have socialized little in those years, but we must assume that having now time and money to spare he bought those books he had desired during his employment by Gilbert Wright. We make that assumption based on events noted in *Life and Times* and the speed of his magical development in the very few years following. He managed to find Forman's student and friend, and inheritor of Forman's library and papers, Dr. Richard Napier. Such investigations and research as were needed to reach this point must have taken place during his marriage to the seemingly possessive Ellen. We find evidence of this in his remark in his *Life and Times* that he spent time with Richard Napier and where he writes that he visited Napier from time to time in 1632 or 1633 (that is, before the death of his wife). Furthermore, "… he had me upp into his Library, being excellently furnished with very choice books, …", and we can reasonably assume that among those books were those having belonged to Simon Forman since Napier had inherited them all. This exposure to Forman's work and library would have reinforced Lilly's earlier ambition to study the occult.

Fortune also worked in Lilly's favour because around this time he was given a number of papers and artefacts from which, Ashmole notes in his annotations, preserved in the autograph of the autobiography, Lilly gained his "first knowledge" of the occult arts. His earliest astrological studies began in 1632 when he also began to investigate those who professed to be astrologers wanting "to discover in whose hands and in what condition astrology then was". Most of those he visited were also involved with the occult often involving the summoning of spirits and, according to Lilly, mostly failing to do so. From this we can deduce that astrology and the occult arts were often practised by the same people suggesting that both subjects were seen in the same light and also suggesting that they had popular appeal.

In 1634 Lilly purchased *Ars Notoria*, and he acknowledges that he used one of the prayers in that book to help him with his astrological studies. The prayers contained within *Ars Notoria* are generally considered to be Christianized invocations and so we see Lilly's early application of magical theory. We might also suspect that success resulted from his efforts because during 1634 he already felt confident enough to teach Sir George Peckham astrology, or at least "that part which concerns sickness, wherein hee so profited that, within 2 or 3 months hee would give a very true discovery of any disease; onely by his figures."

Included in this present volume, is, inevitably, Lilly's *Life and Times* to which we refer frequently, but also a previously unpublished work: Lilly's judgement of the nativity of Sir William Wittypoole. This has been added partly to demonstrate that there is still a wealth of material to be discovered and published, but also to offer an example of the man at work in the privacy of the client relationship.

Added to these pieces is our investigation into the so-called enmity between Lilly and John Gadbury which most commentators refer to as a matter of professional rivalry. Again, the lack of an accurate biography has led to a proliferation of this misapprehension and our aim was to correct that and show the facts. It is within that essay that it becomes clear that Lilly's social standing exceeded that of his social class. Within this we find some ground for our assertion that Lilly was closely involved with others of a similar bent in some secrecy. We also suggest that, as with his student Humphreys, Lilly had refused to teach Gadbury his magical method. Gadbury, as was his custom, would have been entirely affronted and took that affront into print.

To the Student in Astrology

My Friend, whoever you are, that with so much ease shall receive the benefit of my hard Studies, and does intend to proceed in this heavenly knowledge of the Stars, wherein the great and admirable works of the invisible and alglorious God are so manifestly apparent. In the first place, consider and admire your Creator, and be thankful unto him, be you humble, and let no natural knowledge, how profound and transcendent soever it be, elate your minde to neglect that divine Providence, by whose all-seeing order and appointment, all things heavenly and earthly, have their constant motion;but the more your knowledge is enlarged, the more do you magnifie the power and wisdom of Almighty God, and strive to preserve your self in his favour; being confident, the more holy you are; and more neer to God, the purer Judgment you shall give. Beware of pride and self-conceit, and remember how that long ago, no irrationall Creature dared offend Man, the Microcosm; but did faithfully serve and obey him, so long as he was master of his own Reason and Passions, or until he subjected his Will to the unreasonable part. But alas! When iniquity abounded, and man gave the reins to his own affection, and deferred reason, then every Beast, Creature and outward harmful thing, became rebellious and unserviceable to his command. Stand fast, oh man! to your God, and assured principles, then consider your own nobleness, how all things created, both present and to come, were for your sake created; no for your sake God became Man: you are that Creature, who being conversant with Christ, lives and reigns above the heavens, and sits above all power and authority. How many pre-eminences, advantages has God bestowed on you? you range above the heavens by contemplation, conceive the motion and magnitude of the stars; you talk with Angels, yes with God himself; you have all creatures under your dominion, and keep the Devils in subjection: Do not then for shame deface your nature, or make yourself unworthy of such gifts, or deprive yourself of that great power, glory and blessedness God has allotted you, by casting from you his fear, for possession of a few imperfect pleasures. Having considered your God, and what you yourself are, during your being Gods servant; now receive instruction how in your practice I would have you carry yourself. As you daily converse with the heavens, so instruct and form your mind according to the image of Divinity; learn all the ornaments of vertue, be sufficiently instructed therein; be humane, curteous, familiar to all, easie of access, afflict not the miserable with terror of harsh judgment; in such cases, let them know their hard fate by degrees; direct them to call on God to divert his judgments impending over them: be modest, conversant with the learned, civil, sober man, covet not an estate; give freely to the poor, both money and judgment: let no worldly wealth procure an erroneous judgment from you, or such that may dishonour the Art, or this divine Science: Love good men, cherish those honest men that cordially Study this Art: Be sparing in delivering Judgment against the Common-wealth you live in. Give not judgment of the death of your Prince; yet I know experimentally, that Reges subjacent legibus Stellarum[2], marry a wife of your own, rejoyce in the number of your friends, avoid law and controversie: in your study be totus in illis[3] that you may be singulus in arte[4]; be not extravagant or desirous to learn every Science, be not aliquid in omnibus[5]; be faithful, tenacious, betray no ones secrets, no, no I charge you never divulge either friend or enemies trust committed to your faith. Instruct all men to Live well, be a good example yourself, avoid the fashion of the times, love your own Native Country: exprobrate no man, no not an enemy: be not dismaid, if ill spoken of, Conscientia mille testes[6]; God suffers no sin unpunished, no lye unrevenged. (Lilly, *Christian Astrology*)

[2]Kings are subject to the laws of the stars

[3]all you can be

[4]singular in skill

[5]knowing a little of everything – a jack of all trades

[6]Conscience is [equivalent to] a thousand witnesses

Anima Mundi

William Lilly and the Soul of the World

On June, 11th 1647, William Lilly concludes the second part of his epic textbook, *Christian Astrology*. Preparing himself and the reader for the third instalment, the *Tractat of Nativities*, he states:

> Assist me O glorious God, for my task is difficult, and thy servant is of little understanding! Few, nay none at all are the helps I expect from any man living (having hitherto had no assistance) but what thy pleasure is, by the universal Anima Mundi, to infuse into my obtuse intellective part that will I candidly deliver without deceit or fraud; (*CA* p486)

By writing these lines and so sharing his hopes and prayers with the reader, William Lilly provides us with a deep insight into his world view and his belief system. From his point of view those two were intrinsically intertwined and inseparable. Born in 1602, Lilly lived on the threshold between the fading era of the Renaissance Magi, Alchemists and Rosicrucians and the first manifestations of the age of reason, which may be typified by the founding of the Royal Society in 1660. To gain a better understanding of his views and to be able to put them into a wider context, it seems appropriate to cast our eyes towards the roots of the tradition Lilly was steeped in. We may begin this by finding out more about the Anima Mundi.

The Soul of the World, originally called *Psyche tou Kosmou*, came to be known in Europe as Anima Mundi. It was first described by Plato in his *Timaeus*, wherein he states that the Soul of the World would be inherent in the whole of the cosmos; the reason for this would be the fact that the Demiurge, Plato's creator-god, had placed it there. This indicates that the cosmos was seen as a living entity, with the Anima Mundi being both, immanent and transcendent, at the same time.

Marsilio Ficino, the famous physician and Platonizing philosopher of the Renaissance, wrote extensively about the Anima Mundi in the third part of his *De vita triplici*, written in 1489. This part of his work, called *Liber De vita coelitus comparanda*, or, "On Obtaining Life from the Heavens", mainly describes ways of attracting benevolent celestial influences which, in most cases, are planetary. Therein Ficino states:

> For according to the more ancient Platonists, from her reasons, the World-soul constructed in the heavens, besides the stars, figures, and such parts of them as are also themselves figures of a sort, and she impressed properties on all these. (*TBL* p245)

The frontispiece of Robert Fludd's *Utriusque Cosmi Maioris*, vol.1, Oppenheim 1617, provides us with a good example how this idea was envisaged:

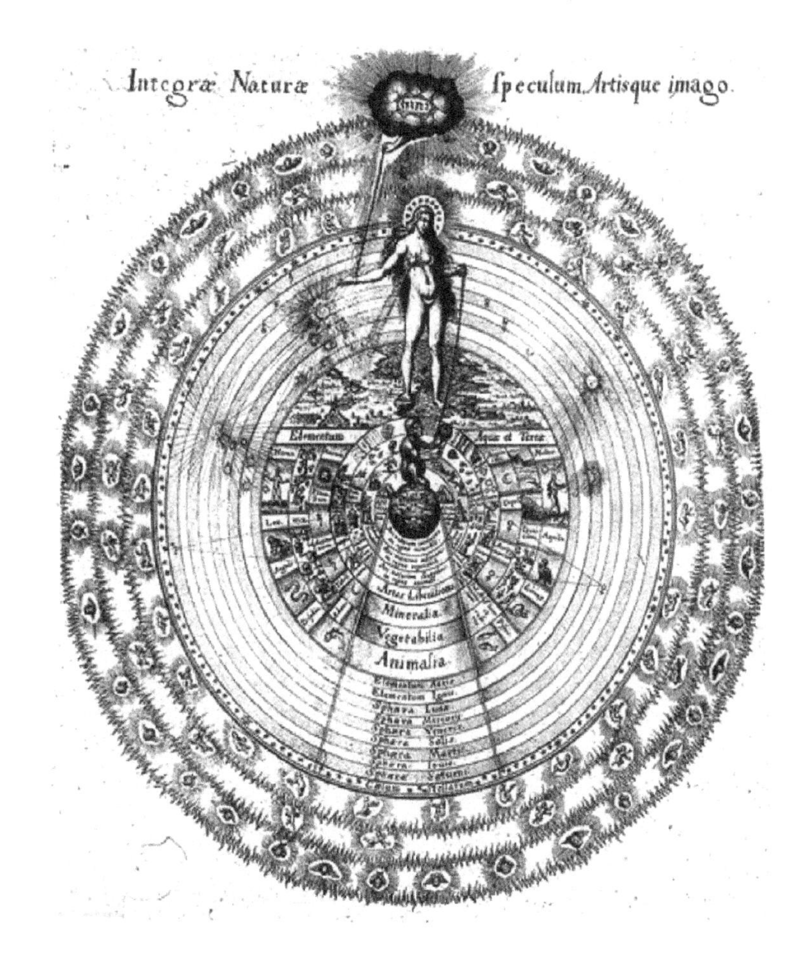

Nature, the mother of all things, depicted as a nude virgin, connects the heavens and the elemental world. She is the Soul of the World, as Fludd explains:

> On her breast is the true sun, on her belly is the moon, […] her heart gives the stars their light and her womb, the spirit of the

> moon, is the filter through which the astral influences reach the earth.

Robert Fludd, who lived between 1574 and 1637, was a respected London physician as well as a universal philosopher and prolific writer in the Neo-Platonist tradition. Fludd became involved in the search for Rosicrucians after the famous *Fama Fraternitatis* was published in 1614. He wrote in defence of their existence and wanted to be accepted into their brotherhood. William Lilly mentions him in his bibliography, appended to *Christian Astrology*:

> [...] and in several other pieces of his Works, has wrote much of Astrology, he may justly be accounted the mirror of our times, and of the Welsh Nation.

Through his statement that he would believe in the Anima Mundi, Lilly provides us with an important piece of information, enabling us to deliver proof of his Neo-Platonist view. This is further corroborated by the fact that he lists several important Neo-Platonic authors in his bibliography. Books on his library shelves included Ficino's *De Vita Triplici*, Paracelsus' *De Summis Naturae Mysteriis* and Cornelius Agrippa's *De Occulta Philosophia.* Although not included in the bibliography of *Christian Astrology*, which was published in 1647, we know that Lilly owned a copy of *Picatrix*, a work which was at the root of magical thinking in Western Europe. David Pingree provides interesting details in his critical Latin edition of *Picatrix*, stating:

> Manuscript M. London, British Library, Sloane 3679. 158 pp. Copied in the early seventeenth century. [...] The manuscript is probably a copy of that acquired by Richard Napier (or Sandy) (1559-1634) of Great Linford. Buckinghamshire, from Simon Forman (1552-1611) in 1599 or shortly thereafter. It was inherited by his nephew, Sir Richard Napier (1607-1676), in 1634, and he, according to a note written by Elias Ashmole (1617-1692) on p. 158, gave it to William Lilly (1602-1681): 'This book was given to Mr Lilly by sr Richard Napier. & I exchanged with him for another of the same written in quarto. E. A.'(*Picatrix*, pxix)
>
> Manuscript N. London. British Library, Sloane 1302. 153 ff. This is probably the manuscript in quarto that Ashmole gave to Lilly in

> exchange for M, and this gift is probably that recorded by Ashmole as having taken place on 5January 1648. (*Picatrix*, pxx)

Another work of interest is Johannes Trithemius' *De Septum Secundeis*, which was first printed in 1508. Lilly translated it and published it as part of his *The World's Catastrophe*, in 1647. We will hear more about this text later on.

Let us first return to Robert Fludd's statement that the "...] heart [of the virgin, which is the Anima Mundi] gives the stars their light and her womb, the spirit of the moon, is the filter through which the astral influences reach the earth." Here we enter the realm of celestial magic which has to be seen as a sub-form of magia naturalis, or white magic. This is diametrically opposed to goetia, or black magic, which does endanger the operator's soul through engagement with bad daemons. That Lilly was familiar with this term can be shown by a quote from the introductory chapter of *Christian Astrology*:

> ...] without exact knowledge hereof, one cannot attaine to any exactnesse in naturall Magick, viz. in gathering Hearbs, or perfecting many other rarities. (CA, p93)

In his *De Vita Triplici*, Ficino gives explanation how the Anima Mundi is making it possible to work celestial or astral magic:

> ...] The World-soul possesses by divine powers precisely as many seminal reasons of things as there are Ideas in the Divine Mind. By these seminal reasons she fashions the same number of species in matter. That is why every single species corresponds through its own seminal reason to its own idea and oftentimes through this reason it can easily receive something from the idea – since indeed it was made through the reason from the idea.[...] And if in proper manner you bring to bear on a species, or on some individual in it, many things which are dispersed but which conform to the same idea, into this material suitably adapted you will soon draw a particular gift from the idea, through the seminal reason of the Soul. (*TBL* p243)

This way of thinking is, of course, rooted in the Hermetic teachings. As G.R.S. Mead points out rightly in his groundbreaking work *Thrice Greatest*

Hermes, it was Ficino who translated the Trismegistic Sermons as early as 1471.

An interesting point worth mentioning is that from this text we can recognise the roots of the underlying principle known to astrologers as the teaching of 'essence'. This concept finds its manifestation in Lilly's table of essential dignities

A table of the essential Dignities of the *Planets* according to *Ptolemy*.

Signs.	Houses of the Planets.		Exaltation.		Triplicity of the Plan.		The Terms of the Planets										The Faces of the Planets.						Detriment.	Fall.
					Di.	Noc.																		
♈	♂	D	☉	19	☉	♃	♃	6	♀	14	☿	21	♂	26	♄	30	♂	10	☉	20	♀	30	♀	♄
♉	♀	N	☽	3	♀	☽	♀	8	☿	15	♃	22	♄	26	♂	30	☿	10	☽	20	♄	30	♂	
♊	☿	D	☊	3	♄	☿	☿	7	♃	14	♀	21	♄	25	♂	30	♃	10	♂	20	☉	30	♃	
♋	☽	N D	♃	15	♂	♂	♂	6	♃	13	☿	20	♀	27	♄	30	♀	10	☿	20	☽	30	♄	♂
♌	☉	N D			☉	♃	♄	6	☿	13	♀	19	♃	25	♂	30	♄	10	♃	20	♂	30	♄	
♍	☿	N	☿	15	♀	☽	☿	7	♀	13	♃	18	♄	24	♂	30	☉	10	♀	20	☿	30	♃	♀
♎	♀	D	♄	21	♄	☿	♄	6	♀	11	♃	19	☿	24	♂	30	☽	10	♄	20	♃	30	♂	☉
♏	♂	N			♂	♂	♂	6	♃	14	♀	21	☿	27	♄	30	♂	10	☉	20	♀	30	♀	☽
♐	♃	D	☋	3	☉	♃	♃	8	♀	14	☿	19	♄	25	♂	30	☿	10	☽	20	♄	30	☿	
♑	♄	N	♂	28	♀	☽	♀	6	☿	12	♃	19	♂	25	♄	30	♃	10	♂	20	☉	30	☽	♃
♒	♄	D			♄	☿	♄	6	☿	12	♀	20	♃	25	♂	30	♀	10	☿	20	☽	30	☉	
♓	♃	N	♀	27	♂	♂	♀	8	♃	14	☿	20	♂	26	♄	30	♄	10	♃	20	♂	30	☿	☿

Practitioners of traditional astrology should be aware that the doctrine of essential dignities is in fact based on Hermetic and Neo-Platonic thinking. But let us look at Ficino's interpretation, as he continues in his own words:

> Always remember, though, that just as the power of our soul is brought to bear on our members through the spirit, so the force of the World-soul is spread under the World-soul through all things through the quintessence, which is active everywhere, as the spirit inside the World's Body, but that this power is instilled especially into those things which have absorbed the most of this kind of spirit. (*TBL* p247)

Here we are reminded of another important author, Heinrich Cornelius Agrippa von Nettesheim. We have already established that Lilly owned an English translation of *De Occulta Philosophia* and have shown elsewhere that he used some of its contents in his own work, *Christian Astrology*. Agrippa collected the wisdom of the wise ones and magicians who came before him and compiled this knowledge in unprecedented form in his magnum opus. A close study of his *Three Books on Occult Philosophy* reveals that his views are built on Neo-Platonic thinking. The world, according to Agrippa, is divided into three parts, namely the elemental, the heavenly and the spiritual part, whereby the lower part is always ruled by the higher one. Consequently a system of steps or links in a chain is built whereby the forces or energies pour out from the higher, more pure, unto the lower. This is represented in the teaching of the correspondences and Lilly devotes chapters VIII to XIV of his *Christian Astrology* to these. A typical Neo-Platonic chain of correspondences would include the appropriate angel, planet, element, animal, plant, metal and stone. For example the correspondences for Saturn are Cassiel – Saturn – air – cat, hare, mouse, dog, wolf, etc. – bearsfoot, wolf bane, hemlock, ferne, etc. – lead – loadstone, black stones.

This brings us to another interesting point which should be investigated. In his *Letter to the Student*, Lilly writes:

> ...] How many pre-eminences, advantages has God bestowed on you? you range above the heavens by contemplation, conceive the motion and magnitude of the stars; you talk with Angels, yes with God himself;

If we look at this quote in the light of Neo-Platonic doctrines, we can see that Lilly had taken on the idea of the steps or chains and applied it by creating an upwards leading chain, consisting of the stars, angels and God, being the highest instance. Lilly mentions angels and we find him writing about them in other places like his *Merlinus Anglicus* of 1676, where he states:

> ...] Nor are the Secundian Intelligences, viz. what Angels then governs, to be omitted in consideration, for the judging of future Events, as to search when he began his Dominion, and how many years since his Government; for there is a very great Mystery in this,

> Trithemius his mensuration of time in those matters doth excel all that I have seen.

Lilly translated Johannes Trithemius' *De Septem Secundeis* into English and published it as part of his *World's Catastrophe* in 1647. Trithemius' work describes "*the Seven Secondary Causes of the heavenly intelligences, governing the Orbes under God*", calling them angels or spirits of the planets. These were originally called daemons of the planets as a quote from Ficino's *Three Books on Life* shows:

> ...] if he employs things which pertain to such and such a star and daemon, he undergoes the peculiar influence of this star and daemon. [...] And he undergoes this influence not only through the rays of the star and the daemon themselves, but also through the very Soul of the World. For the reason of any star and daemon flourishes in her. (*TBL* p245)

Agrippa, who was heavily influenced by Trithemius, recorded them under this name in his *Three Books on Occult Philosophy*. It has to be noted that these daemons have nothing to do with the demons of later popular lore although the debate about the difference between angels and daemons and their role was raging between occultists and clerics with such intensity that it would lead us to far astray if we would try and wade into this discussion. In his *The Occult Sciences in the Renaissance*, Wayne Shumaker provides a clear if slightly simplistic definition stating:

> ...] These intelligences, as every contemporary reader would have known without explanation, are spiritual beings intermediate between God and men: In the Christian view angels, in the Neo-Platonic view daemons. (p113)

That Lilly saw them as intermediaries between God and men can be seen in this quote from *Christian Astrology*:

> If attaine the Philosopher's Stone? [...] but as it is all blessing beyond all blessings upon earth, so I hold, that it is given but to very few, and to those few rather by revelation of the good angels of God, than the proper industry of man. (*CA*, p442f)

In 1503, five years before he would publish *De Septem Secundeis*, Trithemius wrote a manuscript, *Calendarium naturale magicum*, which is kept in Vienna's national library; therein he shows drawings of the sigils attached to the names of these intelligences[7]. Fred Gettings lists them in his *Dictionary of Occult, Hermetic and Alchemical Sigils*:

PLANET	PLANETARY SPIRIT	PLANETARY ANGEL
JUPITER	BETHOR	ZACHARIEL
MARS	PHALEG	SAMUEL
MERCURY	OPHIEL	RAPHAEL
MOON	PHUL	GABRIEL
SATURN	ARATRON	ORIPHIEL
SUN	OCH	MICHAEL
VENUS	HAGITH	ANAEL

One can see that the names of the planetary angels are identical to those later used in *De Septem Secundeis.* But already in 1634 Lilly had an encounter with angels when he purchased a manuscript of the Ars Notoria. In his autobiography he writes:

> ...] One whole year and more I continued a widdower and followed my studys very hard, during which tyme a Scholler pawned unto mee for 40s. Ars Notoria, a large Volumn wrote in Parchment, with the names of those Angells and their Pictures which are thought and believed by Wise men to teach and instruct in all the 7 Liberall Sciences, and this is attained by observing elected Tymes and those prayers appropriated unto the severall Angells. I do ingeniously acknowledge, I used those prayers according to the form and direction prescribed for some weeks, using the word Astrologia for Astronomia, but of this no more. That Ars Notoria, inserted in the

[7]It has been suggested by Adam McLean that this MS would be wrongly attributed to Trithemius. For a full discussion of the subject, see *The Magical Calendar: A Synthesis of Magical Symbolism from the Seventeenth-Century Renaissance of Medieval Occultism*, translation and commentary by Adam McLean, Phanes Press 1994

latter end of Cornelius Agrippa signifyeth nothing, many of the prayers beeing not the same, nor is the Direction unto those prayers any thing considerable. (*Autobiography*, p41)

It has to be noted that Lilly is talking about Agrippa's *Opera Omnia*, published in two volumes, ca. 1620. Vol. 1 includes the spurious 4th book of *De occulta philosophia*, the *Ars Notoria* (by Apollonius, of Tyana), and other works by various authors. Later, in 1657, Robert Turner published his translation of *Ars Notoria*, apparently based on the version appended in *Opera Omnia.* But, as Lilly rightly states, both versions do not include the all important mystical drawings.

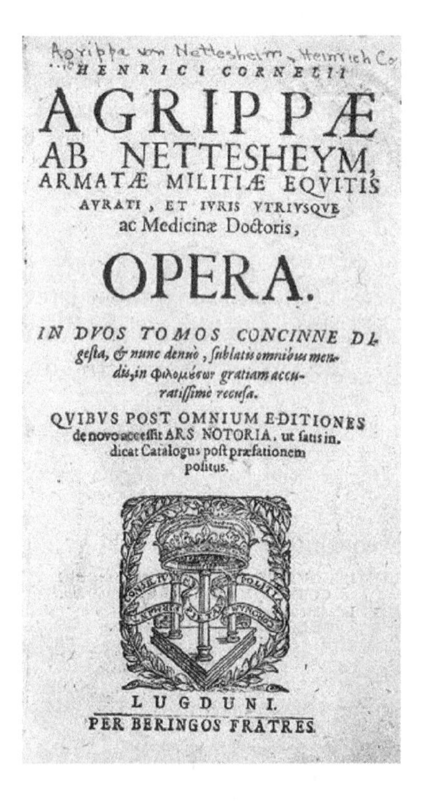
HENRICI CORNELII
AGRIPPÆ
AB NETTESHEYM,
ARMATÆ MILITIÆ EQVITIS
AVRATI, ET IVRIS VTRIVSQVE
ac Medicinæ Doctoris,
OPERA.
IN DVOS TOMOS CONCINNE DIgesta, & nunc denuò, sublatis omnibus mendis, in φιλομαθῶν gratiam accuratissimè recusa.
QVIBVS POST OMNIUM EDITIONES de novo accessit ARS NOTORIA, ut satis indicat Catalogus post præfationem positus.
LUGDUNI.
PER BERINGOS FRATRES.

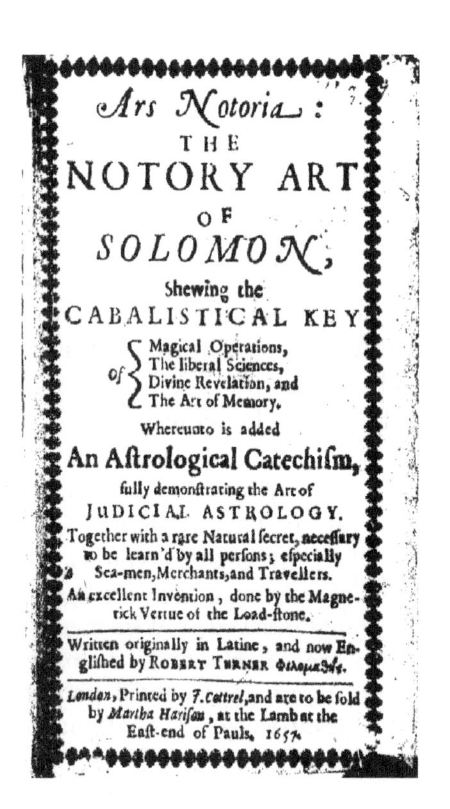
Ars Notoria:
THE
NOTORY ART
OF
SOLOMON,
Shewing the
CABALISTICAL KEY
of Magical Operations, The liberal Sciences, Divine Revelation, and The Art of Memory.
Whereunto is added
An Astrological Catechism,
fully demonstrating the Art of
JUDICIAL ASTROLOGY.
Together with a rare Natural secret, necessary to be learn'd by all persons; especially Sea-men, Merchants, and Travellers.
An excellent Invention, done by the Magnetick Vertue of the Load-stone.
Written originally in Latine, and now Englished by ROBERT TURNER Φιλομαθής.
London, Printed by J. Cottrel, and are to be sold by Martha Harison, at the Lamb at the East-end of Pauls, 1657.

There has always been doubt over the authorship of the fourth book of Agrippa and textual analysis undertaken by Will Erich Peuckert has shown beyond doubt that the fourth book of Agrippa was indeed written by a pseudo-Agrippa, an impostor.

Ars Notoria is a Grimoire of the so called "Salomonic Cycle" and closely related to *Liber Juratus*, sometimes called *Liber Sacratus*, another mediaeval Grimoire. In his A *History of Magic and Experimetal Science,* Thorndike devotes a whole chapter to Solomon and the *Ars Notoria*, writing:

> ...] This calls to mind the passage in The City of God where Augustine speaks of "incantations and formulae composed by an art of depraved curiosity which they either call magic or by the more detestable name goetia or by the honorable title theurgia. For they try to distinguish between these arts and condemn some men, whom the populace calls malefici, as devoted to illicit arts, for these, they say, are concerned with goetia; but others they want to make out praiseworthy as being engaged in theurgy. But they are both entangled in the deceptive rites of demons who masquerade under the names of angels."(vol2, p279ff)

Lilly experimented with the angels of the Ars Notoria and undertook several magical operations. The problems he encountered are mentioned in his autobiography where he states that he

> ...] grew weary of such imployments, and since have burned my bookes, which instructed those Curiositys: for after that, I became melancholly, very much afflicted with the Hypocondriack melancholly, growing lean and spare, and every day worse, so that in the year 1635, my infirmity continuing and my acquaintance increasing, I resolved to live in the country. (*Autobiography*, p43)

William Lilly might have burnt his books dealing with the darker, goetic side of magic and turned his back to conjurations and necromancy. But as the evidence of the books kept in his library and quotes from his *Christian Astrology* and other publications shows, he still was a firm believer in Hermetic and Neo-Platonic doctrines. Like many other Platonists before his time, he may have turned his daemons into angels but he still believed in the Anima Mundi. It has to be understood that without this foundation of natural magic the whole concept of his astrology would have collapsed. In his *Merlini Anglici ephemeris for 1651* we find a summary and fine amalgamation of his beliefs:

> ...] I feare not their bellowing or thundering against me or Astrology, I seek God in his own words, wherein I find no Envy,

> Malice, self-ends, domineering, rebellion against Superiors, or Lording it over tender Consciences commanded, or checking the spirit of any upon whom his holy spirit breaths: In the Gospel of Jesus Christ, I find sweet perswasions, most heavenly directions, that all our Actions be performed with love, charity, meekness, submission and obedience to powers and Authority, sith they are ordained by God." (p A3)

Bibliography:

Autobiography: *The Life of William Lilly student in Astrology, wrote by himselfe in the 66th year of his age, at Hersham in the parish of Walton uppon Thames in the county of Surrey : propria manu.* Transcribed from the autograph by Sue Ward with annotations, commentaries and biographical notes, including Elias Ashmole's addenda, 1998 & 2009.

CA: William Lilly, *Christian Astrology*, Regulus edition, London 1985

TBL: *Marsilio Ficino, Three Books on Life*, critical edition by Carol Kaske and John Clark, Arizona, 1998

Picatrix: *The Latin Version of Ghayat Al-Hakim*, edited by David Pingree, Warburg Institute, London, 1986

The Life of William Lilly student in Astrology,

wrote by himselfe in the 66th year of his age, at Hersham

in the parish of Walton uppon Thames in the county of Surrey : propria manu.

Transcribed from the autograph
by Sue Ward

with annotations, commentaries and biographical notes,

including Elias Ashmole's addenda.

Nativities of some notable persons appended.

Preface

Lilly's "Life" is more a series of anecdotes, or after-dinner stories, than an autobiography. Yet these are points in his life which Lilly thought important to recount. Clearly, this recounting is done largely to satisfy his friend Elias Ashmole, and we see this in his directly addressing Ashmole throughout the body of the work, not just in the dedication.

The information Lilly provides seems to fall into roughly two categories: that relating to his public life, and that relating to his interest in magic and occult matters generally. In this we see again that it is in reference to Ashmole that he includes this material. There is very little of his personal life to be found, and this was probably because Lilly intended that his "Life" should be published.[8] To this day, we know very little about his domestic life, although a picture can be pieced together from his letters to Ashmole (*Notes*) which relate to the latter part of his life after he had settled permanently in Hersham.

In both cases it appears that Lilly is taking this opportunity to tell his side of the story, and he does so in some detail. The importance to him of these matters is evidenced by the amount of that detail he recalls, even to what was said and by whom. Possibly he kept a journal, but none has been found.

To the casual reader, the frequent mention of the acquisition of private libraries and papers, or their ownership and whereabouts, must seem unusual in the context of an autobiography. One is tempted to deduce a conceit on Lilly's part: in addressing his audience, he wants them to know of his involvement in these rather important and scholarly matters. Perhaps even his reference to Ashmole's possession of such documents and books can be viewed in the same way. This explanation is more alluring when we read some of Lilly's remarks concerning the libraries of certain individuals.[9] Certainly, both he and Ashmole went to great lengths, and expense in some

[8]"Memorandum–the lives of John Dee, Dr. Nepier, Sir William Dugdale, William Lilly, Elias Ashmole, esq.,–Mr. Ashmole haz and will doe himselfe: as he told me formerly but nowe seemes to faile." (Aubrey).

[9]John Booker for example (p.38).

cases, to obtain objects of, to them at least, great value. This, however, does not explain the occasions when such collections were apparently freely given to one or other of them.

While we must acknowledge the value placed on printed works at a time when they were still very expensive items, we should also consider the nature of those collections. They seem to fall into the general category of occultism, including astrological, magical, medical and alchemical texts. This in itself offers an explanation of the assiduousness of Lilly and Ashmole in their collecting: to amalgamate and preserve such works in the public arena. We should note the complaints of Lilly and his contemporaries of the exclusivity of the usual repositories of such knowledge, that is, religious institutions such as monasteries. We know how strongly he felt about freedom of access from the dedication and address in *Christian Astrology*. However, I believe that there is a further reason which addresses the matter overall and takes precedence over the personal. The turbulence of the times is witnessed in the destruction of personal and religious estates. Private libraries of individuals and religious houses were lost along with the buildings themselves in some cases.

In his foreword to *Two Antiquaries*[10] Richard Ollard brings this very important consideration to our attention: "[Aubrey] was alive to the possibilities, even, as it seemed to him, the possibilities of violent political change. What that meant for the preservation of irreplaceable documents he had known from his childhood when philistine parsons were still using manuscripts pillaged from monastic libraries at the Dissolution to line pie-dishes or stop up the bungs of cider barrels. As a young man he had seen the wanton destruction of great collections in the Civil War." Even as late as 1688, such upheaval remained a very real possibility and we see this in Aubrey's report of Ashmole's anger at Anthony Wood's apparent refusal to send Aubrey's manuscripts to the museum at Oxford (the Ashmolean) for safety.[11] The reason given for Ashmole's outburst was that because Wood was a Roman Catholic there was a grave risk of his library and papers being seized and possibly destroyed.

---

[10]*Two Antiquaries: A Selection from the Correspondence of John Aubrey and Anthony Wood*, by Maurice Balme, Durham Academic Press, 2001.

Editorial Interventions and Additions

As far as I know, this is the first time that Lilly's own manuscript has been published unchanged and in its entirety. While I am aware that, had the manuscript gone to publication, a printer would have made many changes to the original, I have felt it important to stay as close to it as possible. To this end, I have maintained the margin and footnotes written by Lilly and Ashmole. Sometimes these were simply to clarify certain points, at other times they contained additional information provided by Ashmole as he read the manuscript through. An unknown hand in the marginalia seems to belong to a proof-reader who also makes notes apparently in preparation for the printer. An example of the original page layout is to be found in Appendix 3 and shows how these margin notes were inserted.

There was no standardised spelling in the 17th century, and through this regional accents become apparent. For this reason, I have not modernised the spelling beyond inserting the silent "e" at word endings and a capital "F" to replace "ff". The punctuation remains as in the original except for the inclusion of occasional full-stops and capitalisation of sentence beginnings. This has been done only where it is very clear that this is required and where no punctuation has been used. I have kept in mind that Lilly spent a great deal of time referring to texts written in Latin in which punctuation is little used and capital letters at the beginning of sentences never used.

Contractions of 'which', 'where', 'our', etc. have been expanded to assist reading. Lacunae and illegible script have been checked with the 1715 transcription.

I hope this will aid reading flow and help the reader to a better appreciation of William Lilly.

---

[11]22 December 1688 (MS Aubrey 12, f.2.), from a letter to Wood: "… Mr Ashmole desired to speake with me about it, and is most outrageously angry: and charged mee to write to you, as soon as I could, and to order you to putt the Box in the Musaeum: for he lookes upon you as a P[apist] and sayeth, so does the whole University, … and he sayes, he expects to heare of your being plundered, and papers burnt, …" (*Notes*) With the impending arrival of the protestant William of Orange, the danger was clear.

Additional Documents
Further sources, in transcription, have been appended as follows:

1. Elias Ashmole wrote a continuation of this autobiography with the intention of publishing it along with his own;

2. A table of contents has been added to assist readers in locating various parts of the manuscript. Lilly did include a few chapter headings and these have been maintained;

3. Footnotes to clarify certain points and to provide definitions of archaic words and phrases;

4. Footnoted biographical and anecdotal information of some of the characters is included. The *Oxford Dictionary of National Biography* (OUP, 2004) has been relied upon in most cases. This has been done to broaden the scope of the *Autobiography*, and, as with all other editorial interventions and additions, to help the reader to a greater appreciation of the age in which Lilly lived and prospered.

5. An index of the people Lilly mentions;

6. A copy of Lilly's license to practice medicine is attached to the manuscript and I have therefore included it here;

7. My transcription of Lilly's last will and testament;

8. Lilly's own nativity and directions.

Where they could be found, horoscopes have been included as an appendix. The most reliable sources have been used for these data, and John Gadbury's *Collectio Geniturarum* has been avoided because of his known unreliability with birth data, although reference is made to this text where appropriate.

Acknowledgements
Some years ago, I had intended to publish this transcription and discovered that David Plant had also transcribed the manuscript for a similar purpose. He had gone one step further and had obtained a translation into English of the Latin dedication from Graeme Tobyn. David Plant and I then combined our transcriptions for the purposes of publication although this never took place. I should then offer my thanks and appreciation for the work that Graeme and David did which helped to complete my own transcription of the manuscript.

Bibliography

"Notes": Elias Ashmole (1617-1692): His Autobiographical Notes, his Correspondence, and Other Contemporary Sources Relating to his Life and Work, editor C.H. Josten, Oxford at Clarendon Press, 1966.

"Whitelock": *The Diary of Bulstrode Whitelock 1605 - 1675*, editor Ruth Spalding, Oxford University Press, 1990, 1991.

"OED": *Shorter Oxford English Dictionary*, Oxford at Clarendon Press, third edition, 1972 reprint.

"Lewis & Short": *A Latin Dictionary*, Lewis & Short, Oxford at Clarendon Press, 1951 reprint.

"WWBH": *Who's Who in British History*, ed. Juliet Gardiner, Collins & Brown, London, 2000.

"CH": *Cambridge History of English and American Literature in 18 volumes*, vol. XIV, ed. Ward & Trent et al., G.P. Putnam and Sons, New York, 1907-21.

"NAPL": *The Notorious Astrological Physician of London: Works and Days of Simon Forman*, Barbara Howard Traister, University of Chicago Press, Chicago and London, 2001.

OHE": *Oxford History of England, The Early Stuarts 1603-1660*, Godfrey Davies, OUP, second edition 1959, 1991 reprint , Oxford.

"Aubrey", *Brief Lives*, John Aubrey, ed. Andrew Clark, OUP at the Clarendon Press, 1898.

"Chambers": *Chambers Biographical Dictionary*, 5th ed., Edinburgh, 1990.

"Gadbury": *Collectio Geniturarum*, John Gadbury, London, 1661.

"Britannica": Encyclopedia Britannica 2003.

"ODNB": Oxford Dictionary of National Biography, OUP, 2004

"Harvey": *Nativitas: Astrological Studies*, James Martin Harvey, Triom, Sao Paulo, 1997. 3 vols.

The Autobiography

The Life of William Lilly student in Astrology, wrote by himselfe in the 66th year of his age, at Hersham in the parish of Walton uppon Thames in the county of Surrey : propria manu. Excellentissimo viro Armigero Elias Ashmole. D. D. D.

nos vita meas Laboris.

[Dico - D; Dedico. D; Devoso. D.]

Peragrationes totius vitae mea, tibi (oh illustrissime ac literatissime Armiger Elias Ashmole libenter quamuis laboriosissimas communico) cum quam plurimus ejusdem circumstantias adhuc aut ignotas aut latentes quœ mihi per tot annorum spatium contigerunt; Profiteor me in hisce scribendis omnem sinceritatem observasse nec innaniter aut leviter aliquid scripsisse; non enim nostrœ facultatis aut intentionis fuit, aliquid in lucem proferre, sine matura deliberatione et consulte; scripsi, eo desiderio summopere motus; ut presentis et futuri sciant; Quis fui; ubi natus; quomodo vixi; quibusque studijs versatus fui; Si humanitas vestra candide acceperit hasce subsequentes Chartulas, mirum in modum gaudebo, sin aliter; clementer, prudentiam vestram obsecro, ut qualescunq sint mittentur flammnuis.

Non ignoro, sed optime scio, non est una omnium ad scientiam properantium intentio, nec finis – quidem unus: aliqui enim multa scire cupiunt eo tantum fine, ut sciant: et fructum suœ curiositatis unum et in nihilo consistentem recipiunt: alij, scire volunt propter commodum temporale, ut assequanter dignitates, divitias, et honores; multique hodie ad scientiam se in hunc finem conferre reperiuntur: ex numero horum non fui.

Vester senilis jam amicus, Lillius[12]

---

[12]Translated by Graeme Tobyn.

"To the most excellent man Elias Ashmole Esquire, I dedicate these labours of my life.
I communicate these journeyings of all my life to you, o most illustrious and most learned esquire Elias Ashmole, willingly If most laboriously, together with very many circumstances of the same kind, still either unknown or hidden, which have befallen me through the space of so many years. I declare that in these writings I have observed all sincerity and have written nothing vainly or without due consideration, for it was not my purpose or intention to bring anything to the light without mature deliberation and counsel. I have written especially motivated by this desire, that the present and future should know; Who I have been, where I was born, how I have lived, in what studies I have been versed. If your kindness will freely accept these following papers, I shall rejoice exceedingly; if otherwise, I beg your prudence kindly to commit them to the fire. I am not unaware, but know very well, that all pursuing knowledge have not one intention, nor even one final aim; for some wish to know much as an end in itself – to know, and the fruit of their inquiry they receive alone, nothing more. Others wish to know for their own worldly advantage, that they may pursue high position, riches and honours; many today apply themselves to learning for this end; I was never among the number of these.

Your old and present friend, Lilly"

I was born in the County of Lecester, in an obscure town in the northwest borders thereof called Diseworth, 7 miles south of the town of Derby, one mile from Castle Donnington, a town of great rudeness, wherein, it is not remembred, that any of the Farmers thereof, did ever educate any of their soons to Learning, onely my grandfather sent his younger soon into Cambridge, whose name was Robert Lilly, and died Vicar of Cambden in Glocestershire about 1640.

The town of Diseworth did formerly belong unto the Lord Seagrave, for there is one Record in the hands of my cozen Melborn Williamson, which mentions one acre of Land abutting North uppon the Gates of the Lord Seagrave, and there is one Close called Hall close, wherein the ruines of some antient buildings appear, and particularly where the Dovehouse stood, and there is also the ruins of decayed fishponds, and other out houses. This town came at length to bee the inheritance of Margaret Countess of Richmond mother of Henry the 7th, which Margaret gave the town and Lordshipp of Diseworth unto Christs Colledge in Cambridge, the Master and Fellows whereof have ever since and at present enjoy and possess.

In the Church of this town, there is but one monument, and that is a white Marble stone[6] [13] now allmost broken to peeces, which was placed there by Robert Lilly my grandfather in memory of Jane his wife, the daughter of Mr. Pool of Dalby in the same County, a family now quite extinguished; my grandmothers brother was Mr. Henry Pool one of the Knights of Rhodes, (or Templers), who beeing a Soldier in Rhodes at the taking thereof by Solyman the Magnificent, and escaping with his life, came afterwards into England, and married the Lady Parron, or Perham of Oxfordshire and was called during his life Sir Henry Pool. William Pool the Astrologer[14], knew him very well and remembers him to have been a very tall person, and reputed of great strength in his younger yeares.

---

[13]While Lilly's remarks here refer to the status of this church, Ashmole had a long-standing interest in monuments in English churches.

[14]Lilly appears to have maintained a relationship with this member of his grandmother's family.

The impropriation[15] of this town of Diseworth, was formerly the inheritance of 3 sisters, whereof 2 became Votaries, one in the Nunnery of Langly in the parish of Diseworth, valued at the suppression, I mean the whole Nunnery, at 32^{L} per annum and this sisters part is yet enjoyed by the family of the Grayes, who now and for some yeares past have the enjoyment and possession of all the Lands formerly belonging to the Nunnery in the parish of Diseworth and are at present of the yearly value of 350^{L} per annum. One other of the sisters gave her part of the great Tythes unto a Religious house in Bredon uppon the Hill and, as the inhabitants repoart, became a religious person afterwards. The third sister married, and her part of the tythes in succeding ages, became the Earle of Huntingdons, who not many yeares since sold it to one of his servants.

The Donation of the Vicaridge is in the gift of the Grayes of Langly, unto whom they pay yearly, I mean unto the Vicar, as I am informed, 6^{L} per annum. Very lately, some charitable Citizens have purchased one third portion of the Tythes, and given it for maintenance of a preaching minister, and its now of the value per annum of about £50.

There have been 2 Hermitages in this parish, the last Hermite was well remembered by one Thomas Cook, a very antient inhabitant, who in my younger yeares acquainted mee hearwith.

This town of Diseworth is divided into 3 parishes, one part belongs unto Lockington, in which parish my fathers house, over against the west end of the steeple stands, in which I was born[16]. Some other farmes are in the parish of Bredon, the rest in the parish of Diseworth.

In this town, but in the parish of Lockington was I born, the first day of May 1602; my fathers name was William Lilly, soon[17] of Robert, the soon of Robert, the soon of Rowland etc. My mother was Alice, the daughter of Edward Barham of Fiskerton Mills in Nottinghamshire, 2 miles from

[15]Impropriate: to place tithes or ecclesiastical property in lay hands. (*OED*)

[16]The house still stands, as does the church.

[17]Son.

Newark uppon Trent. This Edward Barham was born in Norwich, and well remembred the Rebellion of Kett the Tanner[18] in the dayes of Edward the sixt.

Our family have continued many ages in this town as yeomen, besides the farme my father and his ancestors lived in, both my father and grandfather had much freehold Land, and many houses in the town not belonging to the Colledge[19], as the Farm wherein they wear all born, doth and is now at this present of the value of 40^{L} per annum and in possession of my brothers soon[20]: but the Freehold Land and houses formerly purchased by my Ancestors was all sold by my grandfather and father, so that now our family depend wholly uppon a Colledge lease.

Of my infancy I can speak little, onely I do very well remember that in the 4th year of my age, I had the Measells.

I was during my minority putt to learn at such Schools and of such masters as the rudeness[21] of the place and country affoarded, my mother intending I should bee a Scholler from my Infancy, seeing my fathers backsliding in the world, and no hopes by plain husbandry to recruit a decayed estate; therefore uppon Trinity tuseday 1613[22], my father had mee to Ashby de la Zouch, to bee there instructed by one Mr. John Brinsly[23], one in those tymes of great abilitys for instruction of youth in the Latin and Greek toungs; hee was very severe in his life and conversation, and did breed

[18]Robert Kett (c. 1492-1549), a yeoman tanner and farmer who led the rebellion in 1549. Following the massacre of the rebels by the Earl of Dudley, Kett was executed.

[19]Christ's College, Cambridge.

[20]Possibly the "Robert" and "William Lilly" referred to in Lilly's will.

[21]Rude: primitive or unsophisticated. (*OED*)

[22]Trinity Sunday fell on 2nd June in 1613.

[23]John Brinsley (fl. 1581-1624) Puritan minister, schoolmaster and an important and influential writer on education. Unusual for the time, but perhaps making an early impression on Lilly, Brinsley emphasised skill and continuing practice in the vernacular. (John Morgan, *ODNB*)

up many Schollers for the Universitys; in Religion he was a strict Puritan, not conformable wholly to the Ceremonys of the Church of England. In this town of Ashby de la Zouch for many yeares together Mr. Arthur Hildersham[24] exercised his Ministry; at my beeing there, and all the while I continued in Ashby, hee was silenced.

This is that famous Hildersham who left behind him a Commentary uppon the 51st Psalm, as also many sermons uppon the 4th of John, both which are printed: hee was an excellent Text man, of exemplary life, pleasant in discourse, a strong enemy to the Brownists[25], and dissented not from the Church of England in any article of faith, but onely about wearing the Surplice, baptizing with the Cross, and kneeling at the Sacrament; most of the people of the town wear directed by his judgment, and so continued and yet do continue Presbiterianly affected; for when the Lord of Loughborough in 1642, 1643, 44 and 45 had his Garrison in that town, if by chance at any tyme any Troopes of horse had lodged within the town, though they came late at night to their Quarters, yet would one or other of the town presently give Sir John Gell[26] of Derby notice, so that ere[27] next morning most of his Majestys troopes wear seised in their Lodgings, which mooved the Lord of Loughboroughmerrily to say, there was not a fart let in Ashby but it was presently carried to Derby:

The several Authors I there learned were these, Sententia Pueriles, Cato, Corderius, Æsops Fables, Tullies Offices, Ovid De Tristibus, lastly Virgill, then Horace as also Cambdens Greek Grammar, Theognis and Homer his Iliads; I was onely entred into Udalls Hebrew Grammar, hee[28] never

---

[24]Arthur Hildersham (1563-1632) Church of England clergyman and puritan, suspected of and punished for nonconformity on a number of occasions.

[25]A name used to refer to those seeking separation from the established Church.

[26]Sir John Gell (baptised 1593, d.1671), a Parliamentary army officer. In 1643 he was made commander-in-chief of parliament's forces in Staffordshire, Warwickshire and Derbyshire, and in 1644 was made governor of Derby. A man of dubious loyalty, he was imprisoned for treason in 1653. At the Restoration in 1660 he was pardoned, possibly as a result of his lending Charles I £900 in gold. (Trevor Brighton, *ODNB*)

[27]Before.

[28]Brinsley.

taught Logick, but often would say, it was fitt to bee learned in the Universitys.

In the 14th year of my age, by a fellow scholler of swart black complexion I had like to have my right eye beaten out as wee wear at play. The same year, about Michaelmas, I gott a Surfett and thereupon a feaver, by eating Beech nutts.

In the 16th year of my age, I was exceedingly troubled in my dreames; concerning my Salvation, and damnation, and also concerning the safety or destruction of my father and mother (their Soules); in the nights I frequently wept, prayed and mourned, for fear my sinns might offend God.

In the 17th year of my age my mother died.

In the 18th year of my age, my Mr. Brinsly was inforced to leave keeping School, beeing persecuted by the Bishops Officers; hee came to London, and then Lectured in London, where hee afterwards died. In this year by reason of my fathers poverty, I was also inforced to leave School, and so came to my fathers house, where I lived in much penury for one year, and taught school one quarter of a year, untill Gods providence provided better for mee.[29]

ex tempore

For the 2 last years of my beeing at School, I was of the highest form in the school, and cheifest of that form; I could then speake Latin as well as English, could make verses uppon any Theam, all kinds of verses, Hexamiter, Pentamiter, Phaleuciums, Iambick, Sapphick, etc. so that if any Schollers from remote Schools came to dispute, I was ringleader to dispute with them; I could capp verses, etc.; if any minister came to examine us, I was brought forth against him, nor would I argue with him unless in the Latin toung, which I found few of them could well speake without breaking

[29]Most of these "accidents" can be found with Lilly's nativity.

Priscians head[30], which if once they did, I would complain to my Master: Non bene intelligit Linguam Latinam, nec prorsus loquitur.

In the derivation of words, I found most of them defective, nor indeed wear any of them any good Grammarians; all and every of those Schollers who wear of my form and standing went to Cambridge, and prooved excellent Divines; onely poor I, William Lilly, was not so happy, fortune then frowning uppon my fathers present condicon, hee not in any capacity to maintain mee at University.

Of the meanes how I came unto London.

Worthy Sir[31], I take much delight to recount unto you even all and every Circumstance of my life, whether good, moderate or evill: Deo gloria.

My father had one Samuell Smatty for his Atturney unto whom I went sundry tymes with letters, who perceiving I was a Scholler, and that I lived miserably in the Country, loosing my tyme[32] nor any ways likely to do better if I continued there, pittying my condition sent word for mee to come speak with him, and told me hee had lately been at London, where there was a gentleman, wanted a youth to attend him and his wife who could write etc.

I acquainted my father with it, who was very willing to be rid of mee, for I could not work, drive the plough, or indure any Country Labour; my father oft would say I was good for nothing.

I had onely 20^{S} and no more to buy mee a new suit, hose, doublet, etc.; my doublet was fustian. I repaired to Mr. Smatty (when I was accoutred) for a letter to my master; which hee gave mee. Uppon Munday 3° April 1620, I departed from Diseworth and came to Lecester, but I must acquaint you before I came away, I visited my Freinds, amongst whom I had given mee about tenn shillings, which was a great comfort unto mee.

---

[30]Violating the rules of grammar. Brinsley promoted disputations on grammar. (*ODNB*)

[31]Ashmole.

[32]"Losing my time", probably "wasting my time".

On Tuseday the 4th of Aprill, I took leave of my father then in Leicester Gaole for debt, and came along with Bradshaw the Carrier, the same person with whom many of the Duke of Buckinghams kindred had come upp with:

Hark, how the wagons
crack with their rich Lading.

It was a very stormy week, cold and uncomfortable, I footed[33] it all along – wee could not reach London untill Palm sunday 9° Aprill, about halfe one houre after 3 in the afternoon, at which tyme, wee entred Smithfeilds; when I had gratified the Carrier and his servants, I had 7^{S} 6^{d} left and no more, one suit of cloathes uppon my back, 2 shirts, 3 bands, one payre of shoos, as many stockings. Uppon delivery of my letter, my Master entertained mee, and next day bought mee a new cloake of which you may imagine (good Esquire[34]) whether I was not proud of; besides I saw and eat good white bread, contrary to our diett in Lecestershire.

My Masters name was Gilbert Wright, born at Markett Bosworth in Lecestershire; my mistris was borne at Ashby Dela Zouch in the same County and in the town where I had gone to School.

This Gilbert Wright could neither write or read, hee lived uppon his Annuall Rents, was of no Calling or Profession, hee had for many yeares been servant to the Lady Paulet in Hertfordshire, and when Serjant Puckering was made Lord Keeper, hee made him Keeper of his Lodgings at White Hall. When Sir Thomas Egerton[35] was made Lord Chancellor, hee entertained him into the same place, and when hee married a widdow in Newgate markett, the Lord Chancellor recommended him to the Company

[33]Footed: walked.

[34]Ashmole.

[35]Sir Thomas Egerton's wife, Lady Elizabeth who died in 1648, was related to a friend of Elias Ashmole (*Notes*).

of Salters[36], London, to admitt him into their Company, and so they did and my Master in 1624, was Master of that Company.

Hee was a man of excellent naturall parts, and could speak publiqly uppon any occasion very rationally and to the purpose: you see now, what profession I was brought upp unto. I write this that the world may know hee was no taylor, or myselfe of that or any other Calling or profession: my worke was to go before my M^{r}. to Church, to attend my Master when he went abroad, to make clean his shoos, sweep the street, fetch faggots and beere when wee had Lodgers, make fires, sweep the house, help to drive Bucks, when wee washed sett water in a tubb from the Thames; I have helped to carry 18 tubbs of water in one morning, weed the garden, all manner of Drudgerys I willingly performed; scrape trenchers, etc. If I had any profession it was of this nature. I should never have denyed my beeing a Taylor[37], had I been one, for there is no Calling so base, which by Gods mercy may not affoard a livelyhood, and had not my master entertained mee, I would have been of a very mean profession ere I would have returned into the Country again. So, this page ends the actions of 18 years of my life.

My Master married this his second wife for her estate, for shee was competently rich, shee married him for considerations hee performed not (nocturnall Society) so that they lived very uncomfortably. Shee was about 70 yeares of age, hee 66 or more, yet never was any woaman more jealous of a husband than shee, insomuch that when soever hee went into London, shee was confident of his going to woomen; by those meanes my life was the more uncomfortable, it beeing very difficult to please two such opposite natures, however, as to the things of this world, I had inough and indured their discontents with much silence.

My Mistris was very curious to know of such as then wear called Cunning or Wise men whether shee should bury her husband? Shee

---

[36]Still in existence today and one of the twelve great Livery Companies of the City of London.

[37]These remarks refer to accusations made by his enemies that his master had been a tailor or scrivener. It is interesting, in a time when social status was of the utmost importance, that Lilly should place himself at a lower status to that of a tailor.

frequently visited such persons, and this occasion begott in mee a little desire to learn something that way, but wanting money to buy bookes, I layd aside those notions, and indeavored to please both M^{r}. and M^{rs}.

Of my mistris death and occasion thereof by meanes of a Cancer in her breast.

In 1622 shee complained of a pain in her left breast, wherein there appeared at first an hard knott no bigger than a small peason[38]; it increased in a little tyme very much, was very hard and sometymes would looke very red; she tooke advise of Chirurgions, had oyles, Cearcloths[39], plates of Lead, and what not; in 1623 it grow very bigg and spread all over her breast, then for many weekes pultises wear applied unto it, which in continuance of tyme broak the skinn, and then aboundance of watery thinn stuff came from it, but nothing else; at length the matter came to suppuration, but never any great store issued forth; it was exceeding noysome[40], and painfull.

From the beginning of it, untill she died, shee would permitt no Chirurgion to dress it but onely my selfe, I applied every thing unto it, and her paines wear so great all the winter before shee died, that I have been called out of my bed 2 or 3 tymes in one night to dress it and change plasters. In 1624 by degrees with sizzers[41] I cutt all the whole breast away, I mean the sinnews and Nerves etc – in one fortnight or little more, there appeared as it wear more flesh, all raw, so that shee could scarce indure any unguent to bee applyed. I remember there was a great cleft through the midle of her breast, which when that fully appeared shee died, which was in September 1624, my Master being then in the Country. His kindred in London would willingly have had Mourning for her, but by advise of an especiall friend of his, I contradicted them, nor would I permitt them to looke into any Chest or Trunk in the house; shee was decently buried, and so fond of mee in the tyme of her sickness, shee would never permitt mee out of her chamber, gave me 5^{L} in old gold, and sent mee unto a private Trunk of hers at a friends house where shee had one hundred pounds in gold; shee bad mee bring it away and take it, but when I opened the Trunk, I found nothing therein, for a kinsman of hers had

---

[38]Pea.

[39]Cerecloth: cloth smeared or impregnate with wax or other glutinous matter. (*OED*)

[40]Noisome: evil-smelling. (*OED*)

[41]Scissors.

been there a few days before, and carried all away; she was in great passion at my relating thereof, because shee could no way gratifie my paines in all her sickness, advised mee to helpe my selfe when she was gone, out of my Masters goods, which I never did.

Courteous Esquire[42]; bee not weary of reading hearof, or of what followes –

When my Mistris died, shee had under her Arme hole a small scarlet bagg full of many things, which one that was there delivered unto mee; there was in this bagg severall Sigills – some of ♃ in Tinn, others of the nature of ♀: some of Iron, and one of Gold, pure Angell Gold[43], of the bigness of a 33ˢ peece of King James coyne; in the Circumference on one side was wrote I mean ingraven: Vicit Leo de tribu Juda Tetragrammaton: + : within the midle there was ingraved, an holy Lamb: in the other circumference, there was, Amraphel. and 3

+ : in the midle, Sanctus Petrus α and Omega.

The occasion of framing this Sigill was thus: her former husband, travelling into Sussex, happened to lodge in an Inn, and to lye in a chamber thereof, wherein, not many months before a country Grasier[44] had layn, and in the night cutt his own throat; after this nights lodging, hee was perpetually and for many yeares followed by a Spirit, which vocally and articulately provoked him to cutt his throat; hee was used frequently to say, I defie thee, I defie thee, and to spit at the spirit; this spirit followed him many yeares, hee not making any body acquainted with it, at last hee grew melancholly and discontent, which being carefully observed by his wife, shee many tymes hearing him pronounce, I defie thee etc., shee desired him to acquaint her with the cause of his distemper: which he then did.

---

[42]Ashmole

[43]An angel was an old coin of high gold content.

[44]Grazier: someone who feeds cattle for market.

Away shee went to Doctor Symon Forman[45] who lived then in Lambeth, and acquainted him with it, who having framed this Sigill and hanged it about his neck, who wearing it continually until hee died, was never more molested by the Spirit: I sold the sigill for 32ˢ, but transcribed the words verbatim as I have related; Sir you shall now have a story of this Symon Forman, as his widdow[46], whom I well know related unto mee:

But before I relate his death, I shall acquaint you something of the man, as I have gathered from some Manuscripts of his own writing.

Of Doctor Symon Forman[47].

Hee was a Chandlers soon in the City of Westminster the soon of, the soon of, etc. and after this fashion, hee reccorded 5 or 6 of his Ancestors.

Hee travelled into forraign Countrys for many yeares, purposely to bee instructed in Astrology, and other more occult Sciences, as also in Phisick, taking his Degree of Dʳ beyond the Seas; beeing sufficiently furnished and instructed with what hee desired, hee returned into England towards the latter end of the raign of Queen Elizabeth, and florished untill that yeare of King James, wherein the Countess of Essex, the Earl of Somersett and Sir Thomas Overbury[48], their matters wear questioned.

only into Holland for a month in 1680 1560 a mistake [EA]

Hee lived in Lambeth with very good repoart of the neighborhood, especially of the poor, unto whom hee was charitable.

---

[45]Simon Forman (1552-1611) astrologer and medical practitioner. This story, as told to Lilly, marks the beginning of a lifelong fascination with Forman for both Lilly and Ashmole.

[46]In 1599, Forman married Jean Baker when she was sixteen years old (*NAPL*). She would have been in her eighties as Lilly wrote this manuscript.

[47]*NAPL* provides interesting supporting information regarding Forman, the editor referring to Lilly's autobiography. It is clear from the former work that Lilly had seen many of Forman's papers.

[48]In 1613 during the scandal following the murder of Sir Thomas Overbury, it emerged that Frances, Countess of Essex and her confidante Mrs. Turner, had visited the astrologer and magician Simon Forman, with a view to procuring respectively the love of the Earl of Somerset and Sir Christopher Maynwaring. [*Thomas* page 278]

Hee was a person that in Horary Questions, (especially Thefts) was very judicious and fortunate, so also in sicknesses, which indeed was his Master peece; in resolving questions about marriage, hee had good Success, in other questions very moderate. Hee was a person of indefatigable paines etc., I have seen sometymes halfe one sheet of paper wrote of his judgment uppon one question, in writing whereof hee used much Tautology, as you may see your selfe (most excellent Esquire) if you read a great book of Doctor Floods[49], which you have, who had all that book from the Manuscripts of Forman, for I have seen the same, word for word, in an English Manuscript sometymes Doctor Willoughbys of Glocestershire[50].

Had Forman lived to have methodized his own papers I doubt not but hee would have advanced, the mathematicall part thereof very completely; for hee was very observant, and kept notes of the success of his judgments, as in many of his figures I have observed.

I very well remember to have read in one of his Manuscripts what followeth.

Beeing in bed one morning (sayth hee) I was desirous to know, whether I should ever bee a Lord, Earl, or Knight, etc. wheruppon I sett this figure following; and thereuppon his judgment, by which hee concluded, that within two yeares tyme, hee should bee a Lord or great Man: but, sayth hee, before the two yeares wear expired, the Doctors putt mee in Newgate, and nothing came.

Not long after, hee was desirous to know the same things concerning his honor or greatshipp. An other figure was sett, and that promised him to bee a great Lord within one yeare. But hee setts down, that in that year hee had

[49]Doctor Robert Fludd (bap. 1574, d.1637) physician, mystic and philosopher.

[50]Possibly Percivall Willughby (1596-1685), physician and obstetrician. He and Lilly were friends from 1640 when Willughby arrived with his family, who seems also to have attended one of Lilly's female relations prior to her death. (Joan Lane, *ODNB*). This Willughby was not from Gloucester and is noted later by Lilly as being from Derby.

no preferment at all; onely I became acquainted with a Merchants wife, by whom I gott weele[51].

There is an other figure concerning one Sir Ayre his going into Turky: whether it would bee a good voyage or not: the Doctor repeates all his Astrologicall reasons, and musters them together, and then gave his judgment, it would bee a fortunate voyage, but under the figure hee concluded, this prooved not so, for hee was taken prisoner by Pyrates ere hee arrived in Turky and lost all.

Hee sett severall questions, to know, if hee should attain the Philosophers Stone: and the figures according to his straining, did seem to signifie as much; and then hee tuggs uppon the aspects and Configurations and elected a fitt tyme to begin his operation; but by and by in Conclusion, hee adds, so the worke went very forward, but uppon the £ of ♂ to Sol[52] – my glass broke, and I lost all my paines: hee setts down five or six such judgments, but still complaines all came to nothing uppon the malignant aspects of ♄ and ♂[XIII].

Although some of his Astrologicall judgments did fayle, more particularly those concerning him selfe, hee beeing no way capable of such preferment as hee ambitiously desired, yet I shall repeat some other of his judgments, which did not fayle, beeing performed by conference with spirits.

My Mistris went once unto him, to know when her husband being then in Cumberland would return, hee having promised to bee at home near the tyme of her Question. After some consideration, hee told her to this effect, Margery, for so her name was, thy husband will not bee at home this 18 dayes, his kindred have vexed him, and hee is come away from them in much Anger, hee is now in Carlile; And hath but 3^d^. in his purse – when hee came home, hee confessed all to bee true, and that uppon leaving his Kindred; hee had but 3^d.^ in his purse.

---

[51]"Well". For Forman's numerous love affairs see *NAPL*.
[52]"...but uppon the square of Mars to Sun..."

[53]"...malignant aspects of Saturn and Mars."

I shall now relate one story more, and then to his Death.

One Coleman, Clerk to Sir Thomas Beamount[54] of Lecestershire having had some liberall favors, both from his Lady and her daughters, bragged of it etc. The Knight brought him into the Starr Chamber, had his servant sentenced to be pillored, whipt, and after during life to bee imprisoned: the sentence was executed in London and was to bee in Lecestershire: 2 Keepers wear to convey Coleman from the Fleet to Lecester.

My Mistris taking consideration of Coleman, and the miserys hee was to suffer; went presently to Forman, acquainting him therewith, who after consideration swore Coleman had layne both with the mother and daughters and besides sayd, that the old Lady beeing afflicted with fitts of the mother, called him into her chamber, to hold down the fitts with his hands, and that hee holding his hands about the breast, shee cryed, Lower, Lower, and putt his hands bilow her belly: and then –

Hee also told my mistris, in what posture, hee lay with the young Ladys, etc and sayd, they intend in Lecester to whipp him to death, but I assure thee Margery hee shall never come there, yet they sett forward to morrow sayth hee.

And so his 2 Keepers did, Colemans leggs beeing locked with an Iron chain under the horses belly – in this nature they travelled the first and second day, on the third day the 2 Keepers seeing their prisoners Civillity the two preceding days, did not lock his chain under the horses belly as formerly, but lockt it onely to one side, in this posture they rode some miles beyond Northampton, when on a sudden one of the Keepers had necessity to untruss[55], and so the other and Coleman stood still, by and by the other Keeper desired Coleman to hold his horse, for hee had occasion also: Coleman immediately tooke one of the swords, and rann through 2 of the horses, killing them stark dead, getts uppon the other with one of their

[54]Sir Thomas Beaumont of Stoughton, Leicestershire (c.1555-1614). His suit in 1607 in the Star Chamber had more to do with John Coleman's allegedly making the affair public knowledge than with the act itself.

[55]To relieve himself.

swords, farewell Gentlemen (quoth hee) tell my M^r. I have no mind to bee whipt in Lecestershire and so went his way.

The 2 Keepers in all haste, went to a Gentlemans house near at hand, complaining of their misfortune, and desired horses of him to pursue their Prisoner, which hee with much civillity graunted, but ere the Horses could bee made ready, the Mistris of the House came down and inquiring what the matter was, went to the stable and commanded her horses to bee unsadled, with this sharp speech –

Lett the Lady Beamount and her daughters live honestly, none of my horses shall go forth uppon this occasion.[56]

I could relate many such storys of his performing, as also what hee wrote in a booke left behind him, viz: This I made the Devill write with his own hand in Lambeth feilds, 1596; in June or July as I now remember.

Hee professed to his wife, there would bee much trouble about Carr and the Countess of Essex, who frequently resorted unto him, and from whose company hee would sometymes lock himselfe in his study one whole day[57].

Now wee come to his death, which happened as followeth; the Sunday night before hee died, his wife and hee beeing at supper in their garden house, shee beeing pleasant, told him shee had been informed hee could resolve whether man or wife should dye first; whether shall I (quoth shee) bury you or no? Oh Trunco, for so hee called her, thou wilt bury mee, but thou wilt much repent it; yea, but how long first? I shall dye (sayd hee) ere Thursday night; Munday came, all was well. Tuesday came, hee not sick. Wednesday came, and still hee was well; with which his impertinent wife much twitt him in the teeth[58].

---

[56]Knowledge of this scandal was widespread.

[57]These remarks refer to the scandal of the murder of Sir Thomas Overbury by Frances Howard, Countess of Essex, in which Forman was implicated posthumously. (*NAPL*)

[58]Twit: taunt. (*OED*)

Thursday came, and dinner was ended, hee very well, hee went down to the waterside, and tooke a payr of Oares to go to some buildings hee was in hand with at Pudle Dock; beeing in the midle of the Thames, hee presently fell down, onely saying, an Impost, an Impost and so died: a most sad storm of wynd immediately following; hee died worth 1200^{L} and left onely one Son called Clement.

X His son Tho: Napper Esq: most generously gave most of these M.S: to EA. [EA]

All his raritys, secret manuscripts, of what quality so ever Doctor Napper of Lindford[59] in Buckinghamshire had, who had been a long tyme his Schollar, and of whom Forman was used to say, Hee would bee but a Dunce: yet in continuance of tyme hee prooved a singular Astrologer and Phisition, [X]Sir Richard Napper now living I beleeve hath all those raritys in his possession which wear Formans, beeing Kinsman and heyre unto Doctor Napper: I hope you will pardon this digression.

After my mistris was dead I lived most comfortably, my M^{r}. having great affection for mee.

The year 1625 now comes on, and the plague exceeding violent[60]; I will relate what I observed, the Spring before it broke forth; against our Corner house[61], every night there would come down about 5 or 6 of clock sometymes one hundred or more boys, some playing, others as if in serious discourse, and just as it grew darke, would all bee gone home; many succeeding yeares, there was no such or any concourse, usually no more than of 4 or 5 in a Company; in the Spring of 1665 the boys and youth of severall parishes in like numbers appeared again, which I beholding, called Thomas Sanders my Landlord, and told him, the youth and young boys of severall parishes did in that nature assemble and play, in the beginning of the year 1625 God Bless us (quoth I) from a plague this year; but then there succeeded one and the greatest ever was in London.

---

[59]Dr. Richard Napier (1559-1634), parson, astrologer and physician and Forman's friend. He inherited all of Forman's precious papers and books which were passed on to his nephew Sir Richard Napier, MD. The latter's son, Thomas, then gave the collection to Ashmole in 1677 (i.e. after Lilly had completed this manuscript). (*NAPL*)

[60]The plague of 1625 was especially severe. (*OHE*)

[61]Lilly's London home.

In 1625 the visitation increasing, and my Mr. having a great charge of money and plate, some his own, some other mens, left mee and a fellow servant to keep the house, and himselfe in June went into Lecestershire, hee was in that year Feffee[62] Collector for 12 poor alms people living in Clement Danes Churchyard, whose Pensions I in his absence payd weekly, to his and the parishes great satisfaction.

My Mr. was no sooner gone down, but I bought a base Viall[63], gott a Mr. to instruct mee; the intervalls of tyme I spent in bowling in Lincolns Inn feilds with Watt the Cobler, Dick the blacksmith, and such like companions; wee have sometymes been at our worke at six in the morning, and so continued untill 3 or 4 in the afternoon, many tymes without bread or drink all that while.

Sometymes I went to Church and heard funerall Sermons, of which there was then great plenty, at other tymes I went early to St. Antolines[64] in London, where there was every morning a Sermon.

The most able people of the whole Citty and Suburbs wear out of town, if any remained, it was such who wear engaged by parish Offices to remain. No habit of a gentleman or woaman continued; the woefull Calamity of that year was greevous, people dying on the open feilds and in the open streets.

At last in August the bills of mortallity[65] so increased that very few people had thoughts of surviving the Contagion; the Sunday before the great bill came forth, which was of 5000 and od hundreds, there was appointed a

---

[62]Feofee: one of a board of trustees holding land for charitable or other public purposes. (OED)

[63] Bass-viol.

[64]St. Antholin's church, Budge Row, Watling Street was a centre for Puritan preachers. The church was destroyed in the Great Fire of 1666.

[65]Lists of those who had died which were posted in public places in each parish.

Sacrament at Clement Danes, during the distributing whereof I do well remember we sang 13 parts of the 119 psalme.[66]

M^{r}. Jacob our Minister, for wee had 3 that day, the Communion was so great, fell sick as hee was giving the Sacrament, went home and was buried of the plague the thursday following. M^{r}. James another of the Ministers fell sick ere hee had quite finished, had the plague, and was 13 weekes ere hee recovered. M^{r}. Whitacre the last of the 3 escaped not onely then, but all the contagion following without any sickness at all, though hee officiated at every funerall, and buried all manner of people, whether they died of the plague or not: hee was given to drink, seldome could preach more than one quarter of one houre at a tyme, etc.

In November my M^{r}. came home, my fellow servants and my diet came weekely to six shillings six pence, sometymes 7$^{s.}$ so cheape diet was at that tyme.

In february of that year my M^{r}. married again one who after his death became my wife. In the same year hee setled uppon mee during my life 20^{L} per annum which I have enjoyed ever since even to the writing hearof.

22: May 1627 my M^{r}. died at the Corner house in the Strand, where I also lived so long. Hee died intestate, my M^{rs}. relinquishing the administration it came to his elder brother, who assigned the estate over unto mee for payment of my Masters debts, which beeing payd, I faithfully returned the remaining part unto his administrator: nor had I one penny of the estate, more than 20^{L} which was allowed me by Contract to undertake the payment of my Masters debts.

Of my marriage the first tyme.

My Mistris had been twice married to old men, was now resolved to bee cozened[67] no more. Shee was of a brown ruddy complexion, corpulent, of but mean stature, plain, of no education, yet a very provident person, and of good conditions. Shee had many Sutors, old men, which shee

[66]Lilly is drawing attention to the long duration of the sacrament; Psalm 119 has twenty-two parts of seven verses each.
[67]Cozen: cheat or dupe. (*OED*)

declined, some gentlemen of decayed fortune, which shee liked not, for shee was covetous and sparing. By my fellow servant shee was observed frequently to say shee cared not, if shee married a man that would love her, so that hee had never a penny, and would ordinarily talk of mee when shee was in bed: this servant gave mee incoragement to give the onsett[68]. I was much perplexed hearat, for, should I attempt her, and bee slighted, shee would never care for mee afterwards; but again, I considered that if I should attempt and fayle, shee would never speak of it, or would any beleeve I durst bee so audacious as to propound such a question, the disproportion of yeares and fortune beeing so great betwixt us: however all her talke was of husbands, and in my presence saying one day after dinner, shee respected not wealth but desired an honest man; I made answer, I thought I could fitt her with such an husband; shee asked mee, where? I made no more ado, but presently saluted her, and told her, my selfe was the man: shee replyed I was too young; I said nay: what I had not in wealth, I would supply in love: and saluted her frequently, which she accepted lovingly, and the next day at dinner made mee sitt down at Dinner with my hatt on my head, and sayd shee intended to make mee her husband, for which I gave her many salutes, etc.

Esquire dogged paper.[69]

I was very careful to keep all things secret, for I well knew if shee should take Councell of any freind, my hopes would bee frustrated, therefore I suddenly procured her Consent to marry, unto which shee assented, so that uppon the 8th day of September 1627 at St. Georges in Southwark I was married unto her, and for two whole yeares wee kept it secret. When it was divulged and some people blamed her for it; she constantly replyed, that shee had no kindred, if I proved kind and a good husband, shee should make mee a Man; if I prooved otherwise, she onely undid her selfe.

In the 3 or 4th yeare after our marriage, wee had strong suites of Law with her first husbands kindred, but overthrew them in the ende.

---

[68]To approach her in the matter.

[69]A note by Lilly to Ashmole at a page ending.

During all the tyme of her life, which was until October 1633, we lived very lovingly, I frequenting no Company at all; my exercises wear sometymes Angling, in which I ever delighted, my companions 2 aged men; I then frequented lectures, 2 or 3 in a weeke, I heard M^r^. Sute in Lombard Street, M^r^. Googe[70] of Black Fryers, D^r^. Mickletwait[71] of the Temple, D^r^. Oldsworth, with others the most learned men of those tymes, and learned in judgment to Puritanisme. In October 1627, I was made free of the Salters Company London[72].

How I came to study Astrology.

It happened one Sunday 1632, as my selfe and a Justice of peace his Clerk wear before Service discoursing of many things, hee chanced to say, that such a person was a great Schollar, nay so learned that hee could make an Almanack, which to mee then was strange; one speech begott an other, till at last he sayd hee would bring mee acquainted with one Evans[73] in Gunpowder Alley, who had formerly lived in Staffordshire, that was an excellent wise man, and studied the black Arts.

The same weeke after, wee went to see M^r^. Evans, when wee came to his house, hee having been drunk the night before, was uppon his bed, if it be Lawfull to call that a bed whereon hee then lay; he roused upp himselfe, and after some complements, hee was content to instruct mee in Astrology; I attended his best opportunitys for 7 or 8 weeks, in which tyme I could

[70]William Gouge (1575-1653) Church of England clergyman and author, recommended to St. Ann Blackriars by Arthur Hildersham (cf.). Usher describes his sermons as the "most celebrated in London". His conformity was questioned and he fell foul of Archbishop Laud on a number of occasions.

[71]Paul Micklethwaite (1588/9-1639) Church of England minister, renowned preacher whose library revealed a wide interest in Jewish studies and included a book written by John Dee. (Nicholas Rogers, *ODNB*)

[72]It is unclear whether this was as a result of his marriage as Lilly tells us that the marriage was kept a secret during this time.

[73]John Evans (b. 1594/5 d. in or after 1659). He had offered tuition in English, Latin, Greek, Hebrew, etc. (Bernard Capp, *ODNB*) '2 August 1675: "Mr: Lilly told me that John Evans who first taught him Astrology informed him that he was acquainted with Kellys [Edward Kelly, John Dee's scryer] Sister in Worcester, & that she shewed him some of the gold her Brother had transmuted. & that Kelley was first an Apothecary in Worcester." (*Notes*).

sett a figure perfectly; books hee had not any except Haly de judicijs Astrorum, and Origanus his Ephemerides, so that as often as I entred his house, I thought I was in the wilderness; now something of the man.

Hee was by byrth a Welshman, a M^{r}. of Arts, and in sacred orders, hee had formerly had a Cure of soules in Staffordshire, but now was come to try his fortunes at London, beeing in a manner inforced to fly for some offences very scandalous committed by him in those parts where hee had lately lived[74], for hee gave judgement uppon things lost, the onely shame of Astrology. Hee was the most perfect Saturnine person my eyes ever beheld, either before I practised or since; of a midle stature, broad forehead, beetle browed, thick shoulders, flatt nosed, full lipps, down looked[75], black curling stiff hair, splay footed; to give him his right, hee had the most peircing judgment naturally uppon a figure of theft, and many other questions that ever I mett with all: yet for money hee would willingly give contrary judgment, much addicted to debauchery, and then very abusive and quarrellsome, seldom without a black eye or one bruise or other, this is the same Evans who made so many Antimoniall Cupps[76], uppon the sale whereof he principally subsisted: hee understood Latine very well, the Greek toung not at all.

Hee had done some Acts above and beyond Astrology, for hee was well versed in the nature of spirits, and had many tymes used the Circular way of invocating, as in the tyme of our familiarity hee told mee.

Two of his Actions I will relate, as to mee delivered.

There was in Staffordshire a young gentlewoaman, that had for her preferment married an aged rich person, who beeing desirous to purchase some land for his wifes maintenance, by this young gentlewoman, his wife, was desired to buy the land in a gentleman her very dear freinds name, but for her use; after the aged man was dead, the widdow could by

---

[74]He had left Enfield, Middlesex under a cloud. (*ibid.*)

[75]Looking downwards.

[76]Cups made of glass of antimony, to communicate emetic qualities to wine. (*OED*) Even though he had been charged with causing the deaths of two of his patients through the use of these cups, Evans continued to offer them for sale as late as 1659. (*ibid.*)

no meanes procure the Deed of purchase from her freind, whereuppon shee applyes her selfe to Evans, who for a somme of money promiseth to have her deed safely delivered into her own hands; the somme was 40 pounds.

Evans applyes himselfe to the Invocation of the Angell Salmon, of the nature of Mars – reads his Lettany in the Common prayer book every day at select houres, weares his Surpless – lives orderly all that tyme; at the fortnights end, Salmon appeared, and having received his commands what to do, in a small tyme, returnes with the very Deed desired, lays it down gently uppon a table where a white cloth was spread, and then beeing dismissed, vanished. The Deed was by the gentleman, who formerly kept it, placed amongst many other of his Evidences in a large woodden Chest, and in a Chamber at one end of the house, but uppon Salmons remooving and bringing away the Deed, all that bay of the building was quite blown down, and all his own proper Evidences torne all to peeces. The second story followeth.

Sometymes before I became acquainted with him, hee then living in the Minories, was desired by the Lord Bothwell[77] and Sir Kellam Digby[78], to show them a Spirit; hee promised so to do, the tyme came, and they wear all in the body of the circle, when lo, uppon a sudden, after some tyme of Invocation, Evans was taken from out of the Room and carried into the Feild near Battersey Causeway close to the Thames.

---

[77]A letter to Ashmole from Lilly: '24 Jan.1667: "...I also in a Trunk, send you the greatest Arcana's any privat person in Euroap hath[,] they wear the 10: years Collection of the Lord Bothwell: given to Sir R. Holborn & by him to mee: I more esteem your love and generous spirit, then all those wear they many more:..." (*Notes*) Lilly may have had this collection of occult books for some time because Sir Robert Holborn, barrister and politician, died in 1648. He was said to be an "avid follower" of astrology and a "devotee" of William Lilly. (D.A. Orr, *ODNB*).

[78]Sir Kenelm Digby (1603-1665), natural philosopher, courtier, virtuoso with a wide variety of interests and academic accomplishments, and one of the founders of the Royal Society, as was Ashmole. Digby was interested in alchemy and had his own laboratory. (Aubrey) A friend and probably a student of Rev. Richard Napier, he later became of student of Thomas Allen at Oxford, also an astrologer. He was a student of Johannes Hunyades the alchemist. (Michael Foster, *ODNB*).

Next morning a Country man going by to his labour and espying a man in black Cloathes, came unto him and awaked him, and asked him how hee came there. Evans by this understood his own condition, inquired where hee was, how farr from London, and in what parish hee was, which when he understood, hee told the Laborer hee had been late at Battersea the night before, and by chance was left there by his freinds.

Sir Kellam Digby and the Lord Bothwell went home without any harme, came next day to hear what was become of him; just as they in the afternoon came into the house, a messenger came from Evans to his wife to come to him at Battersea; I inquired[79] uppon what account the Spirits carried him away, who sayd, hee had not at the tyme of the Invocation made any Suffumigation, at which the Spirits wear vexed.

It happened that after I discovered what Astrology was, I went weekly unto little Brittain[80], and bought many bookes of Astrology, not acquainting Evans therewith.

M[r]. Bedell[A,81] minister of Totenham high cross near London[82], who had been many years Chaplain to Sir Henry Wotton[83] whilst he was Ambassador at Venice, and assisted Pietro Soave Polano in composing and writing the Councell of Trent, was lately dead, and his Library beeing sold into Little Brittain, I bought amongst them my choycest bookes of Astrology. The occasion of our falling out was thus; a woaman demanded the resolution of a question, which when hee had done, shee went her way, I standing

[A]. *Bedwell.*

---

[79]Presumably Lilly enquired of Evans.

[80]Little Britain is an area of London near St. Paul's Cathedral. Then associated with booksellers, as was Paternoster Row and St. Paul's Churchyard a little later.

[81]William Bedwell (bap.1563, d.1632), Arabist and mathematician. He was a close friend of the Huguenot scholar Isaac Casaubon, the father of Meric Casaubon who produced the 1659 edition of John Dee's magical diaries Conversations with Spirits. (*ODNB*).

[82]Tottenham High Cross, a monument rebuilt in 1600, is about five miles from central London, but now within the boundaries of Greater London.

[83]Sir Henry Wotton (1568-1639), diplomat and writer. His first embassy to Venice was in 1604. (A.J. Loomie, *ODNB*).

by all the while and observing the figure asked him, why hee gave the judgment hee did, syth[84] the significators showed quite the contrary, and gave him my reasons; which when hee had pondered, hee called mee Boy, and must hee bee contradicted by such a Novice: but when his heat was over, hee sayd had hee nott so judged, to please the woaman, shee would have given him nothing, and hee had wife and family to provide for; uppon this wee never came together after.

Beeing very meanly introduced[85] [86], I applied my selfe to study those bookes I had obtained, many tymes 12 or 15 or 18 houres day and night. I was curious to discover whether there was any verity in the Art or not. Astrology at this tyme, viz in 1633, was very rare in London, few professing it that understood anything thereof. Let it not repent you (oh noble Esquire) if now I make a short digression of such persons as then professed Astrology, that posterity may understand in what condition I found it, and in whose hands that little that remained, was lodged[87].

There lived in Houndsditch one Alexander Hart, who had been a soldier formerly, a comly old man, of good aspect; hee professed Questionary Astrology and a little of Phisick; his greatest skill was to elect young gentlemen fitt tymes to play at Dice, that they might winn or gett money. I went unto him for resolution of 3 questions at severall tymes, and hee erred in every one.

To speake soberly of him, hee was but a Cheat as appeared suddenly after, for a rusticall young fellow of the Citty, desirous of Knowledge, contracted with Hart, to assist him for conference with a Spirit, and payd him 20^{L} of 30^{L} – the Contract.

---

[84]Since.

[85]To the study of Astrology.

[86]According to Lilly's address to the reader in Christian Astrology, this occurred after only six weeks of instruction.

[87]Readers are referred to Christian Astrology and Lilly's Dedication to Bulstrode Whitelock, as also his Address to the reader therein where Lilly remarks upon this further.

At last, after many delays, and no spirit appearing or money returned, the young man indites him for a Cheat at the old Baily in London, the Jury found the Bill; at hearing the cause, this jeast happened; some of the Bench inquired what Hart did; hee sate like an Alderman in his Gown quoth the fellow, at which the Court fell into a great Laughter, most of the Bench beeing Aldermen.

Hee was to have been sett uppon the Pillory for this Cheat, but John Taylor[88] the water poet, beeing his great freind, gott the Lord Cheife Justise Richardson[89] to beile him ere hee stood uppon the Pillory, and so Hart fled presently into Holland, where he ended his days; it was my fortune uppon sale of his bookes in 1634 to buy Argolls primum mobile for 14s. which I onely wanted.In Lambeth Marsh at the same tyme lived one Captain Bubb, who resolved horary questions Astrologically, a propper handsome man, well spoken but withall covetous and of no honesty, as will appear by this story, for which hee stood uppon the Pillory.

A certain Butcher was robbed going to a faire of 40^{L}; hee goes to Bubb, who for 10^{L} in hand payd would helpe him to the theefe; appoints the Butcher such a night precisely to watch at such a place, and the theefe should come thither; commanded him by any meanes to stop him; the butcher attends according to direction, about 12 in the night, there comes one riding very feircely uppon a full gallop, whom the butcher knocks down, and seized both uppon man and horse, the butcher brings the man and horse to the next town, but then the person whom the butcher attacked, was John, the servant of Doctor Bubb: for which the Captain was indited, and suffered uppon the Pillory and afterwards ended his dayes in great disgrace.

There was also one Jeffery Neve[90] at this tyme student in Phisick and Astrology, hee had formerly been a merchant in Yarmouth and Mayor of the

---

[88]John Taylor (1578-1653) English poet and pamphleteer, known as the 'Water-poet'. (*Chambers*) See also Aubrey.

[89]Sir Thomas Richardson (bap. 1569 d. 1635), judge, was Lord Chief Justice between 1631 and 1635.

[90]Dr. Jeffrey Le Neve (1579-1653), astrologer and medical practitioner. See Gadbury for an opposite opinion of Le Neve's abilities as an astrologer, he also provides Le Neve's nativity.

I have seen his Diploma

town, but failing in estate went into the Low Countrys, and at Franecker took the degree of Doctor of Phisick; hee had some little smattering in Astrology, could resolve a question of Theft, or love question, something of sickness; a very grave person, laborious, and honest; of tall stature and comely featured; hee died of late yeares almost in the very street, near Tower Hill.

Doctor Neve had intention of printing 200 verified questions, desired my approbation of them ere they went to the press, I first would see them, and then give testimony, when I had perused the first forty, I corrected 30 of them, would read over no more, I showed him how erronious they wear, desired his emendation of the rest, which he performed not; these are now in R. Sanders custody, bought by him either of his soon or of a stationer. [WL] But first offered to be sold to me for 20s. When Mr. Saunders died I bought them off his son for less. EA

There was then William Pool[91], a nibbler at Astrology, sometymes a Gardiner, an Apparitor[92], a Drawer of Linnen, as quoifs, handkerchiffs, a plasterer, a bricklayer; hee would brag many tymes hee had been of 17 professions; was very good company for drolling, as yourself very well remember (most honoured Sir).

This William Pool pretended to poetry, and so that posterity may have a taste of it, you shall hear have inserted 2 verses of his own making; the occasion of making them was thus: One Sir Thomas Jay, a justice of peace in Rosemary Lane, issued out his warrant for apprehension of Poole, uppon a pretended suggestion that hee was in Company with some lewd people in a Tavern, where a silver cupp was lost, Anglice[93] stolen: Pool hearing of the warrant, packs up his little Trunk of books, beeing all his Library, and runns to Westminster - but hearing some months after that the Justice was dead and buried, hee came and inquired where the Grave was, and after discharge of his belly uppon the Grave, left these 2 verses uppon it, which hee swore hee made himselfe,

This William Pool was married to Alice How, at St. Georges Church Southwark. Mr Lilly gave her to him. [E.A.]

Hear lyeth buried Sir Thomas Jay Knight,
Who beeing dead, I uppon his Grave did shite.

[91]It seems that this is the same William Poole to whom Lilly was related.

[92]A servant or attendant of a civil or ecclesiastical officer. (*OED*)

[93]In English. (*OED*)

Hee died about 1651 or 1652 at St. Mary Overys in Southwark, and this was part of his last will –

Now I give to Doctor Ardee all my bookes, and one Manuscript of my owne, worth one hundred of Lillys Introduction.

Item, if Doctor Ardee give my wife any thing that is mine, I wish the Devill may fetch him body and Soule: the Doctor terrified with this curse, gave mee all the bookes and his goods, which I presently gave to his widdow: interdum seria jocis.

Now also lived this Doctor Ardee, but his true name was Richard Delahay, formerly an Atturny, hee studied Astrology and Phisick, beeing in necessity, and forced from Derbishire where hee had lived, by the old Countess of Shrewsbury; hee was of moderate judgment both in Astrology and Phisick; hee had been formerly well acquainted with Charles Sledd[94], an Apothecary, who used the Christall, and had a very perfect sight. This Doctor Ardee hath many tymes affirmed unto mee (esto fides) that an Angell one tyme appeared unto him, and offered him a lease of his life for one thousand yeares; hee died about the age of four score yeares, left his widdow who married into Kent^; worth 2 or 3 hundred pounds; William Pooles estate came to 4 or 5 pounds.

Of this Charles Sled there is mention made in Dr. Dees Booke his Discourse with Spirits, set forth by Dr. Causabon. pag. 17.

^to one Moreland.

In the yeares 1632 and 1639, John Booker[95] became famous for a prediction of his, uppon a Solar Eclipse in the 19th degree of ♈ 1633, taken out of Leovitius de magnis conjuntionibus; viz: oh Reges et principes etc. – both the King of Bohemia, and Gustavus of Sweden dying during the effects of that Eclipse.

John Booker was born in Manchester of good parentage, in the year 1601. Was in his youth well instructed in the Latin toung, which he understood very well, he seemed from his infancy to bee designed for Astrology, for

[94] *A True & Faithful Relation of What passed for many Yeers Between Sr. John Dee ... and Some Spirits:...* transcribed by Meric. Causaubon, D.D., London, 1659. Charles Sled is mentioned during one of Dee's "conversations" with a spirit.

[95] John Booker (1602?-1667), astrologer, friend of Ashmole and Lilly.

from the tyme hee had any understanding, hee would bee allways poring and studying Almanacks.

Hee came to London at fitting yeares, and served an apprentiship to an Haberdasher in Laurence Lane London, but either wanting stock to sett up, or disliking the Calling, he left at his trade and taught to write at Hadley in Middlesex severall Schollars in that Schoole; hee wrote singularly well both Secretary[96] and Roman[97]; in process of tyme, he served Sir Christopher Clothro, Knight, Alderman of London, as his Clerk, being a Citty Justice of peace; hee also was Clerk to Sir Hugh Hammersly, Alderman of London, both which hee served with great credit and estimation; and by that meanes became not only well known, but as well respected of the most eminent Citizens of London, even to his dying day.

Hee was an excellent proficient in Astrology, whose excellent verses uppon the 12 months, framed according to the configurations of each month, beeing blessed with success according to his predictions, procured him much reputation all over England; hee was a very honest man, abhorred any deceipt in the Art hee studied; had a curious fancy in judging of thefts, and as succesful in resolving Law Questions; hee was no mean Proficient in Astronomy, hee understood much in Phisick, a great admirer of the Antimoniall Cupp, not unlearned in Chymistry, which hee loved well, but did not practise.

Hee was much inclined to a Diabetes, and in the last 3 yeares of his life was afflicted with a Disentery which at last consumed him to nothing. Hee died of good fame in 1667 – since his disease I have seen one Nativity of his performance, exactly directed, and judged with as much learning as from Astrology can be expected.

they cost mee 140^{L}*.* [E.A.]

His Library of bookes came short of the worlds expectation, wear by his widdow sold to Elias Ashmole Esquire, who most generously gave her farr more money than they wear worth, but out of his respects unto the deceased and his memory, hee most willingly payd her the money; hee left behind him

[96]A type of handwriting used mainly in legal documents of the 15th to 17th centuries. (*OED*)

[97]Of handwriting: round and bold (1601). (*OED*)

2 sons and 2 daughters; hee left in writing very little, but his Annuall Prognostications. Hee began first to write about the year 1630 – hee wrote Bellum Hybermicale, in the tyme of the Long Parlament[98], a very sober and judicious booke, the Epistle thereunto I gave him; he wrote lately a small Treatise of Easter day, a very Learned thing, wherein hee showed much learning and reading; to say no more of him, hee lived an honest man, his fame not questioned at his death.

In this year 1633, I became acquainted with Nicholas Fisk[99], Licentiate in Phisick, who was born in Suffolk near Frammingham[100] Castle, of very good parentage, who educated him at Country Schools untill hee was fitt for University; but hee went not to the Academy, studying at home both Astrology and Phisick, which hee afterwards practised in Colchester, and there was well acquainted with Doctor Gilbert, who wrote de Magnete;[101] hee came afterwards unto London, and excersised his facultys in severall places thereof, (for in his youth hee would never stay long in one house); in 1633 hee was sent for out of Suffolk by Doctor Winston of Gresham Colledge to instruct the Lord Treasurer Westons soons in Arithmetick, Astronomy, uppon the Globes and their uses.

Hee was a person very studious, laborious, of good apprehension and had by his own industry obtained both Astrology, Phisick, Arithmetick, Astronomy, Geometry and Algebra singular judgment; hee would in Astrology resolve horary questions very soundly, but was ever diffident of his own abilitys; hee was exquisitly skillfull in the Art of Directions uppon Nativitys, and had a good Genius in performing judgment thereuppon,

---

[98]The Long Parliament began in 1640.

[99]Dr. Nicholas Fiske (1579?-1659), astrologer and medical practitioner. Sir Robert Holborne was one of his clients. Fiske became a close friend of Lilly; John Gadbury claimed Fiske as his teacher after Fiske's death. His son Matthew Fiske was also an astrologer. See our discussion of Fiske's date of birth and Gadbury's involvement in *Monster of Ingratitude.*

[100]Framlingham.

[101]William Gilbert (1544-1603) first described electricity in his work on magnetism in this book of 1600, it was he who established the scientific study of magnetism and who is often considered to be the father electrical studies. (*Britannica*)

but very unhappy hee was that hee had no Genius in teaching his Schollers[102], for hee never perfected any; his own son Mathew hath often told mee, that where his father did teach any Schollers in his tyme, they would principally learn of him; hee had Scorpio ascending, and was secretly envious to those hee thought had more parts than him selfe; however I must be ingenious, and do affirm, that by frequent conversation with him, I came to know which wear the best Authors, and much to enlarge my judgment, especially in the Art of Directions.

Hee visited mee most days once after I became acquainted with him, and would communicate his most doubtful questions unto mee, and accept of my judgment therein rather than his own; hee singularly well judged and directed Sir Robert Holborns Nativity[103], but desired mee to adjudge the 1st house, 7th and 10th thereof, which I did, and which Nativity is (since Sir Robert gave it to mee) come by your hands and remaines in your Library (oh Learned Esquire); hee died about the 78 year of his age, poor.

In this year also, William Bredon, Parson or Vicar of Thornton in Buckinghamshire was living; a profound Divine but absolutely the most polite person for Nativitys in that age, strictly adhearing to Ptolemy, which hee well understood; hee had a hand in composing Sir Christopher Heydons[104] defence of Judiciall Astrology[105], beeing at that tyme his Chaplain; hee was so given over to Tobacco and drink, that when hee had no Tobacco, he would cutt the Bell ropes, and smoke them.

I now come to continue the story of my own life but thought it not inconvenient to committ unto memory something concerning those persons who practised when first I became a Student in Astrology. I have

---

[102]Fiske's nativity given in *Gadbury*, page 127-8, but is incorrect.

[103]Holborne's nativity given in *Gadbury* page 124.

[104]Sir Christopher Heydon (1561-1623), soldier and writer on astrology. Heydon's nativity given in *Gadbury* page 180.

[105]This manuscript was given to Dr. Richard Forster and following his death in 1616, came into the hands of Nicholas Fiske who was encouraged by Ashmole and Lilly to publish it. (Bernard Capp, *ODNB*).

wrote nothing concerning any of them which I my selfe do not either know or beleeve to bee true.

In october 1633 my first wife died, and left mee whatever was hers, it was considerable, very near to the value of one thousand pounds.

One whole year and more I continued a widdower and followed my studys very hard, during which tyme a Scholler pawned unto mee for 40s. Ars Notoria, a large Volumn wrote in Parchment, with the names of those Angells and their Pictures which are thought and beleeved by Wise men to teach and instruct in all the 7 Liberall Sciences, and this is attained by observing elected Tymes and those prayers appropriated unto the severall Angells.

Among Sir Napiers MS. I had an Ars Notoria written by S. Forman. Large Vellum. [E.A.]

I do ingeniously acknowledge, I used those prayers according to the form and direction prescribed for some weeks, using the word Astrologia for Astronomia, but of this no more. That Ars Notoria, inserted in the latter end of Cornelius Agrippa[106] signifyeth nothing, many of the prayers beeing not the same, nor is the Direction unto those prayers any thing considerable.

In the year 1634 I taught Sir George Peckham Knight Astrology, that part which concerns sicknesses, wherein hee so profited, that in 2 or 3 months hee would give a very true discovery of any disease, onely by his figures; hee practised in Nottingham, but unfortunately died 1635 at St. Winifreds well in Wales, in which well hee continued for so long mumbling his Pater nosters, and Sancta Winifride ora pro me, that the cold struck into his body, and after his comming forth of that well, never spoke more.

In this year 1634 I purchased the moyity of thirteen houses in the strand for 530L.[107].

[106]Robert Turner's 1657 edition; his own translation omitting diagrams essential to understanding the text. It was printed with Agrippa's *Opera Omnia.*

[107]Used as an example in *Christian Astrology* page 219. At today's value this would be approximately £40,000, this amount, however, would not buy one house in London, much less a half share of thirteen.

In November, 18th day I was again the second tyme married, and had 500L portion with that wife; shee was of the nature of Mars.[108]

Two Accidents happened unto mee in that yeare, something memorable.

Davy Ramsey brought an halfe quarter sack to putt the treasure in.

Davy Ramsey, his Majestys Clockmaker[109], had been informed that there was a great quantity of Treasure buried in the Cloysters of Westminster Abbey, hee acquaints Dean Williams therewith, who was also then Bishop of Lincoln; the Dean gave him Liberty to search after it, with this Proviso, that if any wear discovered, his Church should have a share of it; Davy Ramsey finds out one John Scott, who pretended the use of the Mosaicall Rodds, to assist him hearin; I was desired to joyn with him, unto which I consented; one winters night Davy Ramsey with severall gentlemen, my selfe and Scott enter the Cloysters; wee playd the hasell Rods round about the Cloyster; uppon the west side of the Cloysters, the Rodds turned one over an other, an argument that the Treasure was there; the Laborers digged at least six foot deepe, and then wee mett with a Coffin, but in regard it was not heavy, wee did not open, which wee afterwards much repented; from the Cloysters, wee went into the Abbey Church, when uppon a sudden, (there beeing no wynd when we begann) so feirce, so high, so blustering and loud a wynd did rise that wee verily believed the west end of the Church would have fallen uppon us; our rodds would not moove at all, the Candles and Toarches all but one extinguished or burnt very dimly.

This Scot lived in Pudding Lane, and had sometime been a Page (or such like) to the Lord Norris. [E.A.]

John Scott my partner was amased, looked pale, knew not what to think or do, untill I gave directions and commanded to dismiss the Dœmons, which when done, all was quiet again, and each man returned unto his Lodging late about 12 of clock at night: I could never since bee induced to joyne with any in such like Actions.

---

[108]Her nativity can be found in Appendix 4.

[109]David Ramsay (c. 1575-1660), father of William Ramesey (1627-1676?), astrologer and physician, author of *Astrologia Restaurata* (1653).

The true miscarriage of the operation of the business was by reason of so many people beeing present at the Operation, for there was about 30, some laughing, others deriding us, so that if wee had not dismissed the Dæmons, I beleeve, most part of the Abbey Church had been blown down. Secrecy, and intelligent operators, with a strong confidence and knowledge of what they are doing, are the best for this worke.

In the same year 1634 or 1635, a Lady living in Greenwich who had tryed all the known Artists in London but to no purpose, came weeping and lamenting her condition, which was this; shee had permitted a young Lord to have the use of her body, till shee was with child by him, after which tyme, hee could not, or would indure her sight, but commanded his lacquies and servants to keep his door fast shutt, least shee should gett in to his chamber, or if they chanced to see her near his lodging to drive her away, which they severall tymes had done; her desire unto mee was to assist her to see him, and then shee should bee content; whereuppon I ordered such a day, such an houre of that day to try her fortune once more.

Shee obeyed, and when shee came to the Kings bench where the Lord was imprisoned, the outward dore stood wide open, none speaking a word unto her, shee went upp staires, nobody molesting her, shee found the Lords chamber dore wide open, hee in bed, not a servant to bee heard or seen: so shee was pleased. Three days after, shee came to acquaint mee with her success, and then drew out of her pocket a paper full of Ratsbane[110], which had she not had admission unto him that day I appointed, shee would in a pint of white wyne have drunk at the stayres foot where the Lord lodged.

The like misfortune befell her after that, when the Lord was out of prison, then I ordered her such a day, to go see a Play at Salisbury Court, which shee did, and within one quarter of an houre, the Lord came into the same Box wherein shee was – but I grew weary of such imployments, and since have burned my bookes, which instructed those Curiositys: for after that, I became melanchollly, very much afflicted with the Hypocondriack melanchollly, growing lean and spare, and every day worse, so that in the year 1635, my infirmity continuing and my acquaintance increasing, I resolved to live in the country, and in March and Aprill 1636 removed

[110] Rat poison.

my goods unto Hersham where I now live, and in May my person, where I continued until 1641: no notice being taken who, or what I was.

In the yeares 1637 and 1638 I had great Lawsuites both in the Exchequer and chancery, about a lease I had of the annuall value of 80^{L}. I gott the victory.

In the year 1640, I instructed John Humphrys, M^{r}. of Art in the study of Astrology, uppon this occasion. Beeing at London, by accident in Fleet street, I mett Doctor Peircivall Willoughby[111] of Derby; wee wear of old acquaintance, and hee but by great chance lately come to town, wee went to the Miter Tavern in Fleet street, where I sent for old William Pool the Astrologer living then in Ram Alley; being come to us, the D^{r}. produced a bill set forth by a M^{r}. of Arts in Cambridge, intimating his abilitys for resolving of all manner of Questions Astrologically; the bill was showed, and I wondering at it, Poole made Answer, hee knew the man, and that hee was a silly foole; I, quoth hee, can do more than hee; hee see's mee every day, hee'l bee hear by and by, and indeed hee came into our Room presently; Pool had just as wee came to him sett a figure, and then showed it mee desiring my judgment, which I refused, but desired the M^{r}. of Arts to judge first; hee denyed, so I gave myne, to the very great liking of Humfrys, who presently inquired, if I would teach him, and for what? I told him I was willing to teach, but would have 100^{L}. I heard Pool whilst I was judging the figure whisper in Humphrys eare, and swear I was the best in England; staying 3 or 4 days in town, at last wee contracted for 40^{L}, for I could never bee quiet from his sollicitations; hee invited mee to supper and before I had showed him any thing, payd me 35^{L}.

As wee wear at supper, a Client came to speak with him, and so up into his closset hee went with his client; I called him in before hee sett his figure or resolved the question, and instantly acquainted him how he should discover the moles or markes of his Client; hee sett his figure and presently discovers 4 moles the Querent had, and was so overjoyed therewith, that hee came tumbling down the stayres, crying foure by G[112], foure by G, I will

---

[111]See the earlier comment regarding Dr. Willoughby of Gloucester.
[112]"...by God..."

not take one hundred pounds for this one Rule; in six weeks tyme and tarrying with him 3 days in a weeke, hee became a most judicious Person.

This Humphres was a laborious person, vainglorious, loquacious, fool hardy, desirous of all secrets, which hee knew not, inso much that hee would have given mee 200^{L} to have instructed him in some curiositys hee was perswaded I had knowledge of, but Artis est celare Artem, especially to those who live not in the fear of God, or can be Masters of their own Councells: hee was in person and condition such an other as that Monster of Ingratitude my quondam Taylor John Gadbury.[113]

After my refusall of teaching him, what hee was not capable of, wee grew strong, though I affoarded him many Civillitys when ever hee required it, for after the Seige of Colchester, hee wrote a book against mee, called the Antimerlinus Anglicus, married a second wife, his first living in Cambridgeshire, then practised Phisick by a contrary name; having intentions to practise in Ireland, he went to Bristoll, but there understanding the Parlaments forces had reduced that Kingdome, hee came back to London but durst not abide therein, but running from his second wife, who also had another husband, hee went to sea, with intention for Barbados, but died by the way in his voyage.

I had never seen John Booker at that tyme, but telling him one day I had a desire to see him, but first ere I would speak with him I would fitt my selfe with my old Rules and rubb up[114] my Astrology, for at that tyme, and this was 1640, I thought John Booker the greatest and most complete Astrologer in the world: my Scholler Humfrys presently made answer; Tutor, you need not pumpe for your former knowledge, John Booker is no such pumper, wee mett sayth hee the other day, and I was too hard for him my selfe uppon judgment of 3 or 4 questions; if all the transactions happening unto that my Scholler wear in one Volumn, they would transcend

[113]John Gadbury (1627-1704), astrologer. A prolific writer and, although, supported by Lilly early in Gadbury's career, became his enemy. For Gadbury's nativity, see *Gadbury* page 190 and for a close examination of this relationship, see *Monster of Ingratitude.*

[114]Polish, revise or rehearse.

either Guzman, Don Quixot, Lazarillo de Tormes or any other of the like nature I ever did see.[115]

Having now in part recovered my health, beeing weary of the Country, and perceiving there was money to bee gott in London, and thinking myselfe to bee as sufficiently inabled in Astrology as any I could meet with, I made it my business to repair thither and so in September 1641 I did, where all the years 1642 and 1643 I had great leasure to better my former knowledge; I then read over all my books of Astrology, over and over, had very little or no practise at all, and whereas formerly I could never indure to read Valentin Naibod his Commentary uppon Alcabitius, now having seriously studied him, I found him to bee the profoundest Author I ever mett with, him I traversed over day and night, from whom I must acknowledge to have advanced my judgment and knowledge unto that height I soon after arrived at, or unto: a most rationall Author, and the sharpest Expositor of Ptolemy that hath yet appeared.

To excercise my Genius, I began to collect notes and thought of writing some little thing uppon the Conjunction of ♄ and ♃[116] then approaching – I had not wrote above one sheet, and that very meanly, but James Lord Galloway came to see mee, and by chance casting his eyes uppon that rude collection, hee read it over, and so approoved of it, yea so incouraged mee to proceed further, that then and after that tyme I spent most of my tyme in composing thereof, and bringing it in the end unto that Method wherein it was printed 1644: I do seriously now profess, I had not the assistance of any person living in the writing or composing thereof. Mr. Fiske sent mee a small Manuscript which had been Sr. Christopher Heydons, who had wrote something of the conjunction of ♄ and ♃ 1603, out of which, to bring my Method in order, I transcribed in the beginning five or six lines, and not any more, though that graceless fellow Gadbury wrote the contrary; but semel et semper Nebulo et mendax[117].

---

[115]Lilly is here referring to his student's exaggeration and fantasies.

[116]"...Conjunction of Jupiter and Saturn..."

[117]Ever and always a good-for-nothing and a liar.

I did formerly write one Treatise in the year 1639 uppon the Eclipse of the Sun in the 11th degree of Gemini 22° May 1639: it consisted of six sheets of paper, but that manuscript I gave unto my most munificent Patron and ever bountifull freind William Pennington of Muncaster in Cumberland Esquire; a wise and excellently learned person, who from the year 1634 even till hee died continued unto mee the most gratefull person I ever was acquainted with; I became acquainted with him by meanes of Davy Ramsey.

Propheticall Merline

Oh most noble Esquire, let mee now begg your pardon if I digress for some small tyme in commemmorating his bounty unto mee, and my requitall of his freindship, by performing many things successfully for his advantage.

In 1639 hee was made Captain, and served his Majesty in his then Warrs against the Scotts; during which tyme a Farmers daughter beeing delivered of a bastard, and hearing by report that hee was slaine, fathered the Child uppon him; shortly after hee returned, most woefully vexing to bee thus abused when absent; the woaman was countenanced by some gentlemen of Cumberland in this her villany against him, so that, not withstanding hee had warrants to attach her body, hee could never discover her, but yet hunting her from one place to an other, her freinds thought it most convenient to send her to London, where shee might bee in most safety, shee same upp to the Citty, and immediately I had notice thereof, and the care of that matter left unto mee, I procured the Lord Cheif Justice Bramstons warrant and had it lying Dormant by mee; shee had not been in the Citty above one fortnight, but that I going casually to the Clark of the Assizes officer for Cumberland, saw there an handsome woaman, and hearing of her speake the Northern Tone[118], I concluded shee was the party I did so want; I rounded the Clark in his ear, and told him I would give him 5s. to hold the woaman in chatt till I came again, for I had a writing concerned her; I hasted for my warrant and a Constable, and returned into the Office, seized her person before the Clark of Assizes, who was very angry with mee; it was then Sessions at old Bayly and neither Judge or Justice to bee found; at night wee carried her before the Recorder Gardner; it beeing

[118]Accent of the north of England

Saterday at night, shee having no baile, was sent to Bridewell[119], where shee remained till Munday.

On munday morning at old Baily, shee produced Baile, but I desiring of the Recorder some tyme to inquire after the baile, whether they wear sufficient, returned presently and told him one of the baile was a prisoner in Ludgate, the other a very poor man, at which hee was so vexed hee sent her to Newgate, where shee lay all that week until shee could please mee with good suretys, which then shee did, and so was bound over to appear at the next assizes in Cumberland, which she did, and was there sentenced to be whipt and imprisoned one whole yeare.

This Action infinitely pleased Mr. Pennington, who thought I could do wonders, and I was most thankfully requited for it; all the while of this scandalous business, do what hee could, hee could not discover what persons they wear that suppoarted her, but the woamans father comming to London, I became acquainted with him by the name of Mr. Sute, merchant, invited him to a dinner, gott George Farmer[120] with mee, where wee so plyed him with wyne, hee could neither see or feele; I payd the recconing beeing 22s. – but next morning the poor man had never a writing or Letter in his pocket; I sent them down to my freind, who thereby discovered the plotts of severall gentlemen in the business, after which Mr. Sute returned to his old name again.

Mr. Pennington was a true Royallist, whom Charles the second made one of his Commissioners of Array for Cumberland; having direction from mee continually how matters did and would go betwixt the King and Parlament, hee acted warily, and did but signe one only Warrant of that nature, and then gave over; when the tymes of Sequestrations came, one John Musgrave[121], the most bold and impudent fellow, and most active of all the North of England and most malitious against my freind, had gott

[119]Bridewell prison.

[120]Possibly the same person as "G.Farmer" who provided the means for Charles I's attempted escape from Carisbrooke Castle.

[121]John Musgrave (fl. 1642-54), pamphleteer. (David L. Smith, *ODNB*).

this Warrant under Mr. Penningtons hand into his Custody, which affrighted my freind, and so it might, for it was cause inough of sequestration, and would have done it, Musgrave intending and promising him selfe great matters out of his estate; I was made acquainted hearwith, Musgrave beeing in London: by much ado, I gott acquainted with him, pretending my selfe a bitter enemy against

Mr. Pennington, whereat hee very hartily rejoyced; and so wee appointed one night to meet at the 5 Bells to compare Notes, for I pretended much; wee did meet, and hee very suddenly produced uppon the table all his papers, and with all, the Warrant of Array unto which my freind had sett his hand, which when I saw, I marry sayd I, this is his hand I will swear, now have it all, come the other cupp, this warrant shall pay for all; I observed where the warrant lay uppon the table, and after some tyme tooke occasion ignorantly to let the Candle fall out which whilst hee went to light it again at the fire, I made sure of the Warrant and putt it into my bootes, hee never missing it of 8 or 10 days, about which tyme I beleeve it was above halfe way towards Cumberland, for I instantly sent it by the Post, with this freindly Caveat, sinn no more: Musgrave durst not challenge mee in those tymes, and so the business was ended – very satisfactory to my freind, and no less to my selfe.

Hee was besides extremely abused by one Isaac Antrobus, Parson at Egremond, a most evill liver, bold, and very rich; at last hee procured a Minister of that Country in hope of the Parsonage, to article against him in London before the Committee of plundered Ministers; I was once more invited to sollicit against Antrobus, which I did uppon 3 or more Articles –

> that Antrobus baptized a Cock, and called him Pater;
>
> hee had knowledge of such a woaman and of her daughter, viz of
>
> both their bodys, in as large a manner as ever of his own wife;
>
> beeing drunk, a woaman tooke a Corde and tyed it about his
>
> privy members unto a Manger in a stable;

for beeing a continuall drunkard;

hee never preached etc.

Antrobus was now become a great Champion for the Parlament, but at the day of hearing, I had procured aboundance of my freinds to bee there, for the Godly, as they termed themselves, sided with him; the present M^r^. of the Rolls was chair man that day, S^r^. Harbottle Grimston[122], who hearing the fowlness of the cause was very much ashamed thereof; I remember Antrobus beeing there, pleaded hee was in his naturall condition when hee acted so ingraciously –

What condicion wear you in, sayd the Chair man,
when you lay with mother and daughter;
Theres no proof of that, sayth hee;
None but your own confession, sayd the Chairman,
nor any could tell so well;
I am not given to drunkenness (quoth he);

Hee was so drunk within this fortnight (quoth I), hee reeled from one side of the street to the other, heares the witness to proove it, who presently before the Committee beeing sworne, made it good, and named the place and street where hee had been drunk.

So hee was adjudged scandalous, and outed[123] of his benefice, and our Minister had the Parsonage. You cannot imagine how much the routing of this drunken Parson pleased M^r^. Pennington, who payd all charges munificently, and thankfully.

But now follows the last and greatest kindness I ever did him; notwithstanding the Committee for Sequestrations in Cumberland wear his very good freinds, yet the sub-Sequestrators of their own heads and

---

[122]Sir Harbottle Grimston (1603-1685), barrister and politician. In his early years he became a friend of Bulstrode Whitelock. (Christopher W. Brooks, *ODNB*)

[123]Removed from.

without order, and by strength of armes, secured his Iron, his wood, and so much of his personall estate as was valued at 7000^{L}.

Now had I Complaint uppon Complaint, would I suffer my old freind to bee thus abused it was in my power to free him from these villains – I hearuppon advised what was best to do, and was councelled to gett M^{r}. Speaker Lenthall[124] his letter to the Subsequestrators, and command them to bee obedient to the Committee of the County.

Whereuppon I framed a letter my selfe, unto the Subsequestrator directed, and with it my selfe and M^{r}. Laurence Maydwell (whom yourself well know) went to see M^{r}. Speaker unto whom wee sufficiently related the stubbornness of the officers in Cumberland, their disobedience to the Committee and then shewed him the letter, which when hee had read over, hee most courteously signed, adding withall that if they proceeded further in sequestring M^{r}. Pennington hee would command a Serjant at Armes to bring them upp to answer their Contempts: I immediately posted that letter to my freind, which when the absurd fellows received, they delivered him possession of his goods again: and for my paines when hee came to London, gave mee one hundred pounds: hee died in 1652, of a violent feaver.

I did carefully in 1642 and 1643 take notice of every grand action which happened betwixt King and Parlament, and did first then incline to beleeve that as all Sublunary affaires did depend uppon Superior causes, so there was a possibility of discovering them by the Configurations of the superior bodys, in which way making some Essays in those 2 yeares, I found incouragment to proceed further, which I did. I perused the writings of the Antients but therein they wear silent or gave no satisfaction; at last I framed unto my selfe that Method, which then and since I follow, which I hope in tyme may bee more perfected by a more penetrating person than my selfe.

In 1643 I became familiarly know to S^{r}. Bolstrod Whitlock[125] a member of the house of Commons, hee being sick, his urine was brought unto me by

[124]William Lenthall (1591-1662), lawyer and Speaker of the House of Commons. (*ODNB*)

Mrs[rs]. Lisle, wife of John Lisle[126], afterwards one of the Keepers of the great Seal; having sett my figure, I returned answer, the sick for that tyme would recover, but by meanes of a surfett would dangerously relapse within one month, which hee did, by eating of Troute at Mr. Sands house near Leathered in Surrey; then I went daily to visit him, Dr. Prideau dispairing of his life, but I sayd there was no danger thereof, and that hee would bee sufficiently well in 5 or 6 weeks, and so hee was.

Merl. Anglic. [unknown hand]

a. the booke. [E.A.]

Jo. Booker. [unknown hand]

In 1644 I published Merlinus Anglicus Junior, about Aprill, I had given one day the Coppy thereof unto the then Mr. Whitlock, who by accident was reading thereof in the house of Commons ere the Speaker tooke the Chair – one lookt uppon it, and so did many, and gott Coppies thereof, which when I heard, I applied my selfe to John Booker to License it, for then hee was Licenser of all Mathematicall Bookes; I had to my knowledge never seen him before; hee woondred at[a] it, made many impertinent obliterations, framed many objections, swore it was not possible to distinguish betwixt King and Parlament, at last licensed it according to his own fancy; I delivered it unto the Printer, who beeing an arch Presbiterian had five of the Ministry inspect it, who could make nothing of it, but sayd it might bee printed, for in that I medled not with their Dagon[127]; the first impression was sold in less than one week; when I presented some to the Members of Parlament, I complained of John Booker the Licenser, who had defaced my booke; they gave me order forthwith to reprint it as I would, and let them know if any durst resist mee in the reprinting, or adding what I thought fitt, so the second tyme it came forth as I would have it.

I must confess I now found my Scholler Humphrys words to bee true concerning John Booker, whom at that tyme I found but moderately versed in Astrology, nor could hee take the Circles of Position of the planets untill that year I instructed him; after my Introduction in 1647 became publiq, hee

[125]Sir Bulstrode Whitelock (1605-1675), lawyer and politician. Patron and friend of William Lilly who bequeathed his Hersham estate to Whitelock's son, Carlton, at the death of his wife, Ruth.

[126]John Lisle (1609/10-1664) politician, regicide.

[127]Dagon: idol. (*OED*)

amended beyond measure, by study partly, and partly uppon Emulation to keep upp his fame and reputation, so that since 1647 I have seen some Nativitys by him very judiciously performed; when the Printer presented him with an Introduction of mine, as soon as they wear forth of the press: I wish, sayth hee, there was never an other but this in England. Conditionally I gave one hundred pounds for this; after that tyme wee wear very great friends to his dying day.

Introduction. [unknown hand]

In June 1644, I published Supernaturall Sigh[t]s, and indeed if I could have procured the Dull Stationer to have been at Charges to have cutt the Icon or forme of that prodigious Apparition as I had drawn it forth, it would have given great satisfaction, however the Astrologicall Judgment thereuppon had its full event in every particular.

That year also I published the white Kings Prophecy, of which there wear sold in 3 days eighteen hundred, so that it was oft reprinted: I then made Commentary uppon it. In that year I printed Propheticall Merline, and had eight pounds for the Coppy.

I had no further intention to trouble the press any more, but Sir Richard Napper, having received one of Captain Whartons[128] Allmanacks for 1645, under the name of Naworth[129], hee came unto mee; Now Lilly, you are mett with all, see hear what Naworth writes; the words wear, hee called mee an impudent senseless fellow, and by name William Lilly.

Before that tyme I was more Cavalier then Roundhead, and so taken notice of, but after that, I engaged body and soule in the cause of Parlament, but still with much affection to his Majestys person and unto monarchy, which I ever loved and approoved beyond any Government whatsoever, and you will find in this story many passages of Civillity, which I did and indeavored to do with the hazard of my life for his Majesty; but God ordered all his affaires and Councells to have no successes, as in the sequel will appear.

---

[128]Sir George Wharton (1617-1681), royalist astrologer. Friend of Ashmole, enemy, and later, friend of Lilly. (*ODNB*)

[129]Wharton's pen-name.

To vindicate my reputation and to cry Quittance with Naworth, against whom I was highly insensed, to work I went again for Anglicus 1645, which as soon as finished I gott to the Press, thinking every day one month till it was publiq; I therein made use of the Kings Nativity and finding that his Ascendant was approaching to the Quadrature of Mars, about June 1645 I gave this unlucky judgment: if now wee fight, a victory stealeth uppon us, and so it did in June 1645 at Naseby, the most fatall overthrow hee ever had.

In this year 1645 I published a Treatise called the Starry Messenger, with an Interpretation of 3 Suns seen in London 19° November 1644 being Charles the second[130] his byrth day; in that book I allso putt forth an Astrologicall judgment concerning the effects of a Solar Eclipse visible the 11th of August 1645; 2 dayes before its publishing, my Antagonist Cap: Wharton having given his Astrologicall Judgement uppon his Majestys present March from Oxford, therein again fell fowle against mee and John Booker; Sr. Samuell Luke[131] Governor of Newport Pagnell, had the thing came to his Garrison from Oxford, which presently was presented unto my view, I had but 12 houres or there abouts to answer it, which I did with such success as is incredible, and the printer printed both the March and my answer unto it, and produced it to light with my Starry messenger, which came forth and was made publiq the very day of the Parlaments great victory obtained against his majesty in person at Naseby, under the conduct of the Lord Thomas Fairfax.

That booke no sooner appeared, but within 14 days Complaint was made to the Committee of examinations, Miles Corbet[132] the beeing Chairman, my mortall enemy, hee who after was hanged, drawn and quartered for beeing one of the Kings Judges; hee graunts his Warrant, and a Messenger to the serjant at Armes seiseth my person. As I was going to Westminster with the Messenger, I mett Sr. Phillip Stapleton[133], Sr. Christopher Wray,[134]

130Underlined to bring attention to the error, it should read: "Charls the first".

131Sir Samuel Luke (bap. 1603 d. 1670), parliamentary army officer. (*ODNB*)

132Miles Corbet (1594/5-1662), politician and regicide. He was one of nine to be hanged, drawn and quartered following the Restoration of 1660. (Sarah Barber, *ODNB*)

Mr. Denzill Hollis[135], Mr. Robert Reynolds[136], who by great fortune had the Starry messenger sheet by sheet from mee as it came form the Press; they presently fell a smiling at me; Miles Corbett, Lilly will punish thee soundly, but fear nothing, wee will dine, and make haste to bee at the Committee tyme inough to do thy business, and so they most honorably performed, for they as soon as they came satt down and putt Mr. Reynolds purposely into the Chaire, and I was called in, but Corbett beeing not there, they bid mee withdraw, until hee came, which when hee did

I was commanded to appear, and Corbet desired to give the cause of my beeing in restraint, and of the Comittees order; Mr. Reynolds was purposely putt into the Chair and continued till my business was over. Corbet produced my Anglicus of 1645, and sayd there wear many scandalous passages therein against the Commissioners of the Excise in London; hee produced one passage, which beeing openly read by him selfe, the whole Committee adjudged it to signify the errors of Sub-officers but had no relation to the Commissioners them selves, which I affirmatively maintained to bee the true meaning as the Committee declared.

Then Corbet found out an other dangerous place as hee thought, and the words wear thus in the printed book – In the name of the father, Son and holy Ghost, will not the Excise pay the Soldiers; Corbet very ignorantly read, will not the Eclips pay Soldiers, at which the Committee fell hartily to Laugh at him, and so hee became silent.

There was a great many Parlament men there, the Chamber was full; have you any more against Mr. Lilly cry'd the Chairman;

133Sir Philip Stapleton (bap. 1603, d. 1647), politician and army officer. By this time both Stapleton and Holles had considerable influence and power. (Andrew J. Hopper, *ODNB*)

134Sir Christopher Wray (bap. 1601, d. 1646), politician. (*ODNB*)

135Denzil Holles (1598-1680), politician. (*ODNB*)

136Sir Robert Reynolds (1600/1-1678), politician and lawyer. (*ODNB*)

Yes sayth the Sollicitor for the Excise, since his Starry Messenger came forth, wee had our house burnt, and the Commissioners pulled by their Cloaths in the Exchange –

Pray Sir, when was this, asked old S^{r}. Robert Pym, that your house was burnt and the Aldermen abused;

It was in such a week, sayth hee; M^{r}. Lilly, when came your book forth? The very day of Naseby fight, answered M^{r}. Reynolds, nor need hee bee ashamed of writing it, I had it daily as it came forth of the press. It was then found the house to bee burned and the Aldermen abused 12 days before the Starry messenger came forth; what a lying fellow art thou, sayth Sir Robert Pym, to abuse us so, this hee spoke to the Sollicitor; then stood up one Bassell, a Merchant; hee inveighed bitterly against mee, beeing a Presbiterian, and would have had my bookes burnt: you smell more of a Citizen than a Scholler, replyed M^{r}. Francis Drake; I was ordered to withdraw, and by and by was called in, and acquainted, the Committee did discharge mee; but I cry'd with a lowd voice, I was under a messenger; wheruppon the Committee ordered him nor the Serjant at Armes to take any Fees, M^{r}. Reynolds saying, Literate men never pay any fees.

I have 24^{L} per an: in Lecestershire my tennant wrote me word all went for taxes.

But within one week after, I was likely to have had worse success, but that the before named gentlemen stoutly befreinded mee. In my Epistle of the Starry Messenger, I had been a little too plain with the Committee of Lecestershire who, thereof made complaint unto Sir Arthur Hazellrigg[137] Knight for that county; hee was a furious person, and made a motion in the house of Commons against mee, and the business was committed to that Committee whereof Baron Rigby was Chair man; a day was assigned to heare the matter, in the morning whereof, as I passed by M^{r}. Pullens shopp in Pauls Churchyard, Pullen bad, God bee with you; [A]M^{r}. Seldon[138], beeing there and hearing my name, gave direction to call mee unto him, where hee acquaints mee with Hazellriggs humour and malice towards mee,

[137]Sir Arthur Hesilrige (1601-1661), baronet, army officer and politician, a staunch republican.

[138]Probably John Selden (1584-1654) lawyer, politician, historical and linguistic scholar. (*ODNB*)

called for the Starry Messenger, and having read over the words mentioning the Committee, hee asked me how I would answer them; I related what I would have sayd, but hee contradicted mee and acquainted mee what to say and how to answer.

In the afternoon I went to appear, but there was no Committee satt or would sitt, for both Mr. Reynolds and Sr. Phillip Stapleton and my other freinds, had fully acquainted Baron Rigby with the business, and desired not to call uppon mee until they appeared, for the matter and Charge intended against mee was very frivolous, and onely presented by a chollerick person to please a Company of Clowns, meaning the Committee of Lecester; Baron Rigby sayd if it wear so, hee would not medle with the matter, but exceedingly desired to see mee; not long after, hee met Sir Arthur, and acquainting him what freinds appeared for mee, I will then persecute him no further.

A. and named mee by name.

All the antient Astrologers of England wear much startled and confounded at my manner of writing, especially old Mr. William Hodges, who lived near Woolverhampton in Staffordshire, and many others who understood Astrology competently well, as they thought; Hodges swore I did more by Astrology then hee could by the Christall and use thereof, which indeed hee understood as perfectly as any one in England; hee was a great Royallist, but could never hitt any thing right for that party, though hee much desired it; hee resolved Questions Astrologically, Nativitys hee medled not with; in things of other nature which required more curiosity, hee repaired to the Christall. His Angells wear Raphael, Gabriel and Uriel; his life conformed not in holiness and sanctity to what it should, having to deale with those holy Angells.

Beeing contemporary with mee, I shall relate what my X partner[139] John Scott affirmed of him; John Scott was a little skillfull in Chirurgy and Phisick, so was Will Hodges, and had formerly been a Schoolmaster; Scott having some occasions into Staffordshire adressed himselfe for a month or six weeks to Hodges, assisted him to dress his patients, let blood etc. Beeing to returne

X the same Scott as is before mentioned.

[139]It would appear that Lilly refers to Scott as his partner in magical pursuits, although he does not explain this. This might have similar connotations as that of the partnership between John Dee and Edward Kelly.

to London, hee desired Hodges to show him the person and feature of the woaman hee should marry; Hodges carrys him into a feild not farr from his house, pulls out his Christall, bids Scott set his foot to his, and after a while, wishes him to inspect the Christall and observe what hee saw there; I saw, sayth Scott, a ruddy complexioned wench in a red wastcoat drawing a cann of bear. Shee must bee your wife, sayd Hodges; you are mistaken Sir, sayd Scott, I am so soon as I come to London to marry a tall gentlewoaman in old Bayly; you must marry the red Wastcoat, sayd Hodges; Scott leaves the Country, comes up to London, finds his gentlewoaman married; 2 yeares after, going unto Dover, in his return hee refreshed himselfe at an Inn in Canterbury, and as hee came into the Hall or first Room thereof, hee mistook the Room and went into the Buttery, where hee espied a mayd described by Hodges as before sayd, drawing a Cann of bear etc. Hee then more narrowly veiwing her person and habit, found her in all parts to bee the same Hodges had described, after which hee became a Sutor unto her, and was married unto her, which woaman I have often seen[140]; this Scott related unto mee severall tymes, beeing a very honest person and made great conscience of what hee spoke.

An other story of him is as followeth, which I had related from a person which well knew the Truth of it.

A neighbour gentleman of Hodges, lost his horse, who having Hodges advice for recovery of him, did again obtain him. Some yeares after, in a frolliq, hee thought to abuse him, acquainting a Neighbour therewith, viz that hee had formerly lost a horse, went to Hodges, recovered him again, but, sayth hee, it was by chance, I might have had him without going unto him, come, lets go, I will now putt a trick uppon him; I will leave some boy or other at the Townes end with my horse, and then go to Hodges and inquire for him.

Hee did so, gave his horse to a youth with orders to walke him till hee returned; away hee goes with his freind, salutes Mr. Hodges, thanks him for his former curtesy, and now desires the like, having lost a horse very

[140]As this was John Scott's wife, it indicates that Lilly was a frequent visitor to that household, or vice versa.

lately; Hodges, after some tyme of pawsing, sayd, Sir, your horse is lost and never to bee recovered; I thought what skill you had, replies the Gallant, my horse is walking in a Lane at the towns end. With that Hodges swore (as hee was too much given unto that vice) your horse is gone and you will never have him again; the gentleman departed in great derision of Hodges, and went where hee left his horse; when hee came there, hee found the boy fast a sleep uppon the ground, the horse gone, the boys Arm in the bridle.

Hee returns again to Hodges, desiring his ayd, beeing sory for his former abuse; old William swore like a Devill, bee gone, bee gone, go seek your horse: this business ended not so, for the malitious man brought Hodges into the Starr Chamber[141], bound him over to the Assizes, putt Hodges to great expense, but by meanes of the Lord Dudley, if I remember aright, or some other person thereabouts, hee overcame the Gentleman and was aquitted.

Besides this, a gentlewoaman of my acquaintance and of credit in Lecestershire, having lost a pillion Cloth, a very new one, went to desire his judgment; hee ordered her such a day to attend at Mount Sorrell in Lecestershire, and about 12 of clock shee would see her pillion Cloth uppon a horse and a woaman uppon it; my freind attended the houre, and place; it beeing cold shee must need warm herselfe well, and then inquired if any passengers lately gone by the Inn, unto whom answer was made, there passed by whilst shee was at the fire about halfe an houre before, a man and a woaman behind him on horse back; inquiring what Colour the pillion Cloth was of, it was answered, directly of the colour my freinds was of: they pursued, but too late.

In those tymes there lived one William Marsh in Dunstable, a man of godly life and upright conversation, a Recusant[142]; by Astrology hee resolved theevish questions with great success, that was his allmost sole Practise.

[141]Court of the Star Chamber: a court of civil and criminal jurisdiction noted for its arbitrary procedure, and abolished in 1641. (*OED*)

[142]Recusant: a Roman Catholic who refused to attend services of the Church of England. (*OED*)

Hee was many tymes in trouble, but by Doctor Napper[143] his interest with the [X]Earle of Bullenbrook, hee still continued his practise, the sayd Earle not permitting any Justice of peace to vex him.

[X]*Lord Wentworth after Earle of Cleveland.* [E.A]

This man had onely 2 bookes, Guido and Haly bound togather; hee had so mumbled and tumbled the leaves of both, that half one side of every leaf was torne even to the middle, I was familiar with him for many yeares, hee died about 1647.

A word or two of Doctor Napper, who lived at great Lindford in Buckinghamshire, was Parson and had the ~~impropriation~~ *Advowson* [E.A.] thereof; hee descended of worshippfull parents, and this you must beleeve, for when Doctor Nappers brother, Sir Robert Napper, a turky Merchant, was to bee made a Barronet in King James raign, there was some dispute whether hee could proove himselfe a gentleman for 3 or more Descents; By my Soule, sayth King James, I will certifie for Nappier, that hee is of above 300 yeares standing in his family, all of them by my soule, gentlemen, etc. However, their family came into England in King Henry the 8th his tyme: the Parson was Mr. of Arts, but whether Doctorated by degree or Curtesy because of his profession I know not; miscarrying one day in the Pulpitt hee never after used it, but all his life tyme kept in his house some excellent Schollar or other to officiate for him, with allowance of a good Salary: hee outwent Forman in Phisick and holiness of life, cured the falling sickness perfectly by Constellated[144] Rings, some diseases by Amulets etc.

A mayd was much afflicted with the falling sickness, whose parents applied themselves unto him for cure, he framed her a constellated Ring, uppon wearing whereof shee recovered perfectly; her parents acquainted some

[143]Doctor Richard Napier (1559-1634), astrologer, physician and Church of England clergyman. Student and friend of Doctor Simon Forman who bequeathed to Napier all his manuscripts and books in trust for his son Clement. Sir Kenelm Digby was among his circle of friends. Napier bequeathed most of his estate to his nephew, also Richard, later Sir Richard Napier (1607-1676), physician. His son, Thomas, made over all Sir Richard's manuscripts to Ashmole. (Jonathan Andrews, *ODNB*)

[144]Ornamented with stars. (*OED*)

scrupulous Divines with the cure of their daughter; the cure is done by inchantment say they, cast away the ring, its diabolicall, God cannot bless you if you do not cast the ring away; the ring was cast into the well, whereuppon the mayd became Epilepticall as formerly, and indured much misery for a long tyme, at last her parents clensed the Well and recovered the Ring again; the mayd wore it and her fitts tooke her no more; in this condition shee was one year or two, which the Puritan Ministers there adjoyning hearing, never left off, till they procured her parents to cast the Ring quite away, which done, the fitts returned in such violence, that they wear inforced to apply to the Doctor again, relating at large the whole story, humbly imploring his once more assistance, but hee could not be procured to do any thing, only sayd, those who despised Gods mercys wear not capable or worthy of enjoying them.

: the Collect ad on 'ichaelmas y, seems to low of aying unto ngells.

sometyme pon great asions hee d conference th Michael, t very rarely, .

I was with him in 1632 or 1633[145] uppon occasion, he had mee upp into his Library, beeing excellently furnished with very choyce bookes, there hee prayed allmost one hour; hee invocated severall Angells in his prayers, viz. [D]Michael, Gabriel, Raphael, Uriel etc; we parted.

Hee instructed many Ministers in Astrology, would lend them whole Cloakebaggs of books, protected them from harme and violence, by meanes of his power with the Earle of [X]Bullenbrook. Hee would confess my Mr. Evans[146] knew more then himselfe in some things, etc. Sometymes before he died, hee gott his cozen[147] Sir Richard to sett a figure to for when hee should dye; beeing brought him, well, the old man will live this winter, but at the Spring hee will dye; welcome Lord Jesus, thy will bee done; hee had many enemys, Cott, a Doctor of Phisick in Northampton, wrote a sharpe booke of Witchcraft, wherein obliquely, hee bitterly inveighed against the Doctor.

ord ntworth r Earle of veland. A]

Venerable Esquire, this side hath detrimented my penn of your own making and made it useless, what precedes was written with it without emendation; viz. every side.
☽ 25 November 1667 11 h. A.M.

[146]John Evans, Lilly's first tutor in Astrology.

[147]Sir Richard Napier was his nephew, the son of his brother Robert.

In 1646 I printed a Collection of Prophecys, with the explanation and verification of Aquila, or the White Kings prophecy, as also the Nativitys of Bishop Laud[148] and Thomas Earl of Strafford[149], and a most learned Speech by him intended to have been spoken uppon the Scaffold. In this year 1646, after great consideration and many importunitys, I began to fix uppon thoughts of an Introduction unto Astrology, which was very much wanting, and as earnestly longed for by many persons of Quality; something also much occasioned and hastened the impression; viz, the malevolent barking of Presbiterian Ministers in their weekly sermons, reviling the Professors thereof, and my selfe particularly by Name.

Secondly, I thought it a duty incumbent uppon mee to satisfie the whole Kingdom of the Lawfullness thereof, by framing a plain and easy Method for any person but of indifferent capacity to learn the Art, and instruct himselfe therein without any other M^{r}. then my Introduction[150]; by which meanes, when many understood it, I should have more partners and assistants to contradict all and every Antagonist.[151]

Thirdly I found it best as unto point of tyme, because the soldiery wear wholly for it, and many of the Independant party, and I had aboundance of worthy men in the house of Commons my assured freinds, no lovers of Presbitery, which then wear in great esteem and able to protect the Art, for should the Presbiterian party have prevailed, as they thought nothing

[148]William Laud (1573-1645), Archbishop of Canterbury. Lilly presents the horary "*What manner of Death Canterbury should dye?" (CA* p.419) dated 3rd December 1644 (OS). He notes correctly that Laud was beheaded on 10th January 1644/5 (OS).

[149]Thomas Wentworth, first earl of Strafford (1593-1641). Both Wentworth and Laud were beheaded for treason under Acts of Attainder. The traditional form of execution in cases of treason was to be hanged, drawn and quartered, which draws attention to the purpose of Lilly's horary question.

[150]Thus a classical (and expensive) education was no longer required in order to learn Astrology. Lilly had collected together all the information required to become proficient in the art, and then published in the vernacular.

[151]This is an interesting statement where Lilly justifies revealing astrological secrets to non-scholars and the non-professional classes.

less then to bee Lords of all, I knew well they would have silenced my penn Annually, and committed the Introduction unto everlasting silence. Fourth, I had something of Conscience touched my Spirit and much elevated my Conceptions, beleeving God had not bestowed those abilitys uppon mee, to bury them under a bushell, for though my education was very mean, yet by my continuall industry and Gods great mercy, I found myselfe capable to go forward with the work, and to committ the issue thereof unto divine Providence. I had a hard taske in hand to begin the first part thereof, and much labour I underwent to methodize it as it is; I ingeniously confess unto you (Arts great Macænas noble Esquire Ashmole) no mortall man had any share in the Composition or ordering the first part thereof, but my one onely selfe; you are a person of great reading, yet I well know you never found the least trace thereof any Author yet extant.

In composing, contriving, ordering and framing thereof viz. first part, a great part of that year was spent, I again perused all or most Authors I had, sometymes adding, at other tymes diminishing, until at last I thought it worthy of the press; when I came to frame the second part thereof, having formerly collected out of many Manuscripts and exchanged Rules with the most able Professors I had an acquaintance with, in transcribing those papers for impression, I found uppon a strict inquisition, those Rules wear for the most part defective, so that once more I had a new difficult labour, to correct their deficiency. to now rectifie them according unto Art, and lastly considering the multiplicity of daily Questions propounded unto mee, it was as hard a labour as might bee to transcribe the papers themselves with my own hand.

X The name of the person whose Nativity is directed and judged therein is Mr: Thompson, whose father has been sometime an Innkeeper at ye White hart in Newark.

The desire I had to benefit posterity and my Country at last overcame all difficultys, so that what I could not do on one year, I perfected early the next year 1647; and then in that year viz. 1647, I finished the 3rd book of X Nativitys, during the composing whereof, for 7 whole weeks, I was shutt upp of the plague, burying in that tyme 2 maydservants thereof, yet towards November of that year, the Introduction, called by the name of Christian Astrology, was made publique.

I devised the forms and fashions of the severall Schemes. E.A.

There beeing in those tymes some smart differences betwixt the Army and Parlament, the head Quarters of the Army wear at Windsor, whither I was carried with a Coach and 4 horses, John Booker with me, wee wear welcome thither and feasted; in a quarter[152] where the Generall Fairfax[153] lodged, wee wear brought to the Generall, who kindly bad us welcome to Windsor, and in effect sayd this much:

That God blessed the Army with many signal victorys, and yet their work was not finished, hee hoped God would go along with them until his work was done, they sought not themselves, but the wellfare and tranquillity of the good people and whole Nation; and for that end, wear resolved to sacrifize both their lives and their own fortunes: as for the Art wee studied, he hoped it was Lawfull and agreeable to Gods word, hee understood it not but hee doubted not, but wee both feared God, and therefore had a good opinion of us both; unto his speech I presently made this reply:

My Lord I am glad to see you heare at this tyme; Certainly both the people of God and all others of this Nation, are very sensible of Gods mercy, love and favour unto them, in directing the Parlament to nominate and elect you Generall of their Armys, a person so Religious, so valiant. The severall unexpected Victorys obtained under your Excellencys Conduct, will eternize your fame unto all posterity. Wee are confident of Gods going along with you and your Army, until the great worke for which hee ordained you both, is fully perfected, which wee hope will bee the conquering and subversion of yours and the Parlaments enemys, and then a quiet settlement and firm peace over all the whole Nation, unto Gods glory and full satisfaction of tender Consciences. S^r^., as for ourselves, wee trust in God, and as Christians beleeve in him; wee do not study any Art, but what is Lawfull and consonant to Scriptures, Fathers and Antiquity, which wee humbly desire you to beleeve, etc.

This ended, wee departed, and went to visett M^r^. Peeters[154] the Minister who lodged in the Castle, whom wee found reading an idle pamphlett come

[152]Accommodation.

[153]Ferdinando Fairfax (1584-1648), second Lord Fairfax of Cameron and parliamentarian army officer. (*ODNB*)

from London that morning. Lilly thou art hearin, (sayth hee) are not you there allso I replyed; yes that I am, quoth hee – the words concerning mee wear:

From the Oracles of the Sibills so silly
The curst predictions of William Lilly
And Doctor Sybbalds shoo lame filly
Good Lord deliver mee.

After much conference with Hugh Peeters, and some private discourse betwixt us two, not to be divulged[155], wee parted, and so came back to London.

King Charles the first, in the year 1646, 27 Aprill went unto the Scotts, then in this nation, many desired my judgment in the tyme of his absence, to discover the way hee might bee taken, which I would never bee drawn unto, or give any direction concerning his person.

There wear many lewd Mercurys[156] printed both in London and Oxford, wherein I was sufficiently abused in this year 1646; I had then my Ascendant ad £ ♂ and ☽ ad F[157] proprium. The Presbiterians wear in the Pulpits as merciless, as the Cavaliers in their Pamphletts.

At this tyme the most famous Mathemetician of all Euroap M^{r}. William Outred[158] Parson of Albury in Surrey was in danger of Sequestration by the

---

[154]Hugh Peter (Peters) (bap. 1598, d. 1660), Independent minister. Preached in support of Parliament and the army. His closeness to Oliver Cromwell led to his execution for treason in 1660. (Carla Pestana, *ODNB*)

[155]Peters was in favour of the king's execution and actively promoted it and lobbied for support.

[156]Pamphlets often with the word "Mercury" in the title.

[157]"my Ascendant [directed - i.e. by the system of primary directions] to square Mars and the Moon to sextile [that Ascendant]."

Committee of or for Plundered ministers[159] (Ambodexters they weare); severall inconsiderable Articles wear deposed and sworn against him, materiall inough to have sequestred him, but that uppon his day of hearing, I applied myself to Sir Bolstrod Whitlock and all my own old freinds, who in such numbers appeared on his behalfe, that though the Chair man and many other Presbiterian Members wear stiff against him, yet hee was cleared by the Major number: the truth is hee had a considerable Parsonage, and that onely was inough to sequester any moderate Judgment, hee was also well known to affect his Majesty; in those tymes many worthy Ministers lost their Livings or Benefices for not complying with the threepenny Directorys. Had you seen (oh noble Esquire) what pittifull Ideots wear preferred unto sequestrated Church Benefices, you would have greived in your soule; but when they came before the Classis of Divines, could those simpletons but onely say, they wear converted by hearing such a Sermon such a Lecture of that godly man Hugh Peeters, Steven Marshall[160] or any of that Gang, hee was presently admitted.

This Gent: I was very well acquainted with, having lived at the house over-against his at Albury in Surrey 3 or 4 yeares. [E.A.]

In 1647 I published the Worlds Catastrophe, the Prophecys of Ambrose Merline, with the Key wherwith to unlock those abstruse Prophecys, also Tritemius, of the government of the world by the Presiding Angells: these came forth all in one book.

The 2 first wear exquisitly translated by yourself (most learned Sir) as I do ingeniously acknowledge in my Epistle unto the Reader, with a true Caracter of your worth and admirable parts, unto which I refer any that do desire to read you perfectly delineated: I was once resolved to have continued Tritemius for some succeeding yeares, but multiplicity of imployment impeded mee; the study required in that kind of learning must

[158]William Oughtred (bap.1575, d. 1660), mathematician, alchemist, astrologer, Church of England clergyman. He was greatly admired and respected at home and abroad. His students and admirers included Jonas Moore, Seth Ward, Christopher Wren, Laurence Rooke, Thomas Wharton, Elias Ashmole and Lilly. Some of these went on to become founder members of the Royal Society.

[159]This was in 1646. (Frances Willmoth, *ODNB*).

[160]Stephen Marshall (1594/5?-1655), Church of England clergyman, prominent and influential politically.

bee sedentary, of great reading, sound judgment, which no man can accomplish except hee wholly retyre, use prayer, and accompany him selfe with Angelical Consorts.

His Majesty Charles the first having intrusted the Scotts with his person, was for money delivered into the hands of the English Parlament, and by severall Remoovalls was had to Hampton Court about July or August 1647, for hee was there, and at that tyme when my house was visited with the plague, hee was desirous to escape the Soldiery and to obscure him selfe for sometyme near London, the Citizens whereof began now to bee unruly and alienated in affection from the Parlament, inclining wholly to his Majesty, very averse to the Army; his Majesty was well informed of all this, and thought to make good use hearof; besides, the Army and Parlament wear at some odds who should bee Masters; uppon the Kings intention to escape, and with his consent, Madam W:[161] whom you know very well (worthy Esquire) came to receive my judgment, viz: in what quarter of this Nation hee might bee most safe, and not to bee discovered, until himselfe pleased.

Whorewood [EA]

When shee came to my dore, I told her I would not let her come in, for I buried a mayd servant of the plague very lately; I fear not the plague but the Pox, quoth shee, so upp wee went; after erection of my figure, I told her about twenty miles or thereabouts from London and in Essex, I was certain hee might continue undiscovered: shee liked my judgment very well, and beeing herselfe of a sharp judgment, remembred a place in Essex about that distance, where was an excellent house and all Conveniencys for his Reception; away shee went early next morning unto Hampton Court to acquaint his Majesty; but see the misfortune; hee either guided by his own approaching hard fate, or misguided by [AD]Ashburnham[162], went away in

AD. *this Ashburnham was turned out of the house of Commons the 3rd week of Novem. 1667 for taking a bribe of* 500^{L} *of the Merchants; I was informed hearof 26 No. 1667, the very day I did write this side of the paper.*

[161]Lady Jane Whorwood (1614/15-1684), daughter of a minor official in the royal stable, a royalist sympathiser who became a close friend of Charles I. The incidents which Lilly recounts are a few of several attempts that Lady Jane made to secure the king's escape. A letter warning the governor of the Isle of Wight that a ship was leaving the Thames to effect the king's escape added that Lady Jane was aboard that ship and described her as "a tall, well-fashioned, and well-languaged gentlewoaman, with a round visage and pockholes in her face", and Anthony Wood adds that she had red hair. (C.H. Firth, *ODNB*)

[162]John Ashburnham (1602/3-1671), courtier and politician. The bribe of £500.00 was taken from French merchants. (Sean Kelsey, *ODNB*)

the night tyme Westward, and surrendred himselfe unto Hammond in the Isle of Wight.

Whilst his Majesty was at Hampton Court, Alderman Adams[163] sent his Majesty one thousand pounds in Gold, five hundred whereof hee gave to Madam W: I beleeve I had 20 peeces of that very Gold for my share.

I have something more to write of Charles the first his misfortunes, wherein I was concerned; the matter happened in 1648 but I thought good to insert it hear having after this no more occasion to mention him.

His Majesty beeing in Carsebrook Castle[164] in the Isle of Wight, the Kentish men in great numbers rose in Armes and joyned the Lord Goring[165]; a considerable number of the best shipps revolted from the Parlament; the Citizens of London wear forward to rise against the Parlament; his Majesty layd his designe to escape out of prison, by sawing the Iron Barrs of his Chamber window; a small shipp was provided and anchored not farr from the Castle to bring him into Sussex, horses wear provided ready to carry him through Sussex into Kent, that hee might bee in the head of the Army in Kent and from thence to march immediatly to London, where thousands then would have armed for him; the Lady W: came to mee, acquaints mee hearwith; I gott [X]G. Farmer to make a Saw, to cutt the Iron Barrs in sunder, I mean to saw them, and Aqua fortis[166] besides; his Majesty in a small tyme did his work, the barrs gave liberty for him to go out; hee was out with his body till hee came to his breast, but, then his hart failing, hee proceeded no further; when this was discovered,

[X]*He was a most ingenious lock-smith and dwelt in Bow Lane.*

---

[163]Sir Thomas Adams (bap.1586, d.1668), local politician. He was alderman from 1639-1649 and lord mayor from 1645-6. (*ODNB*)

[164]Carisbrooke Castle, Isle of Wight.

[165]George Goring (1585-1663), first earl of Norwich, courtier and diplomat. He captured Colchester for the king and was its commander when it surrendered to Parliamentary forces at the end of August 1648 following a siege. It was to this siege that Lilly and John Booker were sent to boost the morale of the parliamentary army.

[166]Aquafortis (strong water) or nitric acid.

or soon after it, was his Majesty narrowly looked after, and no opportunity after that could bee devised to inlarge him.

About September the Parlament sent their Commissioners with propositions unto him into the Isle of Wight, the Lord William Sea[167] beeing one; the Lady W: came again unto mee from him, or by his consent, to bee directed; after perusall of my figure, I told her the Commissioners would bee there such a day; I elected a day and houre when to receive the Commissioners and Propositions, and so soon as the propositions wear read, to sign them, and make haste with all speed to come up with the Commissioners to London, the Army beeing then farr distant from London and the Citty inraged stoutly against them; hee promised hee would do so; that night, the Commissioners came, and old Sea and his Majesty had private conference till one in the morning; the King acquaints Sea with his intention, who clearly dissuaded him from signing the Propositions, telling him they wear not fitt for him to signe, that hee had many freinds in the house of Lords, and some in the house of Commons, that hee would procure more, and then they would frame more easy propositions: this flattery of this unfortunate Lord occasioned his Majesty to wave the advise I and some others that wished his prosperity had given, in expectation of that which afterwards could never bee gained. The Army, having some notice hearof from one of the Commissioners who had an eye uppon old Sea, hasted unto London, and made the Citizens very quiet, and besides, the Parlament and Army kept a better correspondency afterwards with each other.

Whorewood

Whilst the King was at Windsor Castle, one day walking uppon the leades thereof, hee looked uppon Captain Whartons Almanack; my booke, sayth hee, speakes well as to the weather; one William Allen standing by; what, sayth he, sayth his Antagonist Mr. Lilly? I do not care for Lilly, sayd his Majesty, hee hath been allways against mee, and become a little bitter in his expressions; Sir, sayd Allen, the man is an honest man and writes but what

[167]William Fiennes, first Viscount of Saye and Sele, (1582-1662), politician. It seems unlikely that parliament would have sent Saye to negotiate with the king because it had broken off negotiations in January 1648. This suggests that Saye went secretly and that Lilly was, directly or indirectly, privy to this information, because history records Saye's visit as "rumoured". (*ODNB*)

his Art informs him; I beleeve it sayd his Majesty, and that Lilly understands Astrology as well as any man in Euroap: Exit Rex Carolus.

In 1648, I published a Treatise of the 3 Suns, seen the winter preceding, as also an Astrologicall judgment uppon a Conjunction of ♄ and ♂, 28 June, in 11° 8' of ♊[tcl]. I commend unto your perusall that book and the Propheticall Merlin, which seriously considered (Oh worthy Esquire) will more instruct your judgment De generalibus contingentibus Mundi then all the Authors you yet ever mett with.

In this year for very great considerations the Councell of State gave mee in money 50L and a pension of 100L per annum, which for 2 yeares I recieved, but no more, upon some discontents I after would not or did not require it: the cause mooving them was this; they could gett no intelligence out of France, although they had severall Agents there for that purpose: I had formerly acquaintance with a Secular priest, at this tyme Confessor to one of the Secretarys[169]; unto him I wrote, and by that meanes had perfect Knowledge of the cheifest concernements for France, at which they admired; but I never yet until this day revealed the name of the Person; one occasion why I deserted that employment was, because Scott, who had 800L per annum for intelligence would not contribute any thing to gratify my freind, and an other occasion was, I received some affront from [X]one that was a principall Minister belonging to the Councell of State: Scott was ever my enemy, the other knave died of a Gangrene in his Arme suddenly after.

[X]*Gualter Frost, their Secretary* [EA]

In 1648 and 1649, that I might encourage young students in Astrology, I publiquely read over the first part of my Introduction, wherein there are many things contayned not easily to bee understood.

And now wee are entred into the year 1649; his Majesty beeing at St. James house, in January of that year I begann its observations this:

---

[168]" ...A Conjunction of Saturn and Mars, 28 June, in 11° 8' of Gemini."

[169]Gualter Frost (bap.1698, d.1652) political agent and government official.

I am serious, I beg and expect Justice, either fear or shame begins to question Offenders.

The Lofty Cedars begin to divine a thundering Hericano[170] is at hand; God elevates men contemptible.

Our Demigods are sensible wee begin to dislike their Actions very much in London, more in the Country.

Blessed be God who incourages his servants, makes them valiant, and of undaunted spirits to go on with his Decrees.

Uppon a sudden, great expectations arise, and men generally beleeve a quiet and calm tyme drawes nigh.

In Christmas holy dayes, the Lord Gray of Grooby and Hugh Peeters sent for mee to Somerset house, with directions to bring them 2 of my Allmanacks – I did so; Peeters and hee read Januarys observations –

If wee are not fooles and Knaves, sayth hee, wee shall do Justice, then they whispered. I understood not their meaning till his Majesty was beheaded; they applied what I wrote of Justices to bee understood of his Majesty, which was Contrary to my intention, for ♃+m+ the first day of January became direct, and Ω is a sign signifying Justice; I implored for Justice generally uppon such as had cheated in their places, beeing Treasurers and such like Officers. I had not then heard the least intimation of bringing the King unto Triall, and yet the first day thereof[D] I was casually there, it beeing uppon a Saterday, for going to Westminster every Saterday in the afternoon in those tymes; at white Hall I casually met Peeters; Come Lilly, wilt thou go hear the King tryed? When sayd I; Now, just now, go with mee; I did so and was permitted by the guard of Soldiers to pass up to the Kings Bench; within one quarter of an houre came the Judges, presently his Majesty who spoke excellently well and majestically without impediment in the least

[D] *of his tryall.*

---

[170]Hurricane.

[171]Jupiter ... Libra

when hee spoke. I saw the silver Topp of his staff unexpectedly fall to the ground, was tooke up by Mr. Rushworth[172]; but when I heard Bradshaw[173], the Judge, say to his Majesty, Sir, instead of answering the Court, you interrogate their power, which becomes not one in your Condition, the words peirced my hart and soule, to hear a Subject thus audaciously to reprehend his Soveraign, who ever and anon replyed with great Magnanimity and prudence.

After that his Majesty was beheaded, the Parlament for some yeares effected nothing, either for the publiq peace, or tranquillity of the Nation, or setling Religion, as they had formerly promised; the intervall of tyme betwixt his Majestys death and Oliver Cromwells displacing them, was wholly consumed with voting for themselves, and bringing their own relations to bee Members of Parlament, thinking to make a Trade thereof.

The weeke or 3 or 4 days before his Majestys beheading, one Major Sydenham, who had Commands in Scotland, came to take his leave of mee, and told mee the King was to bee putt to death, which I was not willing to beleeve, and said, I could not be persuaded, the Parlament could find any Englishman so barbarous that would do that fowle Action. Rather (sayth hee) then they should want such a man, these Armes of mine should do it; hee went presently after into Scotland, and uppon the first ingagment against them was slaine, and his body miserably cutt and mangled.

In 1651 I published Monarchy or no Monarchy and in the latter end thereof, some Heirogliphicks of my own, composed at spare tyme by the occult learning, many of those Types having representation of what should from thence succeed in England, and have since had verification. I had not that learning from bookes, or any Manuscript I ever yet mett with

---

[172]Possibly John Rushworth (c.1612-1690), historian and politician. He was implicated, along with William Lilly, of being part of a secret meeting on 29th January 1649 having the alleged intention of persuading the king to repent and accept the justice of proceedings of the high court. (Joad Raymond, *(ODNB)*. The king was executed on 30th January 1649.

[173]John, Lord Bradshaw (bap.1602, d.1659), lawyer, politician, regicide. Appointed Lord President of the High Court of Justice for the trial of Charles I. (*ODNB*)

all, it is deduced from a Caball lodging in Astrology, but so misterious, and difficult to bee attained that I have not yet been acquainted with any who had that Knowledge. I will say no more thereof, but that the Asterismes and Signes and Constellations give greatest light thereunto.

During Bradshaws beeing president of the Councell of State, it was my happiness to procure Capt: Wharton his Liberty, which when hee[AD] understood sayd, I will bee an enemy to Lilly if ever hee come before mee; Sir Bolstrod Whitlock broake the Ice first of all on behalfe of Captain Wharton, after him the Committee unto whom his offence had been committed, spoke for him, and sayd hee might well bee bailed or inlarged; I had labored the Committee the morning of his delivery, who thereuppon wear so civill unto him, especially Sir William Armin of Lincolnshire, who at first woondred I appeared not against him, but uppon my humble request, my long continued Antagonist was inlarged and had his Liberty.

A.D. *Bradshaw.*

In 1651, I purchased 110^{L} per Annum in fee Farm Rents for one thousand and thirty two pounds; I payd all in ready money; but when his Majesty King Charles the Second 1660 was restored, I lost it all again, and it returned to the right Owner; the loss thereof never afflicted mee, for I have ever reduced my mind according to my fortune; I was drawn in by severall persons to make that simple purchase. That yeare I bought it, I had my Ascendant directed unto a △ of ♃[174] first, and in the same year unto Cauda draconis – my ⊕ unto a Quadrate of ☿.[175]

When Colchester was beseiged, John Booker and myselfe wear sent for, where wee incouraged the Soldiers, assuring them the Town would very shortly bee surrendred, as indeed it was; I would willingly have obtained leave to enter the town, to have informed Sir Charls Lucas[176], whom I well

[174]"... a trine of Jupiter..."

[175]"...my Part of Fortune unto a Quadrate of Mercury."

[176]Charles Lucas (1612/13-1648), royalist army officer. A native of Colchester and one of the military commanders during its siege, he was executed after the surrender to parliamentarian forces.

knew, with the condicion of affaires as they stood, hee beeing deluded by fals intelligence: at that tyme, my Scholler Humphrys was therein, who many tymes deluded the Governor[177] with expectations of releefe, but fayling very many tymes with his lyes, at last hee had the Bastinado[178], was putt in prison, and inforced to become a Soldier; and well it was hee escaped so. During my beeing there, the Steeple of St. Marys Church was much battered by 2 Cannons purposely placed; I was there one day about 3 of clock in the afternoon, talking with the Cannoneer, when presently hee desired us to look for ourselves, for hee perceived by his perspective glass there was a peece Charged in the Castle against his worke, and ready to bee discharged; I rann for haste under an old Ash tree and immediatly the Cannon-bullet came hissing quite over us; no danger now, sayth the Gunner, but begone, for there are five more charging, which was true, for 2 houres after those Cannons wear discharged and unluckily killed our Cannoneer and his Montross. I came the next morning, and saw the blood of the 2 poor men lye uppon the planks; wee wear well entertained at the head quarters, and after 2 whole days abiding there, came for London.

But wee prosecute our story again, and say that in the year 1652, I purchased my house and some lands in Hersham in the parish of Walton uppon Thames, in the County of Surrey, where I now live, intending, by the blessing of god, when I found it convenient to retyre into Country, there to end my days in peace and tranquillity, for in London, my practise was such, I had none or very little tyme affoarded mee to serve God, who had been so gracious unto mee; the purchase of the [X]house and Lands and building stood mee in nine hundred and fifty pounds sterling[179].

[X]*since much augmented by him.* [EA]

The Parlament now growes odious unto all men, the Members whereof became insufferable in their Pride, Covetousness, selfe ends, lazyness, minding nothing by how to enrich themselves; much hartburning now arose betwixt the Presbiterian and Independant, the latter siding with the Army, betwixt whose two judgments there was no Medium; now came up

[177]George Goring (cf.)

[178]Punishment of beating the soles of the feet with a stick. (*OED*)

[179]Equal to about £100,000 at current values.

or durst appeared that Monstrous people called Ranters[180], and many other Novell opinions in themselves Hereticall and Scandalous wear Countenanced by Members of Parlament, many whereof wear of the same judgement. Justice was neglected, vice Countenanced, all care of the Common good layd aside; every judgment allmost groaned under the heavy burthen[181] they then suffered; the Army neglected, the Citty of London scorned, the Ministry, especially those who wear Orthodox and serious, honest or vertuous, had no Countenaunce; my Soul begann to loath the very name of a Parlament or Parlament men; there yet remained in the house very able, judicious and worthy Patriots, but they in their silence onely served themselves; all was carried on by a rabble of Dunces, who beeing the greater number, Voted what seemed best to their non intelligent fancys.

In this year I published Annus tenebrosus[182], which booke I did not intitle because of the great obscurity of the Solar Eclipse by so many pratles of to no purpose, but because of those under hand and clandestine Councells held in England by the Soldiery, of which I would never but in generall give any knowledge unto any Parlament Man. I had wrote publiqly in 1650 that the Parlament should not continue, but a new Government should arise, etc.

In my next yeares Anglicus[183], uppon rationall grounds in Astrology, I was bold as to averr therein that the Parlament stood uppon a tottering foundation, and that the Commonalty and Soldiery would join together against them. My Anglicus was for a whole weeke every day in the Parlament house peeped into by the Presbiterians, one disliking this sentence, an other finds an other fault, others misliked the whole, so in the end, a motion was made that Anglicus should bee inspected by the

[180]A religious sect which spurned traditional moral and social values. (*EB*)

[181]Burden.

[182]The Dark Year.

[183]1653.

Committee of plundered minsters, which beeing done, they wear to return its errors to the house, viz: repoart [A] them.

A messenger attached mee by a warrant from that Committee; I had private notice ere the messenger came, and hasted unto Mr. Speaker Lenthall, ever my freind; hee was exceeding glad to see mee, told mee what was done, called for Anglicus, marked the passages which tormented the Presbiterians so highly: I presently sent for Mr. Warren the printer an assured Cavalier, obliterated what was most offensive, putt in other more significant words, and desired to have onely six amended against next morning, which very honestly hee brought mee. I told him my design was to deny the book found fault with, to own onely the six bookes, I told him I doubted hee would bee examined; hang them, sayd hee, all rogues, I'll swear myselfe to the Devill ere they shall have an advantage against you by my Oath.

A. its errors

The day after, I appeared before the Committee, beeing 36 in number that day, whereas it was observed at other tymes it was very difficult to get five of them together. At first they showed mee the true Anglicus, and asked if I wrote and printed it; I tooke the booke and inspected it very heedfully, and when I had done so – this is none of my book, some malitious Presbiterian hath wrote it, who are my mortall enemys, I disown it; the Committee lookt uppon one an other like distracted men, not imagining what I presently did, for I presently pulld out of my pocket six bookes; these I own, the other are counterfett, published purposely to ruine mee.

The Committee wear now more vexed then before; not one word was spoke a good while; at last many of them, or the greatest number of them wear of opinion to imprison mee; some wear for Newgate[184], others for the Gate house, but then one Brown of Sussex, called the Presbiterian Bedle, whom the Company of Stationers had bribed to bee my freind by giving him a new book of Martyrs, hee I say preached unto the Committee this Doctrine, that neither Newgate or the Gatehouse wear prisons unto which at any tyme the Parlament sent prisoners, it was most convenient for the Serjant at Armes to take mee in Custody.

[184]Newgate prison.

Mr. Strickland[185] who had for many yeares been the Parlments Embassador or Agent in Holland, when hee saw how they inclined, spoke thus –

I came purposely unto this Committee this day to see the Man, who is so famous in those parts whereof I have so long continued, I assure you his name is famous all over Euroap, I come to do him Justice, a booke is produced by us, and sayd to bee his; hee denyes it, we have not prooved it, yet will committ him; truly this is great injustice, its like hee will write next year, and acquaint the whole world with our injustice, and so hee well may; its my opinion first to proove the booke to bee his ere hee bee committed.

An other, an old freind of myne, Mr. R.[186] spoke thus –

You do not know the many services this man hath done for the Parlament this many yeares, or how many tymes in our greatest distresses wee applying unto him hee hath refreshed our languishing expectations; hee never failed us of comfort in our most unhappy distresses; I assure you his writings have kept upp the spirits both of the Soldiery, the honest people of this Nation, and many of us Parlament men, and now for a slipp of his penn (if it wear his) to bee thus violent against him; I must tell you I fear the Consequences urged out of the book will proove effectually true; its my councell to admonish him hearafter to bee more wary, and for the present to dismiss him.

Notwithstanding any thing that was spoke on my behalfe I was ordered to stand committed to the Serjant at Armes, the Messenger attached my person, sayd I was his prisoner; as hee was carrying mee away, hee was called to bring mee again, Oliver Cromwell, Leiftennant Generall of the Army, having never seen mee, caused mee to be produced again, where hee steadfastly beheld mee for a good space, and then I went with the Messenger, but instantly, a young Clerk of that Committee askes the

[185]Walter Strickland (1598?-1671), politician and diplomatist. Appointed parliamentary ambassador to the United Provinces in 1642. He was an influential ally of Oliver Cromwell. (Timothy Venning, *ODNB*)

[186]Possibly Sir Robert Reynolds (cf.)

Messenger what hee did with mee; where's your warrant, until that is signed you cannot seize M^{r}. Lilly or shall; will you have an Action of false imprisonment against you?

So I escaped that night, but next day obeyed the warrant. That night, Oliver Cromwell went to M^{r}. R. my freind; What never a man to take Lillys cause in hand but yourselfe? None to take his part but you, hee shall not bee long there; Hugh Peters spoke much in my behalfe to the Committee but they wear resolved to lodge mee in the Serjants Custody. One Millington[187], a drunken member, was much my enemy, and so was Crawley[188] of Chichester, a deformed fellow, unto whom I had done severall Curtesys[189].

Cawley.

Full 13 days I was a prisoner, and though every day of the Committees sitting, I had a petition to deliver, yet so many churlish Presbiterians still appeared, I could not get it accepted; the last day of the 13, M^{r}. Joseph Ash was made Chair man, unto whom my cause beeing related, hee took my petition, and sayd I should bee bailed in despite of them all, but desired I would procure as many freinds as I could to bee there; Sir Arthur Hazellrigg and Major Salloway, a person of excellent parts, appeared for mee, and many now of my old freinds came in; after 2 whole houres arguing my cause by Sir Arthur and Major Salloway and their freinds, the matter came to this point: I should be bailed, and a Committee nominated to examine the Printer; the Order of the Committee beeing brought afterwards to him who should bee Chair man, hee sent mee word; do what I would, hee would see all the Knaves hanged ere hee would examine the Printer: this is this truth of the story.

---

[187]Probably Gilbert Millington (c.1598-1666), barrister, politican, regicide. Reportedly a frequenter of brothels and alehouses, and a drunk. (Richard L.Greaves, *ODNB*)

[188]William Cawley (bap.1602, d.1667), politician and regicide. (*ODNB*)

[189]Favours.

The 16° of February 1653 my second wif[e died, for[190]] whose death, I shed no teares[191]; I had 500^L^ with her as a portion, but shee and her poor relations spent mee 1000^L^.

Gloria patri et filiu et spiritui sancto: sicut erat in principio et nunc et semper, et in secula seculorum: for 20th of Aprill 1653 these enemys of mine, viz: Parlament men, wear turned out of dores by Oliver Cromwell.[A.B]

A.B: *A German Dr. of Phisick, beeing then in London, sent mee this paper: Strophe Alcaica:*

Generoso Dn°. Gulielmo Lillio Astrologo, de dissoluto nuper Parlamento. Quod calculasti Sydere prævio, Miles peregit numine conscio, Gentis videmus nunc Senatum, Marte Togaque gravi levatum:

In tyme of my imprisonment Mr. Rushworth came to visit mee, told mee the Army would do as much as I had predicted unto the Parlament.

In October 1654 I married the third wife[192], who is signified in my Nativity by Jupiter in Libra: and shee is so totally in her condition, to my great Comfort.

In 1655 I was indited at Hicks hall by a halfe witted young woaman; 3 severall sessions shee was neglected and the Jury cast forth her Bill, but the 4th tyme they found it against mee; I putt in Bail to traverse[193] the Inditement; the cause of the Inditement, for that I had given judgment uppon stolen goods and received 2s. and 6d.[194] – and this was sayd to bee contrary unto an Act in King James tyme made.

This mad woaman was putt uppon this Action against mee by 2 ministers, who had framed for her a very ingenious speech, which shee could speake without booke, as shee did the day of hearing the Traverse: shee produced one woaman, who told the Court, a soon of hers was runn from her, that beeing in much affliction of mind for his loss, shee repayred unto mee to know what was become of him, that I told her hee was gone for the

[190]Page torn.

[191]Cf.

[192]Ruth Nedham (Needham).

[193]To deny an allegation in pleading. (*OED*).

[194]Two shillings and sixpence.

Barbados, and she would hear of him within 13 days, which shee sayd shee did.

A second woaman made oath, that her husband beeing wanting 2 yeares, shee repayred unto me for advise, that I told her hee was in Ireland and would bee at home such a tyme and shee sayd hee did come home accordingly.

I owned the taking of halfe a Crowne for my judgment of the theft, but sayd I gave no other judgment but that the goods would not bee recovered, beeing that was all that was required of mee, the party before that, having been with severall Astrologers, some affirming shee should have her goods, others gave contrary judgment, which made her come unto mee for a finall resolution.

At last my enemy began her before-made speech, and, without the least stumbling pronounced it before the Court; which ended, shee had some Queries putt unto her, and then I spoke for myselfe and produced my own Introduction[195] unto the Court, saying that I had some yeares before emitted that book for the benefitt of this and other nations, that it was allowed by Authority and had found good acceptance in both Universitys, that the study of Astrology was Lawfull and not contradicted by any Scriptures, that I neither had or ever did use any Charms, Sorcerys or Inchantments related in the bill of Inditement, etc.

Shee then related that shee had been severall tymes with me, and that afterwards shee could not rest a nights, but was troubled with Beares, Lions and Tygres, etc. My Councell was the Recorder Green, who after hee had answered all objections, concluded, Astrology was a Lawfull Art.

Mistris, sayd hee, what colour was those beasts you wear so terrified with –
I never saw any (sayd shee);
How do you then know they wear Lions, Tygres or beares, replyedhee –

---

[195] *Christian Astrology*

this is an idle person onely fitt for Bedlam. The Jury went not from the Barr[196], brought in No true Bill.

There wear many Presbiterian Justices much for her, and especially one Roberts, a busy fellow for the Parlament, who after his Majesty came in, had like to have lost his life and fortune.

I had procured Justice Hooker to bee there, who was the Oracle of all the Justices of peace in Middlesex.

There was nothing memorable after that happened unto mee until 1658* and month of October, at what tyme Captain Owen Cox[197] brought mee over from his Majesty of Sweden a gold Chain and Medall, worth about 50^L^, the cause whereof was that in the year 1657 and 1658, I had made honorable mention of him, the Anglicus of 1658 beeing translated into the Language spoke at Hamburgh, printed, and cryed about the streets as it is in London.

**1659.* [EA]

The occasion of my writing so honorably of his Majesty of Sweden was this, Sir Bolstrod Whitlock, Knight, uppon the very tyme of Olivers beeing made Protector, having made very noble Articles betwixt Christiana then Queen of Sweden, and the English Nation, was, in his beeing at Stockholm, visited frequently by Charles Gustavus, unto whom Christiana resigned during his aboad, and used with all manner of Civillity by him, in so much as some other Embassadors tooke it ill, that they had not so much respect or equall, unto which hee would reply, hee would bee kind where himselfe did find just cause of merit unto any: hee was a great lover of our Nation, but there was some other causes also mooving my penn to bee so liberall, viz: the great hopes I had of his prevailing, and of taking Copenhagen and Elsinore which, if hee had lived, was hoped hee might have accomplished: and had assuredly

[196]That is, they did not retire to consider their verdict.

[197]Owen Cox (d.1665). Having been a successful and daring parliamentary naval officer, in 1658 Cox joined the naval forces of the King of Sweden, for whom he fought with great success. He was something of a hero, a follower of Astrology, and another member of Lilly's colourful circle of acquaintances. According to John Gadbury (cf.) he had warned Cox of disaster before his loss at sea in 1665. (Bernard Capp, *ODNB*)

done, if Oliver the Protector had not so untimely died, ere our fleet of shipps was returned, for Oliver sent the Fleet of purpose to fight the Dutch, but dying, and the Parlament restored, Sir H. Vane[198], who afterwards was beheaded, had order from the Councill of State, to give Order to the Fleet what to do now Oliver was dead and themselves restored. Vane out of State Policy, gave the Earle of Sandwich direction not to fight the Dutch, Captain Symons, who carried those Letters swore unto mee, had hee known the letters hee carried had contained any such prohibition, hee would have sunk both shipp and letters. Oliver sayd when the fleet was to go forth that if God blessed his Majesty of Sweden with Copenhagen, the English wear to have Elsinore as their share, which, if once I have (sayth Oliver), the English shall have the whole trade of the Baltiq sea, I will make the Dutch find an other passage, except they will pay such customes as I shall impose.

Considering the advantage this would have been to our English, who can blame my Penn for beeing liberall, thereby to have incouraged our famous and noble Seamen; or for writing so honorably of the Swedish Nation who had so courteously treated my best of Freinds S^{r}. Bolstrod Whitlock, and by whose meanes had the Design taken effect, the English Nation had been made happy with the most beneficial Commerce of all Christendome.

I shall conclude about Oliver the then Protector, with whom obliquely I had transactions by his son in law, Mr. Claypool[199]; and to speake truly of him, hee sent one that waited uppon him in his Chamber, once in 2 or 3 days, to hear how it fared with mee in my Sessions business. But I never had of him directly or indirectly either Pension or any the least Somm of money, or any gratuity, during his whole [Protectorship; this I protest to bee true, by the name and in the name of the most holy God.][200]

198 Sir Henry Vane the younger (1613-1662), politician and author, beheaded for treason.

199 John Claypole (Claypoole) (1625-1688), army officer and courtier. Married to Oliver Cromwell's daughter, Elizabeth (bap.1629, d.1658). Close to Cromwell and a prominent supporter.

200 Missing from this copy of the manuscript.

In 1653 before the dissolution thereof[A], and that ere they had chosen any for their Embassadors into Sweden, Mr. Claypool came unto mee, demanding of mee whom I thought fitt to send uppon that Embassy into Sweden. I nominated Sr. B. Whitlock, who was chosen, and 2 or 3 days after, Mr. Claypool came again; I hope, Mr. Lilly, my father hath now pleased you, your freind Sir B. Whitlock is to go for Sweden: But since I have mentioned Oliver Cromwell, I will relate something of him, which perhaps no other penn can or will mention.

A. *Parlament*

Hee was born of generous parents in Huntingdonshire, educated sometyme at the University of Cambridge; in his youth was wholly given to debauchery, quarrelling, drinking etc. quid non; having by those meanes wasted his patrimony, hee was inforced to bethink himselfe of leaving England and go to New England; hee had hyred passage in a ship, but ere shee launched out for her voyage, a kinsman dyeth, leaving him a considerable fortune, uppon which hee returns, pays his debts, became affected to Religion, is elected in 1640 a member of Parlament, in 1642 made a Captain of horse under Sir Phillip Stapleton[201], fought at Edge Hill: after hee was made a Collonel, then Leiftennant Generall to the Earle of Manchester, who was one of the 3 Generalls to fight the Earl of Newcastle and Prince Rupert at York; Ferdinando Lord Fairfax, and Earl Leven the Scott wear the other 2 for the Parlament; the last 2 thinking all had been lost at Marston Moor fight, Fairfax went into Cawood Castle giving all for lost – at 12 at night there came word of the Parlaments Victory, Fairfax beeing then layd down uppon a bed; there was not a candle in the Castle nor any fire; up riseth Lord Fairfax, procures after sometyme paper, inke, Candle, writes to Hull, and other Garrisons of the Parlaments of the success and then slept.

Leven the Scott, askt the way to Tweed; the honor of that days fight was given to Manchester, Sir Thomas Fairfax his Brigade of horse, and Oliver Cromwell his Ironsides, for Cromwells horse in those tymes usually wore head peeces, back and side breast plates of Iron. After this victory, Cromwell became gracious with the house of Commons, especially the Zelots, or Presbiterians, with whom at that tyme hee especially joined, the name Independant at that tyme viz: 1644 beeing not so much spoken of.

201Sir Philip Stapleton (bap.1603, d.1647) politican and army officer.

There was some animosity at or before the fight betwixt the Earle of Newcastle and Prince Rupert, for Newcastle beeing Generall of his majestys forces in the north, a person of valour, and well esteemed in those parts, took it not well to have a Competitor in his Concernments, for if the Victory should fall on his Majestys side, Prince Ruperts forces would attribute it unto their own Generall, viz: Rupert, and give him the glory thereof; but that it happened, Prince Rupert in that days fight engaged the Parlaments forces too soon and before the Earle of Newcastle could well come out of York with his Army, by reason whereof, though Rupert had absolutely routed the Scotts and the Lord Fairfax forces, yet ere tymely assistance could second his Army, Sir Tho: Fairfax and Cromwell had putt him to flight, and not long after, all Newcastles Army.

Amongst the most memorable Actions of that daye, this happened, that one intire Regiment of foot belonging to Newcastle, called the Lambes, because they wear all new cloathed in white woollen Cloth 2 or 3 dayes before the fight, this sole Regiment after the day was lost, having gott into a small parcell of ground, ditched in, and not of easy access of horse, would take no quarter, and by meer Valour, for one whole houre kept the Troopes of horse from entring amongst them at mear push of Pike; when the horse did enter, they would have no quarter, but fought it out, till there was not 30 of them living; those whose happ it was to bee beaten down uppon the ground, as the Troopers came near them, though they could not rise for their wounds, yet wear so desperate, as to gett either a pike or sword or peece of them and to gore the Troopers horses as the came over them or passed by them. Captain Camby, then a Trooper under Cromwell, and an Actor, who was the 3rd or 4th man that entered amongst them, protested hee never in all the fights hee was in, mett with such resolute, brave fellows, or whom hee pityed so much: and sayd, hee saved 2 or 3 against their wills.

After the fight, Manchester marched slowly Southwards etc. but at last came to Newbery fight, which ended, hee came for London, and there accuseth Cromwell beeing his Liefetennant, to the Parlament of disobedience and not obeying his Orders.

The house of Commons acquaint Cromwell hearwith, and charge him, as hee would answer it before God, that the day following, hee should give them a full account of Manchesters proceedings, and the cause and occasion of their difference, and the reason, why Manchester did not tymely moove Westward, for the reliefe of Essex then in the West, who was absolutely routed, inforced to fly, all his foot taken and all his Ordinance, and train of Artillery, only the horse escaping.

Cromwell the next day gave his account to Mr. Speaker in the house of Commons, by way of Recrimination.

That after God had given them a successful victory at Marston over the Kings forces, and that they had well refreshed their Army, Manchester by their Order did moove Southward, but with such slowness, that sometymes hee would not march for 3 days togather; sometymes hee would lye still one day, then two days, whereuppon hee sayd, considering the Earle of Essex was in the West, with what success hee then knew not, hee mooved Manchester severall tymes to quicken his March to the West for reliefe of Essex if hee wear beaten, or to divert the Kings forces from following Essex; but hee sayd, Manchester still refused to make haste, and that one day he sayd, if any man but yourself Lieftennant should so frequently trouble mee, I would call him before a Councell of Warr; wee have beaten the Kings forces in the North, if wee should do so in the West, his Majesty is then undone, hee hath many sons living, if any of them come to the Crown, as they well may, they will never forgett us[AB];[202] after which hee marched not at all, untill hee had Order from the Committee to hasten Westward, by reason of Essex his being lost in Cornwall, which then hee did, and at Newbery fight tis true I refused to obey his directions and order, for thus it was; his Majestys horse beeing betwixt 4 and 5 thousand in a large Common in good order, hee commands mee, Mr. Speaker, to charge them, wee having no way to come at them, but through a narrow lane, where not above 3 horse could march abreast; whereby had I followed his order, wee had been all cutt off ere wee could have gott into any order; Mr. Speaker, and then he wept, (which hee could do toties quoties) I considering that all the visible Army you then had was by this councell in danger to bee lost, refused thus to indanger your mean strength, which now most of all consisted of those horse under my Command, etc.

[AB] *this Major Hamond a man of honor, will justifie as well as my selfe.*

[202] This is meant as an insertion into Cromwell's address, rather than a comment by Lilly.

This his Recrimination was well accepted by the house of Commons, who thereuppon and from that tyme, thought there was none of the house of Lords very fitt to bee intrusted with their future Armys, but had then thoughts of making a Commoner their Generall, which afterwards they did, and elected Sir Thomas Fairfax their Generall and Cromwell Leiftennant Generall, but it was next Spring first; uppon Essex his being lost in Cornwall, I heard Serjant Maynard[203] say: if now the King haste to London wee are undone, having no Army to resist him.[204]

His Majesty had many misfortunes ever attending him, during his aboad at Oxford, some by reason of that great animosity betwixt Prince Rupert and the Lord Digby, each indeavoring to cross one an other, but the worst of all was by Treachery of severall Officers under his Command and in his service, for the Parlament had in continuall pay one Collonell of the Kings councell of Warr, one Leifetennant Collonell, one Captaine, one Ensigne, one or 2 Serjants, severall Corporalls, who had constant pay and duly payd them every month, according to the Capacity of their Offices and places; and yet none of these knew any thing of each others beeing so imployed: there wear severall well wishers unto the Parlament in Oxford, where each left his letter, putting it in at the hole of a glass window, as hee made water in the street; what was putt in at the window in any of those houses was the same day convayed 2 miles off by some of the habit of Town Gardners, to the side of a ditch, where one or more wear ever ready to carry the intelligence to the next Parlament Garrison: I was then familiar with all the Spies that constantly went in and out to Oxford.[205]

But once more to my own Actions; I had in 1652 and 1653 and 1654 much contention with Mr. Gatacre[206] of Redriff, a man indued with all kind

---

[203]Probably Sir John Maynard (1604-1690), lawyer and politician, friend of Bulstrode Whitelock. (*ODNB*)

[204]Such detail as Lilly provides in this account demonstrates how well informed he was politically and militarily.

[205]This presents a fascinating glimpse into the intrigue of espionage and intelligence gathering. No less interesting is Lilly's admitting to knowing them all, further demonstrating his closeness to the power centre at that time.

of Learning, and the ablest man of the whole Synod of Divines in the Orientall Toungs.

The Synod had concluded to make an exposition uppon the Bible, some undertook one book, some an other; Gatacre fell uppon Jeremy, uppon making his Exposition on the 2 verse of the 10th Chapter – Learn not the way of the heathen, and be not dismayed at the signes of heaven, for the heathen are dismayed at them.

In his annotations thereuppon, hee makes a scandalous exposition, and in express termes, hints at mee, repeating verbatim 10 or 12 lines of an Epistle of mine in one of my former Anglicus. The substance of my Epistle was that I did conceive the good Angells of God, did first reveale Astrology unto mankind, etc. but hee in his Annotations calls mee blind Bussard, etc.

Having now Liberty of the Press, and hearing the old man was very Cholerick, I thought fitt to raise it upp and onely wrote I referred my discourse then in hand to the discussion and judgment of sober persons, but not unto Thomas Wiseacre, for Senes bis pueri[207]: these very words begott the writing of 42 sheets against my selfe and Astrology. The next year I quibbled again in 3 or 4 lines against him, then hee printed 22 sheets against me. I was persuaded by Doctor Gawdy, late Bishop of Excester, to let him alone, but in my next yeares Anglicus, in August observations, I wrote, Hoc in tumbo jacet Presbiter et Nebulo[208]; in which very month hee died.

Severall Divines applyed themselves unto mee, desiring me to forbear any further vexing of Mr. Gatacre, but all of them did as much condemn him of indiscretion, that in so sober a peece of worke as that was, viz: in an annotation uppon a Sacred text of Scripture, to particularise mee in that

[206]Thomas Gataker - he changed the spelling from "Gatacre" - (1574-1654) Church of England Clergyman and scholar. He was widely known in London and appears to have bequeathed a book to Bulstrode Whitelock's wife. (Brett Usher, *ODNB*).

[207]Old men are twice boys.

[208]In this way the Presbiterian and idler lies dead in the tomb.

dirty language; they pittied him that hee had not better considered with himselfe ere hee published.

Dean Owen of Christ Church in Oxford, hee also in his sermons had sharp invectives against mee and Astrology; I cryed quittance with him by urging Abbot Panormiton his judgment uppon Astrology, contrary to Owens, and concluded, An Abbott was an ace above a Dean.

One Mr. Nye of the Assembly of Divines, a Jesuiticall Presbiterian, hee bleated forth his judgment publiqly against mee and Astrology; to bee quit with him, I urged Causinus the Jesuit his approbation of Astrology, and concluded, sic canibus catulos[209] etc. In some tyme after, the Dutch Embassador was offended with some things in Anglicus, presented a Memoriall to the Councill of State that Merlinus Anglicus might bee considered, and the abuses against their Nation examined; but his paper was not accepted of, or I in any way molested.

In Olivers Protectorship, I wrote freely and satyricall inough; hee was now become Independent, and all the Soldiery my freinds, for when hee was in Scotland the day of one of their fights, a Soldier stood with Anglicus in his hand, and as the severall Troopes passed by him, Lo, hear what Lilly sayth, you are in this month promised victory, fight it out brave boys, and then read that months prediction.

I had long before predicted the Downfall of Presbitery, as you (most honored Sir) in the figure thereof in my Introduction[210], may observe, and it was uppon this occasion: Sir Thomas Middleton[211] of Chark castle[212], enemy to Presbitery, seeing they much prevailed, beeing a Member of the House, seriously demanded my judgment, if Presbitery should prevail or not in England? and the figure printed in my Introduction, will best give you an account, long before it happened, of the sinking and fayling of

[209]Thus from the dogs, the pups.

[210]The horary "If Presbytery shall stand?" (11th March, 1646/7 OS), *CA*, p.439.

[211]Sir Thomas Myddelton (1586-1666), parliamentarian army officer. (*ODNB*)

[212]Chirk Castle, Denbighshire.

Presbitery: so will the 2nd page of my Heiroglyphicks; those men, to bee serious, would preach well, but they wear more Lordly then Bishops, and usually in their parishes more Tyranicall then the great Turke.

Of the year 1660 the Actions whereof, as they wear remarkable in England, so wear they no less then very memorable as to my particular fortune and person.

Uppon the Lord Generall Monke his returning from Scotland with his Army into England, suddenly after his coming to London, Richard Cromwell, the then Protector, his Authority was layd aside and the old Parlament restored; the Councell of State satt as formerly; the first Act they putt the Generall uppon was to take down the Citty of Londons Gates and Portcullises, an Act which the Generall sayd was fitter for a Janizary[213] to do then for a Generall; yet he effected the Commands received, and then lodged in the Citty with his Army; the Citizens tooke this pulling down of their Gates so heinously, that one night the ruder sort of them procured all the Rumps of beefe and other baggage, and publiqly burnt them in the streets, in derision of the then Parlament, calling them that now satt, the Rump: this hurliburly was mannaged as well by the Generalls Soldiers as the Citizens; the Kings health was publiqly drunk all over the Citty, and confusion to the Parlament; the matter continued until Midnight, or longer, the Councill of State sitting at white Hall had hearof no knowledge, until Sir Martin Noell[214], a discreet Citizen, came about nine at night and then first informed them thereof; the Councill could not beleeve it, until they had sent some Ministers of their own, who affirmed the verity thereof; they wear at a stand and could not resolve what to do; at last Nevill Smyth came, beeing one of them, and publiqly protested, there was but one way to regain their Authority, and to bee revenged of this affront, and to overthrow the Lord Generall Monk, whom now they perceived intended otherways then hee had pretended; his Councell was, to take away Monks Commission and to give present Commission to Major Generall Lambert to bee their Generall, which Councill of his, if they would take and putt it speedily in execution, would putt an end to all the present mischiefs; the Councell in generall did all very well approove Nevill Smyths judgment, but presently, upp starts Sir Arthur Hazellrigg, and makes a sharp invective against Lambert, and concluded hee would rather perish under the King

[213]Probably referring to the child-soldiers of the Turkish empire.

[214]Sir Martin Noell (bap.1614 d.1665), financier and merchant. (*ODNB*)

of the Scotts[215] power then that Lambert should ever any more have Command under the Parlament.

The Lord Generall suddenly after, brings in the long secluded Members to sitt in Parlament, beeing persons of great judgment and formerly inforced from sitting therein by the Soldiery and connivance of those who styled themselves the Godly party of the Parlament. These honorable Patriots, presently voted his Majestys coming into England, and so hee did in May 1660; but because Charles the Second[A] now King of England, soon of Charles the first, grandchild of King James first, King of great Brittany; was so miraculously restored, and so many hundreds of yeares since prophecied of by Ambrose Merlin, it will not bee impertinent to mention the Prophecys themselves, the rather because wee have seen their verification.

A. *1667*

Ambrose Merline his prophecy, wrote about 990 yeares since.

Hee calls King James, the Lyon of Righteousness, and sayth when hee died or was dead, there would raign a noble White King; this was Charles the first; the prophet discovers all his troubles, his flying up and down, his imprisonment, his death, and calls him Aquila: what concerns Charles the second, is the subject of our discourse: In the Lattin Coppy, its thus;

Deinde ab Austro veniet cum Sole super ligneos equos, et super spumantem inundationem maris, Pullus Aquilœ navigans in Brittaniam.

Et applicans statim tunc altam domum Aquilœ aquilœ sitiens, et cito aliam sitiet.
Deinde pullus Aquilœ nidificabit in summa rupe totius Brittanniœ: nec juvenis occidet, nec ad senem vivet.

This in our old coppy is englished thus:

After, then shall come through the South with the Sun, on horse of Tree, and uppon all waves of the Sea, the Chicken of the Eagle, sailing into

[215]Charles II.

Brittain, and arriving anon to the house of the Eagle, hee shall show fellowship to them beasts.

After, the Chicken of the Eagle shall nestle in the highest Rooch of all Brittain; nay hee shall naught bee slain young: nay hee naught come old: and other Latin Coppy, renders the last verse thus;

Deinde pullus Aquilœ nidificabit in summo rupium, nec juvenis occidetur, nec ad senium perveniet: there is after this, pacificato regno, Omnes occidet: which is intended of those persons putt to death that satt as Judges uppon his fathers Death.

Verification;

but he landed in Dover, a Port in ye South part of England. [E.A.]

His Majesty beeing in the Low Countrys, when the Lord Generall had restored the secluded members, the Parlament sent part of the Royall Navy to bring him for England, which they did in May 1660; Holland is East from England, so hee came with the Sun; wooden horses are the English shipps. Tunc nidificabit in summo rupium,

The Lord Generall and most of the Gentry of England mett him in Kent, and brought him unto London, then to White hall; hear, by the highest rooch, some write Rock, is intended London, beeing the Metropolis of all England. Since which tyme, unto this very day I write this story, hee hath raigned in England, and long may hee do hearafter. 10th Dec. 1667.

Had I leasure, I might verifie the whole preceding part concerning King Charles: much of the verification thereof is mentioned in my Collection of Prophecys printed 1645, but his Majesty beeing then alive, I forebore much of that Subject: not willing to give offence; I dedicated that booke unto him, and in the conclusion thereof, I advised his return unto Parlament, with these words: Fac hoc et vives. There was also a Prophecy printed in 1588 in Greek Caracters exactly deciphering the long troubles the English Nation had from 1641 until 1660, and it ended thus:

And after that, shall come a Dreadfull dead man, and with him a Royall G (its Gamma in the Greek, intending C in the Latine beeing the 3rd letter of the Alphabett) of the best blood in the world, and hee shall have the Crown, and shall sett England on the right way, and putt out all Heresys.

Monkery beeing then extinguished above 80 or 90 yeares, and the Lord Generalls name beeing Monk, is the Deadman. The royall G or C is Charles the second, who for his extraction may bee sayd, to bee of the best blood in the World.

Thes 2 prophecys wear not given vocally by the Angells, but by inspiration of the Christall in Types and figures, or by apparition the Circular way, where at some distance the Angells appear representing by formes, shapes and Creatures what is demanded; it is very rare, yea, even in our dayes, for any Operator or Master to have the Angells speake articulately, when they do speak, its like the Irish, much in the Throat.[216]

What further concerns his Majesty will more fully bee evident about 1672 or 1674 or at furthest 1676.

And now unto my own Actions in 1660.

In the first place my Fee Farm Rents, beeing of the yearly value of 120L, wear all lost by his Majestys coming to his Restauration; but I do say truly, the loss thereof did never trouble mee, or did I repine thereat.

In June of that year, a new Parlament was called, whereunto I was unwillingly invited by 2 messengers of the Serjant at Armes; the matter whereuppon I was taken into Custody, was to examine mee concerning the person who cutt off the Kings head, viz: the late Kings.

Sr. Daniel Harvey of Surrey gott the business mooved against mee in great displeasure, because at the Election of new Knights for Surrey, I procured the whole town of Walton to stand and give their voices for Sr. Richard

[216]This reads as almost an aside and yet it reveals Lilly's knowledge and experience of magical practices.

Anslow[217]; the Committee to examine mee wear Mr. Prinn[218], one Collonell King[219], Mr. Richard Weston[220] of Grays Inn.

Onslow.

Gods providence appeared very much for mee that day, for walking in Westminster Hall, Mr. Richard Pennington, soon of my old freind Mr. Wm: Pennington, mett me, and inquiring the Cause of my beeing there, sayd no more, but walked upp and down the Hall, and related my kindness to his father unto very many Parlament men of Cheshire and Lancashire, Yorkshire, Cumberland and those Northern Countrys, who numerously came upp into the Speakers Chamber and bad mee bee of good comfort; at last hee meets Master Weston, one of the 3 unto whom my matter was referred for examination, who told Mr. Pennington hee came purposely to punish mee and would bee bitter against mee; but having it related, viz: my singular kindness and preservation of old Mr. Penningtons estate to the value of 6 or 7 thousand pounds, I'le do him all the good I can, I thought hee had never done any good, let me see him, and let him stand behind mee where I sitt.

I did so; at my first appearance, many of the young Members affronted mee highly, and demanded severall scurullous questions. Mr. Weston held a paper before his mouth, bad mee answer nobody but Mr. Prinn; I obeyed his Command, and saved my selfe much trouble thereby, and when Mr. Prinn putt any difficult or doubtful Querie unto mee, Mr. Weston prompt mee with a fitt answer: at last after all most one houres tugging, I desired to bee fully heard, what I could say, as to the Person who cutt Charles the first his head off. Liberty beeing given mee to speake, I related what follows, viz:

That the next Sunday but one after Charles the first was beheaded, Robert Spavin Secretary unto Leiftennant Generall Cromwell at that tyme, invited

---

[217]Sir Richard Onslow (bap.1601, d.1664), politican. (*ODNB*)

[218]William Prynne (1600-1669), pamphleteer and lawyer.

[219]Possibly the Colonel King referred to as a "rabid presbyterian" (Andrew Sharpe, *ODNB*).

[220]Sir Richard Weston (1620-1681). judge and politician. (*ODNB*)

himselfe to dine with mee, and brought Anthony Peirson[221] and severall others along with him to dinner; that their principal discourse all Dinner tyme was onely, who it was that beheaded the King; one sayd it was the Common hangman, an other Hugh Peeters; others also wear nominated, but none concluded.

Robert Spavin, so soon as Dinner was done, tooke mee by the hand and carried mee to the South window; sayth hee, these are all mistaken, they have not named the man that did the fact: it was Leiftennant Collonell Joyce[222], I was in the Room when hee fitted himselfe for the worke, stood behind him when hee did it, when done went in again with him; there's no man knows this but my Mr., viz: Cromwell, Commissary Ireton and myself; doth not Mr. Rushworth know it, sayd I; no, hee doth not know it sayd Spavin: the same thing Spavin since had often related unto mee when wee wear alone;[223] Mr. Prinn did with much Civillity make repoart hearof in the house; yet Norfolk, the Serjant, after my discharge, kept mee 2 days longer in Arrest, purposely to gett money of mee, hee had six pounds and his Messenger 40s. and I was attached but uppon the Sunday, examined on Tuseday and then discharged, though the Covetous Serjant detayned mee until Thursday: by meanes of a freind, I cryed quittance with Norfolk, which freind was to pay him his Salary at that tyme, and abated Norfolk 3 pounds, which wee spent every penny at one Dinner, without inviting the wretched Serjant.

But in the latter end of the year, when the Kings Judges wear arraigned at the old Baily, Norfolk warned mee to attend, beleeving I could give information concerning Hugh Peeters; at the Sessions I attended during its continuance, but was never called or examined: there I heard Harrison, Scott, Clement, Peeters, Hacker, Scroop and others of the Kings Judges[224],

---

[221]Anthony Pearson (bap.1627, d.1666), Quaker administrator. In 1648 he was Sir Arthur Hesilrige's secretary. (Richard L.Greaves, *ODNB*)

[222]George Joyce (b.1618), parliamentarian army officer.

[223]Historians dispute Spavin's account based largely on Spavin's unsavoury character. The identity of the two executioners has never been discovered.

[224]Those who presided at the trial of Charles I.

and Cook the Sollicitor who excellently defended himselfe; I say I did hear what they could say for themselves, and after heard the sentence of Condemnation pronounced against them by the incomparably modest and learned Judge Bridgman, now Lord Keeper of the great Seal of England.

One would think my troubles for that year had been ended, but in January 166½ one Everard, a Justice of Peace in Westminster, ere I was stirring, sent a Serjant and 34 Muskiteers for mee to white Hall, hee had twice that night seised about 60 persons, supposed Phanatiqs, very despicable persons, many whereof wear aged, some wear waterbearers, and had been Parlament Soldiers, others of ordinary Callings; all these wear guarded unto white Hall into a large Room till day light, and then committed to the Gate house; I was had into the gard Room, which I thought to bee Hell, some therein wear sleeping, others swearing, others drinking[225] Tobacco; in the Chimney of the Room I beleeve there was 2 bushells of broken tobacco pipes, allmost halfe one load of Ashes. Everard about 9 in the morning comes, writes my Mittimus for the Gate house, then shows it mee, I must be contented, I desired no other Curtesy, but that I might be privately carried unto the Gate house by 2 Soldiers, that was denyed. Amongst the miserable Crew of people, with a whole Company of Soldiers, I marched to Prison, and there for 3 houres was in the open ayre uppon the ground where the Common house of Office came down; after 3 houres I was advanced from this stinking place up the stayres, where there was on one side a company of rude, swearing persons, on the other side many Quakers, who lovingly entertained mee.

As soon as I was fixed, I wrote to my old honored freind Sir Edward Walker[226], Garter King at Armes, who presently went to Mr. Secretary Nicholas[227], and acquainted him with my condition, hee ordered Sir

---

[225]Should be "smoking".

[226]Sir Edward Walker (1612-1677), herald. George Wharton calculated his nativity in 1645. Although Lilly's friend, Walker wrote him a letter of reprimand for Lilly's publication of *Monarchy or No Monarchy* in 1651. (Hubert Chesshyre, *ODNB*).

[227]Sir Edward Nicholas (1594-1661), government official.

Edward to write to Everard to release mee, unless hee had any particular information against mee, which hee had not; hee further sayd, it was not his Majestys pleasure that any of his Subjects should bee thus had to prison without good cause showed before. Uppon receipt of Sir Edwards letter, Everard discharged mee, I taking the Oath of Allegiance and Supremacy; this days worke cost mee 37^{s}. Afterwards Everard stood to bee Burgess for Westminster, sent to me to procure him voices[228]; I returned answer that of all men living, hee deserved no curtesy from mee, nor should have any.

This side of paper hath spoiled 2 penns.[229]

In this year 1660, I sued out my pardon under the broad Seal of England, beeing so advised by good Councell, because there should bee no obstruction; I passed as William Lilly, citizen and Salter of London; it cost mee 13$^{L.}$ 6$^{s.}$ 8$^{d.}$.

There happened a verification of an astrologicall judgment of mine in this year 1660, which because it was predicted 16 yeares before it came to pass, and the year expressly nominated, I thought fitt to mention.

In page 111 of my Prophetical Merline, uppon three sextill aspects of

♄ and ♃[230] made in 1659 and 1660, I wrote thus –

This their freindly salutation comforts us in England; every man now possesses his own Vyneyard; our young youth growing unto Mans estate, and our old men live their full yeares. Our Nobles and Gentlemen roote again; our yeomanry, many yeares disconselated, now take pleasure in their husbandry: the Merchant sends out shipps and hath prosperous Returns; the Mechanick hath a quick Trading; hear's allmost a new world, new Laws,

[228]Supporters or votes.

[229]Lilly's note at the end of the page.

[230]" ...Saturn and Jupiter..."

new Lords; now my Country of England shall shedd no more teares, but rejoyce with, and in the many blessings God gives or affoards her Annually.

And in the same booke, page 118, over against the year 1660, you shall find –

A Bonny Scott acts his part,
The Long Parlament would give Charles the Second no other tytle then, King of Scotts.

I allso wrote to Sir Edward Walker Knight, Garter King at Armes, in 1659, hee beeing then in Holland –

Tu, dominusque vester videbitis Angliam, infra duos Annos[231] – for in 1662 his ☽ came by Direction to the body of the ☉.[232]

But hee came in uppon the Ascendant directed unto the △ of ☉ and Antiscion of ♃[233] – and happy it was for the Nation hee did come in, and long and prosperously may hee raign amongst us, it beeing the prayer of – William Lilly.

On 1663 and 1664, I had a long and tedious Law Sute in Chancery, MC comming to [of ♄:[234] and the occasion of that Sute was concerning houses, and my enemy though aged, had no beard, was really Saturnine – we came unto an Hearing February 166¾ before the Mr. of the Rolls Sr. Harbottle Grimston, where I had the Victory, but no Costs given mee.

My adversary not satisfied with that Judgement, petitioned that most just and honorable man, the Lord Chancellor Hyde, for a Rehearing his cause

[231] You, and your lord will see England, below two years.

[232] "...his [Charles II] Moon came by Direction to the body of the Sun."

[233] "...unto the trine of Sun and Antiscion of Jupiter...".

[234] "...comming to square of Saturn..."

before him; it was graunted, and the 13th June 1664 my M.C. then directed to [of ♀ and ☉,[235] his Lordshipp most judiciously heard it with much attention, and when my Adversarys Councell had urged these depositions which they had against mee, his Lordship stood upp and sayd –

Heares not one word against Mr. Lilly –

I replyed, My Lord, I hope I shall have Costs, Very good reason sayth hee and so I had, and at my departure out of Court, putt off his hatt and bad God bee with you.

but in other things he hath been very foul, as in the articles drawne up by the Parliament against him it appears. Which articles I presume you have not seen, otherwise you would have been of another mind. [E.A.]

This is the month of December 1667 wherein by misfortune hee is much traduced and highly persecuted by his enemys, is also retyred, however not in the least questioned for any indirect judgment as Chancellor in the Chancery, for there was never any person satt in that place, who executed Justice with more uprightness, or judgment or quickness for dispatch, then this very noble person from his enemys, and in good tyme restore him unto all his Honors again: from my Soule I wish it, and hope I shall live to see it – Amen: fiat oh tu Deus justiciæ.

In 1663 and 1664 I was made Churchwarden of Walton uppon Thames, setling as well as I could the affaires of that distracted parish, uppon my own Charges[236], and uppon my leaving the place forgave them 7 pounds odd money due unto mee.

In 1664 [obliteration] I had an other Law Suite, with Captain Colborn, Lord of the Manor of Esher concerning the Rights of the parish of Walton; hee had newly purchased that Manor and having 150 acres of grounde formerly Park and wood ground, lying in our parish, conceived hee had Right of Common in our parish of Walton; thereuppon hee putts 300 sheep uppon the Common, part whereof I impounded; he replevins them, gave mee a Declaration; I answered it; the Tryall was to bee at the Assizes in Kingston in Aprill 1664; when the day of Tryall came, hee had not one

[235]"...my M.C. then directed to square of Venus and Sun,..."

[236]Meaning "at my own cost."

witness in his cause, I had many; whereuppon, uppon conference, and by mediation, hee gave mee eleaven pounds for my Charges sustained in that Suite, whereof I returned him back $50^{s.}$ – $40^{s.}$ for himselfe and tenn shillings for the poor of the parish hee lived in. This I did at my own cost and charges, not one parishioner joyning with mee: I had now M.C. unto [of ♀ and ☉[237], both in my second, Ergo I gott money of this thing, a Suite. Sir Bolstrod Whitlock gave mee Councell.

Now I come unto the year 1665, wherein that horrible and devouring plague so extremely raged in the City of London; 27th of June 1665, I retyred into Country unto my wife and family[238], where since I have wholly continued, and so intend by permission of God; I had, before I came away, very many people of the poorer sort frequented my lodging, many whereof wear so civill as when they brought water, viz: Urine, from infected people, would stand purposely at a distance. I ordered those infected and not like to dye Cordialls, and caused them to sweat, whereby many recovered. My Landlord of the house was afraid of those poor people, I nothing at all, hee was desirous I should bee gone; hee had 4 children, I took them with mee into Country and provided for them; six weekes after I departed hee, his wife and many servants died of the plague.[239]

In Monarchy or no Monarchy, printed 1651 I had framed an Heirogliphick, which you may see in page the 7th representing a great Sickness and mortallity; wherein you may see the representation of people in their winding sheets, persons digging Graves and Sepulchres, Coffins etc. All this was performed by the more Secret Key of Astrology, or propheticall Astrology.

In 1666 happened the miraculous Conflagration in the City of London whereby in 4 days the most part thereof was consumed by fire. In my

---

[237] "...unto square of Venus and Sun."

[238] By "family", Lilly means those of his household.

[239] The plague was particularly severe in 1665 and it is interesting to note that Lilly had sent his wife, Ruth, and his household to Hersham before him. He himself had been staying in rented accommodation, suggesting that he had either sold or let his London home in The Strand.

Monarchy or no Monarchy, the next side after the Coffin and Pickaxes, there is Representation of a great Citty all in flames of fire, the memoriall whereof some Parlament man remembering, thought fitt to send for mee before that Committee which then did sitt for examination of the Causes of the fire, and whether there was no Treachery or design in the business, his Majesty beeing then in Warr both with the French and Dutch: the Summons to answer before that Committee was as followeth; Munday 22nd October 1666

At the Committee appointed to enquire after the causes of the late fires;

Ordered:

That Mr. Lilly do attend this Committee on Friday next beeing the 25th of October 1666, at two of the clock such Questions as shall bee then and there asked him.

Robert Brooke.

By accident I was then in London when the Summons came unto mee; I was timerous of Committees, being ever by some of them calumniated, upbraided, frowned, and derided; however I must and did appear; and let mee never forgett that great affection and care yourselfe (Oh most excellent and learned Esquire Ashmole) showed unto mee at that tyme; first your affection, in going along with mee all that day, secondly your great paines and care in speaking unto many worthy Members of that Committee your acquaintance, that they should befreind mee, and nott permitt mee to bee affronted, or have any disgracefull language cast uppon mee. I must seriously acknowledge your persuasions so prevailed with those Generous Soules, that I conceive there was never more Civillity used unto any then my selfe, and you know, there wear no small numbers of Parlament men appeared when they heard I was to bee there.

Sir Robert Brooke spoke to this purpose;

Mr. Lilly, this Committee thought fit to summon you to appear before them this day to know if you can say any thing as to the Cause of the late fire or whether there might be any designes therein, you are called the rather hither, because in a book of yours long since printed, you hinted some such thing by one of your Heirogliphicks; unto which I replyd,

May it please your Honors; after the beheading of the late King, considering that in the 3 subsequent yeares the Parlament acted nothing which continued the settlement of the Nation in peace, and beeing the generallity of people dissatisfied, the Citizens of London discontented, the Soldiery prone to Mutiny, I was desirous according to the best knowledge God had given mee, to make inquiry, by the Art I studied, what might from that tyme happen unto the Parlament and Nation in generall; at last having satisfied myselfe as well as I could, and perfected my judgment therein, I thought it most convenient to signifie my intentions and Conceptions thereof, in Forms, Shapes, types, Heiroglyphicks etc. without any Commentary, that so my judgment might bee concealed from the Vulgar and made manifest onely unto the wise, I hearin immitating the examples of many wise Philosophers who had done the like.

Sir Robert, sayth one, Lilly is yet sub vestibulo, I proceed further (sayd I), having found, Sir, that the City of London should be sadly afflicted with a great plague, and not long after with an exhorbitant Fire, I framed those 2 Heiroglyphicks as represented in the book, which in effect have prooved very true.

Did you foresee the year, sayth one – I did not sayd I, or was desirous, of that I made no scrutiny, (but you see, that its in the next page). I proceeded – Now Sir, whether there was any designe of burning the Citty or any employed to that purpose, I must deale ingeniously with you, that since the fire, I have taken many paines in the search thereof, but cannot or could give my selfe any the least satisfaction therein, I conclude, That it was the onely finger of God: but what instruments hee used thereunto, I am ignorant.

Exit Lillius.

finitur ☿ 18. Dec: 1667[240]

The Committee seemed well pleased with what I spoke and dismissed mee with great civillity.

Since which tyme, no memorable Action hath happened unto mee, my retyrement impeding all concourse unto mee. I have many more things to communicate which I shall do as they offer themselves to memory.

In anno 1634 and 1635, I had much familiarity with John Heginus, Doctor of Phisick, a Dutchman, an excellent Scholler and an able Phisition, not meanly versed in Astrology; unto him for his great Civillity, I communicated the Art of framing Sigils, Lamens, etc and the use of the Mosaicall Rodds: and wee did create several Sigills to very good purpose, I gave him the true Key thereof, viz: instructed him in their Forms, Caracters, Words, and last of all, how to give them Vivification, and what Number or Numbers wear appropriated to every planet[241]: cum multis aliis in Libris veterum latentibus; aut perspicue non intellectis[242].

I was well acquainted with the Speculator of John-a-Windor, a Scrivener sometymes living in Newbery; this Windor was clubfisted, wrote with a penn betwixt both his hands, I have seen many bonds and bills, wrote by him; hee was much given to Debauchery, so that at sometymes, the Dœmons would not appear to the Speculator; hee would then Suffumigate, sometymes to vex the Spirits, hee would curse them, fumigate with Contrarys; uppon his examination before S^r^. Henry Wallop K^t^.[243], which I have seen, hee sayd hee once visited D^r^. Dee in Mortlack, and out of a book that lay in the window, hee coppied out that Call which he used when hee invocated –

---

[240]Lilly's note at the end of the page: "finished Wednesday 18th December 1667."

[241]Lilly again provides evidence of the extent of his studies and abilities in these magical matters.

[242]With many other ways hidden in the books of the ancients; or not clearly understood.

[243]Sir Henry Wallop (1568-1642), politican.

it was that – which near the beginning of it hath these words, per virtutem illorum qui invocant nomen tuum Hermeli – mitte nobis tres Angelos, etc.[244]

Windor had many good parts, but a most lewd person. My Mr. Wright knew him well, and having dealings in those parts, made use of him as a Scrivener.

Oliver Withers servant to Sr. H. Wallopp, brought upp a Windors examination unto London purposely for mee to peruse. This Withers was Mr. Fisks Scholler 3 yeares more or less to learn Astrology of him, but beeing never the wiser; Fisk brought him unto mee, by showing him but how to judge one figure, his eyes wear opened; hee made the Epistle before Dr. Neves booke, now in Mr. Sanders hands, was very learned in the Latine, Greek and Hebrew toungs, I desire you, Esquire, to translate that Epistle.

Born in London. Cambridge

Having mentioned Doctor John Dee[245], I hold it not impertinent to speak something of him, but more especially of Edward Kelly[246], his Speculator. Doctor Dee himselfe was a Cambro-Brittain, educated in the University of Oxford; hee tooke his degree of Doctor[247], afterwards for many yeares in search of the profounder studys, travelled into Forraign parts.

To bee serious hee was Queen Elizabeths Intelligencer and had a Salary for his maintainance from the Secretary of State; hee was a ready witted man, quick of apprehension, very learned, and of great Judgment in the Latin and Greek Toungs; hee was a very great Investigator of the more Secret Hermeticall learning, a perfect Astronomer, a curious Astrologer, a serious Geometrician; to speake truth, hee was excellent in all kinds of learning.

---

[244]Through the virtue of those who are calling your name Hermeli - send to us three angels, etc.

[245]John Dee (1527-1609), mathematician, astrologer, antiquarian. He appears to have gained his doctorate in medicine in Prague in 1584 or 1585. (R. Julian Roberts, *ODNB*)

[246]Sir Edward Kelley (1555-1597/8), alchemist.

[247]Ashmole has inserted a cipher character (or two) in this margin note which appears to translate as "this" or "this in". It seems to refer to the university where Dee obtained his doctorate.

With all this, hee was the most ambitious person living, and most desirous of fame and renown, and was never so well pleased as when hee heard himself stiled, Most Excellent. Hee was studious in Chimistry, and attained good perfection therein, but his servant, or rather Companion Kelly outwent[248] him, viz: about the Elixir or Philosophers Stone: which neither Kelly or Dee attained by their own labour and industry; it was in this manner Kelly obtained it, as I had it related from an antient Minister, who knew the certainty thereof from an old English Merchant, resident in Germany at that tyme both Kelly and Dee wear there.

Dee and Kelly, beeing in the confines of the Emperors Dominions in a Citty where resided many English Merchants, with whom they had much familiarity; there happened an old Frier to come to Doctor Dees lodging, knocking at the dore, Dee peeped down the stayres; Kelly, tell the old man I am not at home. Kelly did so; the Fryer sayd, I will take an other tyme to waite uppon him; some few days after, hee came again; Dee orderd Kelly if it wear the same person to deny him again; he did so, at which the Frier was very angry, tell thy Mr. I came to speak with him and to do him good because here is a great Scholler and famous, but now tell him he putt forth a book and dedicated it to the Emperor; (its called Monas Heirogliphicas[249]) hee understands it not; I wrote it my selfe, I came to instruct him therein, and in some other more profound things; do thou Kelly come along with mee; I will make thee more famous than thy Master Dee.

toad -

Kelly was very apprehensive of what the Frier delivered and thereuppon suddenly retyred from Dee and wholly applied unto the Frier, and of him either had the Elixir ready made or the perfect method of its preparation and making; the poor Frier lived a very short tyme after; whether hee died of a naturall death, or was otherways poisoned or made away by Kelly, the Merchant who related this did not certainly know. How Kelly died afterwards at Prague you well know[250]; hee was born at

---

[248]Surpassed.

[249]*Monas Hieroglyphica,* Antwerp c.1564. It is this book that Dee claimed to have written in twelve days.

[250]It is reported that Kelley died from injuries sustained while attempting to escape imprisonment.

Worcester, and had been an Apothecary; not above 30 yeares since; hee had a sister lived in Worcester who had some gold, made by her brothers Projection.

Doctor Dee lived at Mortlack in Surrey, very poor, inforced many tymes to sell some book or other to buy his dinner with, as Doctor Napper of Lindford in Buckinghamshire oft related, who knew him very well.

I have read over his book of Conference with Spirits, and there by perceive many weaknesses in the mennay of that way of Mosaicall learning: but I conceive, the reason why hee had not more plain resolutions and more to the purpose was because Kelly was very vicious, unto whom the Angells wear not obedient or willingly did declare the Questions propounded: but I could give other reasons: but they are not for paper.

I was very familiar with one Sarah Skelhorn, who had been Speculatrix unto one Arthur Gauntlett about Grays Inn Lane, a very lewd fellow, professing Phisick; this Sarah had a perfect sight, and indeed the best eyes for that purpose I ever yet did see; Gauntlets bookes after hee was dead wear sold, after I had perused them, to my Scholler Humfrys; there wear rare notions in them; this Sarah lived long tyme even until her death with one M^rs^. Stockman in the Isle of Purbeck, and died about 16 years since; her M^rs^. one tyme beeing desirous to accompany her mother the Lady Beckonsfeild unto London, who lived 12 miles from her habitation, caused Sarah to inspect her Christall to see if shee, viz: her mother, was gone, yea or not; the Angells appeared and showed her mother opening a trunk and taking out a red wastcoat, whereby she perceived shee was not gone; next day shee went to her mothers, and there, as shee entred the Chamber, shee was opening a trunk and had a red wastcoat in her hand. Sarah told mee oft, the Angells would for some yeares follow her and appear in every room of the house, until she was weary of them.

This Sarah Skelhorn, her Call unto the christall begann,
Oh ye good Angells, onely and onely, etc.

Ellen Evans, daughter of my Tutor Evans, her Call unto the Christall was thus
O Micol, o tu Micol, regina Pigmerorum, veni, etc.

Syth I have related of the Queen of Fairyes, I shall acquaint you that its not for every one, or every person that those Angelicall Creatures will appear unto, though they may say over the Call, over and over; or indeed is it given to very many persons to indure their glorious aspects; even very many have failed just at that present when they are ready to manifest themselves; even persons otherwise of undaunted spirits and firme resolutions are hearwith astonished and tremble, as it happened not many yeares since with us; a very sober discreet person of vertuous life and Conversation was beyond measure desirous to see something in this nature; hee went with a freind into my Hurst wood; the Queen of Fairyes was invocated; a gentle murmuring wynd came first; after that, amongst the hedges a smart whirlwind; by and by, a strong blast of wynd blew uppon the face of the Freind – and the Queen appearing a little[251]. No more I beseech you (quoth the freind) my hart fayles, I am not able to indure longer; nor was hee, his black curling hair rose up, and I beleeve a bullrush would have beat him to the ground; hee was soundly laughed at, etc.

in a most illustrious glory.
[E.A]

[251]Ashmole's comment here suggests that it was he who witnessed this event.

+ *Mr. Gilbert Wakering gave him his Berrill when hee dyed; it was of the largeness of a good big Orange, set in silver with a Cross on the top and another on the Handle, and round about engraved the names of these Angells, Raphael, Gabriell, Uriell.* [E.A.]

Sr. Robert Holborn Kt.[252], brought once unto mee Gladwell+ of Suffolk, who had formerly had Sight and Conference with Uriel and Raphael; but lost them both by carelessness, so that neither of them both would but rarely appear and then presently bee gone, resolving nothing; hee would have given mee 200L to have assisted him for their recovery, but I am no such man. Those glorious Creatures, if well commanded and well observed, do teach the Mr. anything hee desires; Amant secreta, fugiunt aperta[253]. The Fairys love the Southern side of Hills, Mountains, Groves, Neatness and cleanliness in apparrell, a strict diet, an upright life, fervent prayers unto God, conduce much to the assistance of those who are curious these ways.

+ *from these MS he gained his first knowledge.* [EA]

It hath been ever my happiness to meet with many Raritys in my tyme, unexpectedly; I had a sister lived in the Minorys, in that very house where formerly had lived one Evans, not my Tutor, but an other farr exceeding him in Astrology and all other occult Learning, questioned for his life, about 1612; I am sure it was when the present Earle of Manchesters father was lord Chief Justice of England; he was found guilty by a peevish Jury, but petitioning King James by a Greek petition as indeed hee was an excellent Grecian, by my Soule, sayd King James, this man shall not dye, I think he is a better Grecian than any of my Bishops; so his life was spared, etc. My sisters Mr., a new modelling the house, breaking up a window, under which wear Evans secret manuscripts, and 2 molds in brass, one of a man, the other of a woaman, I bought Molds and+ books for five shillings; the secrets wear wrote in an imperfect greek Caracter, but after I found the Vowells, all the rest wear presently clear inough.

You see, most worthy Sir, I write freely, its out of the sincerity of my affection, many things wrote by mee having been more fitt for a Sepulture then a Book.

But
Quo major est virorum prœstantium, tuj similium inopia; eo mihi charior est, et esse debet amicitia tua: quam quidam omnibus officijs, et studijs, quae a summa benevolentia possunt, perpetuo colam.

---

[252]cf. footnote 97.

[253]They love remote places, they flee from open spaces.

However, who study the curiositys before named, if they are not very well versed in Astrology, they shall rarely attain their desired Ends. There was in the late tymes of trouble, one Morlack, who pretended unto Speculation, had a Christall, a Call of Queen Mab, one of the Queen of Fairys; hee deluded many thereby, at last I was brought into his company; hee was desired to make invocation, hee did so; nothing appeared or would, 3 or 4 tymes in my company hee was putt uppon to do the worke, but could not; at last hee sayd, hee could do nothing as long as I was in presence, I at last showed him his error, but left him as I found him, a pretended ignoramus.

I may seem to some to write incredibilia, be it so, but knowing unto whom and for whose onely sake I do write them, I am much comforted therewith, well knowing you are the most Knowing man in these Curiosities of any now living in England and therefore it is my hope, these will bee a Present well becomming you to accept.

Præclara omnia quam difficilia sint, his prœsertim temporibus, (Celeberrime Armiger) non te fugit.

And therefore I will acquaint you with one memorable story related unto mee by Mr. John Marr[254], an excellent mathematician and Geometrician, whom I conceive you remember, hee was servant to King James and Charles the first.

At first when the Lord Nappier of Marchiston made publiq his Logarithms, Mr. Briggs[255] then Reader of the Astronomy Lecture at Gresham Colledge London, was so surprised with admiration of them, that hee would have no quietness in himselfe, until hee had seen that noble person the Lord Marchiston, whose onely invention they wear; hee acquaints John Marr hearwith, who went into Scotland before Mr. Briggs, purposely to bee there when those 2 so learned persons should meet at Edinborough: Mr. Briggs appoints a certain day when to meet at Edinborough, but fayling thereof,

[254]John Marr, clerk of the kitchen to the Prince of Wales, later Charles II. He was highly skilled in mathematics and had constructed sun-dials for the king. (Christopher J.Scriber, *ODNB*)

[255]Henry Briggs (bap.1561, d.1631, mathematician.

the Lord Nappier was doubtfull hee would not come; it happened one day as John Marr and the Lord Nappier wear speaking of Mr. Briggs; Ah John, sayth Marchiston, Mr. Briggs will not now come; at the very instant, one knocks at the Gate, John Marr hasted down and it prooved Mr. Briggs, to his great contentment; hee brings Master Briggs upp into my Lords chamber where allmost one quarter of an houre was spent, each beholding the other allmost with admiration, before one word was spoken.

At last Mr. Briggs begann

My lord, I have undertaken this long journey purposely to see your person, and to know by what Engine of witt or Ingenuity you came first to think of this most excellent helpe unto Astronomy, viz: the Logarithms, but My Lord beeing by you found out, I wonder nobody else found it out before; now known, it is so easy: hee was nobly entertained by the Lord Nappier, and every summer after that during the Lords beeing alive this venerable man Mr. Briggs went purposely unto Scotland to visit him; Tempora non mutantur.

These 2 persons wear worthy men in their tyme, and yet the one, viz: Lord Marchiston, was a great Lover of Astrology, but Briggs the most Satyricall man against it, that hath been known; but the reason hearof I conceive was, that Briggs was a severe Presbiterian, and wholly conversant with persons of that judgment, whereas the Lord Marchiston was a generall Schollar and deeply read in all Divine and humane Historys: its the same Marchiston who made that most serious and learned exposition uppon the Revelation of St. John, it beeing the best that ever yet appeared in the worlde.

Ashmole's Addendum to the Manuscript

This far proceeded M^r^: William Lilly in setting downe the account of his Lyfe, with some other things of Noate: now shall be added something more which afterwards happened during his retyrement at his House at Hersham, untill his death.

He left London in the year 1665 (as he hath before noted) and betooke himselfe to the study of Phisick, in which having arrived at a competent degree of Knowledge, assisted by dilligent observation and practise, he desired his old friend M^r^. Ashmole, to obtayne of his Grace Doctor Shelden then Lord Archbishop of Canterbury, a Lycence for the practise of Phisick; which upon application to his Grace, and producing a +Testimoniall under the hands of two Phisitians of the Colledge in London on M^r^: Lillys behalfe, he most readily granted.

+ *8: Octob: 1670.* [E.A]

Hereupon he began to practise more openly, & with good success, & every Saterday rode to Kingston, where the poorer sort flockt to him from severall parts & received much benefit by his advice & prescriptions, which he gave them freely & without money; from those that were more able he now and then received a Shilling, & sometymes an halfe Crowne, if they offered it to him, otherwise he demanded nothing: and in truth his Charity toward poore people was very great, no less then the care & paines he tooke in considering & weighing their particular Cases, & applying propper remedies to their Infirmities, which gained him extraordinary credit & estimation.

[E.A.]

From Ashmole's Autobiographical Notes...,

[16 August 1674]

He [Lilly] was of a strong Constitution, & continued generally in good health, till the 16th: of August 1674, when a violent humour discovered it selfe in red spots all over his Body, with litle Pushes in his head. This, in the Winter following was seconded by a distemper, whereof he fell sick, & was let blod in the left foote, a litle above the Ankle.

[18 December 1674]

Mr: Lilly fell sick, & was let blood in the left foote a litle above the Ancle (new Moone the day before, & the Sun Ecclipsed).

[20 December 1674]

Mr: Lilly had a great paine in his left Leg which lasted 24 houres, & put him into a great Feaver.

[20 - 28 December 1674]

The 20th of December following, a humour descended from his head by his left side from 8 a'clock at Night till the next Morning, & then staying a while in the calfe of his Leg, at length descended toward his Toes, the anguish whereof put him into a Feaver. This humour fixed in two places on the top of his left foote (one in that where he was let blood two daies before) which (upon application of Plegets[256]) growing ripe, they were lanced by Mr: Agar of Kingston his Apothecary[257] (& no less a skilfull Chirurgeon) after which he began to be at ease, his Feaver abated, & within five Moneths the Cure was perfected.

[7 November 1675 and later] *28. Dec:*

[256] Pledget: a small compress, often covered in some medicament, for applying over a wound or sore. (*OED*)

[257] Thomas Agar (d.1703?), he was the first mayor of Kingston on Thames, 1685-6, and bailiff twelve times. Agar is mentioned in Lilly's will and referred to as his "son" in his correspondence with Ashmole. As there is no evidence of Lilly's ever having children, we might assume that he viewed Agar as his son. Certainly, use of terms such as "family" often referred to whomever made up the household and included employees and those for whom the householder was responsible. Such a term might also refer to a more esoteric relationship such as that between Ashmole and William Backhouse.

The 7th: of November 1675. he was taken with a violent fitt of Vomiting, for some houres, to which a Feaver succeeded, that continued 4 Moneths; this brought his Body exceeding low, together with dimnes in his Eyes, which after occasioned him to make use of Mr: Henry Coley as his Amanuensis to transcribe (from his dictates) his Astrologicall Judgments for the yeare 1677. but the Monethly Observations for that yeare, were written with his owne hand sometyme before, though by this tyme he was grown very dim sighted. His Judgments & Observations for the Succeding yeares till his death (So also for the yeare 1682) were all composed by his directions, Mr: Coley coming to Hersham the begining of every Sommer, & staied there, till by Conference with him, he had dispatched them for the Press: to whome at these oppertunities, he comunicated his way of Judgment & other Astrologicall Arcana's.

[Early 1681]

In the yeare 1681. he had a Flux, which weakned him much, yet after some tyme his strength encreased, but now his sight was wholy taken from him, not having any Glymmering as formerly.

[4 June 1681]

The 4th: of June Mr: Ashmole went to visit him, & found he knew him, but spake litle, & some of that scarce intelligible; for the Palsey began now to seize upon his Tongue.

[8 June 1681]

The 8th: of June he lay in a great Agony, insoemuch that the Sweat followed drop after drop, which he bare with wonderfull courage & patience (as indeed he did all his sicknes) without Complaint.

[9 June 1681]

3H: A:M: Mr: Lilly died.

And about 3 a'clock the next Morning he dyed, without any shew of trouble or pangs; imediately before his breath went from him, he Sneezed three tymes.

He had often in his lyfetime desired M[r]: Ashmole to take care of his Funerall, & now his Widdow desired the same; whereupon M[r]: Ashmole obteyned leave from Sir Mathew Andrews (who had the Parsonage of Walton) to bury him in the Chancell of that Church.

[10 June 1681]

The 10th: of June his Corps were brought thither & received by the Minister (in his Surplis) at the Lichegates, who passing before the Body into the Church, read the first part of the Office for the Buriall of the dead. In the reading Deske he said all the Evening Service & after performed the rest of the Office (as established by Law) in the Chancell at the Interment which was about 8 a'clock in the Evening, on the left side of the Communion Table, M[r]: Ashmole assisting at the laying him in his Graue, whereon afterwards he placed a faire black marble Stone...[258]

[12 June 1681]

Shortly after his death, M[r]: Ashmole bought his Library of Bookes of M[rs]: Ruth Lilly (his Widdow & Executrix) for 50li: he having oft tymes in his lyfe tyme exprest that if M[r]: Ashmole would giue that summe, he should haue them.

---

[258] This marble stone and its inscription can still be seen at St. Marys Church, Kingston upon Thames.

Appendix 1

Transcription of Lilly's Licence to Practice as a Physician

Gilbertus Providentia Divina Cantuarionsis Archioprscoque totiuo Angliœ Primao et Metropolitanus Ditecto Nobio in expo[?] Gulielmo Lilly in Medicinio Professori Salutem gratia et bene dictionem. Cum ex fidedigna relacone acceperimuo Te in arte sive facultato Medicinœ – non modicum tempuo versatum fuisse multsque de salute et sanitate corporio vere desperatio (Dea omni potente adjuvente) subvenisse, eosque sanasse, Necnon in aste quodcamque multaque agitaque laudabili testimonia pro experientia fidelitate, diligentia et industria tuio circa curao quao ressoperia opagendao in hujusmodi Arte Medicinœ merita commendatum esse Ad practicandigiti et exercandi deam Artem Medicinœ in et -- totam Provinciam n-am Cant (civitate Londinium et circuitu septem Milliarum eidem proxadjacon tantummodo exceptio) ex causio prœdictio et alijo ---- in hac gote justo moventibuo Prœstito primituo ap te Juramento de agnascendo Regiam supremam potestatem in causio ecclesiasticio et temporabibuo ac de renuntiando refutando et recusando omni omnimodœ Jurisdicconi, protestati authoritati et supioritati forneio juxta vim formam et effectum Statuti Parliamenti hujuo inclyti Regni Angliœ in ea gote editi et provisi quantum nobio -- Statuta hujuo Regni Angliæ liceat et non abiter neque alio modo Te admittimuo et approbamuo, Tibque Licentiam et Facultatem nostra in hac gote Tenore Prœsontium quamdiu Te bene & laudabili ior gessorio benigne concedimus et elargimur. In cujus rei Testimonium Sigillum (quo in hac gote utimur) prœsontibus apponifreimuo.

Dat: Undecimo die Mensie Octobrio Anno Domini 1670. Nostraque Translationio Anno Octavo.

Radulphus Snowe

et Reg: [?]

Edmundus Sherman

Rich: Lloyd Sur.

Appendix 2

Last Will and Testament of William Lilly

In the Name of God Amen – William Lilly –

I William Lilly of Hersham in the Parish of Walton upon Thames in the Countie of Surrey Student in Astrology being at the writing hereof of perfect memory doe make and ordaine this my last will and Testament in manner and forme following rendring my Soule into the hands of God in the Body I leave to be buried at the diffraction of Ruth Lilly my wife, my worldly Estate I thus disposest of I give and bequeath unto Ruth Lilly my wife during her naturall life all that parcel of Ground called the Hurst wood containing by estimation Eighteene Acres be it more or lesse and all the profitts thereof. It I give and bequeath unto Ruth Lilly my wife during her naturall life the Close called Conyers adjoining to the Hurst wood and all the profits thereof. It. I give and bequeath unto my said wife during her naturall life all thos sic closes called Roberts lane Closes being by estimation fifteene Acres be they more or lesse and all the profits thereof. It. I give and bequeath unto my said wife during her naturall life the wood Leacroft and the Corner Leacroft and the Three Closes called Glinons [?] lying all together and containing by estimation Two and Twenty Acres be they more or lesse and all the profits thereof: the reversion and reversions of all which said Lands after the decease of Ruth Lilly my said wife I give and bequeath unto Carlton Whitlock Sonn of Sir Boulstrode Whitlock Kt. and to his heires and Assignes forever. It. I give and bequeath unto my Brother Robert Lilly the sume of Five pounds. It. I give unto William Lilly his Sonne the Summe of Twentie Shillings. Item I give unto my Sister Suzan Benton the Sume of Tenn Shillings. It. [deleted, see below]

All which said Legacies to be paid within one yeare next after my Decease. It. I desire of my wife that she will give unto Mary Willson at the day of her marriage Twenty pounds for a peece of Plate. Item I will unto everyone of my Six servants the Sume of Twenty shillings a peece. It. I give unto the Poore of the Parish of Walton Towne the Summe of Five pounds at the Day of my Buriall by my good Friend Thomas Best. It. I give and bequeath unto the Poore of Hersham and Burwood the sume of Five pounds to be distributed by Henry Rogerson and John Coles at the day of my Buriall. It. all the rest of my Goods Cattelle Chattels Reall and Personall moveables and immoveables plate money jewels houshall stuff Library of Bookes or whatever is knowne to be mine I give and bequeath unto Ruth Lilly my wife whome I nominate my full and sole Executrix of this my last Will and Testament hereby revoking and renouncing all former wills and Testaments by me in anywise heretofore made or declared. In witness hereof hereunto I have Subscribed my name and set my seale the Fifth of January in the Six and twentieth yeare of the Raigne of our Soveraigne Lord King Charles the Second One thousand Six Hundred and Seventy fower: William Lilly: Sealed declared and delivered up by the said William Lilly in the presence of those witnesses whose names are Subscribed Thomas Agar, Henry Rogerson.

Obliterated

Ann Rogersuns Legacy of £5: - - - - by me William Lilly: 8° Jan: 1677/8: Richard Stevens, Thomas Teel: William South.

Appendix 3

The following image shows how the Ashmole's marginalia were included, although they were not always on separate pieces of paper.

175

In this year 1634 I purchased the moiety of thirteen houses in the Strand for 530li.

In November 30th day I was again the second time married, and since 500li portion with that wife, she was of the nature of Mars.

Two accidents happened unto me in that year, something memorable.

Davy Ramsey his Maties clockmaker, had been informed that there was a great quantity of Treasure buried in the Cloyster of Westminster Abbey, hee acquaints Dean Williams therewith, who was also then Bishop of Lincoln. The Dean gave him liberty to search after it, with this Proviso, that if any were discovered, his Church should have a share of it. Davy Ramsey findes out one John Scott who pretended the use of the Mosaicall Rodds, to assist him herein. I was desired to joyn with him, unto which I consented. One winter night Davy Ramsey with severall gentlemen, myself and Scott entered the Cloysters, wee played the hazell Rods round about the Cloyster, upon the west side of the Cloysters the Rodds turned one over another, an argument that the Treasure was there. The laborers digged at least six feet deep, and then wee mett with a Coffin, but in regard it was not heavy, wee did not open, which we afterwards much repented. From the Cloysters wee went into the Abby Church, where upon a suddon, (there being no wynd when wee began) so feirce, so high, so blustering and loud a wynd did rise, that wee verily beleived the west end of the Church would have fallen upon us, our rodds would not move at all, the candles and torches all but one extinguished, or burned very dimly. John Scott my partner was amazed, looked pale, knew not what to think or doe, untill I gave directions, and command to dismiss the Daemons, which when done, all was quiett againe, and each man returned unto his Lodging, late about 12 of clock at night. I could never since be induced to joyne with any in such like actions.

William Lilly

The true miscarriage of the business was by reason of so many people being present at the operation, for there was above 30. some laughing others deriding us. so that if wee had not dismissed the Daemons, I believe [illegible]

Clockmaker

[illegible]

Davy Ramsey brought an half [illegible] sack [illegible]

Appendix 4
Nativities

Most of the following nativities have been calculated from the data provided in various sources as quoted. However, only those which are copies of originals can be accepted as accurate representations of what the astrologer delineated.

N.B. Charts are here calculated in the Julian Calendar using astrological software. When the year number is near to changing in March, the software makes no allowance for that, so year numbers have been advanced by one where necessary. For example, William Oughtred was born on 5th March 1574 (JC), software will make up for the difference with the Gregorian Calendar, but in this case the year will be 1575 in modern accounting where the year begins on the 1st January.

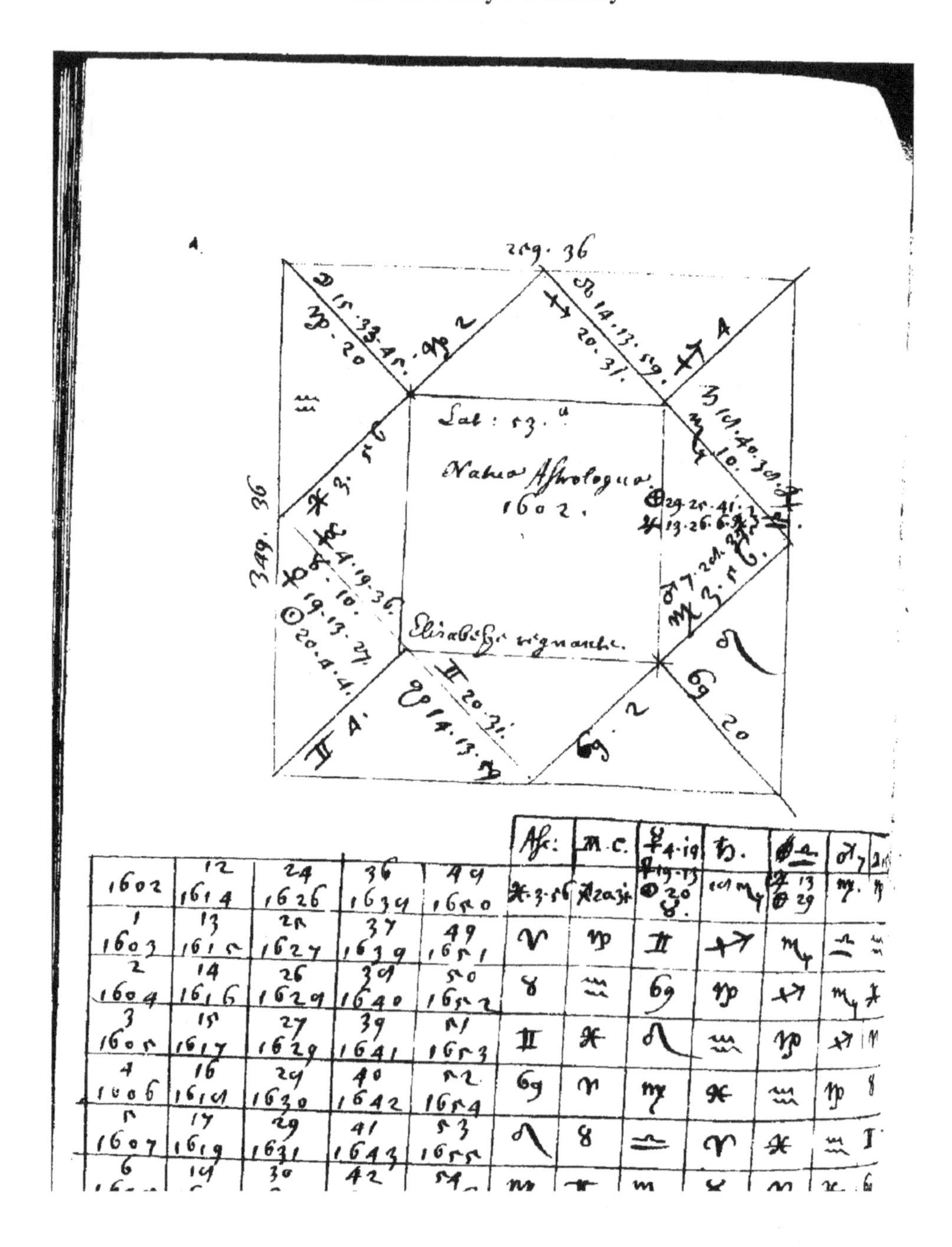
Lat: 53.
Natus Astrologus
1602.
Elizabetha regnante.

Elias Ashmole

The first of the two nativities of from *Notes* where Professor Josten provides a facsimile which is partly in Ashmole's hand. The second whilst very similar shows differences and is from Lilly's full delineation of Ashmole's nativity.

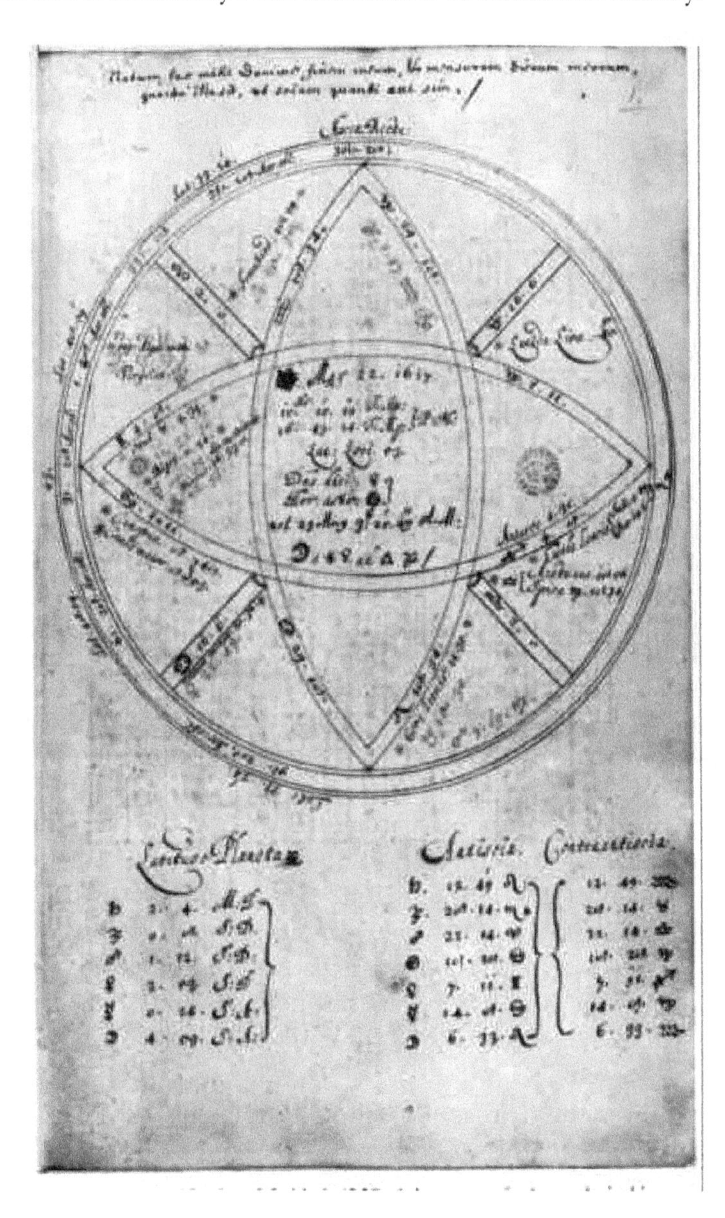

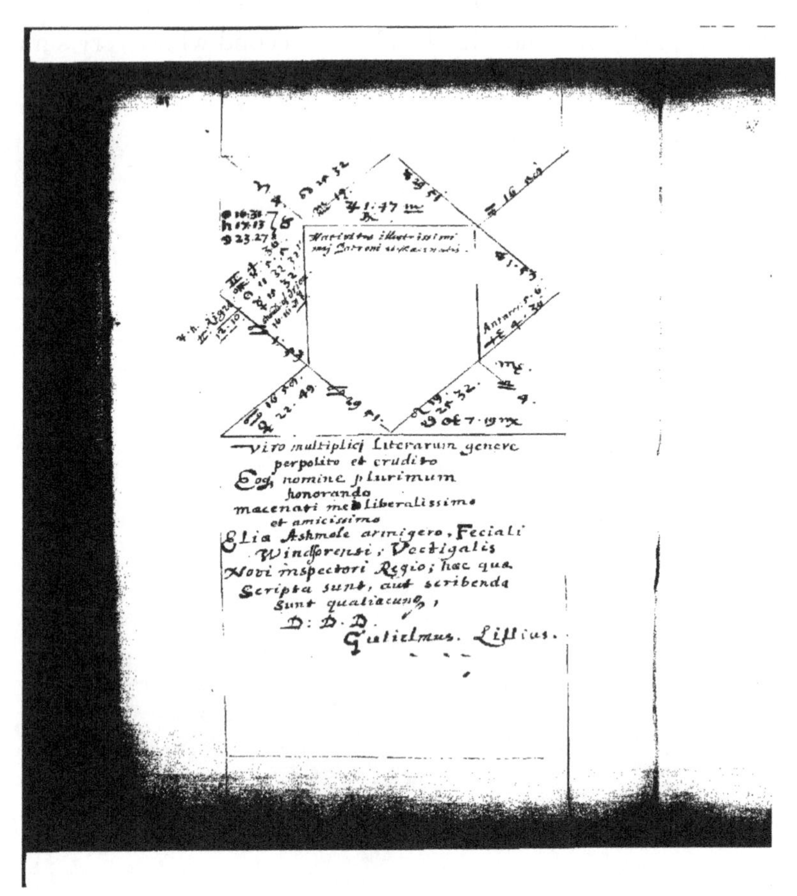
Viro multiplici Literarum genere
perpolito et erudito
Eoq. nomine plurimum
honorando
macenati meo liberalissimo
et amicissimo
Elia Ashmole armigero, Feciali
Windsorensi, Vectigalis
Novi inspectori Regio; haec quae
Scripta sunt, aut scribenda
sunt qualiacunque,
D: D. D.
Gulielmus. Lillius.

There is some confusion regarding the year of Booker's birth. The new year began at the Vernal (Spring) Equinox which, of course, varies annually. However, in 1600, 1601, and 1602 the Equinox occurred on the 10th March (OS). Around the time of the year change annotations would be made as 1600/1, 1601/2, and 1602/3. In each of the following examples the date, given by Booker's contemporaries, is noted as 1601. This has led to confusion as to whether this means 1600/1, or 1601/2.

Aubrey gives the date as "March 23, 1601, 20h 10' P.M." (*Aubrey* 112), and Gadbury repeats this (*Gadbury* 181). Harvey draws no conclusions, but accepts "with reservations" the year as 1600/1 (*Harvey* 1:116). Josten quotes the *Dictionary of National Biography* giving the year as 1603 (*Notes* 401), the *DNB* provides a source for that year as a nativity in the Ashmolean MSS. The revised edition (*ODNB*) gives a date of 1602 without quoting the source. Ashmole gives no clue (Notes). Harvey comments that in the 1822 edition of Lilly's *Life and Times* there is an engraving of Booker which includes his personal sigil. Around that sigil is his birth date and time which is exactly the same as that provided by Aubrey and Gadbury.

Booker was a personal friend of William Lilly and Elias Ashmole, and it would be a safe assumption to make that they would know his birth data accurately, then passing it on to Aubrey. Therefore the following nativity is calculated for 8.10 am 24th March 1600/1 (OS) at Manchester.

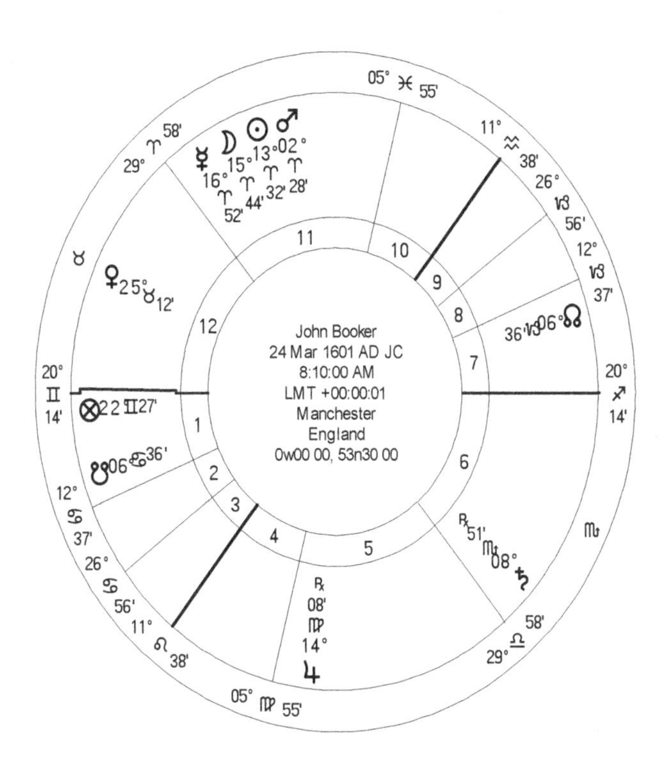

Doctor John Dee

Aubrey provides these data attributing it to a copy he made from "John Dee's papers in the hands of Elias Ashmole (*Aubrey* 211). "Johannes Dee, natus Londini, 1527, Julii 13, 4h 2' P.M.".

The following chart was reproduced in *The Queen's Conjuror* by Benjamin Wooley and was found in the Ashmolean collection in the Bodleian. A note in Ashmole's hand reads, "Calculated by Mr. Streete". This implies that the chart was not simply copied from an original, but recalculated which presents something of a problem. While this is not the place to enter into a discussion of the mathematics of astrological calculations, it is an opportune moment to extend my opening remarks.

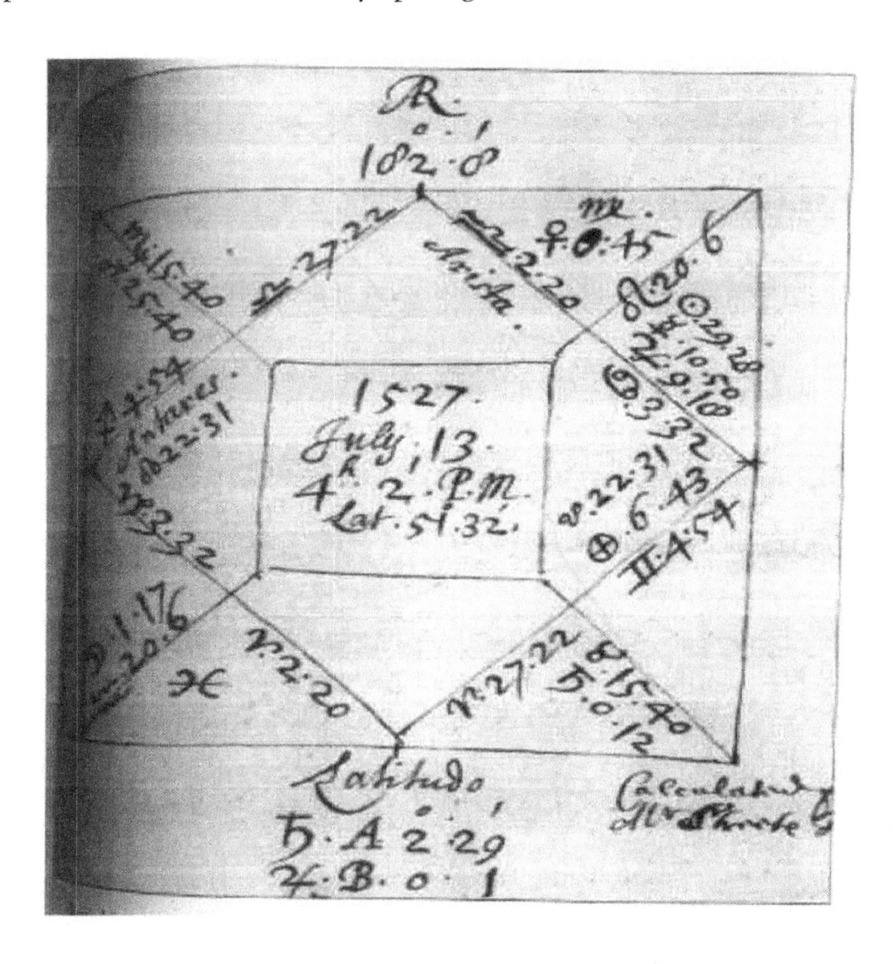

Streete's calculations closely approximate those resulting from the use of computer software. All house cusp positions using the Regiomontanus system are within three minutes of arc of each other. Likewise the planetary positions are within twenty minutes of arc, except Mercury which holds a difference of one and a quarter degrees. However, we should not be misled by the similarity between the mathematician's results and those of the computer. It is unusual for there to be such a close comparison.

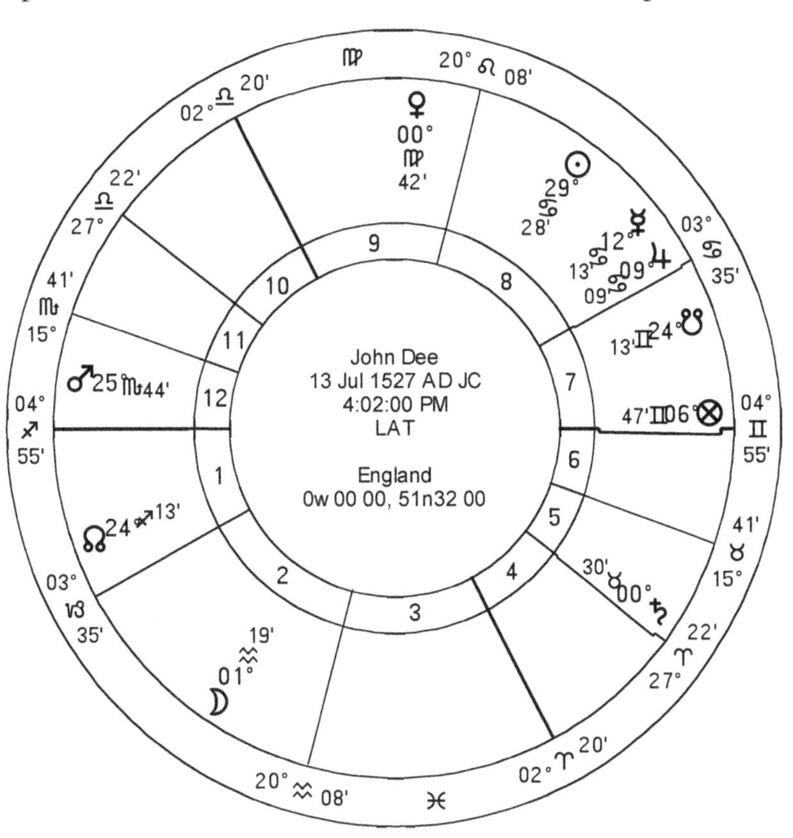

Thomas Streete (1622-1689)[259] was acknowledged and respected as an astronomer and mathematician. Although not a member of the Royal Society his work on longitude was recommended and recognised by some of its leading members. His astronomical tables (*Astronomia Carolina: a New Theorie of Coelestial Motions*, 1661) were highly praised and continued to be the foremost of their kind into the 18th century. The *ODNB* provides an enthusiastic appreciation of Street's work. Aubrey notes that "He had the true motion of the moon by which he could doe it - (he hath finished the tables of the moon and also of Mercury, which was never made perfect before)..." (*Aubrey* 238).[260]

The accuracy of Dee's nativity when compared to modern computations suggests that the talented Streete did indeed recalculate this horoscope and did not copy it from Dee's original. This presents the aforementioned problem that this might well not be the same horoscope that Dee himself calculated. We would do well to remember that the heavens do not always conform to the programmer's algorithm whereas the astrologers of old would often combine observation with mathematics. Therefore, if Dee's own copy of his horoscope is different from Streete's calculations that does not mean that Dee was wrong.

---

[259]Aubrey provides a clear example of how date notation can become confused (see John Booker's nativity). He notes his birth as 5th March 1621, i.e. before the year changed at the Spring Equinox to 1622.

[260]Aubrey also provides Streete's birth data as "natus March 5th, 1621, at 5h 43' 12" P.M., latitude 51° 46'. Streete was born in Cork, Ireland."

Sir Kenelm Digby

We rely again on Aubrey's reading of documents having belonged to Richard Napier and in the hands of Ashmole. Ashmole quotes as follows: "Sir Kenelme Digby natus July 11, 5h 40' A.M. 1603, 14 Leo ascending,". He goes on to note that there is another horoscope giving the time and Ascendant as 4h A.M. and 26° Cancer rising, and furthermore that there are two other horoscopes with Leo and Cancer ascending. (*Aubrey* 1:224) Harvey provides one further birth time of 5.30 a.m., but unusually does not provide his source (*Harvey* 1:124).

Digby was born at Gayhurst in Buckinghamshire and the following horoscope is calculated for 52°N which is reasonably accurate, but in any case reflects the common use of this latitude for locations south of Leicester. It appears that longitude was inconsistently applied and obviously not from the Greenwich meridian instituted later.

The following calculation uses the time of 5.40 a.m. simply because of its appearance of having been rectified from the 'rounded' half-hour alternatives. This does not assume that this birth time is correct, but rather accepts that this might have been the basis of the horoscope delineated by the astrologer. Moreover Aubrey describes him as "...such a goodly handsome person, gigantique [very tall] and great voice, and had so gracefull elocution and noble address, etc., that had he been drop't out of the clowdes in any part of the world, he would have made himselfe respected.", which descriptions are traditionally more suited to the sign of Leo than to Cancer.

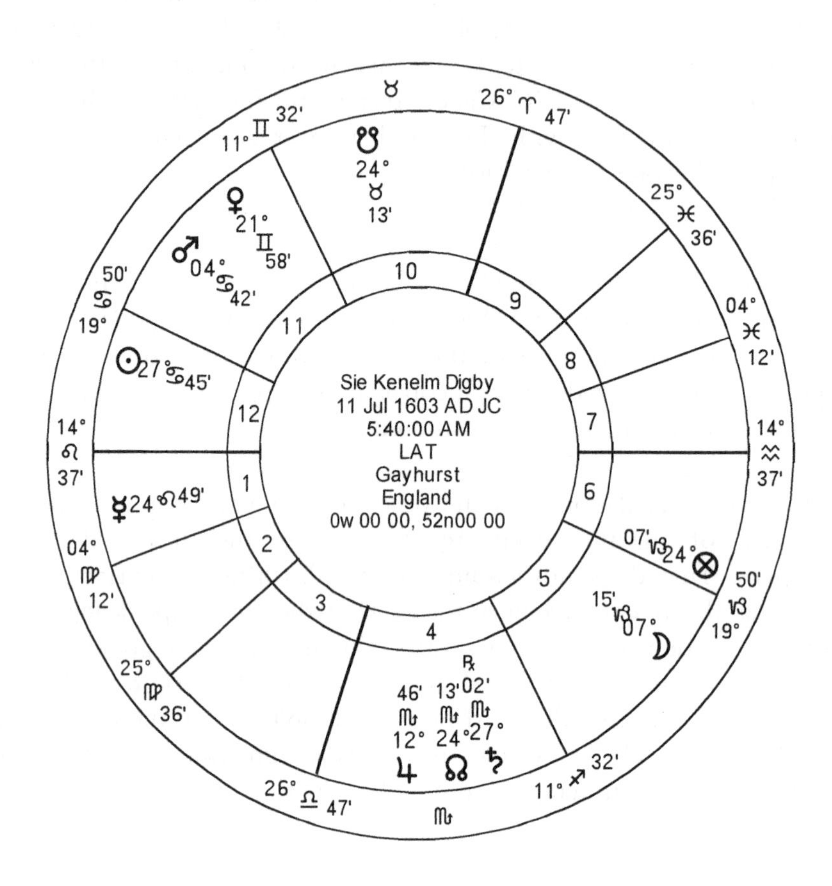
Sie Kenelm Digby
11 Jul 1603 AD JC
5:40:00 AM
LAT
Gayhurst
England
0w 00 00, 52n00 00

Dr. Simon Forman

"Bodleian MS. Ashm. 206. Fol. 218. has Forman's nativity by himself:

Simon Forman the Sonn of Maria and Willm. Borne 1552. 7 post merid at 45 mite post 9. Sub latitud. 51.30.31 31 decebr. The positions given by Forman for himself are these:" (*Harvey*, a list of the positions then follows.)

The following chart is a copy of that in Forman's own hand in the above-mentioned manuscript.

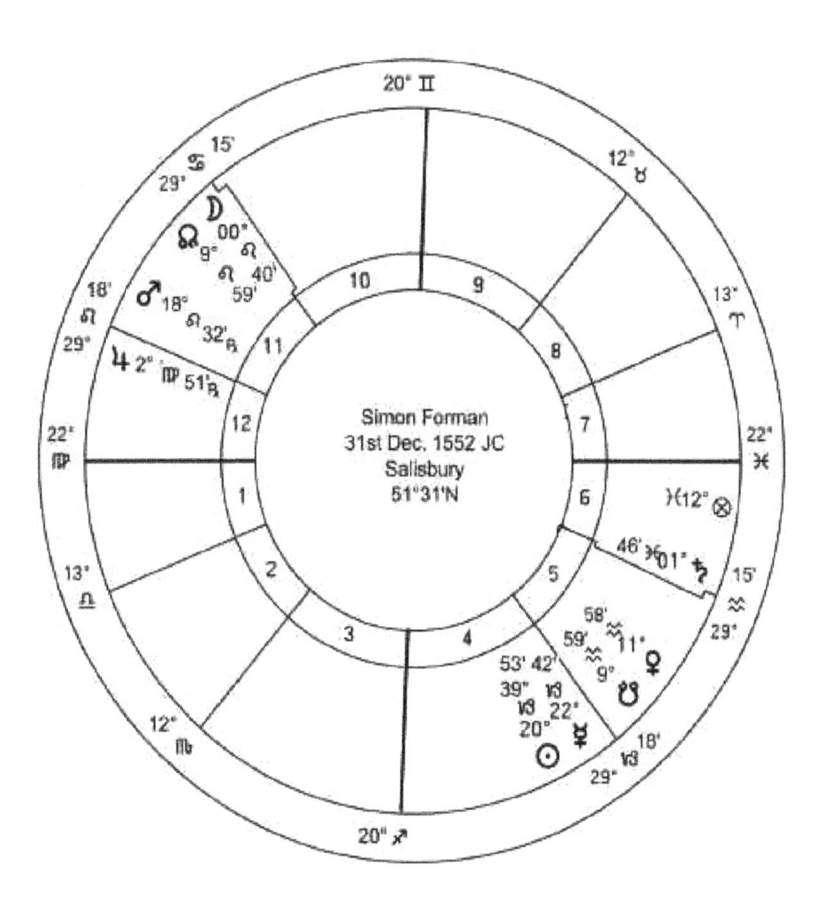

Doctor Richard Napier

"Dr. Richard Napier:- he was no Doctor, but a divine (rector Lindfordiensis) and practised physick – natus Maii 4, 1559, 11h. 4' P.M. in urbe Exoniae." (*Aubrey*)

The following chart is speculatively based upon these data, "Exoniae" being Exeter in Devon.

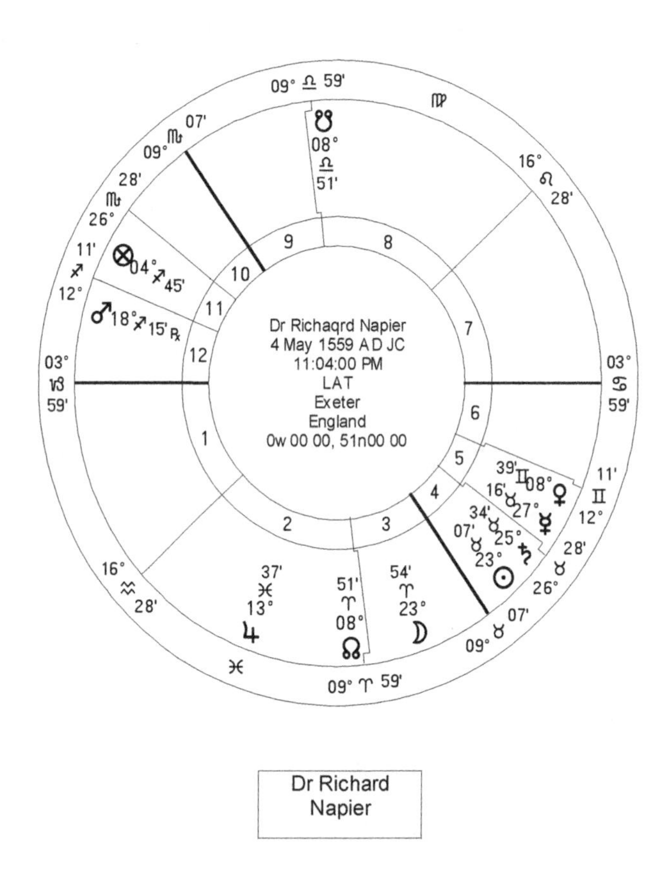

Ruth Nedham (Needham)

"MS. Ashm. 394 contains 276 ff. of transcriptions in Ashmole's hand. At fol. 109.v. is the following:

'Nativity of Ruth 3[d] wife of M[r]. W[m]. Lilly, with M[r]. Hen: Coley's Judgm[t]. Thereon. Nata 29. Ap: 1629 11[H]. 28. P.M. 2 â q 7 ad p # & o 5 sub Lat. 51°32' ' Here follows Coley's figure... I neglected to note the places of the fixed stars."'

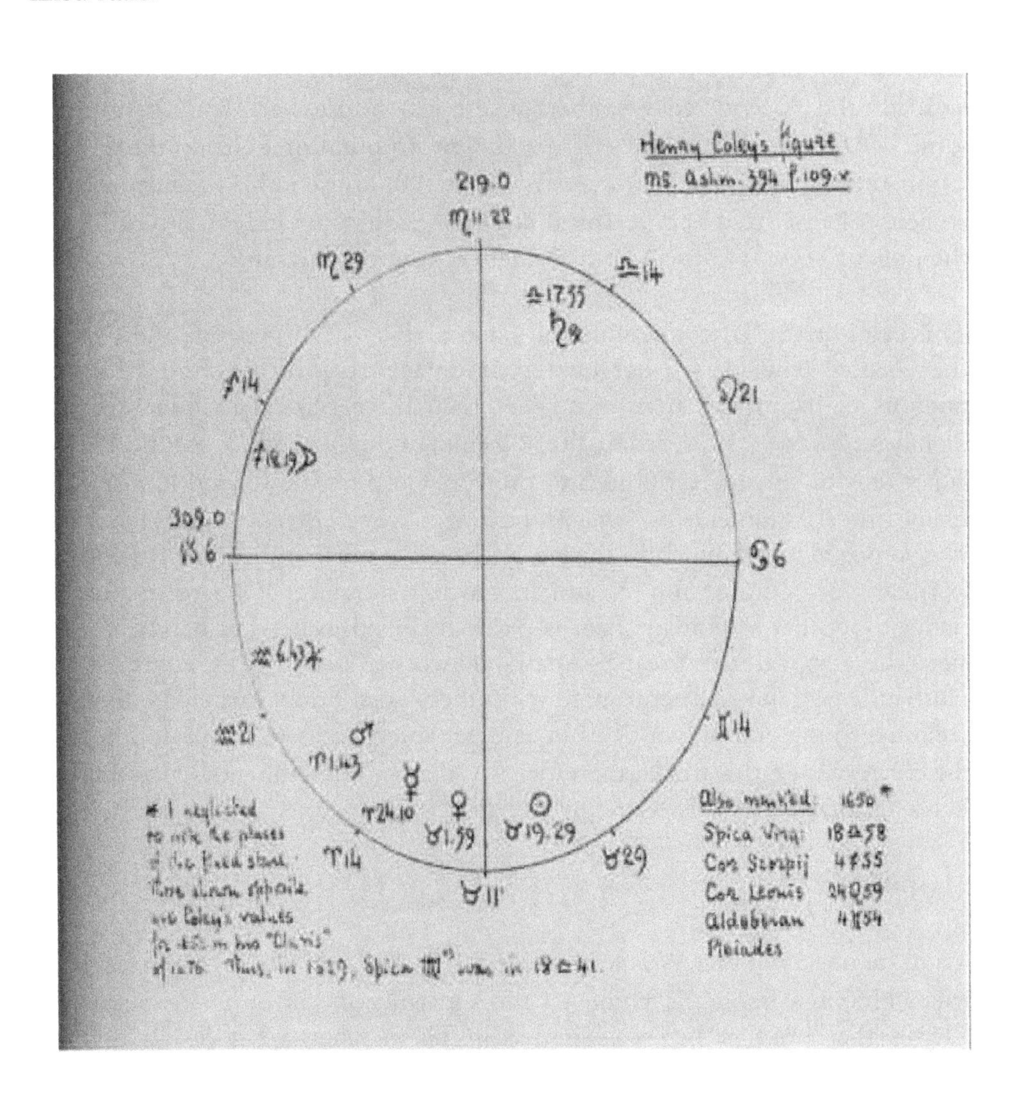

'Tis very p[ro]bable this may be the true position of the Heavens, at the Birth of the Native (or neere it) I shall not be positive in regard the day is not exactly given. The native is moderately well described by the sign J and W in G with the Virgins Spike [Spica], in ' to R, to which may be added the position of V in K. in the Ascendant, w[ch] never failes (in a Naturall Sence) to give a very obliging temper, disposition & deportment: & further I add, that S in A in pfect $ to the R, adornes the Intellect, & gives the Native a most sereene understand[g] above the generallity of her Sex (w[ch] is excellently verefied in the Native & this I may boldly affirme without flattery. Now that she may be of a crazy Consitution the " of W & S may very well intimate, as the one being Lord of the Ascend[t.] & the other of the sixt house, very aptly denote the same. – And for the stricktnes of her Judgm[t.] In point of Religion the afores[d]: Configuracõn also the position of W. In the 9th house in his Exaltacõn neere so benevolent a fixed Star (ie Spica) & Retrograde in my Judgm[t.] (according to the Rule of second Causes) doth eminently promote the same.

This being premised concerning the Face of Heavin in generall, the Fate of the Native (considering her quality & capacity oif Birth) should be very ppitious & happy; for here is no less then three planets in their essential dignities, also V (partly Lord of the seconde) in the Ascend[t.] & second House, is not only in ' to the R, but in $ to the very Cusp of the second House, with many other Arguments w[ch] might be vuged very considerable. Hence the Native neede not doubt but (during lyfe) to live much above the frownes of Fortune, very comfortably & and in much tranquility, & heere it must be understood, that a Womans Fate is partly included in her Husbande. – Now since there appeares so great Sympathy betweene the Natives Geniture & her Husbande (as I am well acquainted with) there is no doubt but the Native may continue to the end of her daies in as great splendor as whe will desire, as to the concernes of this world, therefore this may be something of encouragem[t.] Unto her that her Fate is Naturally so happy –

11 Aprill 1680

Tis to be observed that W is now neere in " to he [sic] Ascend[t.] by Transit, & will within few moneths come to the Quartile of his opposite place, w[ch] advises the native to be exceedingly carefull to prserve her health & keep from cold. W in D may afflict the Stomack & consequently the Head, but when he is once pasd out of D into E I hope she wilbe more healthfull, ye rarely so strong in Body as might be wished, yet moderately cheerfull & pleasant to her owne great content, & the satisfaction of her tender Husband, & this I comit you both to Gods proteccõn, most heartily wishing you both health & long lyfe, & finally eternally felicity hereafter. H.C.'" (*Harvey*)

William Oughtred

Aubrey provides the following information (*Aubrey* 105): "Gulielmus Oughtred natus 5 Martii 1574, 5h P.M.". Using this data the chart below is speculative.

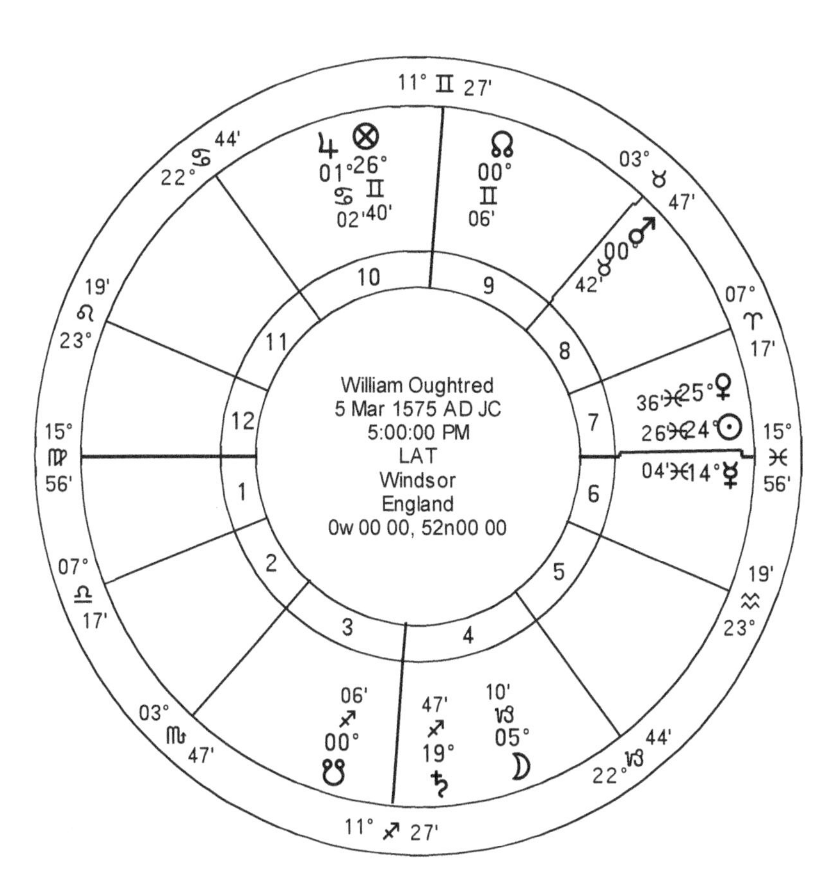

The Nativity of Sir William Wittypoole

Rectified and Directed by

William Lilly

From an unpublished manuscript in MS Ashmole 356

Transcribed and annotated

by

Sue Ward

Acknowledgements
Thanks must go to Mr. David Jones, Curator of the Ipswich Museum. Through informal conversations and his generosity in handing over some of his own research into the Withipoll family, my knowledge of Sir William is greatly enhanced.

My gratitude also to William Lilly, who was wise enough to keep an eye on posterity (us) which preserved this manuscript for our study and education.

Preface

This manuscript is a source of fascination filled as it is with Lilly's attempts to rectify not only an unknown birth time, but also an unknown birth year. The rectification process requires a detailed list of events in the life of the native (the person whose birth details are to be analysed), then a laborious and lengthy process of adjusting the calculations follows in order to correct or rectify the birth time and date. It is not a task to be undertaken lightly and most modern astrologers avoid it even with the advantage of computer software. However, it was common practise to rectify every nativity to find or confirm the birth time.

As you read you will see that Lilly may well have been mistaken with his starting point, but the letter at the end of the delineation explains the problem he had had to deal with. Wittypoole's mother appears to have noted down his date of birth some six years after the event and seems to have mistaken the year. At this time, and for some years to come, the civil year corresponded closely to the astrological year. Wittypoole being born at the beginning of that year in early April, the year notation properly being 1595/6, it might well have been a slip of the pen. His birth date remains unconfirmed, although that given by Lilly is accepted by C.H. Josten, the editor of *Elias Ashmole: His Autobiographical Notes....*

Lilly's prediction of the native's death was far off the actual year of 1645. However, the delineation itself is revealing and demonstrates Lilly's artistry. In this document we are privileged to watch as he produces his work for a client and not for publication – this is the best kind of judgement of all. Those readers who are well-versed in Lilly's work will notice that his technique differs little from that of his later years. They will recognise the ease with which he deals with the nativity, the profections, directions and, on occasion, eclipses, and integrates them into very few, but succinct descriptions and predictions.

He works through his arguments for the rectification smoothly and thoroughly and it is interesting to see that he leaves space for the client to note actual events in the judgement itself. This would have enabled Lilly to adjust his rectification if needed, and demonstrates that he made allowance for error on his part. Also of note is the language Lilly uses when making predictions: it is one of suggestion based upon astrological configurations and political context, that is, the wider world.

Although this manuscript is bound with a letter to Wittypoole, it seems never to have been delivered. The covering page notes that it was given by Lilly to Ashmole in 1657, and it is signed by Ashmole, so there need be no doubt about that (the delineation was completed in 1643). I have no explanation for this, but it might be that there never was an opportunity to give it to Wittypoole before he died just two years after its completion. Given that Lilly passed on this document to Ashmole, it appears that Lilly suffered no embarrassment in so doing. Indeed, knowing how keen both of them were to collect as many nativities as possible, I assume that this was for that collection – which makes little sense if the data were wrong. In fact, this delineation was given to Ashmole along with two others, one of which was that of William Pennington who had a long-standing friendship with Lilly. It is thus difficult to accept that Lilly's gift was at all frivolous or careless. The question remains and speculation is pointless; however, there is one more interesting piece of information. In 1662 Gadbury published his *Collectio Geniturarum* in which he publishes Wittypoole's nativity which I present here with Gadbury's comments.

Gadbury's Delineation

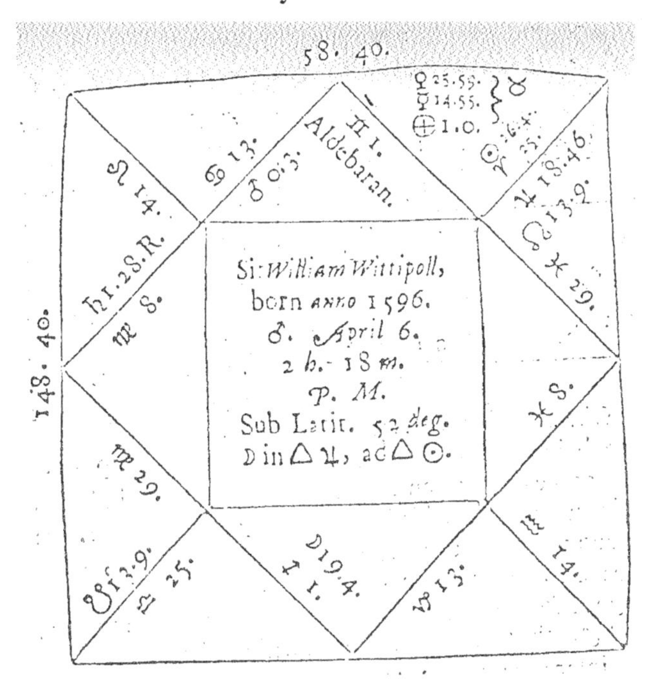

... This Nativity was given to me for the true one of this worthy Person; but any Accidents belonging thereunto, I could never obtain, excepting this, – that he had the hard hap to be engaged in Duels often; in which engagements, three Men were slain by him. It cannot but be [by] ill provoking him, that hath many Planets above the Earth; especially if they shall be in the dignities, or in any Aspect of ♂, or near eminent fixed Stars; as most of them are in this Geniture. Howbeit, this worthy Native should by his Nativity have been a Person of a Noble Nature, hating to do or commit any dishonourable Act: for he hath ☿, his chief significator, in the House of ♀, and in Platique Conjunction with her in the ninth House, in Trine to the Ascendant. It is true, the Moon in ♐, in Trine to ♃ her Dispositor, and to the Sun in ♈ his Exaltation, and the House of ♂, might denote him of spirit and courage so great, that he would scorn to pass by Injuries or Affronts without taking notice of them: but that is an Argument of an inclination and Minde rather honourable, then unworthy or low-orbed. And indeed in all his Geniture, there is not one Argument of an Inclination in him to Homicide, though it was his grand Mis-fortune (most probably through high and insolent Provocations) to have his Hands stained with the Blood of three Men.

Having not other Accidents to verifie this Nativity in particular, I shall forbear all further Discourse hereof.

Gadbury states that the nativity was given to him, but that would not have been by Lilly because Gadbury had made himself Lilly's enemy[261]. Although there are differences in the results of the calculation, presumably because Gadbury had not had sight of the chart itself, the birth time is identical with that found by Lilly through rectification. This can only mean that this is Lilly's data, and perhaps that Gadbury obtained the data by dubious means. It is quite clear that Gadbury knows very little about Wittypoole, but the family must have had some influence for Gadbury to offer such flattery[262]. It is true that Lilly held Wittypoole in some regard, but he was under no illusion about the nature of the man, which seems to have been choleric in the extreme. There are numerous references to this throughout the delineation.

It appears that Wittypoole had been a patron to Lilly, because Lilly dedicates his first "book" to him. In *England's Propheticall Merline*, published in 1644 that dedication runs as follows.

To the honourable and truly Magnanimous,
Sir William Wittypoll *knight*, increase of health and all Wordly Felicity.

Worthy Sir,

---

[261]For a full analysis of this relationship and of Gadbury himself, see *Monster of Ingratitude.*

[262]Idem.

Be pleased to receive this my maiden Dedication (of the ensuing discourse) as a thankfull Testimony of those due respects I really owe unto you; for those manifold favours I hav received from you, since, by means of the virtuous *Robert Tolmach* Esquire, I had first acquaintance with you.

Some, I know, may, and will wonder at this presumption of mine; let them so do: the integrity of my own heart howsoever, empty of all sordid or by- respects, will not suffer me to mistrust your charitable construction, or favourable entertainment of these my loving intentions towards you: be your selfe pleased; let the censorious vulgar frown, or act their silly parts, and I care not.

The Subject matter is of an Art (not so contemptible, as either the illiterate Divine, or sturdy Mechanick, do fancy) or is it altogether unknown to your self; for your frequent conversation with the learned in forraign parts, and your own judgment, guided by your reason, do inform you, that *Astrologie* is no vaine or triviall learning, if rightly understood, and handled by an able hand. For honour of the *English* Nation, I wish the work had been more absolute and compleat; such as it is, I present it, with my Cordiall love to your generous self, and hope in aftertimes it shall be no dishonour, that you were the loving Patron, and very friend,

Sir, Of your much Oblieged Servant,

WILLIAM LILLY

Of note is that the Civil War had been in progress for two years when this was published and Lilly was a supporter of Parliament, where Wittypoole was a Royalist. This says as much about Wittypoole as it does about Lilly. This is of particular interest with regard to Gadbury's betrayal of Lilly, which is often partly, and largely incorrectly, explained by their political and religious differences. Indeed, Lilly's ever-widening circle of friends, supporters and associates was most definitely not exclusively Protestant and Parliamentarian.

William Wittypoole

There are various spellings of this name, but the modern descendants, I am told, prefer the spelling "Withypoll". That said, very little is known about the subject of this astrological delineation; the sparse information that is available has been gathered by David Jones, the Curator of the museum at Ipswich. This is housed partly in the former Withypoll residence at Christchurch.

Sir William seems to have led a colourful life, as Lilly's judgement reports, " I have mett with no Nativity hitherto, that since the 30th yeare of age hath had so many cross and perverse direccons, and they continue yeare by yeare till you dye so that seldome you have two yeares of quietness." Debts, legal battles, bad judgement and treachery were all a part of Sir William's life. Even after death problems continued because Sir William died intestate which occurred because Wittypoole was writing a new will when he died, apparently interrupted by his sister, Lucy.

The legal challenges which followed Wittypoole's death were between his daughter Elizabeth (allegedly excluded from the will) with her husband Leicester Devereux, and Sir Henry Fenton with Ptolemy Tollemache (various spellings), both beneficiaries of the original will. A number of people were called to give evidence regarding Wittypoole's intentions, and among them appears William Lilly, noted as a gentlemen (in the formal sense) of St. Clement Danes.

Records held in the National Archives[263] show that in 1643 a petition had been made by Wittypoole, thus:

> Petition of Sir William Withipoll. During petitioner's absence Leicester Devereux, who married petitioner's sole daughter and heiress, without any colour of title forcibly entered his house at Ipswich, and possessed himself of all the writings and evidences concerning petitioner's manors and lands of inheritance. Prays that Sir Walter and Leicester Devereux may be forced forthwith to make restitution, and that petitioner may be protected.

Clearly, the relationship between father and daughter had deteriorated by this point. A separate record states:

> Sir William states that during his absence beyond seas, Leicester Devereux who married his sole daughter and heiress entered his house at Ipswich and possessed himself of goods to the value of £3000 and all his deeds, and claims to have seized the papers under a pretended marriage agreement.[264]

This offers a reason of an unfulfilled marriage settlement made by the father at his daughter's marriage.

However, there was a counter petition made by Leicester Devereux's father in the following year against Wittypoole. In April 1644, both men had made their answers, the Devereuxs (father and son) were to present evidence that before her marriage *she was in possession of her father's house and housekeeper* and she had been trusted with the care of some household goods which had belonged to her late mother[265]. However, by May Wittypoole was requesting permission not to attend for his own petition because of ill health. In June the committee reported on the matter, and then:

---

[263]House of Lords: Journal Office: Main Papers 1509-1700

[264]Records found by David Jones.

> 25 June 1644 -- Affidavit of Leicester Devereux, that the trunk delivered to Mr Browne, Clerk of the Parliament, contains the whole of the deeds and writings which have come into deponent's hands belonging to Sir William Withypoole.

There is no further mention in these records of whether or not Wittypoole recovered the documents and goods, but it seems likely, although in August there is another petition made by him *concerning his cause against Devereux*. Given Wittypoole's choleric nature, it is unlikely that he would give up a fight even though he was very ill. It is unclear how this matter concluded, but Wittypoole died in the August of 1645 and his daughter and her husband were petitioning again just four months later for possession of Wittypoole's estate.

Gadbury reports that Wittypoole killed three men in duels, whilst this is possible, Gadbury is an unreliable witness and is likely only to have been repeating what he had been told. David Jones has found evidence of one proposed duel which seems almost to have degenerated into a pitched battle between the soldiers of the two antagonists. The affair in 1628 was so serious that it was brought to the king's attention. Wittypoole was found guilty of manslaughter, but received the king's pardon. However, the king was unhappy about the result and there appears to have been wider repercussions afterwards. In a later incident during 1635, Wittypoole is said to have killed Sir Arthur Gorge's second.

Lilly advises Wittypoole a number of times against rash or violent action, and against misplacing his trust. Although this might incline us to believe that Wittypoole was only a hot head who liked his pleasures far more than was good for him, we should note the manner in which this delineation is written. Lilly speaks in astrological terms to his client, something only done if the client understood these terms. In his dedication to Wittypoole, Lilly remarks on the latter's knowledge of astrology obtained through his travels overseas. Also, notable is that Lilly uses Latin for some of his comments and, although not as much as I have seen in another delineation, it does indicate that Wittypoole had had a decent education. This was not necessarily the case even for gentry and minor nobility, particularly where

[265] Idem.

there interests lay in more physical pursuits; hunting appears to have been a favourite for Sir William.

As this delineation is partly a rectification, we should expect a reasonable amount of biographical information. The reason for saying this is that the life events required from childhood would have been supplied by the native. We might assume that Sir William provided biographical information up to the end of 1642, the year before the delineation was completed, although it doesn't always appear so. Lilly seems to provide information which might prompt Wittypoole's memory as well, or where the native was too young to remember.

One important type of event required for a rectification is that of preferment or promotion. At the age of twelve, Wittypoole was sent to court to attend Prince Henry, heir to the throne of James I of England. It is recorded that before he acceded to the English throne, James took his son, Henry, out of the care of his mother. James feared that Roman Catholic Anna would influence Henry's religious upbringing. James surrounded his son with Protestant attendants, and one of these was to be William Wittypoole. In 1605, Henry entered Magdalen College, Oxford, and it is known that he loved education and listening to sermons. We must assume then that William was of a suitable education and inclination to be admitted to Henry's court. It is also known that anyone who swore in front of Henry was made to pay a financial penalty to an 'alms box', what these days would be referred to as a swear box. From this we might deduce that William's upbringing taught him good manners, decorum and the use of moderate language. His time with Henry would also have augmented his education and worldly knowledge, as well as the "manly exercises" to which Lilly refers of fencing, hunting and horsemanship.

In 1610 Lilly notes "a desire to travel...which was also performed", so this may have been the end of William's attendance on Prince Henry, the year in which the latter was invested as Prince of Wales. In 1612 however, the Prince died of typhoid fever at the age of eighteen years. We might assume that this was the end of William's career at court, especially as Lilly's chronology suggests that these following years were spent in leisurely pursuits and "a continuance with the flesh". However, David

Jones has found that in 1623 William appears to have been in the service of Prince Charles who had inherited all of his brother Henry's titles and was, thus, heir to the thrones of England and Scotland.

In 1619, at the death of his father, William inherited the family titles and properties and in 1621 married Jane Stanhope, deemed to have been a good marriage which augmented the Wittypoole estates. They had two children, Edmond who died in infancy in 1634, and Elizabeth who was married to Leicester Devereux in 1642. It is possible to deduce from this that she was the first born possibly a year or two after her parents' marriage.

The duel of 1628 preceded many years of legal actions and debts which required the sale of lands. This culminated in the aforementioned petitions relating to his daughter's husband and father-in-law, persisting beyond Sir William's death.

Editorial interventions

The layout of the manuscript is reproduced here, although pagination has been introduced where none was. Page length does not correspond to the original, but each year begins on a new page as there.

I have left the spellings alone, believing this to add to the character of the work. Contractions such as "p^{r}formed", have been given in full to aid the flow of reading, but astrological abbreviations and initials remain as written in the original. This is because it provides a clear indication of the level of Sir William's astrological education and understanding. Latin phrases have been freely translated in footnotes, but not where it is found in the noting of astrological configurations, such as "ad ter" ("to the term of"). Illegible words are shown thus: [...].

The punctuation is erratic, but I have intervened only occasionally for clarity of meaning.

Lilly's letter to Sir William is now at the front of the delineation where originally it was appended to the back, so that the reader might gain a little more insight and context into the problems Lilly faced.

Lilly's Letter to Sir William Wittypoole

Sir,

Although I am confident of the yeare 1596 yet have I considered the yeare 1595 and erected the Scheame of heaven according to Art, and have also varied it divers manner of wayes, to satisfie my selfe least I should still runne the wrong way. Theres no tyme of the day of your supposed birth that yeare that will come neare truth, but 3 quarters before twelve, a limit of tyme so farr dissenting from the proper handwriting of your reverend mother, that it might greatly call in question her memory, which could not bee so defective both in measure of tyme in yeare and day, syth it was in the compass of six yeares when she wrote yt: I have perfected the Nativity upon assurance, that you weare borne 1596 uppon Tuseday 6th Aprill 2° 18 PM for first it agrees with the Trutine of Hermes, 2^{ly} it accordeth with the Animodar of Ptolomey to a degree, 3^{ly} the accidents do all come neare, if not exactly to the direccons.

The number of yeares naturally allotted you, are 69 theres one dangerous direccon may shorten 3 or 4. The judgment of Mounseur might bee true according to the Basis hee wrought on, but having missed 2 whole yeares of the Radix, I know hee will fall short almost xxty [twenty] in measuring the period of life, and yet no errour in the man, syth the tyme given him was false, but admitting the yeare 1594 for certaine and concludes you in this yeare; I know Art Lymitts you more, which you shall not need to doubt of; and so I present

Sir these weake indeavours, And am

Your servant: ℒ

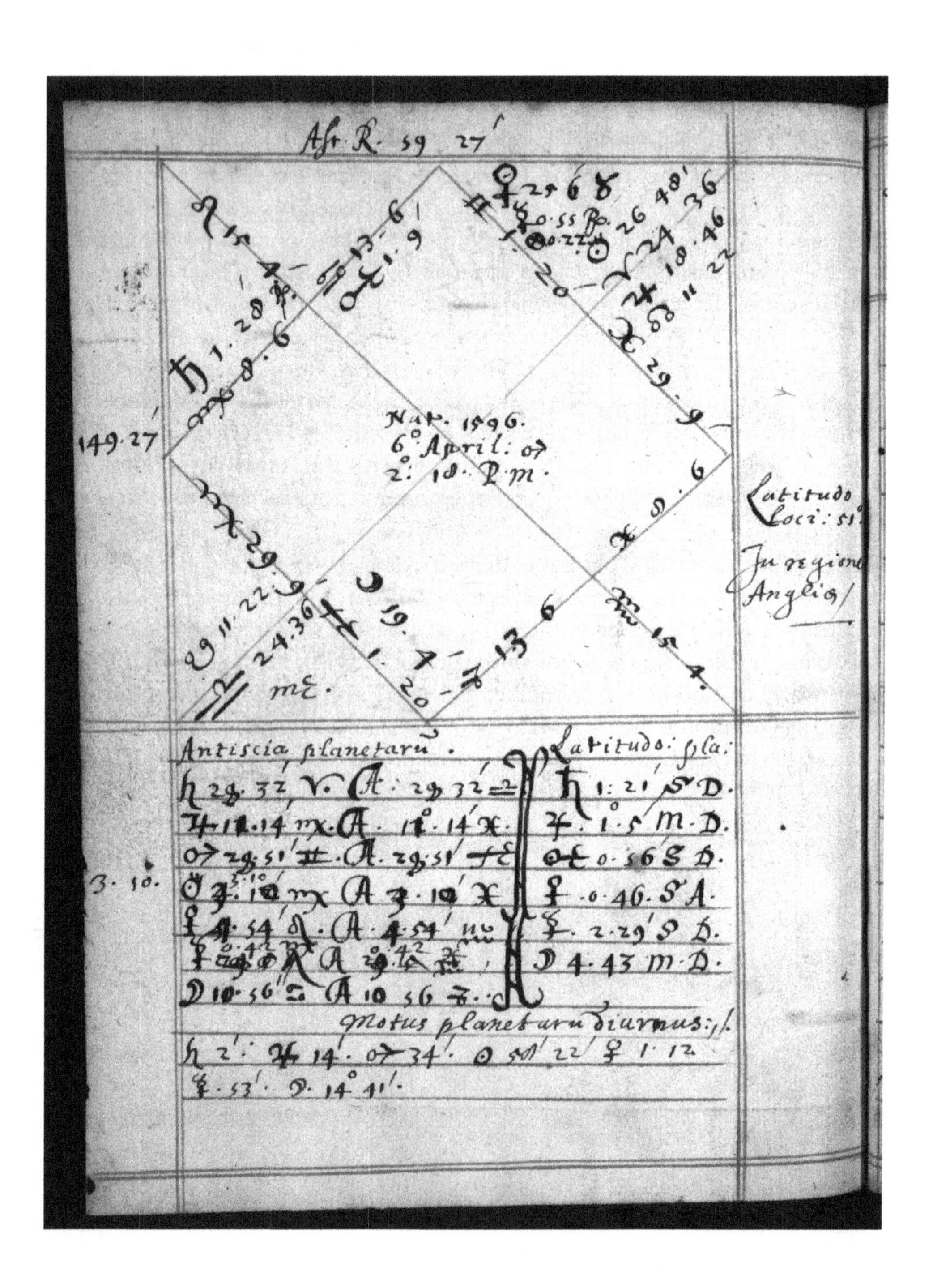
Nat. 1596.
6° April:
2: 10 P.m.
Latitudo
Loci: 51°
In regione
Angliæ
Antiscia planetaru.
Latitudo pla:
Motus planetaru diurnus:

Table of Profections Nat. 1596 6. Apr: ♂ 2.18 P.M.					8.6'	M. Coeli 1.20	☉ 26.48	☽ 19.04	0.22
1596	12 1608	24 1620	36 1632	48 1644	♍	♊	♈	♐	♉
1 1597	13 1609	25 1621	37 1633	49 1645	♎	♋	♉	♑	♊
2 1598	14 1610	26 1622	38 1634	50 1646	♏	♌	♊	♒	♋
3 1599	15 1611	27 1623	39 1635	51 1647	♐	♍	♋	♓	♌
4 1600	16 1612	28 1624	40 1636	52 1648	♑	♎	♌	♈	♍
5 1601	17 1613	29 1625	41 1637	53 1649	♒	♏	♍	♉	♎
6 1602	18 1614	30 1626	42 1638	54 1650	♓	♐	♎	♊	♏
7 1603	19 1615	31 1627	43 1639	55 1651	♈	♑	♏	♋	♐
8 1604	20 1616	32 1628	44 1640	56 1652	♉	♒	♐	♌	♑
9 1605	21 1617	33 1629	45 1641	57 1653	♊	♓	♑	♍	♒
10 1606	22 1618	34 1630	46 1642	58 1654	♋	♈	♒	♎	♓
11 1607	23 1619	35 1631	47 1643	59 1655	♌	♉	♓	♏	♈

Ascendant directed		Asc. ob.	Arke of direc.
♍ 8. 6’		149 27	
Antis. ♃	11.14	153 56	4 29’
Ter ♃	13.0	156 01	6 34
Ter ♄	18.0	163 05	13 38
□ ☽	19.4	164 38	15 11
Ter ♂	24.0	171 33	22 6
△ ♀	26.6	173 10	23 43
Do: 2:^{m}	29.9	178 49	29 22
♎			
Ter ♄	0.0	180 0	30 33
♂	1.9	181 40	32 13
Ter ♀	6.0	188 27	39 0
Ter ♃	11.0	195 30	46 3
☋	11.22	195 54	46 27
☌ ♀ 2.9 in lat. Spicam ♍	18.33	207 39	58 12
☍ ♃ cum Lat.	18.46	205 40	56 13
si lat.	-------	206 31	57 4
Ter ☿	19.0	206 49	57 22
✱ ☽	19.4	206 37	57 30
Ter ♂	24.	213 54	64 27
☍ ☉	26.48	217 52	68 25

Medium Cœli		Asc. R[266]	Arke of direc.	
1.20' ♊		159 27		
□ ♄	1.29'			
Cum lat. Oculus ♉ S.Lat.	 4.30'	 62.30	 3.03	
Cum lat. ter ♃	------- 7.0	63.33 65.09	4.06 5.42	
Hircus ter ♀	------- 14.0	72.11 72.38	12.44 13.11	
Si: Hum. Orionis ✶ ♃ si. pos. orio.	 18.46	72.46 74.18 77.54	13.19 14.51 18.27	
☍ ☽ Cum Lat	19. 04	77.30	18.03	
ter ♄	sine lat. 21.0	78.10 80.12	18.43 20.45	
ter ♂	25.08	84.33	25.06	
✶ ☉	26.48	86.28	27.01	1623
Antis,♂ [note?]	28.51	88.50 89.50	29.23 29.23	
ter ♂ ♋	0.0	90.00	30.33	
✶ ☿	29.18 ♊ 0.	89.14 91.0	29.47 31.33	
Corpus ♂	1.09	91.14	31.47	
✶ ♄	1.28	91.30	32.03	
ter ♃	6.0	96.33	37.06	
Can. major Antis. ☽	------ 10.56	97.07 101.30	37.40 42.03	
Do: XI et ter ☿	13.06	104.10	44.43	
Canis minor □ ♃	------- 18.46	109.53 110.21	50.26 50.54	
Hercules ter ♄	------- 27.0	110.31 119.03	51.10 59.36	
♌ ter ♄	 0.0	 122.12	 62.45	
□ ☿	0.55	123.06	63.39	
Præsepe et		124.37	65.10	∫ ♋ ter ♀20.111.39'. 52.12

117.57
118 50

[266]Right ascension

Asellos	125.16 125.46	65.49 66.19	✶♀ 25.6. 58.30 □☉ 26.48 59.23
Antis. ♀ 5.34	127.58	68.31	
Ter			
ter			

☉ secunde s.s.[267]	Desc. Ob.[268]	Arke of ye æqat.	Polus 30°
26:49' ♈	31° 9'		
Contrantis. ♄ 28.32	33.15	2.06	
ter. ♀ ♉ 0.0	34.55	3.46	
Partem ⊗ 0.22	35.10	4.01	
Corpus ☿ Cum Lat. 0.55	35.10	4.01	
⚹ ♂ 1.09	35.57	4.58	
△ ♄ 1.28	36.20	5.11	
ter ☿ 8.00	44.22	13.13	
ter ♃ 15.00	52.41	21.32	
Caput Algol 20.	58.0	26.51	
Pleyades & ♄ 22.0 Cum lat.	61.04 61.50	29.55 30.41	
Pleyades sine Lat.	63.17	32.08	
Corpus ♀ 64.0	64.0	32.51	
ter ♂ 26.	65.50	34.41	
♊ Medium Cœli 1.20	72.0	40.51	
□ ♄ 1.28	72.10	41.0	
Cum cal. Oculus ♉ 4.30	73.0 75.0	41.51 43.51	
ter ♃ 7.0	78.54	47.45	
ter ♀ 14.08	87.05	55.56	
⚹ ♃ 18.46	91.42	60.33	
Cum lat ------- ☍ ☽ si. 19.04 Lat.	89.38 92.0	58.29 60.51	
ter ♄ 21.0	95.09	64.0	
ter ♂ 25.0	99.40	68.31	
⚹ ☉ proprium 26.48	101.20	70.11	
Antis. ♂ 28.51	104.04	72.55	
ter ♂ ♋ 0.0	105.11		
⚹ ☿ 0.55	106.0		
☌ ♂ 1.09	106.06		

[267]"secunde signorum seritus" – "in the order of the signs." In other words, direct.

[268]Oblique descension.

☉ Contra ordinem[269]		Des. Ob.	Ark of yᵉ æquat.
☉ 26° 48' ♈			
ter ♂	21.0	24.22	
△ ☽	19.04	22.06	
Corpus ♃	18.46	22.06	
ter ☿	14.0	16.12	
☊	11.22	13.05	
ter ♀	6.0	6.56	
ter ♃	0.0	0.0	
♓		360.0	
ter ♄	30.0		
⚹ ♀	25.06	354.2	
ter ♂	24.0	353.04	
□ ☽	19.04		
ter ☿	18		
CA ♃	11.14		
ter ♃	10.		
CA ☉	4.12		
☍ ♄ cum lat.	1.29		
△ ♂	1.09		
⚹ ☿	0.55		
ter ♀	0.0		

[269] "Against the order [of the signs]." Otherwise, converse.

☉ secunde s.s.[270]		Desc. Ob.[271]	Arke of y^{e} æqat.	Polus 30°
26:49' ♈		31° 9'		
Contrantis. ♄	28.32	33.15	2.06	
ter. ♀ ♉	0.0	34.55	3.46	
Partem ⊗	0.22	35.10	4.01	
Corpus ☿ Cum Lat.	0.55	35.10	4.01	
✶ ♂	1.09	35.57	4.58	
△ ♄	1.28	36.20	5.11	
ter ☿	8.00	44.22	13.13	
ter ♃	15.00	52.41	21.32	
Caput Algol	20.	58.0	26.51	
Pleyades & ♄	22.0	61.04	29.55	
Cum lat.		61.50	30.41	
Pleyades sine Lat.		63.17	32.08	
Corpus ♀	64.0	64.0	32.51	
ter ♂	26.	65.50	34.41	
♊ Medium Cœli	1.20	72.0	40.51	
♄	1.28	72.10	41.0	
Cum cal.		73.0	41.51	
Oculus ♉	4.30	75.0	43.51	
ter ♃	7.0	78.54	47.45	
ter ♀	14.08	87.05	55.56	
✶ ♃	18.46	91.42	60.33	
Cum lat	-------	89.38	58.29	
☍ ☽ si. Lat.	19.04	92.0	60.51	
ter ♄	21.0	95.09	64.0	
ter ♂	25.0	99.40	68.31	
✶ ☉ proprium	26.48	101.20	70.11	
Antis. ♂	28.51	104.04	72.55	
ter ♂ ♋	0.0	105.11		
✶ ☿	0.55	106.0		
☌ ♂	1.09	106.06		

[270]"secunde signorum seritus" – "in the order of the signs." In other words, direct.
[271]Oblique descension

☉ Contra ordinem[272]	Des. Ob.	Ark of y^e æquat.
☉ 26° 48’ ♈		
ter ♂ 21.0	24.22	
△ ☽ 19.04	22.06	
Corpus ♃ 18.46	22.06	
ter ☿ 14.0	16.12	
☊ 11.22	13.05	
ter ♀ 6.0	6.56	
ter ♃ 0.0	0.0	
♓ ter ♄ 30.0	360.0	
⚹ ♀ 25.06	354.2	
ter ♂ 24.0	353.04	
□ ☽ 19.04		
ter ☿ 18		
CA ♃ 11.14		
ter ♃ 10.		
CA ☉ 4.12		
☍ ♄ cum lat. 1.29		
△ ♂ 1.09		
⚹ ☿ 0.55		
ter ♀ 0.0		

[272]“Against the order [of the signs].” Otherwise, converse.

Luna s. seritus[273]	Des. Ob.	Ar. æq.	Desc. ☽ Si. Lat: 252.27
19° 04' ♐	254.06		
ter ♄ 20.0	253.27	0.39	
ter ♂ 25.0	258.48	4.42	
△ ☉ 26.48	260.43	6.37	
CA ♂ 28.51	259. 260.0	5.00 5.54	
ter ♀ ♑ 0.0	264.13	10.07	
△ ☿ 0.55	265.10	11.04	
☍ ♂ 1.09	265.36	11.40	
△ ♄ 1.28	265.53	11.47	
ter ☿ 6.0	270.48	16.42	
CA ☽æ Cum Lat. 10.56	275.43	21.37	
ter ♃ 12.0	277.25	23.19	
Do: 5tanus 13.06	278.40	24.34	
□ ♃ 18.46	284.52	30.46	
ter ♂ 19.0	285.11	31.05	
ter ♄ 25.0	291.48	37.42	
△ ♀ 25.06	291.54	37.48	
□ ☉ 26.48	293.25	39.19	
ter ♄ ♒ 0.0	297.18	43.12	
□ ☿ 0.55	298.20	44.14	
CA ♀ Cum Lat. 4.54	303.21	49.15	
ter ☿ 6.0	303.52	49.46	
ter ♀ 12.0	310.22	56.16	
⚹ ♃ 18.46	317.20	63.14	
⚹ ☽ 19.04	317.37	63.51	
ter ♃ 20.0	318.54	64.48	
□ ☿ 25.06	324.18	70.09	
ter ♂ 26.0	325.14	71.23	
⚹ ☉ 26.48			
CA ☿ 29.0			

[273]Following the order of the signs.

☽ Contra ordine[274]	Des. Ob.	Ar. æq.	Pol. 13.
19° 04' ♐	254.06		
△ ♃ 18.46	253.10	0.56	
ter ☿ 14.0	247.07	6.59	
ter ♀ 8.0	240.57	13.09	
Cor ♏ sine Lat. Cum Lat. 30	239.23	14.43	
Si. Lat. --- □ ♄ 1.29	237.25 234.17	16.41 19.49	
ter ♄ ♏ 30.0	232.54	21.12	
ter ☿ 27.0	229.58	24.08	
☍ ♀ Cum Lat. 25.06	228.33	25.33	
ter ♀ 21.0	224.14	29.52	
ter ♃ 14.0	217.42	36.24	
ter ♂ 6.0	210.27	43.39	
△ ✶ ♄ 1.28	206.28	47.38	
△ ♂ 1.08	206.15	47.51	
☍ ☿ Cum Lat. et si. 0.55	206.39	47.26	
♎ ter ♂ 30.0	205.11	48.55	
Antis: ♄ 28.48	203.30	48.36	
☍ ☉ 26.48	202.30	51.36	
ter ☿ 24.08	200.01	54.05	
✶ ☽ 19.04	195.48	58.18	
Spicam ♍ 18.40	196.09	57.57	
☍ ♃ Cum Lat. 18.46	195.0	59.06	
☋ 11.22	189.34	64.32	
ter ♀ 11.9	189.06	65.0	
ter ♄ 6.0	184.56	59.10	
□ ♂ 1.08	180.55	73.11	

[274]Against the order of the signs.

⊗ s:s:s:[275]	Des. Ob.	Ar. æq.	Pol. 28.
⊗ 0.22 ♉34.32	34.32		
Caput Algol 20.	57.21	22.49	
Pleiades cum lat. 24.20	61.08	26.36	
Corpus ♀ 26.06	63.15	29.43	
M. Cœli 1.20'	70.41	36.10	
□♄ 1.29	70.54	36.22	
Oculus ♉ Cum Lat. 4.29	72.17	37.45	
⚹♃ 18.46	90.30	55.58	
☍☽ C. Lat. 19.04	89.0	54.28	
⚹☉ 26.48	99.52	65.20	
Corpus ♂ ♋ 1.08			
⚹☿ et ⚹♄ 1.28			
Antis. ☽ 10.56'			
Do: XI 13.06			
□♃ 18.46			
⚹♀ 25.06			
□☉ 26.48			
⊗ Cont. Ordinem			
Corpus ♃ ♈ 18.46	21.10	13.22	
△☽ 19.04	21.34	13.44	
☊ 11.22	12.30	22.02	
□♂ 1.08 ♓	1.07	33.25	
⚹♀ 25.06	354.21	40.11	
□☽ 19.04	347.44	46.48	
CA ♃ 12.14	339.50	54.32	
CA ☉ 4.12	331.10	63.22	
☍♄ 1.28	327.30	67.02	

[275] As before: following the order of the signs.

△♂ et ✶☿ 1.08			

An Astrologicall judgment upon the Annuall Direccions of the precedent Genesis

By reason of some malevolent occurse of ☉ to the Contrantiscium of ♄ the second yeare prooved to have ended with difficulty in breeding teeth, and some childish diseases etc.

In the yeare 1601: of the native Currant 5: the ☉ in ☍ to ♄ in Revolut. et Asc. ad Antiscium of ♃, et ☉ ad Corpus ☿ et ✶ ♂; et ☽ ad ter. ♂ its probable to have beene a yeare of much infirmeness, and that you then gott that small impediment (in Lingua), but the significators and Promittors in moveable signes argue the diseases weare of severall natures, and of no Continuance; principally the affliction was a soare throat, the ytch, scabby head etc.

In Anno 7° et Domini 1602; ☽ ad △ ☉: provision of a school Master and the native apt to learne, in which Course of life with good health and content of mynd, it seemes the native Continued without any eminent alterations in life and fortune, until the yeare of our Lord God 1607: vide folio proximo[276].

1607 and 12th of age: ☽ ad ☿ Lord of the 10th you now came to attend Prince Henry: where it is probable you had much respect; but in the Latter end of that yeare and beginning of the next ☽ ad ☍ ♂; might indanger health, and by distemper of the humours, occasion a malignant feaver, or some extreame surfett by intemperancy of diett; the Constellation also incites to quarrel with your Companions, and a desire to learne horsemanship and fencings, and all manly excercises, and diverts the mynd from learning and all goodness, etc.

1608 and 13 Currant; according to Capacity and place, much Love and freindshipp at Court etc.

1609 and 14th of your age, ⊗ to the body of ♃: some gift from the Prince or person of quality, very much in favour, but M. Cœli to a fixed starr of

[276]see the next page

malitious influence, some envye at your well doing, and aspersions cast upon your good name.

1610 and 15 Currant of age: ⊗ ad △ ☽ et Asc. profectio ad tertiam Radicis[277]: a desire to travell augmented by ♀ in the Revolution ad Locum ♃ which was also performed, and somewhat South etc. from the place of birth.

.1611 and 16th Currant: Asc: ad □ ☽ et ☽ ad Cor ♏.. Discontent in your travell, by meanes of some freind in some suddaine danger by water, a tast of the feminine sex, infamy and anger thereupon. A surfett by too much eating Crude fruits, as also, by the being of the Promittors in bycorporeall signes frequent visiting and oft remoove from one place to an other etc.

1612 and 17th of your age. ☽ ad Cor ♍ without Lat. et ad ter. ☿ upon some suddaine occasion, or malecontentedness, the Native takes a journey North East, which I conceive was into England.

1613 and 18th vexed and restrayned by auncient people in purse etc. uppon this a desyer to see the world.

1614 and 19th Currant: M. Cœli ad ⚹ ♃. ☉ ad ☊: et M.C. ad ☍ ☽: et sine et Cum Lat[278]: honour at first where you then resyded, both from men and weomen; very many favours from noble persons towards the latter end of the yeare: the first Infortunium at Florence; M.C. ad ☍ ☽ yet more properly in the beginning of the next viz. 1615.

1615 and 20th of your age, the mothers anger is stirred upp against you, dayly infamy by too frequent accompanying the female sex; and perhaps some disease thereby.

1616 hath no direccions: you participate of the former.

---

[277]the profected Ascendant to its radical term

[278]with and without latitude

1617 and 22: Currant; the ☽ and Contrantiscium ☽. too frequent meetings with good Company, and a continuance with the flesh, and those desyers and in danger of a disease thereby.

1618 and 23rd of age. ⊗ to ☊ and Caput Algol. Asc. ad ter ♂: a delight in hunting, hawking, etc. and though no aspect show the actions of this yeare yet I believe they weare merry and manly etc.

1619 and 24th of age, many motions for a wife, frequent visiting, friends and kindred; intimate affection from a beaue Lady; and I conceive the Asc. ad △ ♀ gave the Knighthood towards the Latter end of this and beginning of the 25th of age; and much honour and respect where ever you came.

In 1620 and 25 wholly devoated to Courtship, hunting, pleasure, and delights of youth etc.

1621 and 26th of your age. ☽ ad ☍ ♀: Crossed by weomen in the hopes of marriage, etc. familiar with a Lady, envy, and ignominy ex inde[279]. A journey intended, but not performed, more then in our Kingdome etc.

1622 and 27th of your age, the ☉ to Caput Algoll might with violence kill the father[280], and accidentally indanger the native by some suddaine quarrel or some dangerous fall from horses. ⊗ to the Pleijades, might involve his estate in trouble yet the aspects show some suddaine preferment to bee neare, Continued and augmented by M. C. ad ✶ ☉ so that I conceive your marriage of a great concernment was much about this tyme, and the rather for that ♂ and ♀ weare in the Revolution in ☌ in the radicall degree of ♀ as also an Eclipse of the ☉ in 25 ♈, after this yeare until 1625 wee have no direccons at all.

1625 and 30th year Currant.

---

[279]from thence

[280]It is generally assumed that his father died in 1619, a hereditary peer. It is strange that Lilly was unaware of that accepting that this would have been a notable event in Sir William's life.

M. Cœli ad Antis. ♂ some ma[r]tiall honour; ⊗ ad ♀ some increase in substance by the death of some woaman etc. eyther now you settle your selfe to house keeping, or are plentifully furnished with all manner of beaue furniture, busy in writing letters, conversant with Lawyers, etc. very much respect from all the gentry wheresoever you come, and given to pleasure as hunt etc.

1626 and 31st of your age Asc. ad ter ♄ et M.C. ad ter ♂ . ☉ ad Plejjades et ☽ ad □ ♃.

These aspects and direccons, deprave the humours, & corrupt the blood, so that some feaver or the small pockes might afflict you, dissention and quarrelling more than usually had beene; the disfavour of noble persons, a sensible alteracon of fortune, all things beginning to go headlong to Confusion. Many suites in law etc.

1627 and 32° of age. A yeare herein your fortune was variable, by the falseness of friends, and untrue reports; a yeare naturally inclining to keepe souldiers and such like Company, and to bee active in Military affayres; the Midheaven hastening to a conjunction of Mars, might give period to the mothers life, with many other accidents etc.

1628 33 Currant began on Palme Sunday 6 Aprill. M.C. ⚹ ♄. ☉ ad Pleijades, Medium Cœli ad Corpus ♂. Horosc. ad □ ♂ and in the end of that yeare

M.C. to the body of ♀. heares naturall direccons for every accident that befell; which induceth mee togather with the handwriting of a Judicious Lady to believe that the yeare, moneth, and day now handled is the true tyme of the birth.

Infortunium magnum hoc Anno[281]

1629 and 34 of age. ⊗ to the □ of ♂ wast of substance, sale or mortgage of land, overchargd with debts, etc.

1630 1631 and part of 1632: these yeares threaten nothing but Consumption in estate, cozening by ill servants, solicitors, and other Agents: many law suites, and oppression with debts, etc.

1633 and 38 of age: inclinable to travel, M.Cœli ad ter ♃ et ad Canem Majorem, et ☉ ad ✶ ♀. Heares much conversation with honourable people, popular affection, much employment, many visits to your Kindred, and the sight of many countys in England.

1634 39 yeare, ☽ ad △ of ♀: a journey beyond sea, but ♂ in ♏ in the Revolution procures that frivolous quarrel with Sir A. Gorge[282], as also obstructions and the wynd chollick; or choler in the bowels: etc.

1635 and 40 of your age, the ascendant was under the termes of ♀. But ☽ ad ☉, as also a Lunar Eclips neare the degree ascending; so the conflict beyond sea that yeare is proper [?] for the place; danger is threatned to the right eye, but you overcame.

1636 41 of age, ⊗ ad ✶ ♀ oft remoovall from one place to an other, etc. the mynd desirous to see many Countrys.

1637 and 42 of age. ☉ ad □ ♄: a mind full of discontent, disrespected by friends, some dishonour by vulgar Clownes, or people of no great fortune and this publique, a sensible wast of patrimony, etc. fitte of the Cramp, wynd chollicke, etc. want of many necessary things.

1638 and 43 of age: M.C. ad Antis. ☽ againe move the mynd to travel further, the favour of some great person for advance therof.

---

[281]"Great infortune this year." This was the year of the duel following which Sir William was found guilty of manslaughter.

1639 44 of age. ☉ ad □ ☽ et ad Oculum ♉: suddenly in danger in your travels, the mynd much perplexed etc.

1640 and 45 of age. ☽ ad □ ☿ angry at the falseness of Lawyers, and your former acquaintance, much detriment by theire meanes, vexed about writings, bills, and accounts, letters etc., a yeare that affoarded plentifull cause of Complaint against some former freinds, a desire to returne home, but no aspect of force to effect.

1641 46: and acquisition of new acquaintance, and hopes of better dayes; it's a good revolution, onely ♄ passing by transit the radicall degree of the 7th house might about this tyme cause sickness if not death to the wife.

1642 47 of age. ☉ ad ter. ☿, letters oft writt to little effect, Asc. ad ter ♃ good hopes of bettering your fortune, but from this yeare 1642 till November 1643 the person of the native suffers by the malitious effects of Asc. ad ☋ in the second house of whose influence see presently.

[282]It was this man who was challenged to a duel by Wittypoole during which he killed Gorge's second. Again, it is unbelievable that Lilly would have been unaware of this fact, or perhaps this was a separate incident.

1643 and 48 yeare of age.

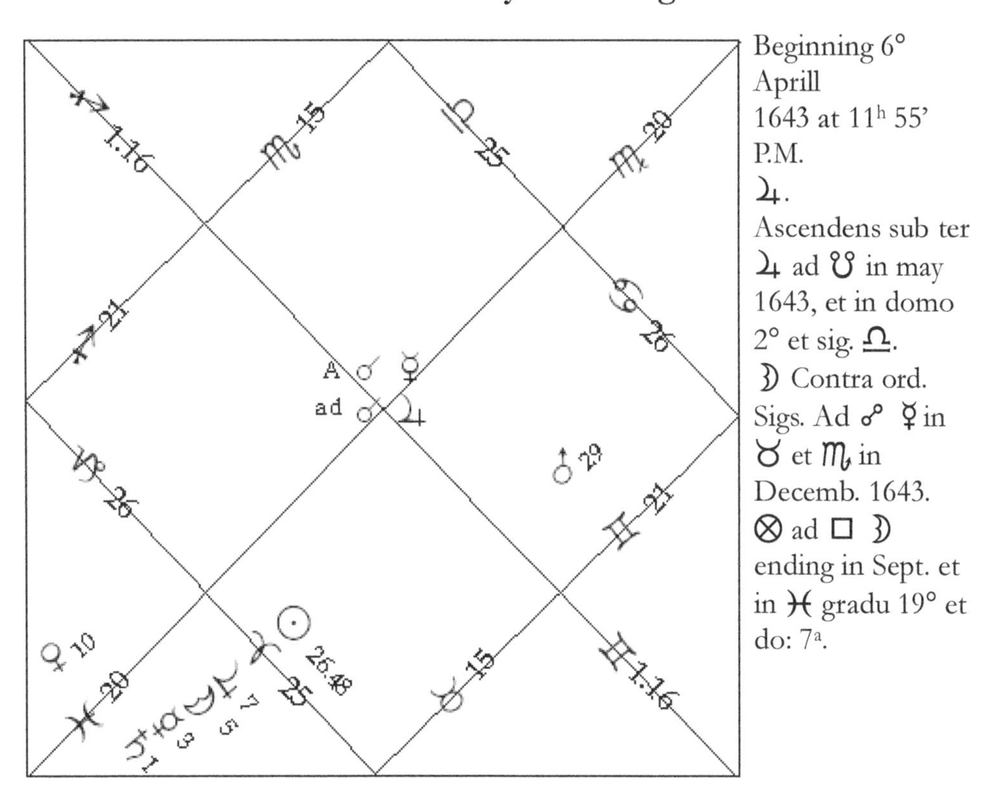

Beginning 6° Aprill 1643 at 11^{h} 55' P.M. ♃. Ascendens sub ter ♃ ad ☋ in may 1643, et in domo 2° et sig. ♎. ☽ Contra ord. Sigs. Ad ☍ ☿ in ♉ et ♏ in Decemb. 1643. ⊗ ad □ ☽ ending in Sept. et in ♓ gradu 19° et do: 7[a].

Neither perfect health or much sicke, the wynd chollicke, ill digestion, the stomack full of crude melancholy humours, distemper in the raynes and kidneys; the mynd variously afflicted, the more by oppression of wynd fuming into the head, etc. Losse in estate and opposed by vulgar fellows, or generality of people, by friends, by weomen; Controversy with men of Authority, with young men, with solicitors and Atturneys, about writings, accounts, evidences and Manuscripts; unkindness with or by reason of Kindred or alliances, many false rumours fathered on you, these end not till November or somewhat after. Unless you are assured of his fidelity, entrust no man that hath an eminent Cutt or blemish in his face: a small matter will for some moneths cause you to bee more then formerly subject to surfett, or [...] hurt by the least disorder in diet, now sooner then you weare woont: weare you young, you would hardly avoyd the Gonorhœa, or the pyles in Ano:

if you love yourselfe be carefull of your Company, ne specis amicitia venenum detur[283]: Asc ad ☋ hoc promittitt.[284]

Turne over

[283]Lest he sees friendship produce poison

[284]Promises this

About August or neare the middle of this 48th yeare, the ☽ comes to ⚹ of ♄: and also a △ of ♂. It may seeme both in health and fortune by these aspects the nature is drawing neare better tymes, but I conceive the effects of these direccons will more manifestly appeare the succeeding yeare.

What is promised by the Revolution.

Weare not the tymes ill, and the direccon of more force then ye Revolution You would ere the expiracon of the yeare recover much detained from you: this inclines those that have beene averse to you, to feel your friendship; danger of death, or of other detention, there is nowe, either by sickness or otherwayes, you need not doubt anything for the vigour of the ill intended is past, and hath expressed its malice in treachery, lyes, deceipt, etc.

This vacuum I leave that you might at the yeares end insert the most principall actions__________________[285]

[285]As previously mentioned, this would allow Lilly to refine the rectification.

49 yeare 1644 beginning Friday 5° Aprill 16:25 PM

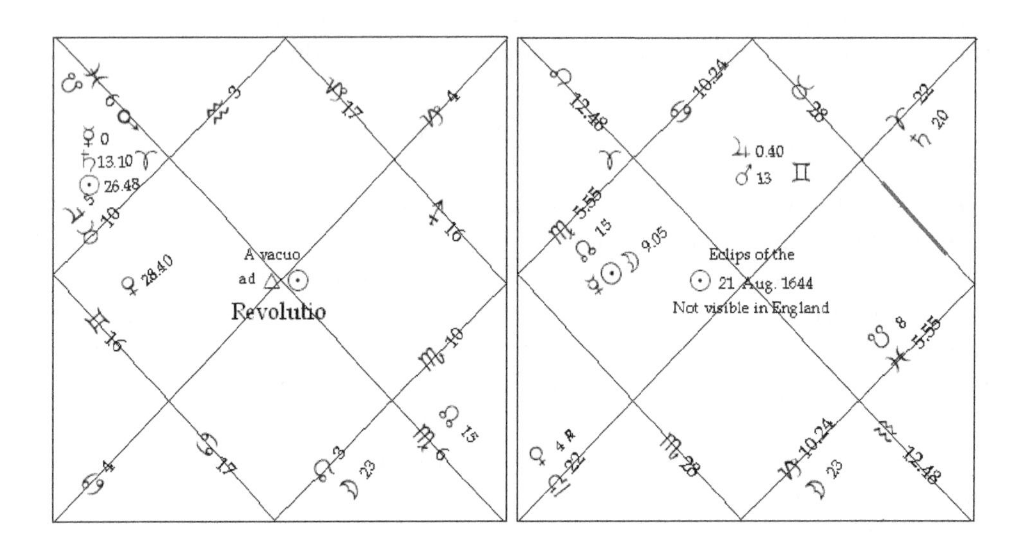

The unkindness betwixt your soon[286] and you seeme to have no sudden period in all points, though each others vigor will bee allayed in mediation of friends: the latter part of the 48th yeare (weare the tymes propitious) would bee spent in letting leases, and agitation with tenants, in building or repayring houses, or new furnishing one; it would bee a seasonable tyme to deale with such men, for they would bee more plyable then at other tymes; and more profit would arise to the nation and it would bee advantageous to treat with those kinds of men this 49th yeare, also, the ☽ to △ of ♂ may cause the native to delight in horsemanship, to consort with Captains and Souldiers, usually it gaines preferment in martiall affayres, and inclines a greater delight then ordinary to hawk, hunt, and to exercise those kinds of sportes, as also it stirs up the facultyes to wanntonesse and to desire the Love of gentlewomen etc. & to travel.

It is a yeare, wherein by meanes of your friends, your selfe shall be reconciled to some of your kindred, and if the tymes [illegible insertion] make some freindly journey North west to some of their houses, you will have one of your speciall enemys imprisoned and perhaps a short red hayred man: avoyd suretiship[287] this yeare. ♃ and ♀ both in the ascendant, may imbolden you all this yeare to go on with confidence and assurance of victory, and to have your owne lawfull desires in any thing you undertake.

Now for the Eclips, which is in August 1644, and the influence it may have on your person or actions; my opinion is so that by meanes of a false oath, you may bee in danger of loosing some portion of land; but shall not, and for that ☿ receiveth both the ☉ and ☽ in his house, and hee is in Corde ☉S[288] your selfe shall end and deride many troubles, or have many of your ould inveterate enemys &c. at your mercy; but ♃ in the degree Culminating at the byrth, should change this forme of life into a better, and should resettle you in all your rights, notwithstanding the hatefull presence of ♂ in the 10th,

[286]Wittypoole's son Edmond is said to have died in 1634 whilst still an infant and yet Lilly predicts further troubles between father and son. The implication is that previously there had been difficulties between them and is likely to refer to his son-in-law.

[287]Acting as a guarantor.

[288]"Corde Solis": in the heart of the Sun, or cazimi.

which intimates some seizure of part your lands eyther by Law or Authority etc. There will bee some sensible alteracon in your Constitution nor neede you feare any danger, though usually the Eclipses designe out some eminent action or other; the body may upon this change of temper bee more fitt and prepared for action, etc. and the Spirits move quicke and nimble by ☽ ad ter ♂: if in October you find any sensible alteracon, advise betimes, but I conceive there will bee no great need: you must beware of women kindred in matters of secrecy, else not.

50 yeare of age. Beginning 6° Aprill 1645 00 PM.

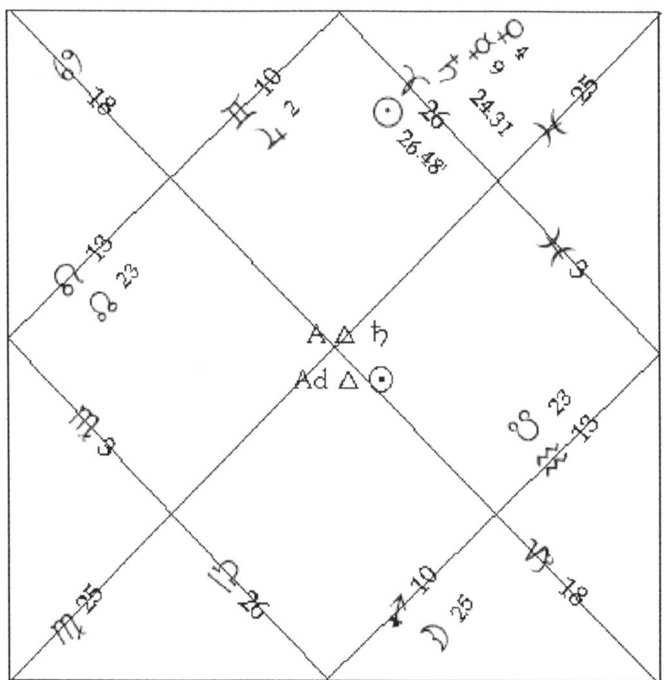

This yeare will partly accord with the former, for both are guided by the same direccons, this yeare affoarding none at all but the judgment of the Revolution.

An exaltacon above your enemys, and new acquaintance with honourable persons is most [...] designed this yeare.

Unless vexed with too frequent Company of weomen and their causes, I hope (the tymes still Considered) you will find this a comfortable yeare, I am confident you shall this yeare end many law suites to your owne content; if it bee a tyme wherein honour or preferment is styrring, expect your share, you cannot miss yt. You will live to see the downfall of very many [of] your malitious enemyes, and that this yeare: lawyers and Clergy men will befriend you; your excess in diet and wyne will incline your hands to a shaking or kind of Palsy; refraine the occasion etc. you may have a touch of the toothach, and a little weakeness in your right eye, occasioned by a chollericke humour.

51 yeare & Domini [...] Christi 1646

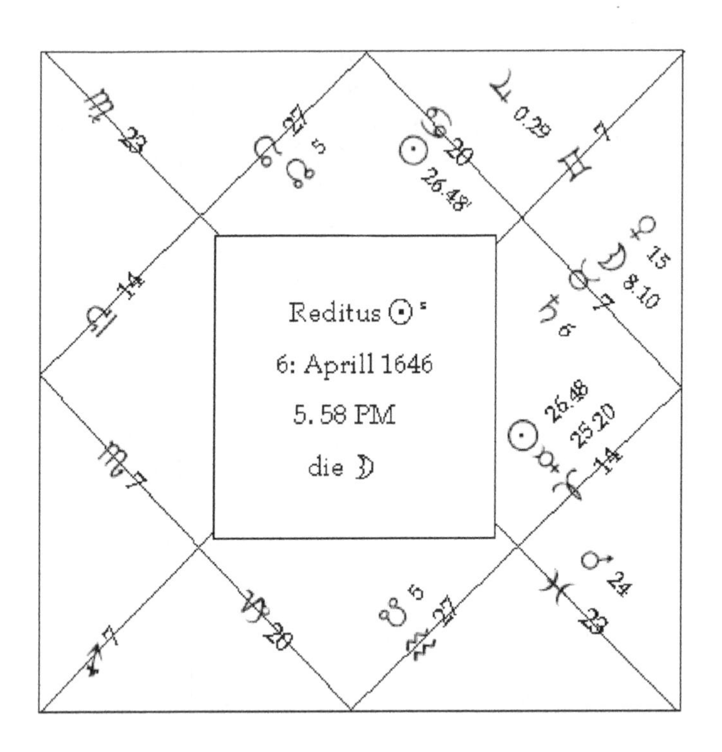

Eclipsis ☉ˢ on 20 ♋

6.11' PM
2 July 1646
Directions ~
Medium Cœli ad Canem Minorem octo. 1646
Ad □ ♃ mart. 1646
☉ CA 6 decemb. 1646

This may bee a fitt yeare to treate about a wife:[289] a whole yeare ♃ is in ♋ take your tyme.

[289]Wittypoole may have been widowed as Lilly was preparing this.

A symptome of the goute affrights you; and flegme or a waterish humour is now more predominant then formerly; Let the Phisition purge wynd & flegme. Beware of untrusty servants this yeare, bee without a theefe if you can: a flaxen hayred man will bee now a knave. Much about these tymes, the English affayres begin to settle[290]. Some sorrow concerning your daughter, shees likely to bee sicke. False oaths will bee frequent against you, and solicitors, Lawyers, gentlemen and Divines (if any bee left) will be eagerly bent against you, I conceive this yeare prepares matter for the succeeding, and a plot may bee layd how to cozen you of some portion of Land, or of part of your inheritance, but because the Eclips doth happen neare the 7th house; this yeare malice is rewarded until the effects of that Eclips have operation which will bee 1647 in or about July. You must procure money for expenses as the succeeding yeare wherein the former direccons will more plainly manifest their influences etc.

[290]This is an interesting prediction concerning the Civil War then in progress.

52 yeare 1647

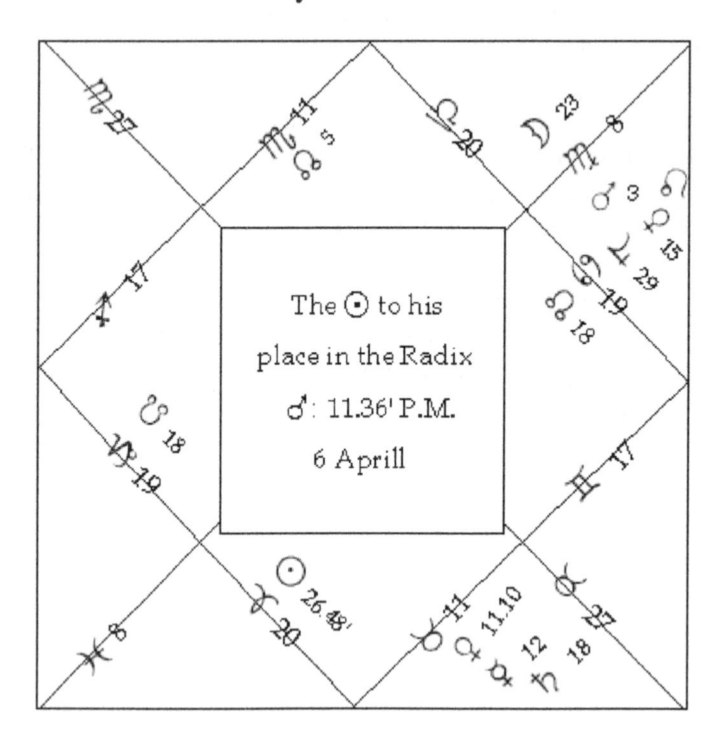

Extreamely apt to quarrel, and as malitiously provoked: your owne discretion guided without passion, may exceedingly availe you in these two yeares passages; of which I trust your wisdome will Consider etc.

Suddenly when least expected, your selfe and freinds sett at variance, by a [wretched?] servant and malitious kinsman; from hence arise suites in Law, and you vexed with the Judges unjust sentence, or some Magistrates unjust act against you. Some patrimony unless heedfuly prevented, wrested from you, by a powerfull hand, if not a Kinge (if Kings bee at that tyme[291]); its good to beware of entrusting your estate into the hands of freinds, especially Clergy, Lawyers, or Souldiers, all is gone if you confide those men; Preferment not contemptible will be offered you, the best for you is to bee quiet, to accept none, but live retired, for your acceptance of any office, will inevitably bring

[291] Again, an interesting political statement which seems to predict the Interregnum.

you to endless troubles, by some rash and unadvised act purposely intended to confound you. You shall finde many persons of quality to envy you: and towards the end of the yeare unless heedfully prevented a fitt or symptome of the Palsy and oppressed with wynd in the miseraicks or small gutts, and ill stomack, and the stone in the raynes and kidneys to purpose. Molested by a sisters soon, etc.. Therefore this yeare speakes fayre to all but trust very few, whether of Consanguinity or other it matters not. Weakeness in your eyesight.

52 Yeare

There may bee some treaty for a wife. I cannot promise performance. Beware of popular tumults, and willingly provoake not the wrath of a great Lady or Countess against you; it may please God you may make better use of her, by connivance etc., and so disgrace those that intend it for you.

53 yeare of age.

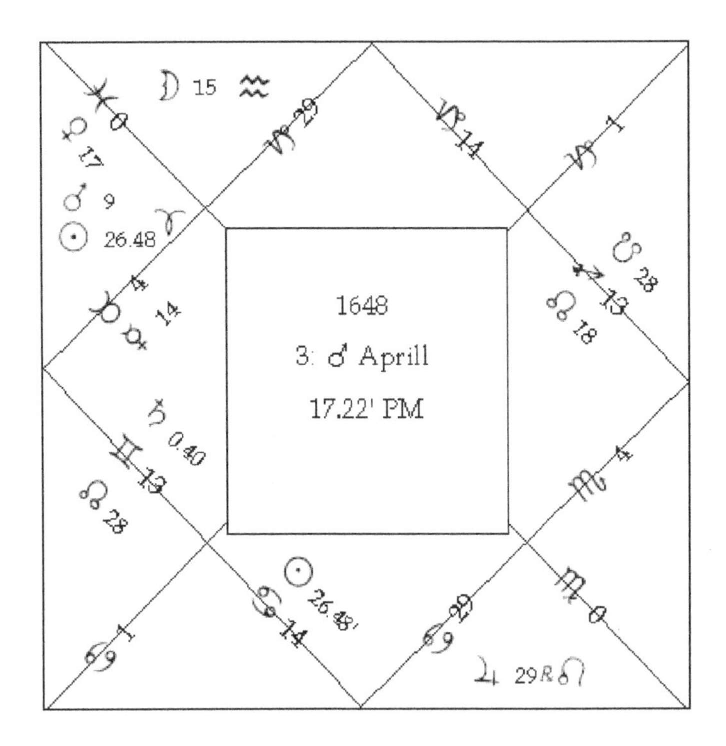

53 yeare of age and Ano: dom: 1648.

Your sober carriage in the 2 last yeares, begins to bring things to good effect as is signified by M. Cœli ad ter ♀.

This yeare perfectly concludes what was begun in the former, and advise you to beware of a soare throat. Perfectly such as the last yeare was, this will bee, for no new matter appears.

54 Annus et Annus Christi 1649.
♃ 5 Aprill. 23:10' PM

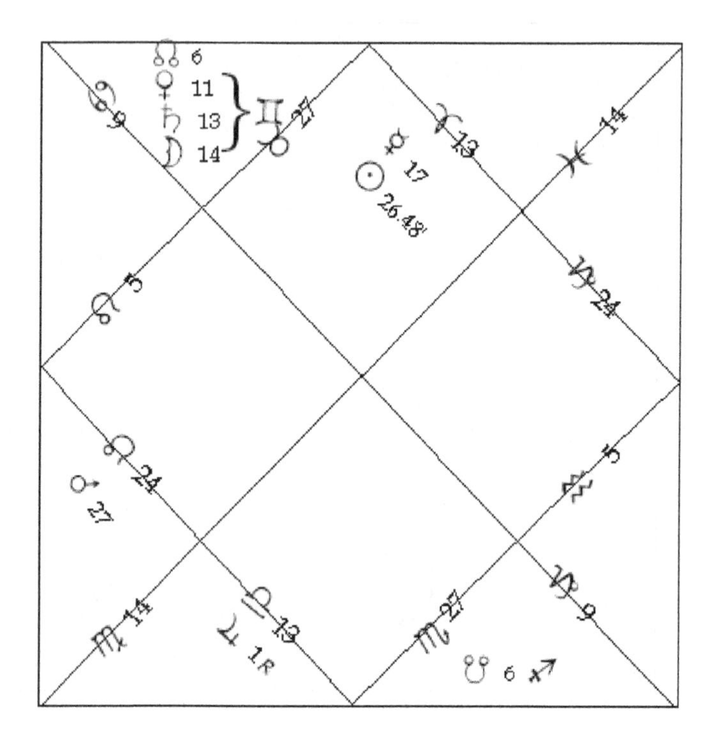

⊗ ad Contrantis.

♃

In question by some man of the Church about an Advowsion or some church matter, hee causeth expence of money; some debts perhaps for suretyshipp are called for; yourselfe grow a little melancholy by fitts; subject to a shaking in your hands, and some frigidity in your joints, your Venerious joints: but you are too hard for the man of God and overthrow him. Theres no direccon to manifest more, unlesse ♂ in the second in △ to the ☉; give you some bountifull favour from an eminent person (prince or King or otherways intytuled[292]) which I advise now to accept, because both honour and money will follow etc. you may bee molested with Lawyers for debts etc.

[292] "or otherways intytuled", another hint as to the shape of things to come.

55 yeare of age. 1650 4.58 PM. ♄ 6 Aprill

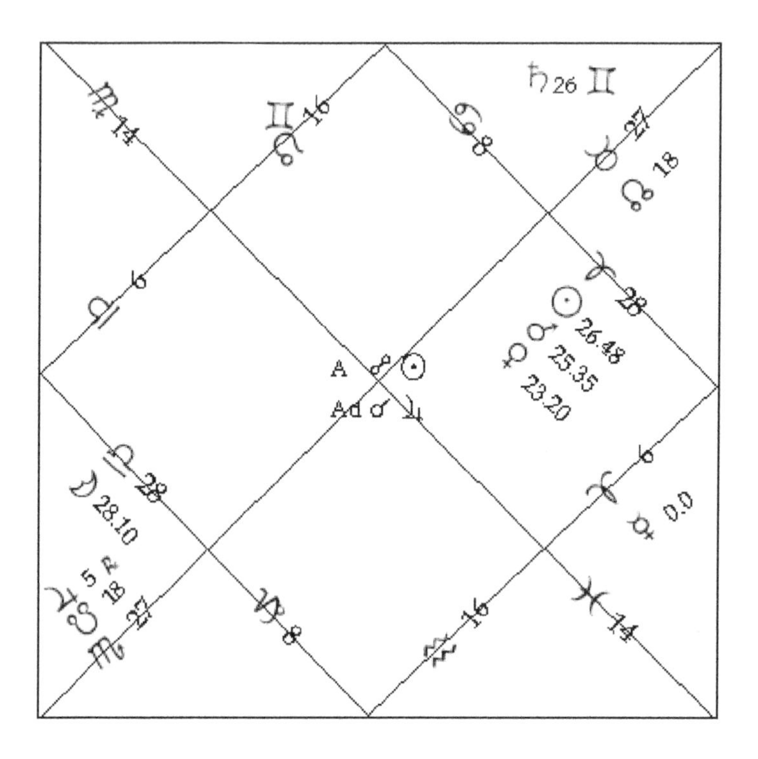

ad ter. ♃
ad ter ☿
Fight no Duells this yeare.

☽ ad ☍ ☉s
troubled with dimness of sight.

Intemperateness in your pleasure, will bring you to fitt of the stone in the kidneys; your Uritories seeme to bee full of gravel; ♂ so neare the ☉ and ♀ Lady of the asc. going to ☌ with him and after to Combustion, intimates a feaver or tertian. Phisitians may doubt your Life; but for as much as the ☽ is separating from the ☍ and is departing his beames, and the hatefull ☍ of ♂ as also for that the ☉ is hastening from ♂, you will not dye of this infirmness, but perfectly recover. Yet shall you find a sensible fayling of your former vigour, and the spirits weake. I shall be confident you may by a wary prevention in your diet, much lessen the causes which may produce such events for this infirmness now threatned, will come by disorder and too much indulging your appetite as is promised both by the Revolution and Profectionall Scheame.

⊗ ad ☍ ☽ vulgar or Common people will cozen you in contracts and bargaines, or in taking new Leases; many will indeavour to molest your quiet; yet with some wrangling you hold your owne.

Annus Climactericus 56 1651

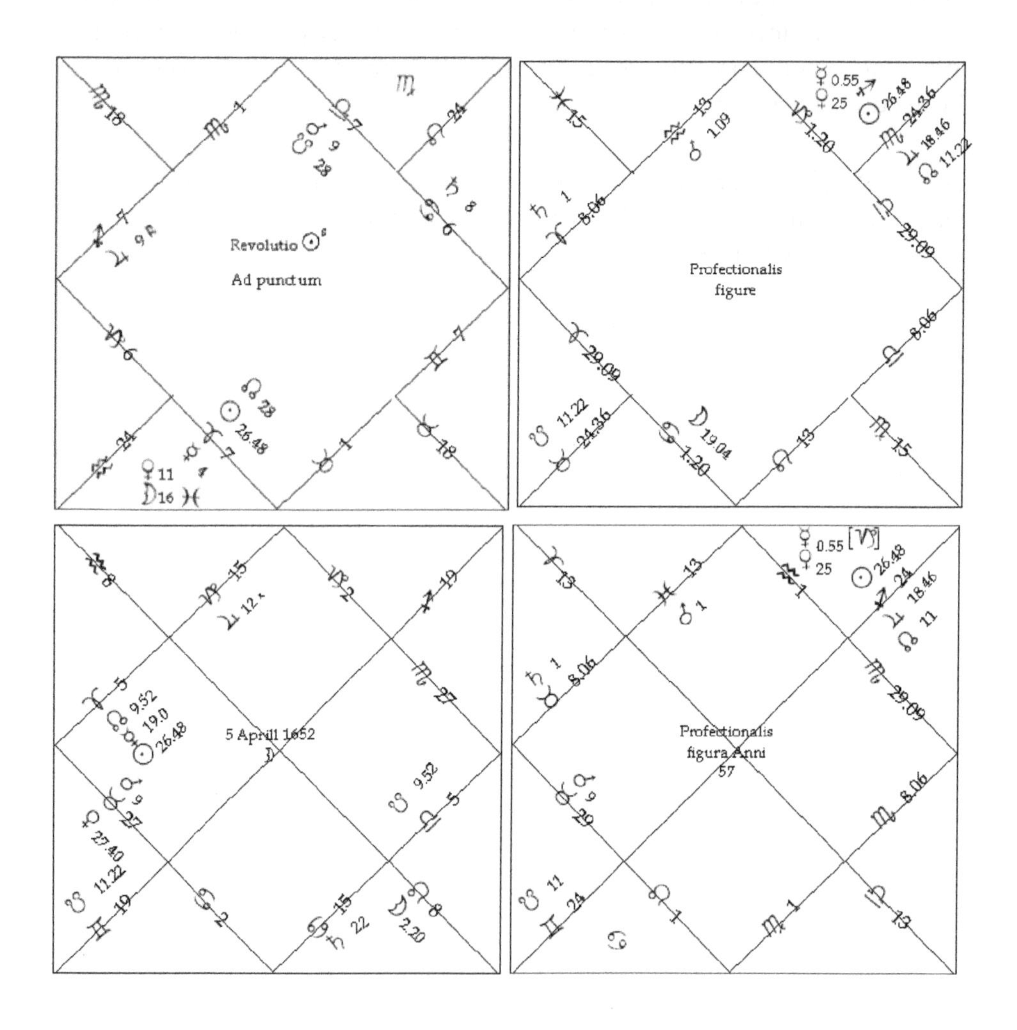

⊗ ad ✶ ♃: This is a Climactericall yeare, and held by many to bee dangerous, for it consisting of 8 tymes 7 yeares. ☉ ad ter ♀: shee have no killing direccon to impeach the natives health; but a flaxen hayred Phisition will carelessly cause much distemper to the native, and give contrary Phisicke; Lett not the native without cause or mearely in wantonness bee advised by that sorte of men, ♃ in the ascendant, may casually heate the blood, but no neede will bee of medicine. Heare seemes a recuperation of some lands or the like formerly in question, good success against a whole Jury of Lawyers; these begin to bee Courteous – a wonder. Bee not acquainted at Court (if any now bee[293]), for some most scandalous untruth will bee vented against your honour, by a perfidious freind; but I beleeve the □ of ♄ to him will hang him. Bee carefull of yourselfe the 24 and 25th of June 1651 and some dayes before and after, least by overheating yourselfe you prejudice your person.

[293] A repeated reference to the possibility of the end of monarchy. These references are of added interest because Sir William was a Royalist.

57 Yeare currant 1652

I was desirous to satisfie my selfe concerning this yeare, with all the inventions Art could thinke of[294]; and I finde no direccons pointing out so much as the least touch of sicknesse; yet the ascendant is drawing neare the ☍ of ♃, partly the destroyer of life; but the perfect aspect is not till the succeeding yeare; but sometimes it happens, the effects precede the cause, as heare it may do, because of the swift motion of ♃ in the Radix. You must then expect a sickly Autumne, being more then usually afflicted with paine in the backe, shortness of breath, and imperfection in the Lungs, coughes which bring upp no moysture, for the Lungs begin to consume, and the Cransie vexeth you. You may bee fearefull of an Apoplexy, stone in the bladder, etc.

[294]This implies that Sir William had been told previously that he would die or be very ill during this year. Perhaps this was predicted by the "Monsour" mentioned in the letter.

57 yeares

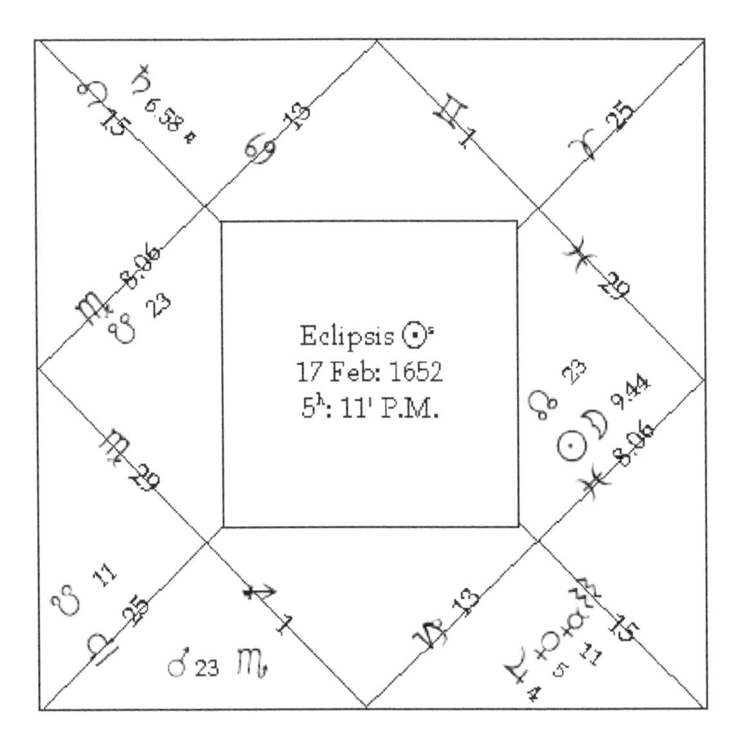

If in August and Sept. 1652 you begin to find some symptoms of these diseases; carefully advise with the Phisitian in tyme; in February, nearer the degree descending, which when that Eclips begins to worke, will indanger your health, for I finde ☋ in the ascendant of that Eclips. After Christmas you begin to bee melancholy, dull, and very captious, in march (if you find this true) purge melancholy from the intestines for the disease is from there, and let not black choler gett an habitt !

Sir, if you find this judgment verified this yeare, then you may bee confident of evading the next, but if so bee you have good health this 57th yeare, the effects remaine to bee fulfilled in the subsequent.

58 yeare 1653

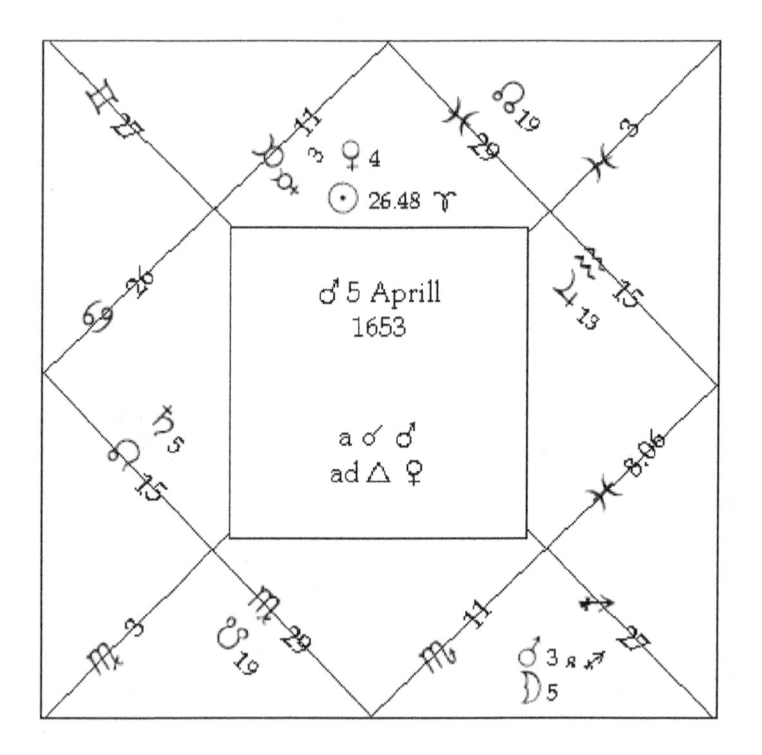

End all differences in words, but not in blowes this yeare.

Ascendens ad ☍ ♃ cum lat: 19: Aprill 1653:

If you escaped the last yeare, which you might well do because the aspect was not in full force, provide in tyme for ☽ with ♂ and Cor ♏; threatens a violent feaver, if not some flux of blood. If a feaver, lett blood, whatever the Doctor say: the disease will begin violently, upon this aspect. You will not dye I conceive this yeare although the ascendant is in the termes of the infortune. Towards the middle of this yeare, do you remove for change of ayre, for so much is signified by Asc. ad ✶ ☽ somewhat North East.

You should bee molested this yeare by your owne kindred, by clergy men, by gentlemen and Lawyers, by some nobleman for a portion of Land; but you will have Divines against you in Religion, or for some church living. Some would judge by ☽ with ♂ you would bee in danger by poison; but the poison will consist of nothing but full cupps of wyne[295], and of this bee confident, yet bee carefull.

Towards the latter end of the yeare, you will perfectly recover both health and victory etc., yet I should advise to begin to sett things in order; because after this tyme, you will be subject to many infirmnesses, and the gout especially, but all those accidentally, and seldome any of long Continuance. But bee carefull of thyselfe all December January and February and March 1653 of relapsing; for then in February the ascendant comes to ☍ of ♃ without Latitude so that it may bee doubted you will now and then have some touches of the maladyes before recited until the beginning of your 59th yeare, of which reade in the next.

[295]Lilly repeats his warnings about excess of drinking and diet with some humour.

59 yeares 1654

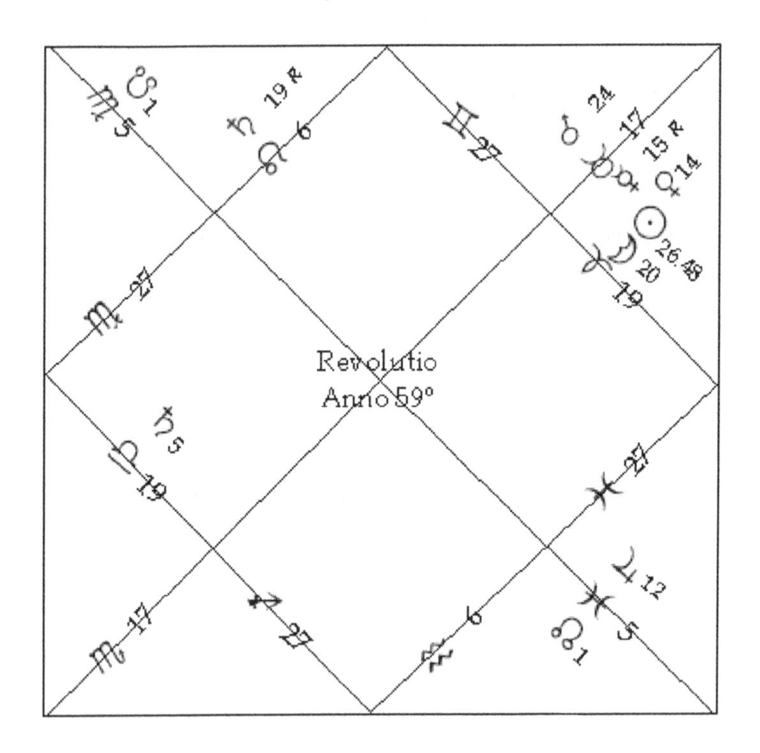

An Eclipse of the ☉ this yeare in August, visible over all Europe, after which the game begins; the longest swords takes all.[296]

Ascendens sub ✶ ☽ ad ter ♀ et spicam ♍ :

☽ ad ✶ proprium et ad spicam ♍ Contr. Or. Sig.[297]

M. Cœli ad ✶ ☿ in medio Anni.

☉ ad ☍ ☽ cum Lat. in medio Anni.

[296]A prediction of war in Europe.

[297]Against the order of the signs.

If God have prolonged your life to this yeare, as I doubt not of; and if now unmarried then this yeare promiseth a wife with aboundance of worldy estate with her; heare are direccons intend you wonders in all manner of felicity.

Your yeares are not so many to refuse such a business, whereas there is the ☉ directed to an ☍ of ☽, it taketh no place in operation till the next yeare.

Expect all manner of honour, happiness and what your hart desires, upon this yeares direccons.

60 yeare 1655

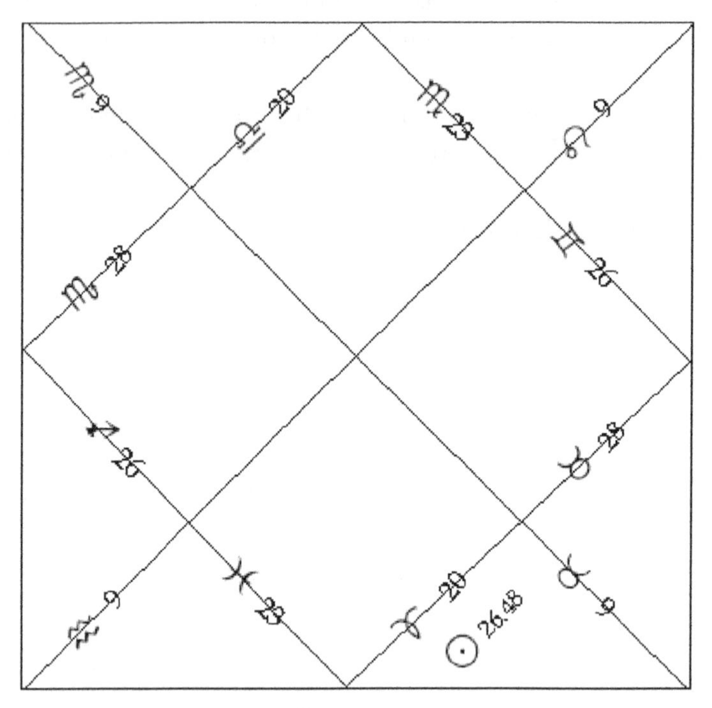

I have no Ephemeris for this yeare.[298]

I find upon better consideration, this is not the yeare of death: onely a small feaver or sore mouth etc.

Perhaps all may end in a bloody flux, or you may bee in feare of an ulcer in the kidneys: but no such thing.

☉ ad ☍ ☽ 9 August 1655 Cum Lat. Et ☽ ad ☍ ♃ Contra ordinem sig:[299]

Et in fine Anni M. Cœli ad □ ☉ et ter ♄

[298]The chart is shown as in the manuscript with only house cusps and the Sun's position shown.

[299]Against the order of the signs.

Tis probable this will bee a yeare of much sorrow unto you: by occasion of sicknesse for the ☉ to ☍ of ☽ in the 4th and ☽ ad ☍ ♃ in the 8 and 9th are in my judgment forerunners of death. The beginning of your sickness should bee by some fall from your horse whereby you may indanger your right thigh, and one of your Armes: if not also your left eye; now much afflicted in the old griefes, and aches in the joynts, some lameness, much opposition and envye from vulgar fellows, and a direct deserting one auncient acquaintance, a yeare of instability in the goods of fortune; where you little mistrusted there you find most treachery: some scandal putt upon you by a slutt: viz an ill woaman.

Plenty of law suites:
In danger of arrests.

61 **62**

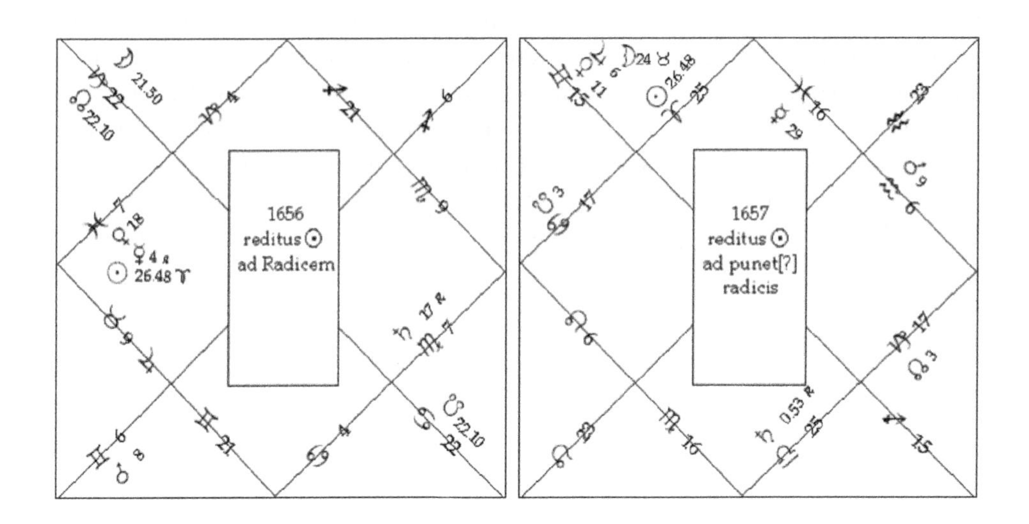
1656
reditus ☉
ad Radicem
1657
reditus ☉
ad punet[?]
radicis

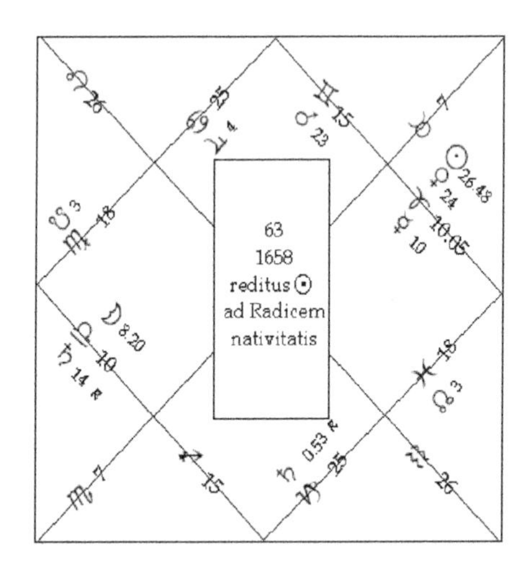
63
1658
reditus ☉
ad Radicem
nativitatis

Annus magnus Climactericus.

The sixtye first, sixty second and 63 yeare of your life have few direccons, now do the Revolutions threaten more then some vexation in Law suites: the success wherof will bee ambiguous in the 62 of your age, yet the ☽ in her exaltacon in the 11th gives hopes of excellent success, All your 63 year ♄ passeth ♎ in ☍ to the Radicall place of the 1 and in the second house of your Revolution. Much disturbance by your tenants, by Artificers, or Mechanicall fellows, and the rabble of Atturneys; some peece of forgery by them acted: A simple Judge doth you a discourtesy, being corrupted, as ♂ in ♊ doth demonstrate [...] you receive some blemish in honour, but its revenged by a great man, if any Grandees bee then in being. Backsliding in estate for a tyme. I find no danger of death any of those yeares. The sixty second will bee worst, by reason of some wynd obstructing the passages, and fuming into the head, etc. But a small appetite now to meate, a weake stomacke and that full of Crude humours, etc. Turne over.

64 yeare 1659

Wherein it seemes by reason of the ☽ to a ⚹ of ♃ and to her owne ⚹, you enjoy your health and are chearefull, delight in good company, yet are more religious then formerly, you have much respect with the gentry and yeomanry where you live, and in probability change your habitacon for a tyme; nothing ill this yeare unlesse Atturneys play the knave with you, and so stir up your choler, which will now arise fast inough without vexation etc.

65 yeare 1660

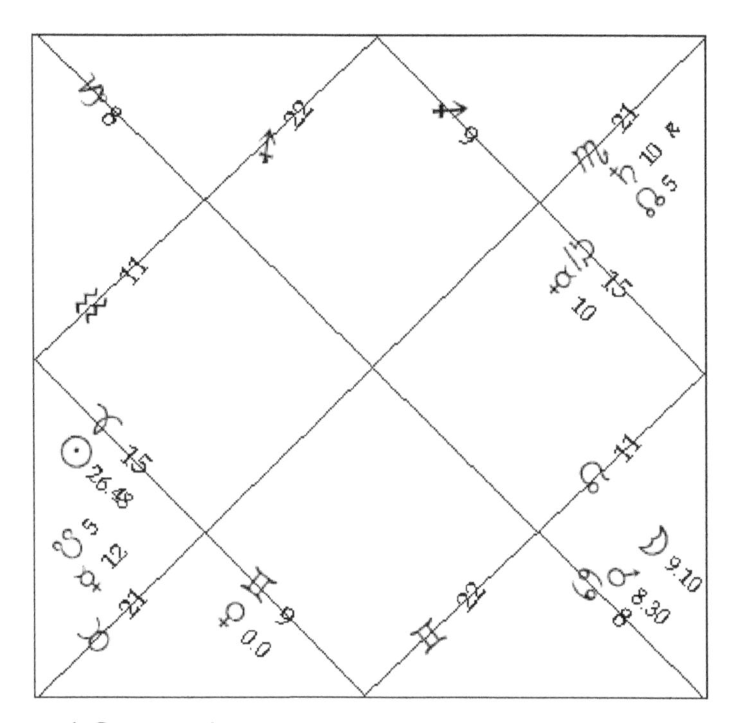

Asc ad ter ♂ ☉ ad ter ♄
ad ☍ ♄ in 1° ♓ et ♏
ad ☋ in ♎ 11

Annus fatalis

The temperature of body do now quite vary, these hatefull aspects depraving the humours, and destroying the vitall and radicall virtues, causing fearefull dreames, and spreading melancholy into all parts of the body, that humour solely predominating, the ☌ of ♂ with ☽ in the 6 begetts ill digestion, and oppression in the stomacke; it turnes after to a feaver, a small one, (vomiting weare good) this is augmented by a swelling tympanicall humour, in the belly, after falling into the leggs, and thighs; so that a dropsy is feared, in prevention wherof, the Physition causeth the dropsy to strike upp to the hart; and so in or about 26 or 30 November 1660 I conceive you may submit to death. And yet the Alchocoden giveth you 69 yeares to live: but certainly if you escape this yeare, in the 66 of your age and 1661 you will bee in danger of loosing your eye sight; and if God deprive you not then of life you may attaine to the 69th of your age and of our Lord God 1664: at what tyme the Ascendant hath occurse to the ☍ of the ☉ whose meane yeares are then determined.

Certainly ☊ and ♃ in the 8th do both promise a naturall and quiet kind of death, in your bedd and owne habitacon. I have mett with no Nativity hitherto, that since the 30th yeare of age hath had so many cross and perverse direccons; and they continue yeare by yeare till you dye; so that seldome you have two yeares of quietness. As an Artist, (but a man) I am confident you shall not dye till about 65 of your age, perhaps not until 69th: heare being so many yeares elapsed, I hold it not fitt to give a generall judgment[300], but conclude all in Annuall direccons of Accidents. And say moreover where the Antiscium of ♃ and of ☉ are in the ascendant and ♃ have dominion of death: the native shall dye a fayre death etc.

Finis 24 August
1643.

[300]Interestingly, Lilly refuses to go further with the judgement because it is so far into the future.

Sir William's Nativity

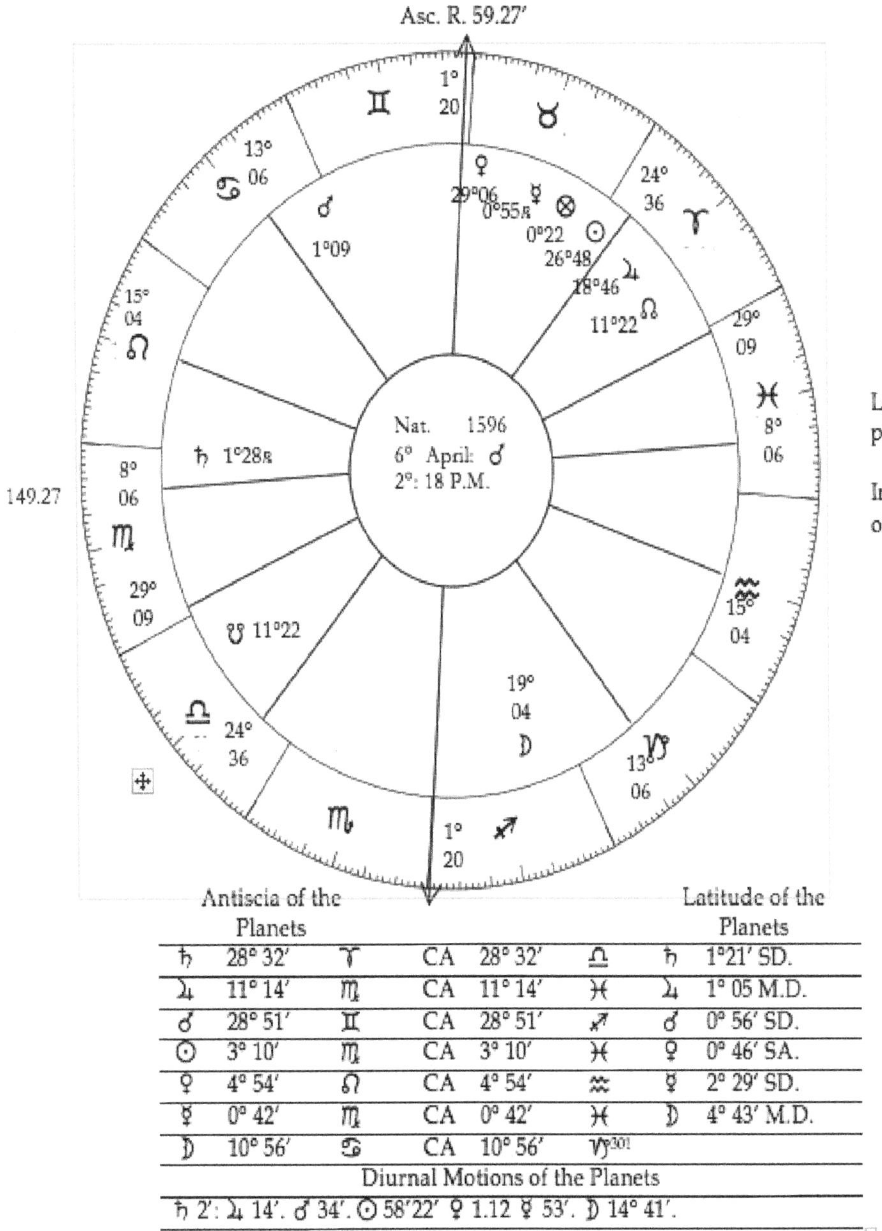

Latitude of the place: 51° […]

In the country of England.

Antiscia of the Planets						Latitude of the Planets	
♄	28° 32′	♈	CA	28° 32′	♎	♄	1°21′ SD.
♃	11° 14′	♍	CA	11° 14′	♓	♃	1° 05 M.D.
♂	28° 51′	♊	CA	28° 51′	♐	♂	0° 56′ SD.
☉	3° 10′	♍	CA	3° 10′	♓	♀	0° 46′ SA.
♀	4° 54′	♌	CA	4° 54′	♒	☿	2° 29′ SD.
☿	0° 42′	♍	CA	0° 42′	♓	☽	4° 43′ M.D.
☽	10° 56′	♋	CA	10° 56′	♑[301]		

Diurnal Motions of the Planets
♄ 2′: ♃ 14′. ♂ 34′. ☉ 58′22′ ♀ 1.12 ☿ 53′. ☽ 14° 41′.

Beyond the Great Fire: Lilly and Ashmole

by

Sue Ward

We know too little about William Lilly and his work, but we know enough to avoid constant references to his prediction of the Great Fire of London. As much of an achievement as this might seem, it has become hackneyed and his achievements go beyond that. So, in order to broaden our working knowledge of Lilly, I will offer some lesser known horoscopes and documents with the aim of improving our understanding of the man through his relationship with Elias Ashmole and through his own nativity which I present here. Sometimes more questions are raised than answered, but at least we will have a clearer understanding of what those might be.

In this original research I shall be referring to primary sources in all cases: Lilly's own autobiography in manuscript[301] and Ashmole's autobiographical notes[302]. Manuscript references are provided where relevant.

Lilly's involvement in post-Restoration politics

We begin later in Lilly's life in 1673, at the advanced age of 71 years. After the Restoration in 1660, Lilly, like many other prominent Parliamentary supporters of the Civil War years, found it advisable to exercise caution in his public life. Charles I had promised that, with the exception of the regicides, there would be no reprisals; even so, in 1660 and again in 1661, Lilly was in trouble with the authorities. In the first case he was called before a Parliamentary committee to give evidence regarding Charles I's execution because it was thought that Lilly might know who the executioner had been; in the second case, he was arrested for "fanaticism"[303]. So, his caution was well-founded although he continued undeterred to publish his annual almanacs with their mundane predictions. But had his enthusiasm for, and involvement in English politics faded? Had he lost his influence and power?

---

[301]MS Ashmole 421

[302] *Elias Ashmole: His Autobiographical and Historical Notes,* ... Ed. C.H. Josten, OUP, 1966.

This essay provides evidence of Lilly's continuing interest and involvement in public affairs, and of his close connection with the powerful.

The following horoscope[304] is a clear demonstration of Lilly's enduring authority. While we cannot say for certain that Charles II knew that Ashmole was consulting his friend regarding the King's concerns, it seems likely that he did. This judgement clearly shows Ashmole's attempt to fulfil the King's wishes, therefore it would not be true to say that Charles intended that Lilly should give judgement on this matter.

[303]A term relating to religious beliefs and, during this period of the new Act of Uniformity, often aimed at Nonconformists.

[304]MS Ashm. 436 10v

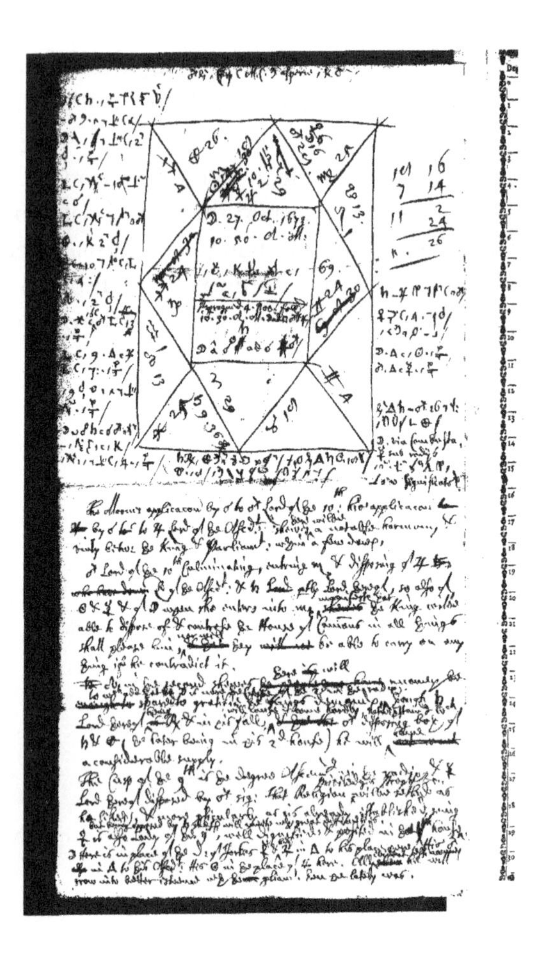

"10H. 50 the Parliament meeting after the Prorougation the King made a Speech."

The horoscope is set for the time the King began his speech at the opening of Parliament. Professor Josten's opinion is that the notes in longhand are a draft of the judgement the King had asked Ashmole to make. Josten also thinks it likely that this consultation went on for a longer period because there are other similar matters with which Ashmole concerns himself and which can be found in his *Autobiographical Notes*....[305]

The king had prorogued Parliament in April 1671, their first meeting having been in January of that year. During the prorogation another war with the Dutch had erupted and the king needed to finance the military action urgently. His reason for recalling Parliament was solely to obtain money for the war. In February of 1673 Parliament did vote for an amount of money, but it was to be spread over three years on condition that the king complied with certain requests. One of these was the Test Act by which every holder of civil or military office had to take the sacrament of the Lord's Supper according to Church of England custom. It was also required that the oaths of supremacy and allegiance had to be sworn, along with a declaration against transubstantiation which was guaranteed to be refused by all Roman Catholics. These conditions were severe, and they brought about the resignation from the admiralty of the King's brother James.[306]

---

[305]For example, MS Ashm. 1136, f. 159v and MS. Ashm. 240, f. 263.

[306]*The Later Stuarts 1660 - 1714*, Sir George Clark, OUP, Oxford.

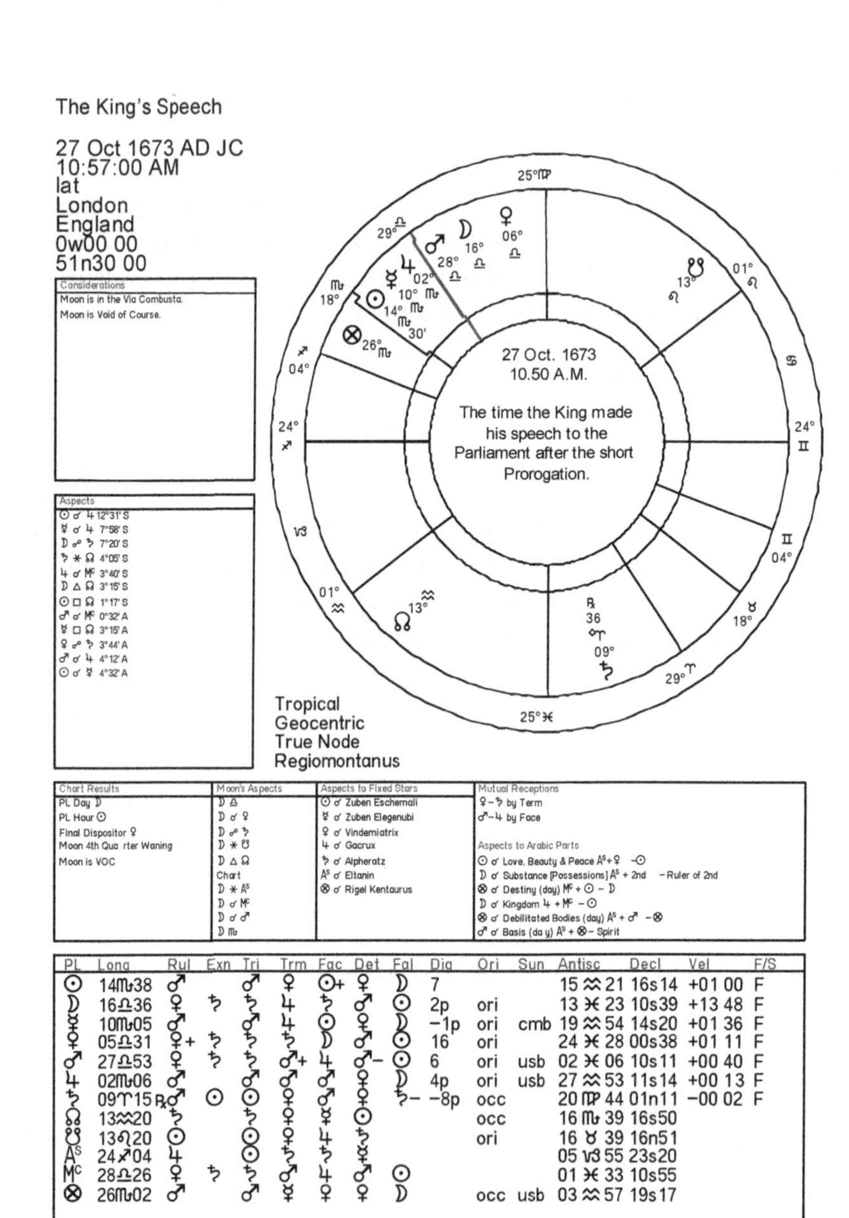

PL	Long	Rul	Exn	Tri	Trm	Fac	Det	Fal	Dig	Ori	Sun	Antisc	Decl	Vel	F/S
☉	14♏38	♂		♂	♀	☉+	♀	☽	7			15♒21	16s14	+01 00	F
☽	16♎36	♀	♄	♄	♃	♄	♂	☉	2p	ori		13♓23	10s39	+13 48	F
☿	10♏05	♂		♂	♃	☉	♀	☽	−1p	ori	cmb	19♒54	14s20	+01 36	F
♀	05♎31	♀+	♄	♄	♄	☽	♂	☉	16	ori		24♓28	00s38	+01 11	F
♂	27♎53	♀	♄	♄	♂+	♃	♂−	☉	6	ori	usb	02♓06	10s11	+00 40	F
♃	02♏06	♂		♂	♂	♂	♀	☽	4p	ori	usb	27♒53	11s14	+00 13	F
♄	09♈15℞	♂	☉	☉	♀	♂	♀	♄−	−8p	occ		20♍44	01n11	−00 02	F
☊	13♒20	♄		♄	♀	☿	☉			occ		16♏39	16s50		
☋	13♌20	☉		☉	♀	♃	♄			ori		16♉39	16n51		
As	24♐04	♃		☉	♄	♄	☿					05♑55	23s20		
Mc	28♎26	♀	♄	♄	♂	♃	♂	☉				01♓33	10s55		
⊗	26♏02	♂		♂	☿	♀	♀	☽		occ	usb	03♒57	19s17		

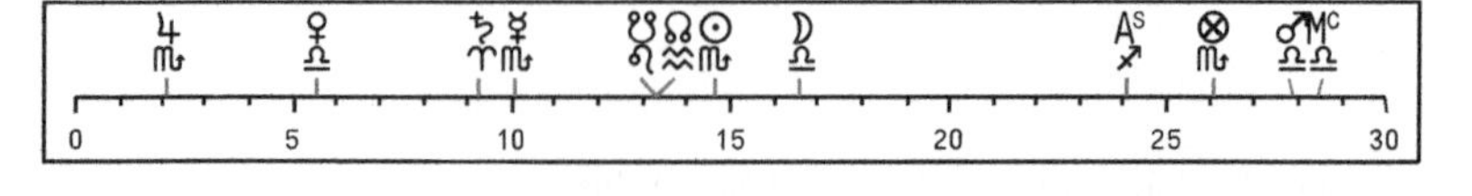

When the Test Act had received royal assent in March, Parliament adjourned. By its next meeting, to which Ashmole's chart refers, the Prince of Orange had deployed agents to excite more opposition.[307] So, the King's anxiety is understandable. Charles gave ground and Parliament had its way, and although the King got his money, in the following year of 1674, Parliament withdrew England from the war.[308] This had further serious ramifications for Charles; the war with the Dutch had been joined to support the French, whose king had been subsidising Charles. If Charles could not send military support to the French then the subsidies would cease. It is interesting to keep these important historical points in mind in relation to Lilly's letters to Ashmole on the subject before considering the final judgement.

"30 Oct. 1673[309]
A letter from William Lilly to Ashmole 'in sheer lane':

'Charissime Patrone, et Ptolemee,

I have seriously weighed and considered your profound judgment, uppon the figure sent mee, and I am very glad of the honor his Majesty did you, but more satisfied at your prudent and well grounded answer about the success – which certainly will correspond with your grave judgment. Mars on the cusp of the M.C. will asperse his honor – and because hee disposeth of Part of Fortune: they will bee ill satisfied with the dispose of monyes, etc. Moon and Mercury are for the Parl: the most inferior planets / Moon in via combust. – Mercury sub radiis, going to combustion, Trine Saturn, And Mars. Saturn Rx. will pass the bill when least expected. Or when Sun Lord of the 8. – South Node in the 8. they will not give plentifully but plead poverty of the subject.

But it is Actum agere to add to what you have sayd.'"

"3 Nov. 1673[310]
A letter from William Lilly to Ashmole 'in sheer lane':

---

[307] *King Charles II*, Arthur Bryant, London, 1936.

[308] *History of England*, G.M. Trevelyan. London 1976.

'Doctissime Patrone

I long to hear what was done on Friday, I fear his Majestys occasions found Difficulty: it was malus dies. you will find Mars in the 10th: many aspersions uppon – but when the male aspects separate – melius sperandum / the Presb. have frequent meetings, more then of late, pray much for the Parliament – the hand of Joab[311] is in all these difficultys – vincet qui patitur - …'"

"6 Nov. 1673[312]
A letter from William Lilly to Ashmole 'in sheer lane' — '& a Hamper':

'Docte Patrone

Vincit qui patitur. our Novembers observations[313] come near the present Matters now agitated. You mistake the Significator of the King – had the Chauncellor onely spoke, you had been right – but himself speaking hath no other Significator but the Lord of the ascendant – which you may know, by the 4 Votes – all which reflect on his Majestys honor etc., its true, when Kings speake, the Sun hath some signification- but in the main, is still the Asc. and his Lords- and this is Naturall-well: I hope well, and am positive for his Majesty in all conferences- assured that those prophetick spirits who long since hinted at him, have delivered nothing but Divine oracles, which shall in fullness of tyme bee verified.: but syth the tymes are so ticklish, I shall acquiess – Oh Saturn in Aries – and the late Comet therein but syth wee may not be publiq, wee will bee silent in private – however great judgments are impending – this – tibi tantum[314]. …'"

The Judgement
Chart square: "The time the King made his speech to the Parliament after the short prorogation".

Beneath that: "Prorogued 4. Nov following 10H. 30' A.M. ☽ ad £ ♂ & ♃."

[309]MS Rawl. D. 864, ff. 61-62v

[310]MS Rawl. D. 864, ff. 63-64v

Above the figure: "♂ upon the Cusp of M.C. will asperse the King's honour." [Extracted from Lilly's letter.]

Beneath the figure: "♄ Rx, Money will be had when least expected perhaps upon △ ♄☉, 18 Nov. ☋ in the 8 They will not give plentifully but plead poverty". [Extracted from Lilly's letter.]

"Upon △ ♄ and ♂ 26 Decem: the bill may pass for money." [Extracted from Lilly's letter.]

"The Moons applicacon by conj. to ♂ Lord of the 10th: his applicacon by conj. to ♃ Lord of the Ascendant shewes there wilbe a notable harmony & unity betw: the King & Parliament within a few daies"

In this passage Ashmole is referring to the King as Mars, ruler of the 10th.

There is no application of the Moon to Mars, they are out of joint moieties. Here and throughout these and Lilly's comments, they address the actual movements of the planets in the heavens, which is usual in mundane matters.

"♂ Lord of the 10th culminating, entring ♏ & disposing of ♃ Lord of the Ascendant & ♄ partly Lord thereof, so also the ☉ & ☿ & ☽ when she enters into ♏ manifests that the King wilbe able to dispose of and controle the House of Commons in all things, shall please him, nor will they be able to carry on any thing if he contradict it "

Ashmole is again putting the king to the 10th house. He is saying that the king will be in control because Mars is on the MC and rules it, and that it will soon enter its own sign strengthening it further. Also, the Sun, Mercury and Jupiter are all in Scorpio and in the 10th, so the King will be able to dispose of all of these in due course, as also when the Moon changes signs.

"☊ in the second shewes there will meanes bee to which add that the"

---

[311]Referring to 2 Sam. XIV. 19.] i.e. someone putting word's into another's mouth, or manipulating the situation from behind the scenes.

[312]MS Rawl. D. 864, ff. 65-66v

The 2nd house according to Ashmole represents Parliament's finances, so he says that they have enough money.

> ☽ is ad___ the Cuspe of the 2nd in the radix [it is at 16° Libra in the event and the natal 2nd is at 11° Libra] spared ["enough to" is deleted] to gratifie the Kings Demands enough though ♄ Lord thereof being Rx. & in his fall will cause it to come hardly, which ♂ disposing both of ♄ and ⊕ (the former being in his 2nd house [of the nativity]) he will have a considerable supply.

The Moon is separating from an aspect with the king's natal 2nd house which is at 11° Libra. He thinks this shows that there will be enough money granted to satisfy the king's demands. Although, because Saturn is Rx. and in fall and is ruler of the event 2nd it will be difficult to obtain. But Mars disposes of both the ruler of the 2nd and the Part of Fortune which is in the natal 2nd, so he judges that the king will get a large sum of money.

> The Cusp of the 9th is the degree Ascending in the radix & ☿ Lord thereof disposed by ♂ sig: that Religion Priviledges & Prophets wilbe settled as hee likes, & wars particularly as is already established seeing ♀ is also Lady of the 9th well dignified and posited in the 9th house, But being opposed by ♄ ____ will _____ with great difficulties. ☽ herein is in place of the Duke of Yorkes ☿ & his ♃ in △ to his place there. His ♂ in △ to this Ascendant. His ☉ in the place of ♃ here. All evident testimony he will grow into better esteeme with the parliament then he lately was.

These remarks refer to the nativities of both King Charles and his brother James, the latter having been unpopular for some time and an avowed Roman Catholic.

It is clear why Lilly disagreed with Ashmole. His last letter on the subject of the 6th November 1673 seems to refer to a different or incomplete judgment made by Ashmole, to that referred to in Lilly's letter of the 30th October where he is in agreement with Ashmole.

---

[313] The observations for November in his almanac for 1673. Interestingly he writes of "Clandestine treaties in many countries, underhand transactions, Counsels, neither pleasing the people or many of their Superiors."

The king obviously could not "dispose of" and "control" Parliament because, as already mentioned, Parliament insisted on strict conditions and later withdrew England from the war with the Dutch. And so the king's 'special relationship' with the King of France was brought to an end.

Lilly's relationship with Ashmole

One of the things made clear from the above correspondence is the trust that each had in the other. Lilly was able to confide in his friend even though their politics differed; nevertheless, Lilly would not accept incorrect astrology and continues to instruct Ashmole. We know that theirs was a close and enduring friendship. It began when, during the evening of Friday, 20 November 1646, Jonas Moore (the famous mathematician and Royalist) introduced Ashmole to Lilly. Ignoring the prohibition on Royalist officers, to whose ranks Ashmole had belonged, he returned to London on 30 October 1646.

It is interesting that this followed so soon after Ashmole had joined a Masonic lodge on 16 October 1646. Josten's comments are also interesting; he writes:

> "Perhaps his newly acquired masonic connexions had influenced Ashmole's decision. Certainly, on his return to London, his circle of friends soon included many new acquaintances among astrologers, mathematicians, and physicians whose mystical leanings might have predisposed them to membership of speculative lodges, yet it is not known if any of them belonged to the craft. To many orthodox minds the study of mathematics and astrology, which to all intents and purposes still were but two aspects of one discipline, savoured of heresy and atheism, a suspicion which might easily have fostered the formation of mathematicians' lodges or other secret societies, yet no evidence supporting such a conjecture is known."

I would venture to take this further and argue that such a group could well have centred around a mutual interest in the study of the hermetic sciences. We know of Ashmole's longstanding practice of alchemy, as we do Lilly's

---

[314]"you only" or between us.

early magical practices. It is a "conjecture" which often arises when considering William Lilly's life and his wide circle of friends and acquaintances which seems to have flourished in spite of religious, political and social differences. This is especially outstanding when we consider the upheavals of the period which often focused on these differences.

Ashmole notes on 2 January 1647[315] "At night I dreamed that Mr. Lilly had assured me, he would procure me Jupiter [Mrs March[316]] by his art." Josten thinks that "art" probably means magic, but when referring to the period some twelve years earlier, Lilly says in his autobiography: "…and since have burned my bookes, which instructed those Curiositys: for after that, I became melancholly, very much afflicted with the Hypocondriack melancholly, growing lean and spare, and every day worse, so that in the year 1635, my infirmity continuing and my acquaintance increasing, I resolved to live in the country, and in March and Aprill 1636 remooved my goods unto Hersham wher I now live, and in may my person, wher I continued until 1641, no notice being taken who or what I was…"

The "curiositys" to which Lilly refers related, in one instance, to his assisting a pregnant lady to gain access to her estranged lover and perhaps were not the same as the "art" to which Ashmole refers. Nevertheless, he tells us that he burned those books, implying that he had ended those activities. It is difficult to believe that Lilly would burn his books, especially considering how expensive and highly prized books were. Ashmole's reference to Lilly's "art" also suggests that he had not discontinued these practices. One of the reasons for Lilly's departure from London was to lead a quieter life, without fame and publicity, but his renown extended beyond his astrological abilities.

In his autobiography, Lilly tells us that he began his astrological education with the astrologer-magician John Evans in 1632. In 1634 Lilly acquired a parchment book known as *Ars Notoria*, a well-known grimoire attributed to Solomon. He explains that it has "the names of those Angells and their Pictures which are thought and beleeved by Wise men to teach and instruct in

[315]MS Ashm. 1136, f.219

[316]Ashmole pursued this lady for marriage.

all the 7 Liberall Sciences and this is obtained by observing elected Tymes and those prayers appropriated unto the several Angells. I do ingeniously acknowledg, I used those prayers according to the form and direction prescribed for some weeks, using the word Astrologia for Astronomia, but of this no more." Lilly began teaching Astrology in this same year; whether his rapid progress in Astrology was due to natural or supernatural means is open to speculation, but he seems to imply it was a least partly due to the latter.

Lilly was already in high standing when Ashmole arrived in London, but it has always been assumed that it was because of the part he had played as Parliament's astrologer. We should now consider whether Lilly's status and influence was based on something along with his renown as an astrologer.

At the beginning of their acquaintanceship things did not run smoothly. Ashmole was a friend of Lilly's rival and enemy George Wharton[317], whose Royalist pamphlets ran the latter into numerous scrapes with Parliament. On 19th November 1646, the day before he was introduced to Lilly, Ashmole asks the horary question: "*Whether it will be any prejudice for me to publish Wharton's errors against Lilly.*" Wharton had produced two such almanacs in 1647 supposedly revealing Lilly's astrological errors. So on the day before his first meeting with Lilly, Ashmole begins to have second thoughts about this joint enterprise. Unfortunately, either Ashmole's grasp of astrology was not very good, or it was too late to turn back.

[317]Ashmole had met Wharton in Oxford in 1645. Ashmole had begun his studies at Brasenose College, and Wharton was already an established astrologer.

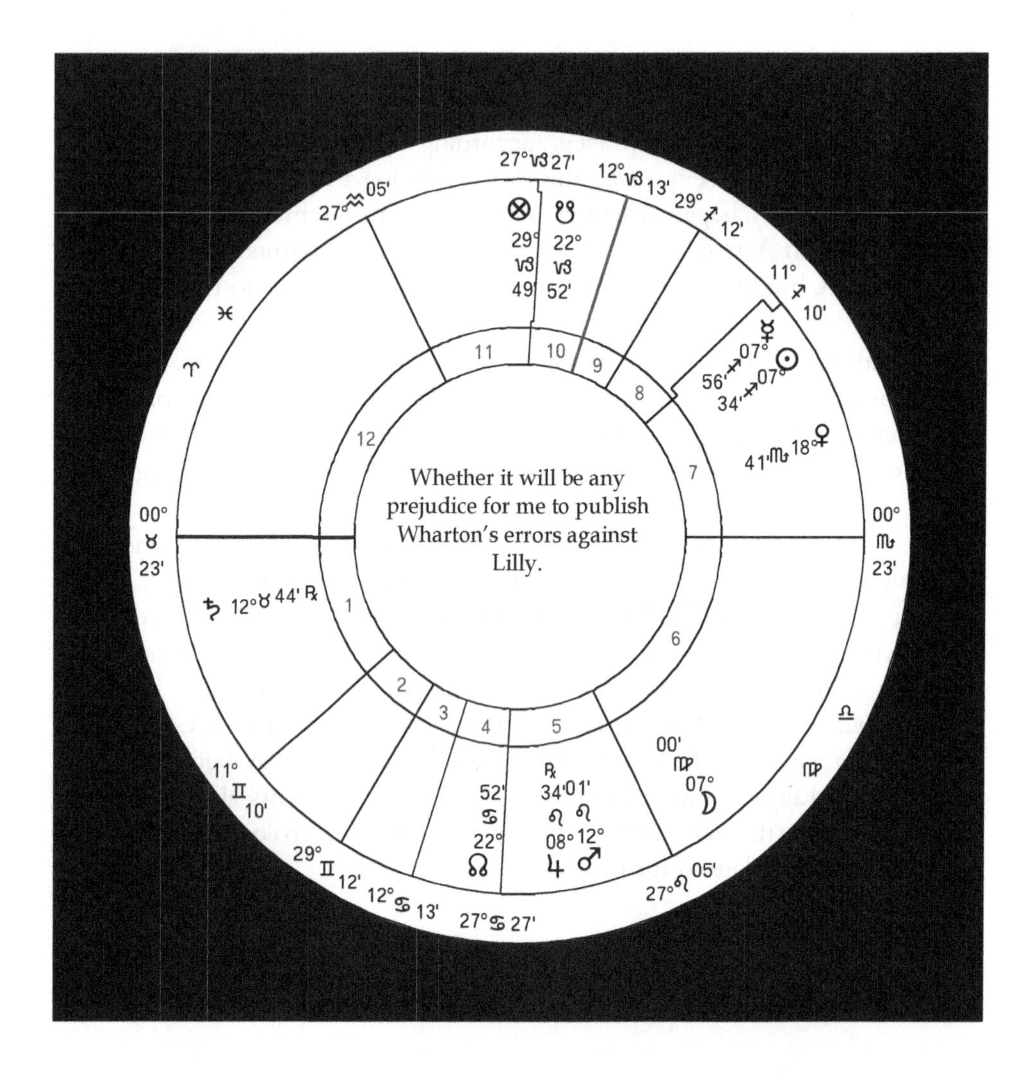

The Ascendant is very early, and because this is not a copy of the chart Ashmole judged, but a calculation based on his data, we cannot be sure what he was examining. Taurus is a sign of short ascension, rising in about an hour, so allowance must be made for the possibility that late degrees of Aries rose. Either way it is not a good start. An early Ascendant, especially with Saturn there, suggests that the querent should delay any decision. If Ashmole is signified by Venus we see that he is in detriment and opposes the 1st house. In other words, he puts himself in a position where he damages himself, and has put himself into the hands of his enemies. Notably, Saturn rules the 11th and 12th houses, perhaps signifying pretended friends, but certainly bringing scandal to Ashmole through a friend.

If late degrees of Aries rise and he is Mars, then we see a conjunction with Jupiter (peregrine and an accidental infortune because it rules the unfortunate 8th and its other sign of Pisces is intercepted in the unfortunate 12th). But this is a separating conjunction, and the next application of Mars is with Saturn. Actually, this is a mutual application which indicates a sudden event, and as the malefics are involved, a sudden, evil event would be anticipated. Saturn remains the ruler of the 11th and 12th houses and is in the 1st, so the previous delineation maintains. Therefore, he should have judged that such an action was prejudicial to him. I would speculate that late degrees of Aries rose and that the die had already been cast.

A year later, on 16th November 1647[318], the horary perfected and Ashmole notes: "This morning Lilly told me of my discovering his secrets to Wharton." Josten also notes that Ashmole does appear to have supplied Wharton with information which provided the latter with his ammunition, so Ashmole did not simply publish the pamphlet. Two months after that on 5 January 1648[319], Ashmole writes: "This evening I delivered to Mr. Lilly Picatrix[320] and was reconciled with him."

We might speculate on how Lilly perceived Ashmole's treachery when we consider Lilly's "Epistle to the Reader" in *The World's Catastrophe* (1647): "But one day, happily complaining of my want of convenient time, to Translate these succeeding Treatises unto Elias Ashmole Esquire, my noble Friend, … This worthy Gentleman no sooner heard my complaint, but offered Balsom to the wound, and most humanely and courteously proferred his learned indeavours…" Lilly continues in praise of Ashmole's abilities, "…that being in years so young, should understand and distinguish terms and names, so obsolete, and not frequently vulgar; and yet hath he rendred them in our mother-tongue in so compliant and decent Phrase, as might well have become an Antiquary of double his years.".

---

[318]MS Ashm. 1136, f.205

[319]MSAshm. 1136, f.184

We also know that Ashmole had worked with Lilly on *Christian Astrology*[321] which was published in November 1647. In that same month Lilly confronted Ashmole. Whether Lilly had provided Ashmole with paid employment is unknown, but it is possible as Ashmole was in need of money. He had not yet procured an advantageous marriage and he still had not resumed his law practice. Lilly had been betrayed by the person he had tried to help and who had been working closely with him, perhaps even under his personal tutelage and protection.

Although they had been reconciled, a month and a half later on 19th February 1648[322] Ashmole had further cause for concern: "At noon I received the book written in the behalf of Mr. Lilly. At 2: after noon I first read it. Now scandal threatens to fall upon me upon the £ of ♄ and ☿ which was the 18th day." This "book" was in fact a pamphlet supposedly written by a cavalier officer[323]. It answered and refuted Wharton's allegations in his pamphlet against Lilly.

This reply was published in London in January 1648, and moreover it has been suggested that Lilly himself wrote it. However, in the postscript the anonymous author relates a meeting he had with Wharton subsequent to the publication of Wharton's broadside:

> I met Wharton since my last coming to towne, and inquiring of the man seriously, wheretofore he thus abused Lilly about Hows, and why he imputed such ignorance to him, when as all men who read his writings know otherwise, … he sincerely professed, that he did much admire Lilly's parts, but knew not how to be revenged of him otherwayes then by thus aspersing him, and that he was importuned hereunto by one M. and by one Ashinole [the "in" is almost certainly a printer's misreading of "m"] an Atturney, as for his part he protested he knew no one thing of it either true or false. He further sayd that if he mentioned not Lilly in his Mercuries [the name of Wharton's almanacs], they would not sell;…"

---

[320]A grimoire of astrological magic.

[321]In one of Ashmole's notes in the manuscript of Lilly's autobiography he says: "I devised the forms and fashions of the severall schemes."

On the same day Ashmole drew a horary for the question: "Whether that book was of Lilly's contriving and whether he be not a secret enemy or public enemy of mine …, 2 ♍ ascending."[324]

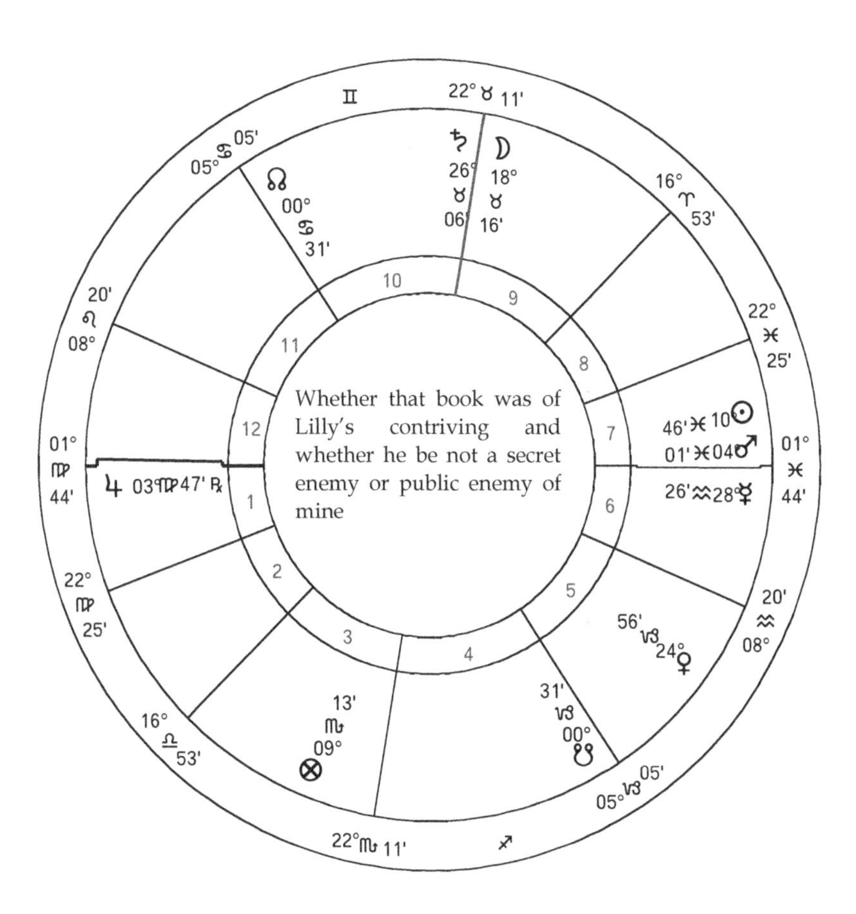

[322]MS Ashm. 1136, f. 185v

[323]MS Ashm. 546

From the question, it is clear that Ashmole is wondering how long Lilly had known about his complicity with Wharton, especially when he mentions "a secret enemy". It is possible that Lilly had known about it for some time and had awaited the publication of *Christian Astrology* before dealing with Ashmole's treachery. Either Lilly hid his knowledge from Ashmole throughout their reconciliation, or the second pamphlet supporting him did indeed reveal information that Lilly had not been privy to. If that is so then clearly Lilly could not have written it himself.

In this chart we know the Ascendant that Ashmole calculated, but care is still required with all the other house cusps. He says that it was 4 hours after noon, but to achieve this Ascendant I have used a time of 4.30 pm.

The notable thing about this horary is the angularity; all but Venus are angular. Our problem here is in deciding which planet Ashmole considered to be Lilly's significator. It is tempting to view the question in two parts: did Lilly have something to do with the writing of the pamphlet, and is he an enemy to Ashmole? If Lilly *had* been connected with the publishing or writing of the pamphlet, then by necessity it would mean that he was Ashmole's enemy. However, it is also possible that Lilly was Ashmole's enemy and yet had nothing to do with the pamphlet.

Using the astrological rules given by Lilly (*Christian Astrology* p. 384), where a potential enemy is named, the 7th and its ruler are significant. Judging by the Sun and Mars in the 7th, I suggest that Ashmole had more than just Lilly to fear. Mercury and Jupiter, significators of the two parties, are in a mutually applying opposition. Of this Lilly says: " *the enmity, difference or controversie is approaching, is not yet over, will grow to a greater height then now it is, and the party enquired after* [Lilly in this case], *doth what in him lyes to thwait and crosse the occasions of the querent.*" In other words, this opposition, because it is applying, means that Lilly is going to do everything he can to obstruct Ashmole. This is more so, since the aspect is mutually applying which is a sudden and ill application arguing that a great deal of contention and animosity were to follow.

---

[324]MS Ashm. 1136, f. 185v

Moreover, Lilly says that if the ruler of the 7th (Jupiter) is in conjunction or in aspect with any planet which is in square or opposition to the ruler of the Ascendant (Mercury), or the Moon, without reception, then "the quesited is averse and an enemy to the querent". In this chart, Jupiter is in aspect by mutually applying square with Saturn and Saturn is in square to Mercury; worse still is that Saturn disposits Mercury. So, we have both arguments for Lilly's being Ashmole's enemy. There is no need to consider the secret enemy part of the question, because since he has named Lilly, the rules refer back to the 7th house.

What needs to be considered in this chart is the prominence of Saturn; it is in the 10th and is fairly strong because of its mutual reception with Venus and because of its position. Venus is in the Saturn ruled 5th, the turned 11th of Lilly's assistants. We should also note that the 7th cusp is close to Lilly's natal Ascendant. So, I think that there is no doubt that Lilly was doing everything he could to neutralise, and possibly avenge, Ashmole's disloyalty.

Mercury and Jupiter in each other's houses show direct confrontation, but whereas Mercury is moving further into Lilly's hands, Lilly is retrograding out of Ashmole's. In fact, after Ashmole collides with Jupiter, he is confronted by a dignified Mars, and as he does that, he becomes combust and is obliterated by the Sun: Ashmole is vanquished.

As to whether or not Lilly wrote the pamphlet or was complicit in its writing and publishing remains uncertain. It seems doubtful that Lilly wrote it; his style of writing was well known, and a letter from him is printed in the same pamphlet. He may well have known that it was going to be published, but whether he caused it to be published is doubtful. We might consider that he had little need to extend himself in his own defence because he had many friends who would do that for him as is indicated in Ashmole's horary chart. The last passage referring to the conversation the author was supposed to have had with Wharton, is interesting. Either Wharton *did* say those things, or it was based on detailed information from someone else of Ashmole's involvement. It is noticeable that the prominent and exalted Moon, the carrier of messages, is ruler of the 11th of Ashmole's friends.

It is unlikely that either pamphlet changed anyone's mind about Wharton or Lilly. But these allegations (that Lilly had tricked a lady into marrying his client), were very dangerous for Lilly, and had to be countered.

On the 14th March 1648 Wharton was imprisoned, and there is a suggestion that Ashmole suspected Lilly of causing the arrest. Notice that the Moon in the preceding horoscope signifies Ashmole's friends and after its trine to Venus, it runs straight into Saturn of imprisonment. Saturn and Venus are co-operating through mutual reception. The Moon also applies to the friend's 12th.

Wharton escaped Newgate in September 1649 but was recaptured on 21st November 1649. The next day Ashmole approached Lilly on Wharton's behalf, and that is the first mention we find of their meeting since February 1648. So, their estrangement had been prolonged, although Ashmole had attended at least two Astrologers' Feasts during this period and it is possible that they had met there.

Ashmole recounts that when he had apprised Lilly of the situation regarding Wharton, Lilly replied: "himselfe very sorry, because he knew … it was intended to hang him, and most generously (forgetting the quarell that had been betweene the Captaine and him) promised me to use his Interest with Mr: Bulstrode Whitlock (his Patron) to obteyne his release." Without labouring the point, Lilly achieved this, although Ashmole insists that he had to "constantly solicit" Lilly's assistance.

The ice seems to have been broken because on 26th January 1650 Ashmole proposed a horary question to Lilly[325]. Then on 7th April[326] he asks the horary question, "Whether Mr. Lilly will prove a real friend to me in the suit against Sir Humphrey?" which gives evidence of his having approached Lilly for personal assistance. A little later that month on 29th April 1650[327] he notes that at about 8.30 am he gave "chambers to Lilly". Presumably meaning that Lilly had come to him for legal services. However, on the same day, Ashmole

[325]MS Ashm. 374, f. 6v

[326]MS Ashm 374, f. 25

posed another horary question to Lilly, and again on 7th May 1650. Then, at the publication of Ashmole's book *Fascilus Chemicus*, Lilly's name is the first in a list of names, possibly of Ashmole's friends, who were to receive a copy.

[327]MS Ashm. 374, f. 31v

Lilly's nativity

A further indication of the strengthening of their friendship is demonstrated when Ashmole and Lilly together visited Dr: Ardee on 3rd June 1650[328]. Ashmole asked at least one further horary of Lilly leading to the horary of interest here. Their friendship had been repaired enough for Lilly to reveal his natal data to Ashmole. However, their reconciliation was not complete and Ashmole remained distrustful of Lilly because his note for the 25th September 1650 at 8.10 am[329] records the following rather well-known horary:

"Whether Mr. Lilly told me true last night, when he said that he had ♓ ascending and ⊕ in 1 ♏ in his nativity."

---

[328]MS Ashm. 1136, f. 22v

[329]MS Ashm. 374, f.66

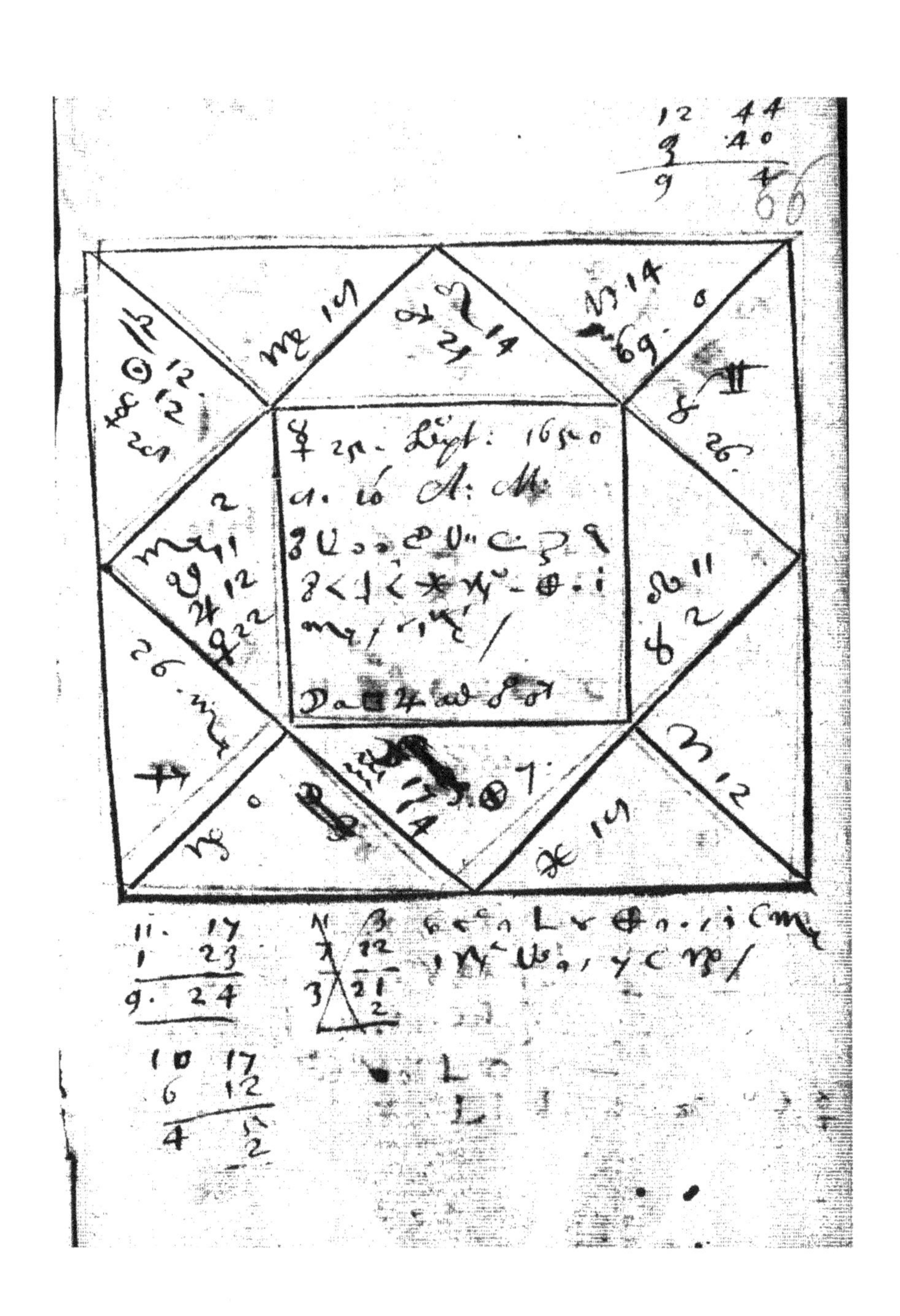

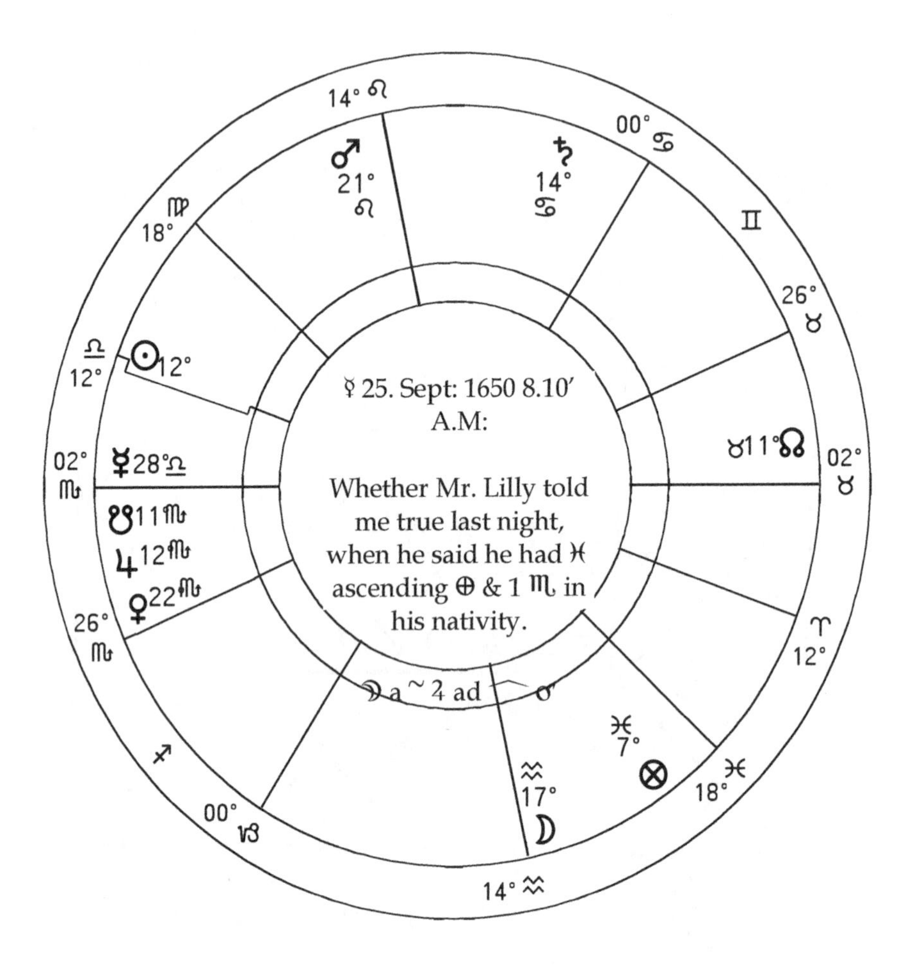

Again, using *Christian Astrology* (p.192) for the judgement, most arguments in this chart are of truth, others plead the opposite.

Ashmole attempted to rectify Lilly's horoscope resulting in an Ascendant of 25° Virgo. "He saith he hath 3.56 of ♓ ascending in his nativity."

"This scheme I believe is the truer, for midheaven came to the ⊕ as well as △ to ☽ at one time, and when he married first he had a good estate with his old wife." (MSAshm. 312). But at another point Ashmole gives Lilly's Ascendant as 3° 56' Pisces, indicating that he had by that time accepted Lilly's word. Gadbury's rectification[330] is well known, even being included in the Regulus facsimile edition of *Christian Astrology*; the Ascendant there is 4° 36' Pisces.

Fortunately, we have Lilly's horoscope and accidents used by himself[331] which Ashmole copied and seems to have acquired following Lilly's death. At the end of Lilly's list of directions, the last entry being for 1664, Ashmole writes: "Thus far Mr. William Lilly's nativity was directed by himselfe. He dyed the 9 of June 1681 of dead palsey.", implying that Ashmole accepted this horoscope as correct. Josten also notes that it is likely that this is the true scheme and that Ashmole's suspicions were unfounded. I agree that it is the true nativity, but I doubt that Lilly gave Ashmole the whole truth. However, finally, we have the nativity of William Lilly, Astrologer.

---

[330]*Collectio Geniturarum*, John Gadbury, 1662, London.

[331]MSAshm. 394, f.108v

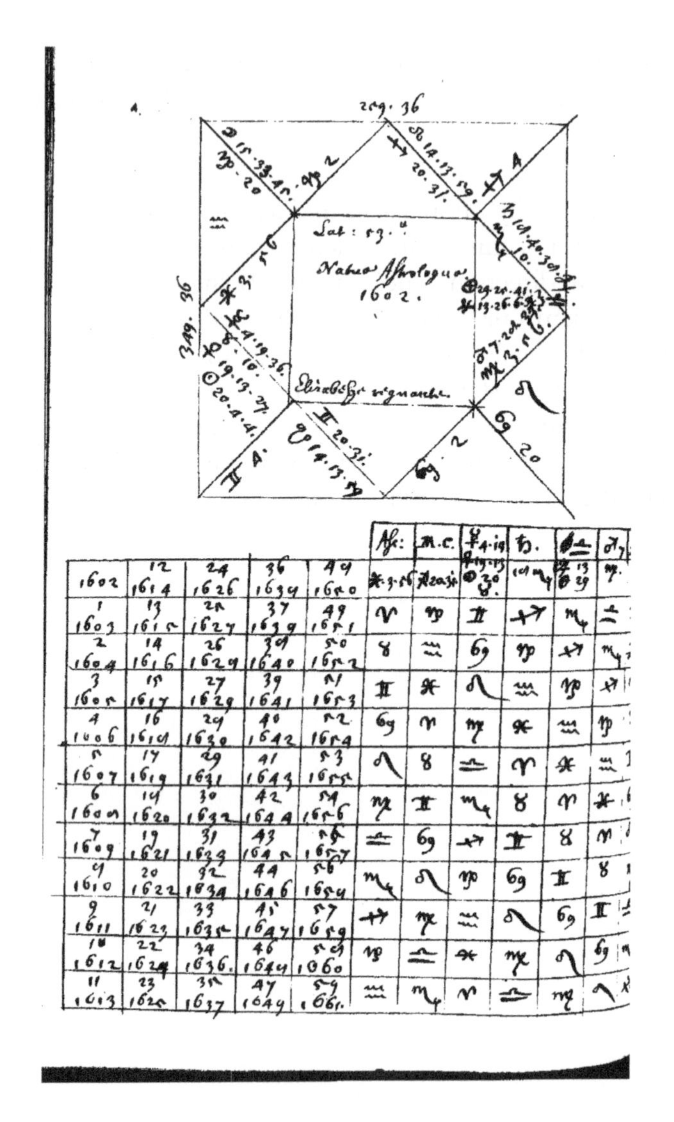

Figure 1: Lilly's nativity with a list of profections

Each planet is calculated precisely to seconds of arc, and the Part of Fortune is placed at 29°26' Libra. So, Lilly did tell the truth about his Ascendant, but perhaps he still did not trust Ashmole completely. The Part of Fortune is calculated from the positions of the Ascendant, Sun and Moon, so by giving Ashmole the incorrect position, Lilly cast doubt on those three very important positions. In fact, with the Part of Fortune itself and the

Midheaven, Lilly caused uncertainty about what are known as the five Hylegiacal places which are crucial for directions. Such a device would also ensure that should anyone ever publish his nativity – as Gadbury did – Lilly would always know the source of that information.

The following reproduction shows part of Lilly's directions.

Anni Domini	Ascend.	Med. Coeli	☉ Direct	☉ Convers	☽ Direct	[illegible]	⊕ Direct	⊕ Convers	♄ Direct	♃ Direct	♂ Direct	♀ Direct	☿ Direct	Anni aetatis
	3 ♓ 56	20 ♐ 31	20 ♉ 4	20 ♉ 4	15 ♍ 34	[illegible]	29 ♎ 26	29 ♎ 26	10 ♏ 41	13 ♎ 26	7 ♍ 29	19 ♉ 13	4 ♉ 19	
1602				[illegible] 45			[illegible]	[illegible]	[illegible] 47	[illegible] 23	[illegible]			0 / 1602
1603	[illegible]						[illegible]	[illegible]		[illegible]	[illegible]	[illegible]		1 / 1603
1604	[illegible]		[illegible] 4				[illegible]	[illegible] 7		[illegible] 37	[illegible]	[illegible]	[illegible]	2 / 1604
1605	[illegible] 57		Pleiades 0	[illegible]		[illegible]	[illegible]	[illegible]			[illegible]		[illegible]	3 / 1605
1606	[illegible]	[illegible] 36	[illegible] 56	[illegible] 48		[illegible]	[illegible]	[illegible]		[illegible]	[illegible]	[illegible]	[illegible]	4 / 1606
1607	[illegible]	[illegible]		[illegible] 4			[illegible]				[illegible]	[illegible]	[illegible]	5 / 1607
1608	[illegible]	[illegible]	[illegible] 9		[illegible]	[illegible]		[illegible] 24	[illegible]	[illegible]	[illegible] 13	♊		6 / 1608
1609			[illegible]		[illegible]	[illegible]	[illegible]	[illegible]	[illegible] 49		[illegible]	[illegible]		7 / 1609
1610				[illegible]		[illegible]	[illegible]		[illegible] 20	[illegible]	[illegible]		[illegible]	8 / 1610
1611	[illegible]			[illegible] 41	[illegible] 49	[illegible]	[illegible]			[illegible] 38	[illegible] 9			9 / 1611
1612	[illegible]	[illegible] 24	[illegible] 38				[illegible]	[illegible]			[illegible]	[illegible]	[illegible]	10 / 1612
1613	[illegible] 49			[illegible]		[illegible]	[illegible]	[illegible]		[illegible]	[illegible]		[illegible]	11 / 1613
1614	[illegible]	[illegible] 57	[illegible] 41	♈	[illegible] 48	[illegible]	[illegible] 23			[illegible] 30	[illegible] 19	[illegible]	[illegible]	12

Figure 2: a part page of Lilly's directions

Using Lilly's own methods of calculation, it would appear that he had a phlegmatic/sanguine temperament and Jupiter, although weak, is the strongest planet in the chart with the Moon in close second place. We know from his own question about Master B's. houses (*Christian Astrology* p.219), that he himself placed emphasis on this Jupiter.

We see evidence of this temperament in his moving from and to London after his inheritance. He left London in the first place to escape fame, for peace and quiet (phlegmatic), and returned for the opposite reason (sanguine). Eventually he set up home permanently in Hersham.

If we look at the nativity from just one point of view, that of scholarship, he tells us in *Christian Astrology* that neither temperament type make good students, so a mixture will not enhance that. And yet we know that he was an excellent student and scholar. The laziness associated with the phlegmatic temperament is not apparent in what we know of Lilly and in that regard we might accept the detrimented Moon as being obsessively hardworking. It is in square to a sanguine and angular Jupiter which would lift the gloom associated with that Saturnian Moon. However, its application to the sextile of Saturn, repeats the emphasis on work and also reminds of us of his first removing from London due to "*hypocondriak melancholly*".

Although Saturn is in poor condition, we might accept its conjunction with Agena as improving its more malefic qualities. Agena is a first magnitude star of the nature of Venus and Jupiter, and as its nature is not Saturnian but rather the opposite, we might expect a mollification.

Jupiter as the strongest planet rules both the 9th and 10th houses, and is in the sign of Saturn's exaltation. So, there is some justification for describing a scholar of some achievement. We might also note that Mercury, although a long way from the Ascendant, is still in the 1st. But what can be said about Mercury in Taurus? In the system of humours, Mercury is choleric because it is oriental of the Sun. So, we gain another clue about Lilly's speed of thought and sharpness of tongue. When we add that to its trine to Mars in Virgo, we get an image of not only a quick and volatile mind, but one which is also enthusiastic and passionate.

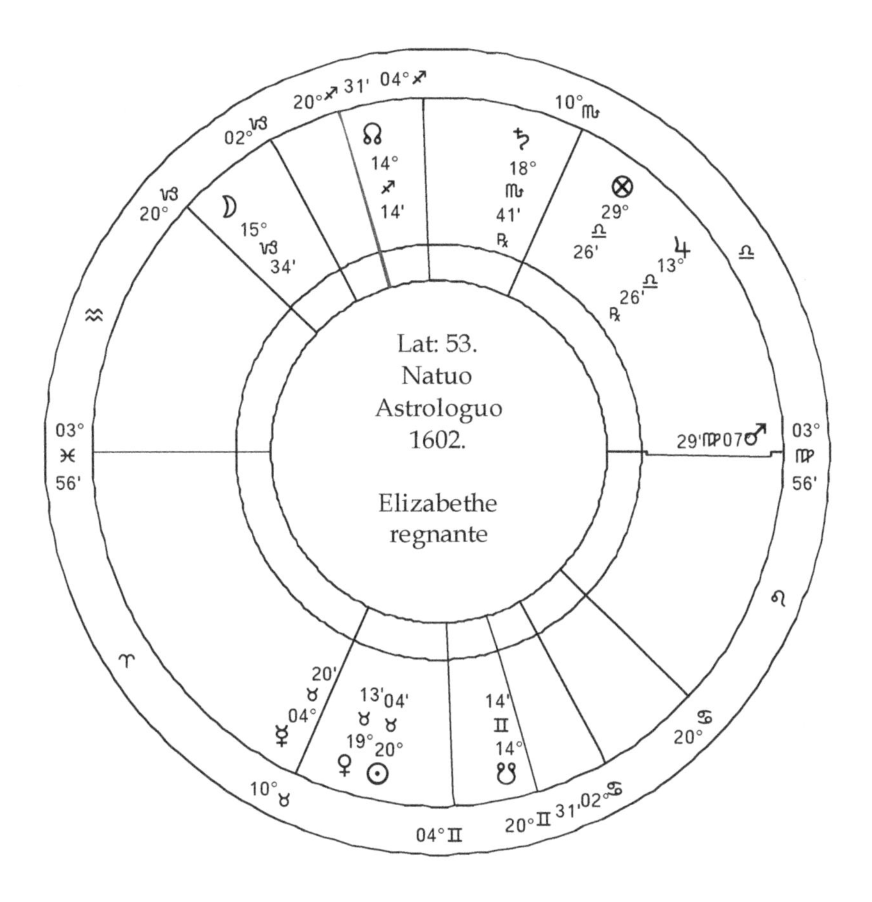

Focusing on Jupiter, we see a likeable, affable man with a generous spirit. We know that he was sociable and a genial host who kept a good table. He had many friends and supporters, and the letters which exist show that he was held in high regard, and that his help was often sought. This idea is supported by Jupiter's dispositor, Venus, which is in its own sign.

1634: a busy year

We might also look briefly at one year in his life and compare it to his own profections and directions. In 1634 he notes the following events in his autobiography, and because of that they must have had a special place in his memory:

- bought Argol's Primum Mobile;
- taught Astrology to Sir George Peckham;
- bought a half share of thirteen houses in The Strand for £530 (Master B's. houses);
- on the 18th November he married Jane Rowley ("of the nature of Mars");
- he, Davy Ramsey and others went to Westminster Abbey and dowsed for treasure;
- at the end of this year, or the beginning of the next he interceded magically for an unmarried and pregnant young woman;
- he developed melancholia which began to affect his physical health and he lost weight. The following year it increased to hypochondriac melancholy;
- his public profile increased to beyond his capacity;
- Davy Ramsey introduced him to Sir William Pennington of Muncaster with whom Lilly became very friendly;
- taught the magical art of constructing sigils, lamens and the use of divining or dowsing rods to the Dutchman John Heginus.

The natural ruler of buying and selling, teaching, magic and astrology is Mercury, as the natural ruler of property (real estate), and melancholy is Saturn. His renown is associated with the Sun and possibly the Moon, and Venus is the natural ruler of love and marriage. Therefore we should find all of these planets activated in his profections and directions, as we should the accidental rulers of these matters in his nativity. This has Jupiter ruling the 1st and 10th houses, Mercury ruling the 7th and 4th houses, and Saturn ruling the 11th and 12th houses, with the Moon ruling the 6th.

His profections for that year had Scorpio on the Ascendant and Leo (natal 8th) on the MC (natal intercepted 6th), Mercury, Venus and the Sun fell in Capricorn (natal 11th and 12th), Saturn in Cancer (natal 5th and 6th), Jupiter and Part of Fortune in Gemini (natal 3rd and 4th), Mars in Taurus (natal 2nd), and the Moon was in Virgo (natal 7th).

Keeping these planets in mind, Lilly notes that in 1634 the Ascendant was directed to the opposition of Saturn, the conjunction of the Sun and the conjunction of Venus. The MC was directed to the 12th cusp. The Sun's converse directions were to the terms of Mercury, the sextile of the Sun, Mercury and the Moon. The converse Part of Fortune met with the contra-antiscium of Saturn (with latitude) and the square of Saturn itself. Jupiter was in sextile to its natal position and conjunct the North Node. Finally, Mars came to the conjunction of Saturn (with latitude).

All of the planets one would expect to find involved in the various events of that year, both naturally and accidentally, are indeed repeatedly prominent, enough to ensure that subjectivity is diminished.

And so, the mutual distrust faded and the friendship held firm for the rest of Lilly's life. There is a touching moment in one of Lilly's letters[332] to Ashmole in 1677, when at the end of giving his general news and before sending love, Lilly writes just two words: "my eys."[333] In that brief but moving comment we can read of Lilly's fears and grief over his rapidly diminishing eyesight, and he confides all of that in his dear friend.

---

[332]MS Rawl. D. 864, ff. 126-7v

[333]MS Rawl. D. 864, ff. 126-7v.

Monster of Ingratitude

by

Peter Stockinger and Sue Ward

Introduction

The primary aim of this book is to correct the myriad errors found in various biographies of William Lilly. We attempt this through the lens of the protracted enmity of John Gadbury towards Lilly. Although the subject matter itself might appear to be trivial and hardly worth our efforts, we use it to demonstrate the far greater problem of poor research and slack scholarship in the history of astrology. As astrologers ourselves, we are aware of the perennial complaint that Academia does not take astrology seriously. In light of this, we would argue that whilst astrologers treat their subject and its history in a lax manner, respect from the Academy will never be forthcoming. Moreover, such laxity has allowed inaccuracies to be perpetuated and, in the biographies of William Lilly, have led to other areas of his work being impugned and maligned.

With any history, accuracy largely depends on the availability of primary sources and on the conclusion the historian draws from them. The fewer there are of the former, the more is subject to opinion. In the case of William Lilly, there is a wealth of material over and above the well-known autobiography[334], so it would be fair for the reader to expect a good deal of accuracy and thus less opinion from the biographer or commentator. So far this has not been the case and we will attempt to redress that imbalance through our investigations here.

---

[334]William Lilly's autobiography has been reprinted many times over the years but, compared to the original autograph, all printed editions are flawed. Sue Ward's full annotated transcription of the autograph can be found herein.

In particular, a reliance on the prolific John Gadbury as a trustworthy historical source has produced the greatest number of misunderstandings and mistakes. His version of events, even relatively minor ones, has been treated as historical fact without, it appears, further investigation. As a result, this has led to, among other things, an insidious, creeping criticism of William Lilly and his work on a much wider scale. For example, in a footnote, Keith Thomas writes:

> Thus William Lilly's *Christian Astrology* (1647), the most influential vernacular treatise of the seventeenth century, was said to be little more than a translation of the medieval Arab astrologer Albohazen Haly filius Abenragel (J. Gadbury, *Dies Novissimus* [1664] p47). Lilly, though claiming that the first part of the book at least was original (Autobiography, p.129), appended an impressive bibliography, which gave some indication of his dependence upon his predecessors.[335]

Thomas refers to the following attack by Gadbury which in fact refers to the latter's accusations of plagiarism against Lilly which we will deal with later on. It reads:

> And for the greater part of his *Christian Astrology*, myself saw in manuscript in the hands of the beforementioned Dr. *Fiske*, which by the Doctor was translated from *Haly, de judiciis astrorum*, as many of L's best Friends know also to be true; and yet has he been so impudent therein, as to print in Pag. 830 of that his book, *That he hath not advised with any man living in any thing comprehended in that Work.*[336]

The context of the above quoted passage is that Lilly is explaining that he had been housebound whilst writing the third book because of the plague to which he lost two servants, and he explains further:

> My great affliction at present conclusion of this Work, bids thee accept my good will, and passe by my very many imperfections in

[335]Thomas, Keith: *Religion and the Decline of Magic*, Penguin Books, England, 1982, p336.

[336]Gadbury, John: *Dies Novissimus*, London, 1664, p 46f.

> the preceding Treatises, having advised with no man living in any thing comprehended in all the three Books.

This appears to link "my very many imperfections" with "having advised with no man living". There are two possible interpretations of this passage: that he had been unable to have the book proof-read or checked and thus there are likely to be many errors, or that he has not referred to the work of any living authority. It is always difficult to know exactly what Gadbury complains about, as here. Is he complaining that Lilly has referred to ancient authors like Haly, or that it had been translated by Fiske? Either way, it is hard to understand why this would contradict Lilly's words. Thomas is correct, the bibliography contained within *Christian Astrology* is very large, but as a scholar himself it is curious that he should find this dubious. Lilly is quite clear about his references and provides his sources in what would now be called a select bibliography[337]. The only originality to which Lilly ever alludes is in the structure of the book, the organisation of the contents and the method of application[338]. Moreover, Lilly was capable of translating these old manuscripts for himself and did. However, he explains quite clearly as follows:

> ...and if my Judgments doe vary from the common Rules of the ANCIENTS, let the Candid Reader excuse me, sith he may still follow their Principles if he please: and he must know, that from my Conversation in their Writings, I have attained the Method I follow.[339]

This needs no translation and is very plain and might have been referred to by scholars such as Thomas, but yet again Gadbury has been preferred.

By way of example of the problem, in his biography[340] Parker apparently quotes directly from Lilly's *Autobiography* and proceeds to produce the quotation of a particular episode. In fact this quotation does not appear in the autograph but in *Monarchy or No Monarchy: the Life and Death of King*

---

[337]Lilly, William: *Christian Astrology*, London, 1647, p833ff.

[338]Ward: William Lilly's autobiography, op. cit. p63

Charles[341]. Parker also nominates Gadbury as Lilly's "rival" when referring to Gadbury's first pamphlet attacking Lilly[342]. No matter how well affected towards Gadbury one is, it is impossible that he could have rivalled Lilly at this point. The analysis of the final episode of Gadbury's attacks on Lilly[343] is skewed and demonstrates little consideration of facts, having decided from the outset that Lilly was less than honest and honourable. For all that, Parker's biography is not presented by him as a scholarly work, as historian Dr. Ann Geneva has pointed out in her PhD thesis[344] which has been published as *Astrology and the Seventeenth Century Mind,* stating:

> ... Familiar to All ... is unsatisfactory, both because of its innocence of footnotes and the alternating credulity and spurious scepticism which inform the author's treatment of his subject.[345]

Therefore it is difficult to understand why scholars rely upon it so frequently and ignore its fictions.

Following the facsimile reprint in 1985 of William Lilly's magnum opus, *Christian Astrology*[346], there has been an increasing interest in Lilly. Since this republication the numbers of both astrologers and non-astrologers commenting on his work, politics and personal life have increased proportionately. The majority of those commentators rely for their information on a limited number of sources: a single biography, subsidiary biographies based upon it, and occasionally on the 18th and 19th century published versions of Lilly's autobiography[347]. This autobiography, first published in 1715 after the autograph continues to be the main source of information regarding Lilly's life. Written in 1667, it is more a memoir to satisfy his friend, Elias Ashmole, and recounts the more notable events and individuals of Lilly's life. It does seem to rely on memory rather than notes taken at the time, and there are places where Ashmole corrects the manuscript in this regard. Lilly gives very little personal detail apart from the opening pages where he outlines his early years, his arrival in London and his marriages. The remainder refers to his career, the political situation of the time and the people he met and knew.

339Lilly, William: *Christian Astrology*, facsimile reprint of 1st ed. 1647, Regulus, Exeter 1985, p143.

The biographers, Derek Parker[348] and Patrick Curry[349], use the published editions as a main source. Curry states that he used the second edition from 1715, while Parker's choice was the edition of 1822, for its ease of accessibility[350]. It is instructive to note that Professor Josten[351] says, "[Lilly's autobiography] has been printed in several editions, none of which is wholly reliable"[352] (this does not refer to Curry's article for the *Oxford Dictionary of National Biography*[353] (*ODNB*) which was published much later and, for the same reason, Geneva's thesis).

Although published nearly thirty years after *Familiar to All*, Curry follows Parker by including many of his sources, for example, Elias Ashmole's *Autobiographical Notes*[354] and Keith Thomas's *Religion and the Decline of Magic*[355], and by not providing the interested historian or astrologer with the exact derivation of the quotations from which they draw their conclusions. While this is standard practise for the *ODNB* where often only a bibliography is provided, the many pamphlets and almanacs written by Lilly and his colleagues are essential for a deeper understanding of the man, but such information as they contain is often buried within them. This might be one of the reasons why succeeding commentators using the above-mentioned biographies as their sources, have never delved more deeply into the subject to learn about the complexities of Lilly's life and his relationships with his contemporaries. A close look at remarks from those commentators, whose articles can be found aplenty on the internet, reveals that none of them has looked much beyond Parker or the *ODNB*. Where they have availed themselves of other source material, all seem to have repeated Parker's rather jaded conclusions. The result of this has been a perpetuation of misunderstandings and inaccuracies.

For example, Parker writes:

> But this had made him [Lilly] enemies, and during the next fifteen years – indeed, virtually for the rest of his life – he was to be attacked by almost every other astrologer in England[356].

[340]Parker, Derek: Familiar To All, William Lilly and Astrology in the Seventeenth Century, Jonathan Cape, London, 1975 p84.

As with a great deal of this biography, there is no given source of this information. It is true that Lilly was attacked numerous times, but there is no evidence whatsoever that it was by "almost every astrologer in England". Indeed, the evidence points to his being supported by them. The names of John Booker, Richard Edlin, Richard Saunders, Henry Coley, Vincent Wing, Jeremy Shakerley come to mind as those of prominent astrologers who were friends, associates or supporters of William Lilly. Most of those named owed a debt to Lilly for his friendship and support. In another remark related to the attacks of Thomas Gataker against Lilly, Parker states that in 1654 Gadbury was "no friend of Lilly"[357], whereas at this time they were most certainly on friendly terms, as we will show.

In order to demonstrate how a more wide-ranging selection of sources can reveal surprising information and lead to alternative conclusions, we shall draw attention to the turbulent relationship between William Lilly and John Gadbury which hitherto has been treated as a protracted exchange of insults between professional and political rivals. We shall show that the enmity which developed had a much different cause than has been supposed and was in reality a very one-sided affair. To explore this relationship properly a thorough examination of Lilly's life and work is required, but we shall limit ourselves here to that biographical information required for a fuller understanding of this particular aspect of Lilly's life[358]. Information found in modern commentaries on this subject is sparse, thus their authors' opinions and conclusions are unreliable. We have investigated, as far as possible, all extant published texts of the period and beyond which refer to the relationship between Lilly and Gadbury.

[341]Lilly, William: Monarchy or No Monarchy: the Life and Death of King Charles, London, 1651, p108.

[342]Ibid, p197.

PART 1
Lilly and Gadbury

Chapter 1 - William Lilly (1602-1681)

[343]Ibid, pp252-256

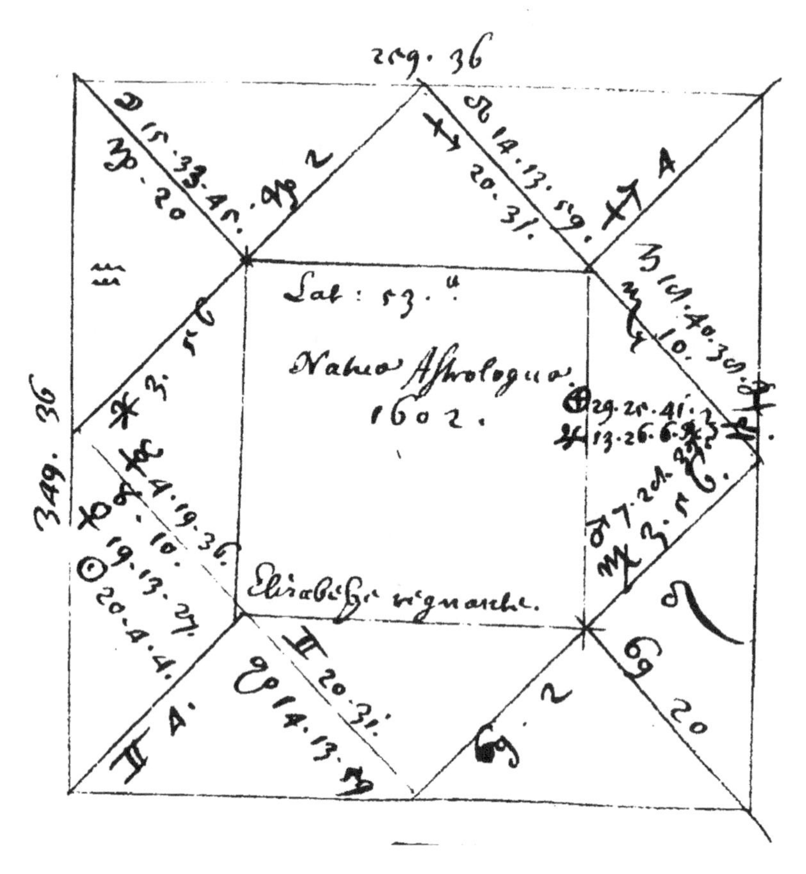

In 1645, in his *Anglicus, Peace or No Peace*[359] Lilly describes himself, through astrology, as a flawed individual, but one who recognised the blessings of his life. Given the relative wealth of personal information that can be drawn from these pages, it is worth reproducing the relevant passage in its entirety:

> **[The criticisms of astrology]** Astrologie, for many years, what with the prevaricate opinion of some scrupulous Clergie-men, and the impostures of some other pretended Astrologers, was cast into that obloquie, few would believe any such thing was in rerum natura [in the nature of things of the world]. Many also conceived we maintained a fatall necessity; a monstrous and terrible Mistake. Not

[344]Geneva, Ann*: England,s Propheticall Merline Decoded*, Dissertation by Ann Geneva, Doctor of Philosophy in History, State University of New York at Stony Brook, 1988

one Author in our Art, whose Works are extant now above the earth, or ever were, was of so corrupt a judgment. We unanimously say, Providence is the Governesse of all things, and that things are affected by providence, not as necessary, but as contingent. What is he, or his name, that is of us, and faith, Events do necessarily ensue upon those things in our power? The Mercurian Vermines of the time must escandalize us, although we hold nothing falls out necessarily, but that it may either be so or not so, as God pleaseth, who is not concluded under any necessity, or his will confined by fatall necessity; for he is Creator of necessity it self. Give us less leave to explain our selves, and we say, that God laid necessity upon the Stars, and they are constrained to keep those regular courses he first limited. These are no Heresies, or am I a Schismatick if I say, God stayed once the course of the Sun and Moon, whereby he shewed, he is not confined to necessity, but that according to his power all things are contingent. I let these things passe. ... The small conceit and opprobrious judgment the English Nation have of Astrologie, had also almost enforced me to silence:

[Need for astrology books in English] But considering it's rather want of Books fitted for the capacities of our English, then any wilfull defect in their understandings, I will write not onely now, but if God spare me life, I will make this Art hereafter perceptible to the meanest, and useful for every vulgar capacity, I hope to the content of the whole Kingdom.

[Astrological errors] Admit these my succeeding Predictions should fail, as they well may, it breeds no Heresie, no Schism: Consider, that we live within this City know not the daily passages thereof in every part thereof, nor can any relate them truely. For Gods sake, let us then have some favour assigned us, if we misse, that fetch our judgments from the Stars, seated in the Heavens: Its a great way thither, you all know. Do we make a Rent in the Church, or disjoint an Arm, or lop off a Branch? Ten thousand errours in Astrologie, summed up altogether with many more, make not up one Heresie.

---

[345]Geneva, Ann: Astrology and the Seventeenth Century Mind, William Lilly and the Language of the Stars, Manchester University Press, Manchester, 1995, p55

[346]Lilly: *Christian* Astrology, op. cit.

[From poverty to comfort] Many desire to know what I am, what's my Religion, how I stand affected to His Majestie, to His Cause; to the Parliament at Westminster, and their Cause. I was native of Diseworth in Leicester shire, and so a Bean-belly. I have cause to blesse God, and so I do, that I ever came to the City of London, which I did the 9 of April 1620. with an hundred pence in my purse, and no more: Per varios casus, per tot discrimina rerum [through various misfortunes and so many crises of affairs]: I am now as I am; have a competency: And yet if any Gentleman or man of quality desire it, I am content to read Astrologie, any part thereof, or to give further satisfaction, &c.

[Education and loyalty] I was Scholar to M. Brinsley of Ashby de la Zouch: all of my form are singular Divines, &c. If an enemy approach this Citie, I'll do my best for London, as Bonatus did for Forolivium, which when Pope Martin strictly besieged, and offered the Citizens bad Conditions, the Astrologer advised to patience, and upon an elected time, commanded his Citizens to issue and charge the enemies, which they did, & victimus omnes, saith he; we routed them all, and so freed the City of an insulting foe, and potent adversaries.

[Religion] My religion is according to the Reformed Protestant Church of England: and although my conversation and dealing in the World hath casually fallen out to be more with the Papist than Protestant (for I am not unknown to Franciscus de Sancta Clara, a most learned man: the liberty of the times I lived in, gave me leave and opportunity to converse with many Franciscans, in whom I found much reality; the Secular Priest I ever found a good fellow and not scrupulous; the Jesuite I never fancied, or much the Dominican: some have accused me of a Church-Papist) yet I professe before Almighty God, I never did encline to any one Popish Tenent, nor did any of the learned I ever met withal, seek my conversion unto them. In these unsetled times, I almost stand unresolved in what posture to steer my course. I read the Bible, run over the 39. Articles But in points now controverted, I rigidly

---

[347]According to the bibliography in *Familiar To All*, Parker used *Mr. Lilly's history of his life and times*, London, 1715, London 1721, Reprinted for Charles Baldwyn, London 1822.

adhere to that pious Tract of Master Hildersham, upon the fourth of John: He can be no Separatist that judicially reads that learned mans Works: He was as knowing a man in his time, as any now living. I was none of those that distracted or disturbed the Parliament about the Earl of Strafford, or ever cried Episcopacie down, or Presbytery up.

[Politics] I have subscribed to all Pensions for Peace, except that of the Virago faction. I gave my voice for Sir Gilbert Gerrard and Sir John Franklyn, Knights of the Shire for Middlesex; I hope they will prove honest Members. Peace, above all earthly blessings, do I wish to this Kingdom. I see deeper into a Milstone then many, and know by what Faction we are divided. I should be glad to see a sickly Commonwealth preserved and restored. Inæquissima Pax, justissimo Bello ante ferenda [I prefer the most unjust peace to the most righteous war]. We shall finde it so. I cannot cleave an hair in sunder; yet I see Peace is convenient. I see ruine approaching, the furious Angels Sword drawn: Here's not a David to pray, not an Abraham to intercede.

[Character] In my Nativity I have Venus in Taurus, in Cazimi with the Sun; I have Mercury in Taurus, and Mars in Virgine, two earthly Signes, the reason why my conceptions are so dull, and my Speech and Discourse so defective: I have Jupiter in Libra, near Spica Virginis, and Saturn in Scorpio, the Moon in Piscibus: I am a piece of a good fellow; my heart is larger than my fortune, and yet I live contented amidst all vexatious Taxes, of which I partake too often. I love money as my servant, I adore it not for my master: I rather give than take, and pitie where I cannot relieve. I partly forsee the evil event of these Intestine Jars: I would willingly contradict the naturall course thereof. My Clymactericall yeer of seven is to me troublesome; my Enneaticall yeer perilous and sickly: I am drawing neer one: the grand Mutations of my whole life ever begun in one of these. To the day of the writing hereof, and its the 12 of December 1644, I have run over more days then fifteen thousand five hundred and fifty nine: Before I attain sixteen thousand four hundred and twenty two days, I shall be in great hazard of my life.

[348]Parker: op. cit.

[349]Curry, Patrick: *Lilly, William (1602-1681)*, Oxford Dictionary of National Biography, Oxford University Press, 2004, accessible via http://www.oxforddnb.com/

[Current political situation] But that yeer which afflicts me, will stagger Monarchy and Kingdom. Its hard to expresse what Anima Mundi is, and yet Unicuique impressus character divinus [it imprints on each one a divine character]. I highly prize Monarchy, and extremely respect the Majestie and Honour attending it. I have just cause, and I do cordially esteem His Majestie now living, and His posterity: the War he maintains and countenanceth against His English and Scotish Subjects, I totally abhor: the end will be bitter. He was the worst of men, that advised his Majestie to decline his presence from Westminster, and his Parliament there residing; Let that man die childless, and his hoar head not go to the Grave or the Sepulchre of his fathers in quiet. But this was decreed long since, and he the instrumentall means of an unhappie Scourge to the English and Scotish people. …

[Publishing difficulties and threats] Should I speak Verity in its proper colours, it might procure me a suppression from writing any more. I am almost more plunged to get my Book licensed, then others to print twenty; and yet no exception in point of Art is taken, but against my expressions: I cannot flatter, I will not: To mince my judgement, and deliver ambiguous stuff, is to lessen the validity of Art. I stand upon the honour of my Nation, and somewhat upon my own repute, &c. I must either speak more then an Angel, or lesse then a Man: Speak what I can, I content not all, am understood by few, sentenced by all: Is there one of a thousand a competent judge for our Art? For the Discourse ensuing, its derived from the Rules of Astrologie; the success and verity thereof will either speak much for it self, or else it deceives me: Yet I tell thee, I never hold that Merchant wise, which adventures all his stock in one Bottom. I would provoke others to do their endeavours as well as my self, and in such a Dialect as is capable of understanding, and not in ambodextrous language, the fault of our predecessours, and of some living. As this Moneth, the later part thereof, and the beginning of January proved, so believe of the succeeding Moneths. Reader, pray for the peace of England, and safety of the City of London. I have much to say, for the benefit of my Countrey; but being curbed in my expressions, I purposely omit what was intended, and silently rest …

---

[350]Parker: op. cit. p263

He was born on April 30th, 1602 (OS) in Diseworth, Leicestershire, where he spent the first eighteen years of his life. He and his family were of yeoman stock but, because of his father's falling into poverty, he had to return home from grammar school in Ashby-de-la-Zouch. It was here that he had been taught grammar, rhetoric, Latin and Greek by the Puritan schoolmaster, John Brinsley[360]. Realising that he would be unable to enter university, and to avoid a life of farming, he accepted an offer made to him by his family's solicitor and moved to London to make his fortune there.

Lilly would spend the next six years as the servant of Gilbert Wright, a member of the Company of Salters, and Lilly's own description of his duties leaves us in no doubt about his lowly status. However, being able to read and write, he became indispensable and impressed his illiterate master with his hard work and honesty. His good fortune really began in 1627 when Gilbert Wright died and after which he successfully courted his master's widow, the much older Ellen Whitehaire, whom he eventually married. She died only six years later which left Lilly with a degree of financial security and thus the wherewithal to buy books and the time to study.

Too much is made of this because, from a modern perspective, Lilly's behaviour may seem materialistic at best and cynical at worst. However, matches were made in much different ways than we understand now, and before the mercies of a Welfare State each had to take care of himself and his family. 'Making a good match' was part of this attempt to survive for both parties. Lilly could not have engineered this marriage, there were too many potential obstacles, indeed they kept the marriage a secret for two years in order to avoid those challenges. Lilly had proved himself to be discreet, dependable and trustworthy and Ellen Whitehaire had grown to know him well. What else is required as the basis for a marriage of this kind? Having accused Lilly of "a nicely managed courtship" in the case of his first wife[361], and then, when referring to the death of Lilly's second wife, Jane, Parker goes on to write, "whom he also probably married for her money." Since Lilly writes very little about his private life, it is difficult to understand the grounds for such speculation. Although Lilly does report in his *Autobiography* that she

[351]Professor C. H. Josten: Historian of science and Curator of the Museum of the History of Science at Oxford. It was he who discovered Ashmole's cipher enabling him to edit and publish *Elias Ashmole: His Autobiographical and Historical Notes, his Correspondence, and Other Contemporary Sources Relating to his Life and Work*. Clarendon Press, Oxford, 1966.

brought 500 pounds as a portion, he further explains that her poor relations cost him over 1000 pounds.

In 1636 Lilly left London. In the letter to the reader in *Prophecy of the White King*, Lilly explains about his departure:

> In the latter part of the year 1635, I was afflicted with much sicknesse, and enforced to betake my selfe in the Countrey to avoid the multiplicity of my acquaintance more than the infirmnesse itself. In April 1636 (I bade adieu to London) it was said by some and believed by many, that I did it to avoid the plague which that yeare ensued.[362]

It is interesting to note that in that very short time Lilly had already achieved considerable renown for his abilities as astrologer and occultist, and that it was this renown which played such a large part in his decision to leave London. But, once recovered, the rural life began to pall and in 1640 Lilly moved back to London and there began to practice as a professional astrologer. He writes about it in 1644:

> Like an Hermit fourteen miles from London I lived neere Oatlands: But the heavens appearing cloudy, and foretelling mee a storme was coming, I left my Country habitation 1640, and came to London, where now I am,[363]

The most frequent reason quoted for his returning to London is the remark made in his *Autobiography*, where he says:

> Having now in part recovered my health, being weary of the Country, and perceiving there was money to be gott in London, and thinking myself as sufficiently enabled in Astrology as any I could meet with, I made it my business to repair thither…

---

[352]Josten, C.H. (ed.): Elias Ashmole, his autobiographical and historical notes…, 5 vols, OUP 1966/67, p162

This, Parker[364] and others repeatedly take as evidence of his "fondness for money". In some ways it does read as though his primary aim was to obtain money in some kind of confidence trick. Yet the rest of the quotation clearly shows that this was far from the truth.

> ...and so in September 1641 I did, where all the years 1642 and 1643 I had great leisure to better my former knowledge; I then read over all my books of Astrology, over and over, had very little practise at all,...

Having "very little practise" means that he rarely took clients and that for over two years. Had he been so fond of money and a trickster or charlatan why did he waste so much time on study? There may well have been an intention to supplement his income having foreseen "a storme was coming", but it cannot have been a primary motive because the "storme" broke in 1642 when the Civil War began.

The events of the years following 1642 would shape the lives of the English beyond recognition for centuries to come. Shortly thereafter in 1644 Lilly published his first pamphlet, *England's Propheticall Merline*[365] and his first almanac, *Anglicus Merlinus Junior*, wherein he states:

> The discourse hath already found some friends, it must now expect as many enemies; I care not, I have avoided almost the termes of Art, that it might appear plaine and easie to the meanest; some things in my Copy the Licenser expunged, its thereby lesse significant: I am contended, it might have appeared in better termes four moneth sooner, had I intended to print.[366]

From the outset Lilly had to confront the frustrations of licensing and censorship. The astrologer John Booker[367] , who was the appointed licenser of mathematical publications and therefore responsible for the censorship of astrological works, demanded rigorous cuts and changes to be made before he allowed the first edition to be published. The second edition of the almanac

---

[353]Curry, op.cit.

[354]Ibid

for 1644, published only weeks later because of high demand, contained the unexpurgated text and the comment referring to the licenser had disappeared. Lilly had taken his complaints about John Booker, who he thought had defaced his almanac, to some of the members of Parliament. They gave Lilly an

> ... order forthwith to reprint it as I would, and let them know if any durst resist mee in the reprinting, or adding what I thought fitt, so the second tyme it came forth as I would have it[368].

Lilly would continue to produce his almanacs on an annual basis until his death in 1681. Although the publication and wide distribution of his *Anglici Merlini* brought him fame, this did not come without a price in that political pressure was applied commensurate with his popularity. The nation was embroiled in a civil war and anybody who could contribute to the 'war effort' was pressed into service. This is not to say that Lilly was unwilling, but there is little doubt that political considerations had to be accounted for. For example, much later in his *Anglicus* of 1673 he writes:

> The Wars still continuing in those years betwixt his Majesty of England and the Dutch; we were desired by some worthy Persons to explain that Prophecy; which in a Manuscript we did, with some other Astrological Observations, upon the present and future estate of the Hollanders, it was ready for the Press; but by some prudent persons it was thought not fit to be made publick; there being then some overtures for Peace.

Shortly before his death Lilly wrote about these pressures in his *Anglicus* of 1677:

> We desire to give no Offence, but such is the peevishness of Men and the Times, That we have been silent in some material Affairs;

---

[355]Thomas: op. cit.

[356]Parker: op. cit. p177

> for We let the Nation know, that since We wrote first, We have been Nine times under Restraint to Our great Cost and Charge.[369]

William Lilly was first and foremost an astrologer and predicted what his art dictated to him. He was content with what life – God – had given him and sought out nothing more. Nowhere in his writings can we find any suggestion of social or material ambition. We recognise that this might be due to careful writing, but given the wealth of material Lilly wrote, there would have been some glimpse of a grasping nature if he had had one.

In giving the astrological detail of his nativity, Lilly mentions that he has the Moon in Pisces which, of course, is incorrect. Gadbury makes much of this in *Collectio Geniturarum*[370] where he accuses Lilly of deliberately trying to mislead. In his view, the Moon in Pisces makes Lilly "a piece of a good fellow", but the Moon in Capricorn imports something else entirely, which is true. He prints a recalculation of Lilly's nativity which although fairly close to Lilly's own, is still incorrect and remains the calculation to which most writers refer. An alternative explanation is that in the printing five words were omitted: "…the Moon *in Capricornus and the Ascendant* in Piscibus". Having given as much detail as he has, it would be unusual indeed for Lilly – or any astrologer – to omit mention of the rising sign. In fact, astrologically speaking, Pisces rising would indicate a pleasant and affable person, to which Lilly alludes, whereas the Moon in Capricorn would not. It is hardly worth considering that Lilly would not be aware of this obvious difference or that many of his readers would be unaware of it. From almost all images that we have of him, he is quite clearly Piscean in appearance and this would not have been lost on his astrologically educated readers. Moreover, he has just written that his "conceptions are dull" because he has Mercury and Mars in earthy signs. For a writer and teacher this would have been more cause for concern had he been minded to try to obscure his shortcomings. Again, we do not suggest that our view is correct, only that there are other ways of approaching William Lilly's life and work.

---

[357]Ibid. p189

[358]Ward: op.cit.

This is not the only time that Lilly mentions the restraints imposed upon him by the Licenser and others. It was unfortunate that he was put under such political pressures which led to many of the difficulties he experienced in his public life. He may well not have been unwilling to add his weight to the cause in all instances, but his peaceable nature and desire for justice often conflicted and seem to have taken him into actions which he regretted later. As early as 1656 Lilly writes:

> [We are] intending therefore (if God spare our life) to retire and end those few years we have yet remaining in quietnesse, piece and tranquillity, we were more sparing; we have had a full experience of the vanity and inconsistency of the Creature; we have known both good and evil fortune: we have been sensible of Liberty and Imprisonment: we have been a Servant to the unthankfull; we have shared in honour and dishonour, notwithstanding all which, we have had all along since 1644.[371]

There are other passages from his later almanacs in which he refuses to be drawn into political or religious debates for the same reason of desiring peace and quiet for his last years. His frankness in discussing the peaks and troughs of his career is disarming, as is his wanting to avoid further trouble with the authorities. Revealing his feelings of having lived too long in the public eye, it is notable that this was written four years before the Restoration and thus without threat or coercion from a vengeful monarch. It also flies in the face of Parker's comments regarding Lilly's opportunistic and self-preserving tendencies[372].

In the same year of 1644, Lilly published *A Prophecy of the White King*, predicting that Charles I, without naming him directly, would be defeated by the forces of Parliament. As a result, Captain George Wharton[373], an astrologer and devoted Royalist, attacked Lilly in his own Almanac for 1645[374]. In the autobiography, Lilly writes:

---

[359]Lilly, William: *Anglicus, Peace or no Peace*, London 1645, pA4ff

[360]John Brinsley (1581-1624)

> I had then no further intention to trouble the press any more, but Sir Richard Napper[375] having received one of Capt. Wharton's Almanacks for 1645, under the name of Naworth, he came unto me: Now Lilly, you are met withal, see here what Naworth writes; the Words were, he called me an impudent senseless Fellow, and by name William Lilly.[376]

This seems to have been the turning point where political pressure, focused through the accusations of George Wharton moulded William Lilly into a Parliamentarian astrologer. To defend his reputation Lilly had little choice but to take sides, as he goes on to explain:

> Before that Time I was more Cavalier than Roundhead, and so taken notice of; but after that I engaged Body and Soul in the cause of Parliament, but still with much affection to his Majesty's Person and unto Monarchy, which I ever loved and approved beyond any Government whatsoever; and you will find in this Story many passages of Civility which I did and endeavoured to do, with the Hazard of my Life for his Majesty: But God has ordered all his affairs and Councils to have no Successes, as in the Sequel will appear.[377]

There is no reason to suggest that this sentiment is insincere; it was not a particularly uncommon political expression. Many considered the king to have been badly advised, not at fault in himself. Many histories have been written about this period and most conclude that the arrest and beheading of the king was the cause of national trauma. In Lilly's case, it was very soon after that Ashmole[378], hitherto a Royalist officer, was introduced to Lilly by a Roman Catholic. These friendships of mixed politics and religions continued whichever party was in power. There is more contemporary evidence to support his remarks than there is to refute them, and biographers might avail themselves of that evidence rather than modern opinions too often based upon slight research.

---

[361]Parker: op. cit. p42

[362]Lilly, William: *A* Prophecy *of the White King*, London 1644, p2

Lilly was a deeply religious man and his astrology was based upon the fact that every action undertaken must be first and foremost to serve God. This quotation from his almanac of 1651[379] gives us an insight into his beliefs and morality:

> I feare not their bellowing or thundering against me or Astrology, I seek God in his own words, wherein I find no Envy, Malice, self-ends, domineering, rebellion against Superiors, or Lording it over tender Consciences commanded, or checking the spirit of any upon whom his holy spirit breaths: In the Gospel of Jesus Christ, I find sweet perswasions, most heavenly directions, that all our Actions be performed with love, charity, meekness, submission and obedience to powers and Authority, sith they are ordained by God.[380]

We are not attempting to portray Lilly as other than an imperfect man, but we do want to demonstrate that there are perspectives other than cynical ones. We should not confuse our modern disaffection from religious and moral standards such as personal honour, with a code of conduct that was commonly expected of the educated classes. Furthermore, we will point out that this was the precise difference between Lilly and Gadbury and with which Gadbury was repeatedly criticised by his contemporaries.

On 12th June 1645, the King was defeated at Naseby, vindicating Lilly's astrological prediction, recounted in his diary by Bulstrode Whitelocke[381] but described by Parker as a "lucky stroke"[382]. Lilly's fame as an astrologer was growing and he was making influential friends who would be of great help to him in the future. As previously mentioned, in 1646 Elias Ashmole was introduced to Lilly by the Royalist Jonas Moore[383]. This is significant because Ashmole, as a Royalist officer, was forbidden to enter London, thus his activities required some caution. It is known that Ashmole assisted Lilly with the production of *Christian Astrology* in terms of the diagrams and charts and Lilly presumably paid him for that work[384]. The beginning of their acquaintanceship was not however without difficulty, but Lilly and Ashmole would become lifelong friends, and the latter would help Lilly out of some

[363]Lilly, William: *England's propheticall* Merline, London 1644

[364]Parker, op. cit. p129

dangerous predicaments after the Restoration of 1660. However, the most influential of William Lilly's friends was without doubt Bulstrode Whitelocke, the Keeper of the Great Seal. In 1643, Lilly had diagnosed Whitelocke's illness from a urine sample which had been brought to him and from which he correctly predicted recovery. After this the two men became firm friends and Lilly had found a patron in Whitelocke who would act in his favour and protect him in times of political turmoil and personal crisis. Lilly showed his gratitude by dedicating his *Christian Astrology* to him and by bequeathing his entire estate to Whitelocke's son, Carlton, following Ruth Lilly's death Presumably, having no children of his own and acknowledging a debt of honour and friendship, Lilly reverted his estate to his friend's son.

From about 1649 onwards, Lilly's fame and reputation were unrivalled by any other British astrologer. He was best known for his annual almanac *Anglicus Merlin* – the most widely read at the time – and for his successful predictions, like the victory of the Parliamentary forces at Colchester. On a personal level he was introduced to Lord Fairfax[385], was acquainted with the famous mathematician William Oughtred[386] and the astrologer and herbalist Nicholas Culpeper[387]. Scientists like the astronomers Vincent Wing[388] and Jeremy Shakerley[389] wrote letters to Lilly seeking his advice. But there were of course critics of William Lilly as well. In 1653, the cleric Thomas Gataker[390] published his *Vindication*[391] in which he criticises Lilly in very strong terms. In his autobiography, Lilly writes:

> In his [Gataker's] annotations thereuppon, hee makes a scandalous exposition, and in express termes, hints at mee, repeating verbatim 10 or 12 lines of an Epistle of mine in one of my former Anglicus. The substance of my Epistle was that I did conceive the good Angells of God, did first reveale Astrology unto mankind, etc. but hee in his Annotations calls mee blind Bussard, etc.
>
> Having now Liberty of the Press, and hearing the old man was very Cholerick, I thought fitt to raise it upp and onely wrote I referred my discourse then in hand to the discussion and judgment of sober

[365]Lilly: ibid

[366]Lilly, William: *Merlinus Anglicus Junior,* London, 1644, first edition, p3, with handwritten date June 12th, on front page and handwritten remark "Booker" next to the quoted text.

> persons, but not unto Thomas Wiseacre, for Senes bis pueri [Old men are twice boys.]: these very words begott the writing of 42 sheets against my selfe and Astrology. The next year I quibbled again in 3 or 4 lines against him, then hee printed 22 sheets against me. I was persuaded by Doctor Gawdy[392], late Bishop of Excester, to let him alone, but in my next yeares Anglicus, in August observations, I wrote, Hoc in tumbo jacet Presbiter et Nebulo [Here in a tomb lies a Presbiter and scoundrel]; in which very month hee died.[393]

However, of greater interest for our purposes here are Lilly's words when commenting later upon Gataker's death:

> We will henceforth meditate Heaven, and are resolved never hereafter to meddle in point of Controversie, or to take notice in print, either of the person or failings of any particular man.[394]

Indeed, as far as can be ascertained, Lilly never did engage his critics in print again. It is true that there are comments made by him from time to time regarding Gadbury, but these are always in response to a particularly violent attack by the latter. Some examples will clarify the matter, but Lilly's words should be borne in mind as we proceed because they express his strength of character, moral standing and his attitude in his dealings with John Gadbury. His replies, such as they are, were in his own defence and never to initiate or prolong a dispute, as we will show. Clearly, Lilly's preference was for a quiet life. Of his 79 years only about 27 were spent living in the hurly-burly of London, with a break of five years living in Hersham in what he termed "obscurity". This is easy to overlook when most biographers and commentators focus on the Civil War years and Lilly's prominence during that period. It would probably be fair to say that he was not always averse to fame and publicity, but his first preference was for a peaceful existence which does not conform to Parker's opinion that he enjoyed or even actively sought out confrontation and contention[395].

---

[367]John Booker (1603 – 1667)

[368]Ward: William Lilly's autobiography, op. cit. p52

Lilly's network of friends, assistants and supporters was wide and reached far beyond London. From the available evidence it is clear that he attempted to help whenever he could; simply put, those who knew him, generally liked him. He appears to have been affable, good-humoured, sociable, generous and compassionate. These characteristics are clearly shown in his letters to Ashmole[396] and in the fact that the later years of his life were given to treating the sick of his local area. He asked no payment for this, and his generosity to the Parish of Walton on Thames whilst a Warden of the Church is recorded by Ashmole.[397] There is enough evidence to contradict opinions such as those recorded in Parker that Lilly "was fond of money"[398]. So far as it is possible to tell, there is no evidence to support this view, quite the contrary in fact. This is not to suggest that Lilly was universally liked or admired or that he did not have enemies. His position, influence and public prominence were bound to attract unwanted attention as were his political affiliations.

Lilly was at the centre of a large group of intelligent and educated men respected in their own fields: mathematicians, physicians, astronomers, astrologers, politicians, gentlemen and aristocrats. This deserves more attention than it has been given, as the evidence suggests that his influence was based upon a superior, or, at least, elevated position within that group and there is little doubt about the esteem in which he was held by its members. Professor Josten also speculates on the matter[399] and we find our own research over many years has led us to a similar conclusion. It is enough to say that Lilly had many supporters and that this is a reflection of his status and influence. It may be true that these diminished after the Restoration, but his popularity did not decline and his close friends remained. His advice and tutelage was still sought by many and his time absorbed with these activities, clients and that of maintaining his *Anglicus*. He never did manage to write all the books he had intended in his earlier years and never achieved a new edition of *Christian Astrology*. Although a second edition of *Christian Astrology* was published in 1659, doubts have to be raised about Lilly's authorisation of it. As early as 1656 Lilly writes in his *Merlini Anglici*:

---

[369]Lilly, William: Merlinus Anglici Ephemeris for 1677, London 1677

[370]Gadbury, John: *Collectio* Genitorum, London, 1662

> … notwithstanding all which, we have had all along since 1644 as general and full a Practice in all the knowne parts of Astrology, as ever any man of this Nation; and if God shall lengthen our dayes, its possible we may put our dear bought experiences into a method for benefit of Posterity: we will only adde this much, that we hear our Introduction unto Astrology is reprinting; if it be so, its without our Knowledge, Consent or Owning; we intended, and intend a serious review and enlargement thereof, upon a second Impression, if ever be by our Consent. But the malicious covetousnesse of those who now have a propriety in it, or have acquired the Copy, or others shall reprint it, we not consenting, we then say, the Booke will come forth, very lame, deficient and contrary to our sober intention of amending its former errors; occasioned then by our being shut up of the Plague.[400]

Although he writes that the second edition would be "corrected and amended", a close comparison of the first and second editions shows that nothing was altered. Even crude mistakes, like the numbering of pages 171 to 175 in reverse order, are retained in the second edition. In 1676 Lilly, who had just recovered from an illness, knew that he would not be able to publish a corrected and enlarged version in his lifetime and wrote in the preamble to Henry Coley's *Clavis Astrologia Elimata*:

> But this Author ... hath now with no small pains and Industry, saved me that labour, in presenting the world with this most compleat piece of Astrology, which (not improperly) he Intitles, A KEY to the whole ART ...[401]

For this reason his later almanacs are all the more important because it is within those pages that he imparted his more treasured astrological aphorisms. Furthermore, perhaps those who want an alternative to *Christian Astrology* as a reference text should give preference to Coley's work over Gadbury's.

---

[371]Lilly, William: Merlinus Anglicus Ephemeris for 1656, London 1656

[372]Parker: op. cit. p145

Chapter 2 - John Gadbury (1627-1704)

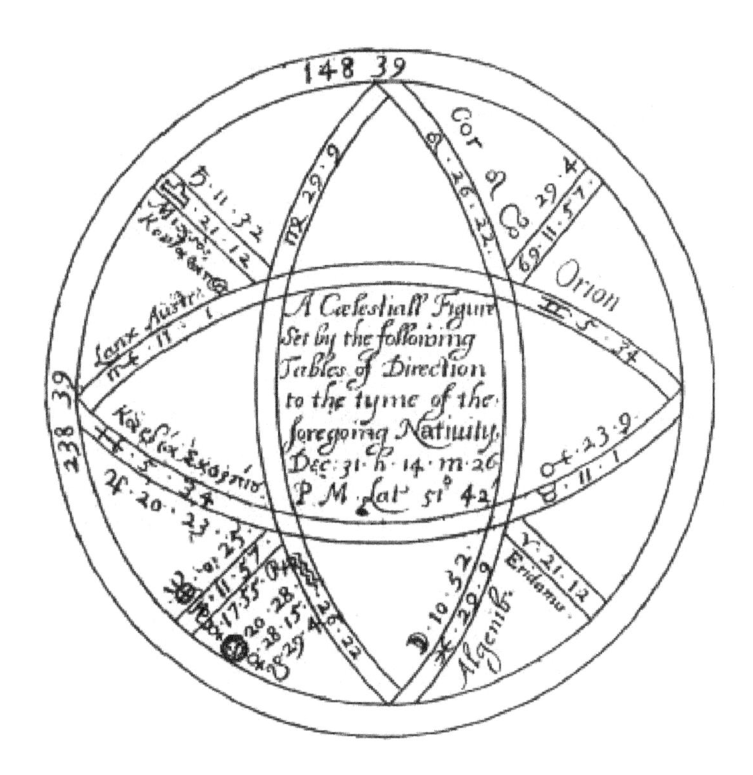

The following comprises an abstract of Gadbury's delineation of his own nativity, speaking in the third person because he writes as though for a client. It is included at length as an autobiographical and primary source which in itself gives support to many of the criticisms made of Gadbury by his contemporaries.

"According to the natives own confession, he has never been driven to an absolute want, nor yet hath he abounded much in riches: and the reason for

[373]Sir George Wharton (1617-1681)

[374]Naworth (Sir George Wharton): A New Almanack, 1645

these aphorisms not exactly taking place, I presume is this: Saturn is superior to Jupiter in the figure, and is exalted above him, and therefore (for a time) abates his good signification. Besides, I remember a rule of Johannes Angelus, which says, He who has Saturn posited in the eleventh of his nativity, shall not attain on any dignity or estate, until he have passed the thirtieth year of his age. And Jupiter and the Part of Fortune also are in the north part of the figure; which denotes the height of the native's felicity and happiness will happen unto him in the later part of his age. Thus you see the adage made good. There is no general, but admits of exception.

"Three planets in the third house (viz. Sun, Mercury and Venus) declares the various dispositions and affections of the brethren and kindred of the native toward him; and shows the native propense to study, and to take short journeys, sometimes for pleasure's sake. But the presence of the Dragon's Tail in the second house denotes many quarrels and dissentions between the native, and his brethren and kindred for you must know that Cauda Draconis infortunat domum ubi invenitur, the tail of the dragon infortunates that house wheresoever he is found.

"The native confesses that he has had many unhappy differences with his brethren, sisters and kindred: and has been cheated and cozened by them to purpose; and that he does many times take short journeys for his pleasure, and is also (as we hinted before) propense to study.

"The native and his father may agree indifferently well, because the Lord of the Ascendant and the Sun (a general significator of fathers) are in trine unto each other, and the Moon is going to the sextile of them both; and it is most true, that generally they agree well enough.

"The native might be born to an inheritance, but will hardly attain it; and if ever, with difficulty: for Mars Lord of the third from the fourth, declares that a brother of the natives father shall obstruct and hinder him, and do much

---

[375]Sir Richard Napier (1607-1676), physician.

prejudice to his father also; for it is a square from fixed signs that he casts unto the cusp of the fourth, viz. the most malicious of all other.

"The native has seriously acknowledged that he was born to £80 per annum, which by a trepan (too long to relate her) his father was necessitated to part with; and this when the native was a childe, and uncapable. And the knavery was acted by a brother of the natives father; who holds part of the same to this day; so that there is no hopes of regaining it.

"Here you see the cusp of the fifth is a fruitful sign, and so is the Ascendant; and the Moon is posited in Pisces, the sign of the fifth, beholding the Ascendant with a perfect trine. Whence it results, that there is a possibility of the natives having children.

"The native acknowledges that he is much subject to the head-ache, and to surfeits, and also to the stone in the reines, etc, and to windy and flatuous humours; and is many times afflicted with the ptisique, but is easily recovered again.

"Mercury, a general significator of servants, is retrograde and combust, and presages the servants of the native to be thievish, and shows they shall deceive him; and Mars, Lord of the sixth in opposition to the Ascendant, denotes the same. But Jupiter casting a trine to the sixth house, and the Moon in sextile with Mars and Mercury, shows they cannot do him much injury before they be discovered.

"The native confesses he has had several servants, and yet never had but one that was honest and true to him; but before they did him much harm, he still had the good fortune to discover them.

"The Lord of the Ascendant in the seventh, and in trine to Venus governess of the seventh, declares a propensity or desire in the native to marry, and shows also that he will put that desire into act. And the Lord of the

---

[376]Lilly, William: The Life of William Lilly, Student in Astrology…, MS Ashm. 421 ff. 178-223.

[377]Ibid

Ascendant and the Moon in reception and her transferring the light of the Lord of the Ascendant to the Lady of the seventh presages the same.

"The Lord of the Ascendant and seventh in trine, and in reception also, declares a very friendly harmony and agreement, between the Native and his wife; and the Moon in the dignities of Venus, viz. her exaltation, the same.

"The native is married as by direction of the Ascendant to the sextile of Venus and he informs me that he and his wife agree very well indeed, and are rarely known to jar or fall at odds.

"The Lady of the twelfth house, and Lord of the Ascendant in trine by reception, denote no great danger of imprisonment to the native: yet it discerns the brethren, kindred, etc. of the native to be the most treacherous enemies he can meet with: but the affliction of Venus verifies the proverb, curst cows have short horns: so although they have a great desire and will to injure and prejudice the native, yet they have small power, so that he need not fear them. I need not speak of other significations of this house, because the native is not concerned herein. He acknowledges that he has been very free from imprisonment, and never suffered above three days restraint (setting aside the time of his minority) in his life; and for his private enemies, he never could yet come to discover any but those of his kindred and familiar acquaintance: but he says also, they never prevailed against him."

Gadbury then moves on to delineate the astrology for the 'native's' 28th (1654) and 31st (1657) years of age.

"[1654] 1. The direction portends a very unsuccessful time unto the native in his estate and goods of fortune especially; and presages, many vain and idle expenses make him subject to thefts, and to lose much by Martial men and things; it also denotes quarrels and controversy between the native and his kindred, for that it falls in the third House; chiefly, with the female sort of them, because it falls in a feminine sign, and near the body of Venus.

---

[378]Elias Ashmole (1617-1692).

[379]Lilly, William: *Anglicus Merlin*, London 1651.

“2. The Revolution concurs in judgment herewith, for Cauda Draconis there is afflicting the Part of Fortune in the second House, and Saturn Lord of the third and fourth of the radix. And the Lord of the second is in the seventh, and the Lord of the seventh in the third house retrograde. But the chief occasion from whence the mischief shall arise unto the native, is discovered by the Moon, as she is governess of the Ascendant, and locally in the eight, in square to Mars Lord of the Ascendant of the Radix in the fifth; which denotes the native to be inquisitious after the wills, legacies, etc. of some persons deceased: But he will certainly lose his hopes and expectations, and spend his money, and all in a vain and frivolous manner; for the heavens do no ways favour or befriend him in any such thing or things this year.

“3. But as Jupiter is Lord of the Revolution, and from the heart of heaven beholds the Ascendant with a trine, and the Sun Lord of the tenth in the radix, with a sextile dexter, and Mars Lord of the Ascendant, with a trine also; the native shall (in this year) notwithstanding all his losses and vexations gain a great many eminent acquaintance, by whose means he shall gain reputation and credit , and a convenient esteem in the place where he lives; by whose means he may withstand many troubles, etc.

“4. And as the ninth of the Radix is the Ascendant of the Revolution, it denotes the native to be inclinable to study arts, and sciences; and it may possibly put him upon some journey, and that north-west; for the Ascendant it self is north; and Mars Lord of the Ascendant of the radix, is in a northerly Sign; but the Moon in a sign westerly: but he will get little or nothing by it; for Mars quartiles the ninth.

“5. Let him be very careful that he neither drink nor riot to excess (for he will this year be inclinable to such courses) for the Moon is near the cusp of the fourth in the eighth of the Revolution, in square to Mars in the fifth, and that from fixed signs; it does indeed threaten a surfeit or fever, which nothing but moderation can prevent.

---

[380]Lilly, William: Merlini Anglici ephemeris for 1651, London 1651

"To the first the native confesses that he was subject to many quarrels and controversies with his Kindred: he says, he was at odds the same year with his mother, went to law with an uncle and sister; and was cozened and cheated by a captain, who, for want of other employment, was his solicitor; and the same year, was troubled with two thievish servants.

"To the second, he acknowledges the occasion of his going to law was a pretended legacy; but he spent much money therein, and to no purpose.

"To the third, he says, that he came into favour that year with many eminent acquaintance, and did gain reputation and credit by them.

"To the fourth, he says, he was much addicted to study, and that not only to one knowledge or science, but many; and he says also, that he did go a journey of fifty or sixty miles exactly northwest; but he confesses he got nothing at all by it, but his labour for his pains.

"To the fifth, he says and confesses, his health was impeded, and that by a surfeit which he got by drinking, and he was in a discrasied condition seven weeks by reason thereof.

"But the principal thing which I admire at, is this: on April the fourth, 1655, the same day did the native, as he professes to me, entertain both his counsel and solicitor; which was the foundation to all the mischief and loss he underwent; and had his nativity been calculated, it might have been prevented.

[1657/8 predictions]

"And that happens in the year 1658 on June the fourteenth day, just about noon. The MC ad trine Venus, portends great pleasure, profit and delight to the native, abundance of new acquaintance, and makes him ambitious of honour and esteem: he hath health of body and peace of mind; and all things

---

[381]Spalding, Ruth (Editor): *The Diary of Bulstrode Whitelocke 1605-1675.* The British Academy/OUP, Oxford 1991 (reprint of 1990)., p167. Referring to 1645, "June. 9. Wh[itelocke] accidentally in the streets meeting with his kind friend Mr. Lilly, who asked him of the newes of the 2 Armies being neer one another, Wh[itelocke] told him it was true, &

succeed prosperously with him; and ere the direction be over, he may have a child. But---

"The Sun ad T. Mars, somewhat contradicts the good presignifed by Venus, and advises the native to beware of rash and head-strong actions, and bids him to be very cautious in his affairs. This is indeed as a cloud before the other Sun-like direction, and may a little dim, but cannot wholly darken it. And so I come to examine the Revolution."

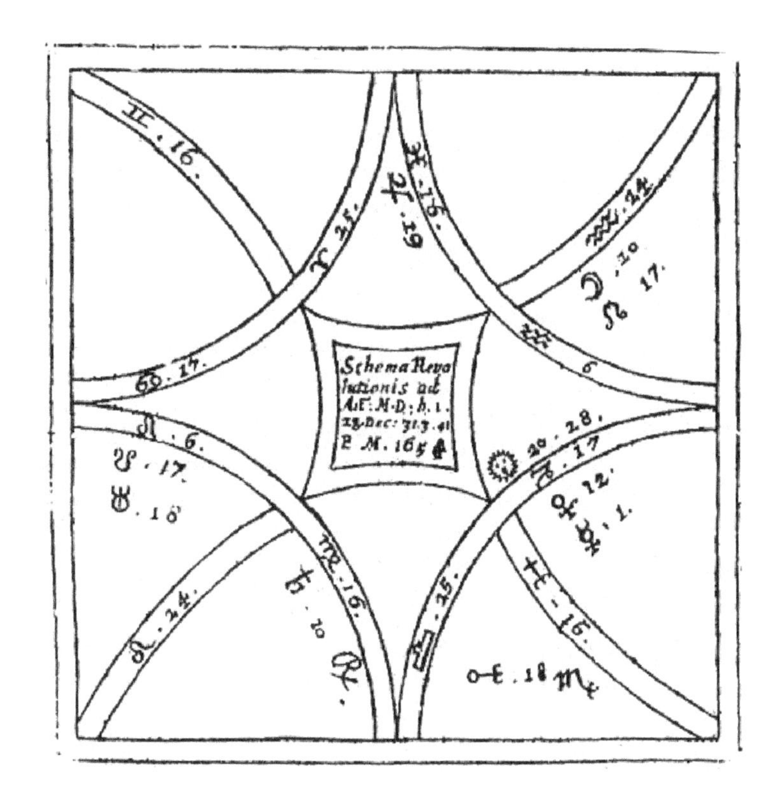

that they were very likely to engage, Mr. Lilly replyed, if they doe not engage before the eleaventh day of this moneth, the Parlem[en] [t] will have he greatest victory that they ever yet had, & it proved accordingly."

"In the Revolution, we have the fourth [house cusp] of the radix ascend, and the Lord thereof in trine to the same, from the eighth of the figure wherein he is exalted; which intimates thus much: That the native shall have or possess some land or estate, or aliquid tale, as a gift or legacy of some person or persons deceased; the return of Venus to the radical place of Jupiter, idem; and the position of Caput Draconis in the tenth, will augment his reputation; and Venus in the eleventh, his hopes, and procure him many feminine friends; and as she is dominatrix of the third house, she portends much peace and quietness between him and his neighbours, etc.

"But here we have the Moon and Mars in conjunction in the second in Aries, and in opposition to Saturn, and square to the Sun and Mercury, which denotes some loss of estate, but also controversies and contentions with elderly clownish people and strangers, and possibly some diminutive trouble and cross in a law-suit, or some controversy; but Venus her sextile to Saturn, and trine to Mars and the Moon, will suddenly appease the fury portended; also her semi-sextile to the Sun and Mercury. Howbeit the square of the Sun and Saturn, and opposition of Saturn and Mars will afflict the body of the native with cholerick-melancholy humours, which may enervate by good medicine and moderate courses, as Venus aspects will denote.

"The return of Mercury to his place, argues some preferment; but because Mercury suffers a double evil in his return, viz. his combustion; and being in the twelfth house, it will be the less, and perhaps the longer deferred.

"To conclude, the year will have much more good then evil in it, and it will be wisdom for the native to take hold of opportunity by the foretop; for … 'tis bald behind. And there is a storm coming, which will (in some measure) darken the Sun-shine of this (I may comparatively call it) golden year that glitters with so many glorious days in it. "

———

[382]Parker: op.cit. p134.

[383]Sir Jonas Moore (1617-1679)

As demonstrated above, biographical information about Gadbury is fairly easily found, but as with that of Lilly, finding reliable information is more difficult. There is evidence to suggest that there were at least two versions of John Gadbury's beginnings: the version he himself preferred and that heard from those who knew him. The story which persisted throughout his life is summed up by John Aubrey[402]:

> Mr. Gadbury the astrologer's father, a taylor, takes the measure of a young lady for a gowne and clappes up a match.[403]

The editor's note appended to this entry shows that Wood[404] provided a less disparaging account:

> Anthony Wood in the *Ath. Oxon.* gives a more correct version of this story. William Gadbury, a farmer, of Wheatley, co. Oxon, made a stolen marriage with a daughter of Sir John Curson of Waterperry. Their son, John Gadbury, was apprentice to an Oxford tailor, before he set up as an astrologer.

Even so, Gadbury was offended by these remarks and threatened to write publicly about the matter[405], implying yet another of his broadsides or pamphlets which, as we will show, had been and would continue to be a fairly frequent activity. In his reply to Aubrey's letter informing him of this, Wood expresses surprise that Gadbury should be upset that it would now be known that he was not Oxford educated, but that his education was "mechanical" and thus would be admired.

However, the story held fast and much later John Partridge[406] plays on it in one of his pamphlet responses to Gadbury's attacks:

> ...and away they sent him to St. Nichols's Colledge, where with the help of a good Tutor, and a whetting Diet, this little thief grew as sharp as a Needle, to the admiration of all the Fellows of that House, and the circumadjacent Colledges, who spent their time in

[384]Lilly: *The Life of* ..., MS Ashm. 421 ff. 178-223. Ashmole's handwritten marginal notes state that he assisted with the "schemes".

[385]Sir Thomas, Lord Fairfax (1612-1671)

> that kind of Study; so that it was generally agreed on as a Gratitude to his Merit, and for the Reputation of his Parts, to confer on him that Honourable Title of *Lousy Jack*; and under this Reputation he was for some time mad Runner General for the whole Society, where he spent a few years to make him fit to take his Degrees at London; to which place he came at a good suitable Age,... [407]

Gadbury had been apprenticed to a tailor named Nichols in Oxford and it is to this that the author is referring. Partridge then mentions obliquely Gadbury's poverty once settled in London and working for a merchant adventurer named Taylor. During this period Gadbury married for the first time and lived near Strand Bridge[408] according to Partridge. In *Doctrine of Nativities*[409], Gadbury presents a table for his own directions, in this Gadbury writes that in 1633 (or 1634) the native "Went to a Lawyer", to which, in his own copy, Lilly adds, "then to a Taylor.". For 1636, the note for that direction is "An Apprentice", to which Lilly adds, "to a Taylor in Oxford called Nicholls." Since Gadbury was born in 1627, this would bring him to seven and nine years of age. Although it seems very young, it was not uncommon for a child in poverty to be apprenticed at an early age. Indeed, one of Lilly's comments in his copy of D*octrine* indicates that the parish had paid for Gadbury's apprenticeship: this might happen in cases of illegitimacy as well as poverty. It might be that the legitimacy of Gadbury's birth had been doubted because of the manner of his parents' marriage. The same table reports that Gadbury, the 'client', married in 1651 and had a child in 1653.

---

[386]William Oughtred (bap.1575, d.1660)

[387]Nicholas Culpeper (1616-1654)

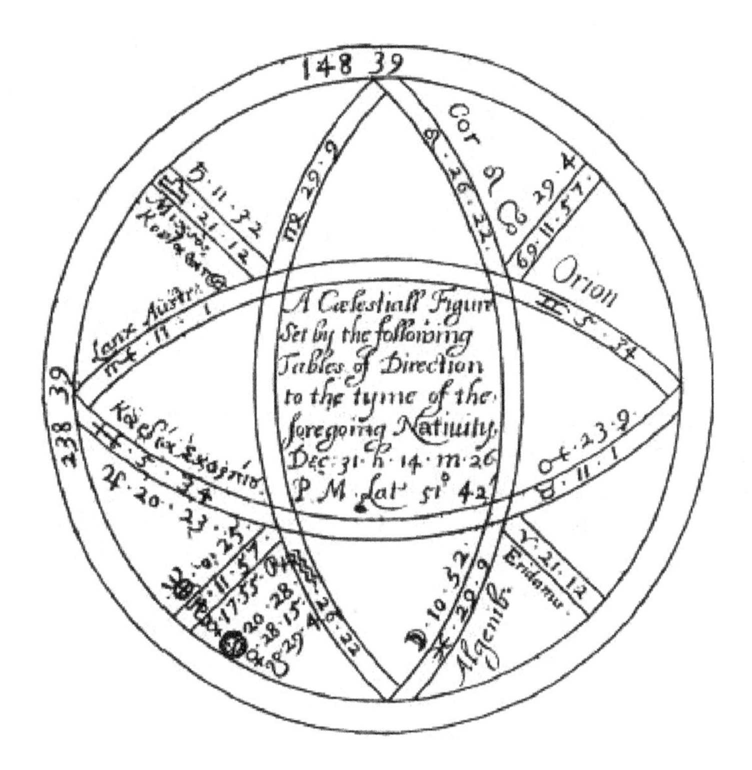

Gadbury's writing career began with a pamphlet, when in 1652 he replied to "Philastrogus"[410] wherein he defended Nicholas Culpeper against the latter's criticisms and demonstrated support for William Lilly amongst others. His arguments supporting astrology and astrologers would have attracted favourable attention from Lilly in particular. One of Lilly's stated aims in publishing *Christian Astrology* was to generate more supporters of astrology that it might survive.

> … I thought it a duty incumbent uppon mee to satisfie the whole Kingdom of the Lawfullness thereof, by framing a plain and easy Method for any person but of indifferent capacity to learn the Art,

---

[388]Vincent Wing (1619-1668)

[389]Jeremy Shakerley (1626-1653?)

> and instruct himselfe therein without any other Mr. then my Introduction; by which meanes, when many understood it, I should have more partners and assistants to contradict all and every Antagonist.[411]

Gadbury's impassioned reply spoke of Lilly's own battle with those who would have cast astrology into oblivion along with those who practised it. This printed reply was Gadbury's opening to the circle to whose membership he aspired. Those early years of his astrological career were promising indeed and his future looked bright as he himself remarked later.

A major breakthrough occurred when in 1656 he and his uncle Timothy published a recalculation of *Hartgill's Tables*[412]. This was followed two years later by his first book as sole author[413] and it is within those pages that we discover more about the man himself. Having presented his nativity as that of a client, we can read his view of his own character and the events of his life up to that date. His retrospective for the year 1654 as his 'directions' referred to it, and his predictions for the year 1658, as we will show, are years of the greatest import both for Gadbury and for our examination here. He began his annual almanacs in 1655 which continued until his death, but his career as an author was varied and prolific. For the moment, this will suffice, but we will refer to others of Gadbury's publications as the need arises.

Gadbury and Nicholas Fiske

One of Gadbury's claims, which has been widely accepted, was that he had been a student of the well-known mathematician and astrologer, Nicholas Fiske. It is reported[414] that Gadbury left London to learn astrology from Nicholas Fiske. The *ODNB* states that this was in 1644 and 1652 and that it took place in Oxford[415], but this is difficult to accept when, in a separate article from the *ODNB*, it is stated that Fiske was resident in London from 1633 until his death in 1659[416]. Added to this is Gadbury's own statement in *Doctrine* that he did not have his nativity in 1654[417] which, if he had been studying astrology from 1644 *or* 1652, he would certainly have calculated. It is

---

[390]Thomas Gataker (1574-1654) church of England minister and scholar.

striking too that Gadbury did not begin to make these claims until *after* Fiske had died.

Also of note is that some scholars[418] accept Gadbury's account of Fiske's date of birth, possibly assuming it to be more accurate having accepted that Fiske was his tutor. This is not unimportant because not only does it reflect on Gadbury's version of events in this case and others, but also on the inconsistency of historical research. Gadbury states[419] that Fiske was 84 years old when he died which places his birth in 1575. Lilly notes[420] that Fiske was 78 years of age when he died – bearing in mind that he and Fiske had been friends for over 25 years – producing a birth year of 1580 or 1581. Fiske himself writes[421] in 1650 that he was "more than seventy", whilst this may mean that he was somewhere between 70 and 80 years of age, it is more likely that he meant between 70 and 71 years of age, which places his birth in 1580. This is supported by the context of the remark because Fiske was complaining about the great delay in publishing this work through political interference; had he been 75 years old, as Gadbury's date of death implies, he would have said so. It is fair to assume that Gadbury did not know how old Fiske was because he did not know him well enough. Of course, it may have been a simple error, but it is one which has been perpetuated.

Some commentators also report that when Gadbury left London to return to his grandfather, he took up his studies at Oxford University, this, too, is inaccurate according to contemporary records[422]. Gadbury did not study at Oxford University, nor did he study under Fiske at Oxford, in fact, it is unlikely that he studied with Fiske at all.

Gadbury's political and religious allegiances appear to have been mutable according to contemporary critics, and, to a certain extent, to Gadbury himself in his delineation of his own nativity in *Doctrine*, "...which very well portends prejudice by religious tenets, or at least, those that are presumed to be so, although they have nothing of true religion in them". A fairly detailed account of this can be found in Partridge[423] (and elsewhere), albeit in the terms of a critic. However, the point of emphasis is that to change one's

[391]Gataker, Thomes: B.D.*His vindicationof the annotations by him published upon these words*, London 1653

[392]Probably Dr. John Gauden (1599/1600?-1662), Bishop of Exeter and later of Worcester.

religion was drastic. It pointed to hypocrisy, inconstancy, unreliability, superficiality and – in a time when one's religion often spoke of more than one's spiritual affiliations – treason. This is particularly notable with Gadbury, because he appears to have changed his political allegiances concurrently with those of his religion. This is apparent in his pamphlets printed after the Restoration[424]. Of course, the greatest of caution was exercised by all noted supporters of the Commonwealth, including Lilly, but Gadbury's words are extreme by any standard, and intended to put clear distance between himself and his former associates.

Descriptions of Gadbury's inconstant and impulsive nature are found frequently, as are those of an uncouth man lacking in intelligence and discrimination. Such characterisations dogged Gadbury for most of his life and likewise his apparently innate ability to turn friends into enemies. Both William Lilly and John Partridge had once been his supporters, but they were educated and intelligent men and could not be bullied into compliance. As we will demonstrate, what Lilly had suggested, largely in private, about Gadbury's astrological abilities, Partridge made public in great detail and with published evidence.

Chapter 3 - Ingratitude

In our time it can be difficult to appreciate how serious an accusation ingratitude was. We live in a capitalist or commercial age when we buy the things we need and suppliers sell them to us for profit; thus gratitude is hardly necessary. We earn our livings with certain safeguards and rights, and the thought of being grateful to an employer is anathema. In the UK the opportunity for destitution and starvation is limited, but in earlier times all but the most wealthy and powerful needed assistance and support. Patronage put food on the table and secured one's livelihood and family. To be ungrateful for this patronage, no matter how well-earned, was considered to be

---

[393]Lilly: ibid, MS Ashm. 421 ff. 178-223.

[394]Lilly, William: *Merlini Anglici Ephemeris for 1655*, London 1655

unforgivable. Gratitude was a debt, an obligation, a responsibility on which one's honour and reputation depended. It may seem strange to modern minds used to individual 'rights' of one kind or another, but we should not confuse the principle of gratitude with servility. There are many letters written to Lilly asking for favours of various sorts wherein the writers *always* proffer their thanks and service. Both parties would expect such a debt to be discharged at some point as a matter of duty.

When Lilly referred to Gadbury as "a monster of ingratitude"[425] it was not a simple angry outburst, he chose his words carefully. This was not a shouted insult, but a quiet accusation pregnant with meaning which would not be lost on his audience. It was a shocking charge which would be made public only in the most extreme of circumstances. It could hardly have been worse had Gadbury been charged with murder.

The epithet of "monster of ingratitude" was not, in fact, original to Lilly, but is a well-known line from Shakespeare's *King Lear* where Lear refers to his daughters' duplicity in pretending love for him. The phrase implies ingratitude of vast and inhuman (monstrous) proportions, a sin going against nature. Shakespeare returns to this theme in his writings a number of times highlighting the importance of the principle, particularly so to parents. Ingratitude is synonymous with treason in social and political terms and this is brought to light again in a commentary on Shakespeare's *Coriolanus*:

> Ingratitude, the theme (or sub-theme) ... is itself a violation of Order, for it is the failing to render what is due to him to whom it is due. Shakespeare has woven the idea of ingratitude into the play, with the effect of once more underscoring the grand theme of Order. The accusation of ingratitude reverberates throughout the play. In Coriolanus, "ingratitude" is a word in the mouths of many. It is an idea in the minds of all. And it is a fault or sin which contributes greatly to the death of the hero and the near catastrophe that befalls Rome itself.[426]

---

[395]Parker: op.cit. p177.

[396]Josten: op. cit.

One of the mainstays of society in ancient Rome was the principle of patronage and the grateful client, and so Seneca's words are clear:

> He is ungrateful who denies that he has received a kindness which has been bestowed upon him; he is ungrateful who conceals it; he is ungrateful who makes no return for it; most ungrateful of all is he who forgets it.[427]

Ingratitude could potentially undermine the very fabric of society, especially one such as that of the mid-17th century which depended on friendship, assistance and support. In astrological terms, the 11th house is presently associated with friendship of an emotional nature, but it had a much broader meaning in earlier ages, including just those qualities mentioned above, or in modern terms: sponsorship. The mention of parents is understandable because it was they who 'bred' ingrates, that is, they not only gave birth to them but also brought them up. On this note, we might remember that William Lilly, who had no children, referred to Thomas Agar as his son[428] which may be speculated as a close relationship of another, more mystical order. Elias Ashmole notes the same when William Backhouse[429] bestowed upon him the honour of calling him "son", Ashmole calling Backhouse "father". This was at a time when Backhouse thought he may be dying and, a short time later, bestowed upon Ashmole the secret of the Philosopher's Stone[430]. It may be that Lilly took a similar view of Gadbury, thus the reference, if it was to King Lear particularly, would have had a double significance. The son had been ungrateful to his father.

So, Lilly's accusation was of great seriousness, the substance of which would have been clearly understood by his contemporaries. Gadbury's pretence of friendship to Lilly and the subsequent betrayal of his trust were summed up in the word "ingratitude", and, in the word "monster" we understand an aberration of nature, a miscreation. But this 'sin' was never forgotten or forgiven even beyond Lilly's death; the accusation survived him in the hands of at least one other[431] demonstrating the gravity and longevity of such a charge.

---

[397]Ibid

[398]Parker: op. cit. p129

In Gadbury's address "To the Reader" in *Doctrine*, he himself writes the following:

> Onely give me leave to signifie to the World, the Assistance I have received in the Compilement of this Treatise, and from whom: which, if I should bury in silence, I might expect the black brand of Ingratitude to be annexed unto my Name for ever.

And so it was.

We can find no other reference to or for the cause of Lilly's displeasure and we will present some of the more notable comments. In fact, even though much was written about the matter over the years, largely by Gadbury, no other cause was ever mentioned. The charge of ingratitude suggests that the problem arose from patronage – although Lilly never uses this word – or a situation resonant with it. Gadbury had accepted favours and kindnesses from Lilly and, not only did he fail to repay him, but also betrayed him and everything that Lilly represented.

Continuing with the theme of friendship, betrayal and ingratitude; a similar rift seems to have arisen between Lilly and Ashmole. Looking at the crucial events, we recognise familiar patterns of behaviour in both parties concerned. The one notable difference is the outcome, as Ashmole seems to have regretted his wrongdoings and made reparation, and finally the two men became close friends until Lilly's death. To begin with the relationship between the two was not a smooth one. One of the main reasons for this was that Ashmole was a friend of Lilly's Royalist rival, the pamphleteering George Wharton, who we have already met in Chapter 2. In her paper *Beyond the Great Fire*[432] Sue Ward analyses the relationship between the two men, Lilly and Ashmole. She shows that even on the day of their introduction, the 19th November 1646, Ashmole was having concerns about his association with Lilly, and he cast a horary chart for the question: '"Whether it will be any prejudice for me to publish Wharton's errors against Lilly?"'[433] In other words, would it harm his new relationship with Lilly were he to support Wharton and his latest pamphlet.

At some point just after this, Ashmole's concern was brought to fruition. Having worked closely with Lilly on the diagrams in *Christian Astrology*, he provided Wharton with detailed information about Lilly, making it possible for the former to use this inside knowledge in his pamphlets against Lilly. At some stage Lilly found out about Ashmole's betrayal and on the 16th November 1647, one year after Ashmole asked his horary question, he noted "This morning Lilly told me of my discovering his secrets to Wharton."[434] So once again Lilly had been betrayed by somebody who was working closely with him and who may well have been supported financially by him, too. This could have been the end of their association, but contrary to the situation with Gadbury, Ashmole was keenly interested in a reconciliation, as he writes on the 5th January 1648: "This evening I delivered to Mr. Lilly Picatrix and was reconciled with him."[435] This particular copy of the book *Picatrix,* formerly belonging to Simon Forman and Richard Napier, would have had been highly prized by Ashmole, it was a very valuable gift indeed. Such a demonstration of contrition and appeasement gives us insight into Lilly's status.

Although now reconciled, Ashmole still had concerns about Lilly's motives, writing: "At noon I received the book written in the behalf of Mr. Lilly. At 2: after noon I first read it. Now scandal threatens to fall upon me upon the square of Saturn and Mercury which was the 18th day."[436] The pamphlet in question was supposedly written by a cavalier officer, answering and refuting Wharton's allegations against Lilly. We will never know for certain if Lilly himself wrote the pamphlet, but it seems unlikely. In this pamphlet Ashmole is identified as being the one who provided Wharton with his information. On the 14th March 1648 Wharton was imprisoned and on the 22nd November 1649 Ashmole approached Lilly on Wharton's behalf. It seems that this was the first meeting of the two men since February 1648, indicating that, although reconciled, it took Lilly a long time until he was able to trust Ashmole again. But at last the ice seems to have been broken and on the 7th April 1650 Ashmole asked the horary question: "Whether Mr. Lilly will prove a real friend to me in the suit against Sir Humphrey?"[437]

[399]Josten: op. cit. p36. "Certainly, on his [Ashmole's] return to London, his circle of friends soon included many new acquaintances among astrologers, mathematicians, and physicians whose mystical leanings might have predisposed them to the craft [Freemasonry]. To many orthodox minds the study of mathematics and astrology, which to all intents and purposes

We can clearly see that, contrary to Gadbury, Ashmole recognised his failings and made deliberate moves to repay Lilly and mend the rift. His intention, at least in part, was to keep his reputation intact and to avoid being judged and stigmatised as another monster of ingratitude.

---

still were but two aspects of one discipline, savoured of heresy and atheism, a suspicion which might easily have fostered the formation of mathematicians' lodges or other secret societies, yet no evidence supporting such a conjecture is known."

PART 2:
King of the Castle

I'm the king of the castle and you're the dirty rascal
I'm the king of the castle, get down you dirty rascal.

This nursery rhyme was the basis of a game whereby one child would take possession of a hillock or mound – the castle – and others would try to push him off. The possessor would recite this rhyme whilst pushing back his attackers. Gadbury created a mound where he might rule supreme, but Lilly stood on a distant mountain.

There are three distinct phases in the Gadbury affair: from 1652 to 1658; from 1659 to 1664; from 1673 to 1677. The first relates to the period of Lilly's support for Gadbury, the second to Gadbury's first period of attacks which began with widespread insults regarding Lilly's abilities and led to accusations of plagiarism, and the third relating to the comment made by Lilly regarding the sign of Scorpio. We will handle these periods separately, chronologically and as they appear in print.

---

[400]Lilly, William: *Merlini Anglici Ephemeris for 1656*, London 1656

[401]Coley, Henry: *Clavis Astrologiae Elimata*, 2nd edition, London 1676, pA2

Chapter 4 - The Beginning 1652-1658

It was at around the time of Gadbury's *Philastrogus Knavery* in 1652 that he met Elias Ashmole. According to his own account : "He was also my most Honour'd FRIEND and PATRON, and I had the Happiness of an Intimate Acquaintance with him near Fourty Years;" [438]. Ashmole died in May 1692 implying that this "Intimate Acquaintance" began in early 1652 or thereabouts. How intimate this relationship was is open to question judging by how Gadbury addresses Ashmole when writing to him in later years.[439] Indeed, Gadbury is seldom mentioned by Ashmole at all, unlike his other friends and associates,

Accepting that Gadbury became acquainted with Ashmole in 1652, it is very likely that this was true of Lilly, too. In fact, it is more likely that Lilly introduced Gadbury and his uncle to Ashmole, pointed out by the quotation below and Gadbury would have, had it been necessary, reminded Lilly of his support in *Philastrogus Knavery*, perhaps expecting some demonstration of gratitude. An ardent and vocal supporter of astrology and one prepared to produce corrected tables as described below, would have been welcomed.

Ashmole and Lilly had been reconciled and their friendship placed on a firm footing, Lilly having assisted with the release of Ashmole's friend, George Wharton in 1649. This was during the period of the Interregnum[440], when it was a dangerous time to be a Royalist, therefore both Ashmole and Wharton would have been in need of friends such as Lilly. The strength of these friendships should not be underestimated; as Wharton discovered, they often meant the difference between life and death.

Gadbury, with his uncle, Timothy, published their edition of Hartgill's astronomical tables[441] approximately four years after their meeting Ashmole. The book is dedicated to Ashmole, and Lilly writes a foreword dated February 1654/5, laudatory poems are included from, among others, John Booker and George Wharton – better credentials could not have been wished

---

[402]John Aubrey (1626-1697), antiquary and biographer.

[403]Aubrey, John, *'Brief Lives', chiefly of contemporaries, set down by John Aubrey, between the Years 1669 & 1696*, edited from the author's MSS by Andrew Clark, Clarendon Press, Oxford 1898.

for. It is unsurprising to see such encouragement and support when correct tables were so rare and so necessary for an astrologer's work. It would be easy to imagine that astrologers leapt at the opportunity to support and encourage such an enterprise.

In this work the authors acknowledge Lilly's assistance:

> In order to its Redaction, we applied our selves unto the most Learned and truly Noble Artist Mr. William Lilly, who no sooner hearing our intentions were to reduce *Hartgils* Tables, but very Nobly and Generously offered us the use of his *Studies*, toward the accomplishment of this so necessary a Work; which was (not only an encouragement, but) a great advantage to us, in this our troublesome Taske.

They had sought out Lilly ("applied ourselves unto") not Ashmole, and they had not yet begun work on the tables. It is from this that we deduce that Gadbury's acquaintanceship with Ashmole followed. It is clear that Lilly was enthusiastic about the project and that other astrologers of his standing followed suit. Although the Gadburys acknowledge that Lilly had handed over his work on the matter at the very beginning of their project, no mention is made of his being John's tutor. We might think that this is evidence of Lilly's word being untrue when he says the contrary. However, they also mention the assistance of Nicholas Fiske who Gadbury later maintained *was* in fact his tutor:

> And let us not be unmindfull of the many civilities of that most eminently Learned Mathematician Doctor *Nicholas Fiske*, who in many parts of the Worke did abundantly assist us, and (to say the truth) had not his encouragements prevailed on us, we had left it off, when we had done a third part of it.

---

[404]Anthony Wood, antiquary (1632 – 1695)

[405]Ibid.

It is of course possible that there had been conversations between them about astrology, but there is no mention of any prolonged association along those lines. Partridge notes[442]:

> He went to Dr. Fisk, to know what the meaning of Jupiter in the 6th House was, and this in the year 1650. Of whom he says, he learnt that little of Astrology that he hath. Utterly disowning his best Master, Mr. Lilly, by whose Assistance (he says in the Epistle to his Doctrine of Nativities) and Favours, he was enabled to compleat that Book, which was printed in the Year 1657. Now do you think that Mr. Lilly's Acquaintance had done him no Service, beside the use of Books in that Seven years? Or do you believe his asking Dr. Fisk that one question, had set him in a Station above the want of other Instructions? If so, he was the adeptest Scholar to one, and the most ungreatful to the other of any man living. But I shall forbear any further Aggravation of that Ingratitude, because the whole Nation is so well acquainted with the thing.

This would have been the place for those acknowledgements, at the beginning of Gadbury's career when good fortune abounded and he had hoped to prosper. A biographer might accept the word of their subject about such matters, but it is clearly challenged by Gadbury's contemporaries. Whilst it is not unknown of course to use any means possible to win a battle of words, the context of these challenges and of those who made them appears never to have been examined.

The Gadburys go on to describe the difficulties they had encountered in completing the work, how tedious and laborious it was. They speculate that Hartgill himself may have taken as long as seven years to complete the original tables. They had Ashmole's patronage, Lilly's work to get them started and Fiske's help along the way. Therefore, we might assume that the Gadburys would not have completed the work in under three years, particularly if we take into account the number of times they almost gave up on it[443]. We might also assume that Lilly would have written his foreword after having had sight of the final proof of the manuscript. So accepting the date

---

[406]John Partridge, astrologer (1644 – c1714)

of Lilly's foreword of 1655, work would have begun after Lilly donated his "studies" to them in about 1652 – the year in which Gadbury says that he met Ashmole. It seems obvious, based on this evidence, that John Gadbury introduced himself to Lilly who then introduced him to Ashmole.

It is interesting that Gadbury chose 1654 and 1658 as examples of predicting upon his own nativity; for him the opportunity of paid employment and astrological tuition were enormously important. He was associated with the most famous astrologer in the country (perhaps equalled only by John Booker) with international renown; he was indeed fortunate. In 1658 his *Doctrine* was published with a recommendation from Lilly *and* Booker, which in anyone's estimation was extraordinary. It is this book which brings us primary source information about the rift between Lilly and Gadbury.

Referred to earlier, William Lilly's own copy of *Doctrine* is extant[444] and in it we find extensive marginalia which provide a fascinating insight into this affair. These notes provide a commentary on Gadbury's text and on the man himself, and give us a wider view of the contention. It is from these notes that we find that Gadbury was in London in 1646 as a "covenant servant" to one John Thorn, a tailor, located "over against the Talbot in the Strand". It is clear from these notes that Lilly's knowledge of Gadbury was far different from that usually published in more recent biographies. It is much in accord with that of Partridge[445] who was close to Gadbury for much longer than Lilly had been.

[407]Partridge, John: *Nebulo Anglicanus, Or the First Part of the Black Life of John Gadbury* London 1693.

To the Reader.

nification of every House: then by his Tables of Right and Oblique Ascentions, his Ascentional Differences, and Declinations, his Tables of Position, thou mayst both take the Circle of Position any Planet is in, and direct every Significator to his proper Promittor; judge the effects of every Direction; with much facility set every Annual Revolution; judge of a Revolutional Figure, &c. with many other material things too large for me to repeat. He is Copious in the whole Work, and in every Subject he handles, very curious; and yet hath not pestered his Book with unnecessary matter, but abundantly compleated it with most material and pertinent Aphorisms and choice Collections through each Page thereof. Knowing the Modesty of the Author, and how little he esteemes the publick applause of Men, I silently pass by many other considerable matters therein contained.

And with much satisfaction to my self, am heartily glad to behold so learned a Production from an English Man; the essential Verity whereof, shall manifest unto Posterity for many Ages, the high Worth and indefatigable Industry of the Author.

In these marginalia the phrase "monster of ingratitude" is found a number of times, the first being on the frontispiece where Lilly has struck through the title of "Philomath" on the by-line and replaced it with "Taylor, & monster of ingratitude". The second occurrence is in Gadbury's address "To the Reader" where he writes:

> When I first of all adventured upon this Task, I made my intention known unto my truly-honoured Friend, Mr. William Lilly, who, upon the hearing thereof, very nobly, and like a true and faithful Propagator of Art and Learning, gave me many encouragements to perfect the thing I intended; and that I might not want the Sight or Assistance of the best Authours, both Arabian and Latine, he most civilly and freely offered me the use of his Studie towards the

[408]Partridge: ibid. The biographical information contained in this pamphlet and *A short Answer to a Malicious Pamphlet*, also by Partridge, can be found at Partridge, John: *A short answer to a malicious pamphlet called, A reply written by John Gadbury*, London 1680.

> Accomplishment hereof; without which signal Favour and Respect, it had been impossible for me to have framed it so perfect as thou now seest it. And I hereby return him my hearty thanks, as the only Testimony of a Grateful Heart, where a Richer Requital is wanting.

Here we see sincere thanks – gratitude – for the great generosity shown to Gadbury by Lilly, to which the latter responds in the margin:

> Just see how this villain requited Lilly in 1659 & 1660 in writing 3 or 4 Libelling pamphlets against him.

We will provide further quotations as evidence that this is the essence of the whole matter: Gadbury published pamphlets against Lilly almost immediately following the publication of *Doctrine* in 1658. Before delving into those, we must look at the other notes which show why Lilly was so offended by Gadbury's betrayal. Having obliterated his own 'signature' at the end of his recommendation of Gadbury to the reader, Lilly notes that he "gave him Directions in the whole". Later, Gadbury writes "These verses have I borrowed from the works of that worthy Poet, Mr. Tho. May.", to which Lilly notes, "tis very true, and all the whole book from Lilly, Origanus, Argol, and Sconer, nothing is this pimping fooles but the Tautology." Further pertinent remarks are: "...witness his several pamphlets against Lilly who was his maker, he is a monster of ingratitude", "The Rascall was a meer poor Taylor till Lilly taught him Astrology in 1654", and, "hee wrought 4 yeares to Lilly, made him new clothes, & mended his old."

This provides further support that the falling out between Lilly and Gadbury was truly brought about by the latter's demonstration of gross ingratitude. There is no reason for Lilly to mention the year of 1654 and that he then began to teach Gadbury if it were not true. Lilly's anger is plain, as was his generosity in providing for Gadbury as he did, but we can find no reason to disbelieve Lilly's comment that Gadbury was closely associated with him between 1654 and 1658. As he did for Ashmole, Lilly gave Gadbury work,

---

[409]Gadbury, John: *The Doctrine of Nativities*, London 1658. Containing Lilly's handwritten comments.

[410]Philastrogus, *Lillies Ape Whipt*, 1652.

and paid him[446], whilst also teaching him astrology. It is clear from Gadbury's preface to his *Doctrine*, that he had relied on Lilly to a considerable degree in its preparation. As previously mentioned Lilly had been unable to produce a revised edition of *Christian Astrology*, thus he was enthusiastic about younger astrologers publishing in his stead.

However, the original recommendation of Gadbury's book does raise doubts about Lilly's judgement. If the book was good enough for Lilly to write about it in glowing terms, why criticise it so strongly later? We must return to Lilly's unfulfilled desire to revise and republish *Christian Astrology*. Gadbury's *Doctrine* was perhaps the best new primer available because Lilly had had the opportunity therein to correct some of the shortcomings of his own text. He specifies his own contributions and those of Origanus, Argol and Schoener. It would be reasonable to assume that Lilly recommended these earlier authors to Gadbury and then gave him access to those books.

So, supported by William Lilly in both work and study, Gadbury was encouraged to pursue a career in astrology. As he himself notes in his natal delineation, he was introduced to people of eminence and influence in various fields of knowledge, religion and politics; Lilly's circle was of men of education, influence and power. It is obvious from the retrospective delineation of his nativity for 1654, that Gadbury himself recognised this. It is also obvious that he was very pleased and excited at the possibilities that this presented. Lilly befriended Gadbury and employed him as his tailor so that he might support himself and his family and taught him between 1654 and 1658, even though this was denied later by Gadbury.

It may be, as has been suggested[447], that Gadbury declined from Lilly because of the latter's more 'magical' attitude towards astrology, or perhaps because of his politics. Gadbury does indeed write along these lines, but it seems more likely that Gadbury was persuaded by his own desire to be on the winning side at all times and by his self-confessed ambition for "honour and esteem", or perhaps through his own "rash and headstrong actions". Certainly Gadbury presents a confrontational and distrustful character, always

---

[411]Ward: op.cit. p63

suspicious of those closest to him. Richard Cromwell resigned as Lord Protector on 25th May 1659, (an interesting date in Gadbury's pamphleteering, as we will show) and Charles Stuart, soon to be Charles II, arrived at Dover exactly one year later. Clearly, Gadbury had convinced Lilly of his sincerity; Lilly was keen to find supporters of astrology with whom it might survive and flourish. But at a time when friends were often all that stood between a person and destitution, when patronage was actively sought, it is odd that Gadbury should discard it. He could after all have maintained his subterfuge and thus Lilly's support. There can be only one reason and that is that he had found a replacement for Lilly, someone Gadbury considered to be more powerful and influential, and the source of greater patronage and one who may have been in better standing with the Royalists. It would seem that Lilly was of no further use.

However, we should also bear in mind that in October of 1659 Lilly was brought the gold medal given to him by the King of Sweden[448] (Lilly gives 1658 as the year[449] which is corrected by Ashmole to 1659). Gadbury makes mention of this on numerous occasions and over a considerable period[450] suggesting jealousy and resentment. *Merlinus Gallicus* was imprinted 1660, but its owner had noted 10th October 1659 as its issue date and it is within this pamphlet that Gadbury gets into his stride with his accusations against Lilly. This corresponds very closely with the date of Lilly's receiving the gold medal and chain, presumably with some advance notice.

One of Gadbury's complaints was that Lilly had used ancient prophecies with which to link Charles Gustav to great victories and that he had not used astrology. This may have been a genuine concern, but it was not the complaint which stands out principally in Gadbury's directory of bitterness, it was the gold medal and chain. The evidence of his own pamphlets support the argument that it was this which turned him against Lilly – a gift from a king widely admired as a hero of the Protestant nations. Gadbury's own ambitions for such recognition transmuted to jealousy and hatred of his benefactor. (Perhaps the real reason that he published the King of Sweden's nativity was an attempt to ingratiate himself with Charles Gustav or some

[412]Gadbury, Timothy & John: *Astronomicall Tables first invented by George Hartgill…*, London 1656.

[413]ibid

other and earn a medal of his own.) This seems a much more plausible reason than political or astrological disputes for the poison which issued from his pen over subsequent years. Gadbury's pamphlets during 1659 and 1660 read from beginning to end as almost frenzied attacks which become increasingly irrational and violent. However, in each he returns to the central theme of the gold medal and chain.

Gadbury had found patrons for his *Doctrine* and *Ephemeris* of 1658, Francis Gregory and William Battine respectively, thus we might reasonably speculate that his confidence had been bolstered. Even so, to reject such a man as Lilly, and not just reject but make an enemy of him, suggests that Gadbury may simply have been overcome by envy; envy is clear in every pamphlet he writes against Lilly. In his very many protests, perhaps too many in the Shakespearian sense, the question is raised as to whether Gadbury was demonstrating regret at his own foolhardiness.

---

[414]For example, Parker: op. cit. and Curry: *Lilly, William (1602-1681), Oxford Dictionary of National Biography*, Oxford University Press, 2004.

Timeline

02.02.1652	Attacks Culpeper, defends WL, et al.	Philastrogus (R. Lilburne): *Lillies Ape Whipt*	1
05.04.1652 (noted: 12.04.1652)	Criticises Lilly's "Black Munday"	Brommerton: *Confidence Dismounted*	2
05.04.1652	Reply to Philastrogus. Defending Culpeper, supporting Lilly	Gadbury: *Philastrogus Knavery*	3
1652	**Gadbury makes Ashmole's acquaintance (according to Gadbury)**		
16.11.1652	Comments on *Black Munday* and *Liilies Ape Whipt*	Lilly: Merlini Anglici, 1653	4
1653	T. Gataker attacks Lilly	Gataker: *Vindication*	5
1654 (1653?)	Gadbury defends astrology and Lilly	Gadbury: *Animal Cornutum or The horn'd beast*	6
1654	T. Gataker attacks Lilly and Gadbury	Gataker: Discours Apologetical	7

[415]Curry: *'Gadbury, John' ODNB* op. cit.

[416]Capp, Bernard: *'Fiske Nicholas' (1579-1659) Oxford Dictionary of National Biography*, Oxford University Press, 2004.

1654	**Lilly teaches Gadbury (according to Lilly)**		
1656	Gadbury praises Lilly	Gadbury: *Coelestial Ambass*ador	8
1656	Publication of Hartgill's Astronomical Tables	Gadbury, J. and T.: *Astronomical Tables*	9
1658	**Lilly receives gold medal from King of Sweden**		
1658	Gadbury, living near Lilly, publishes *Doctrine of Nativities.*	Gadbury: *Doctrine of Nativities*	10

1. (Lilburne, Robert ?): *Lillies ape whipt by Philastrogus. Ephemeris for the year 1652*,London: Printed for W.I. C.I. G.W., 1652.
2. Brommerton, William: *Confidence dismounted; or the astronomers knavery anatomized. By William Brommerton a well-wisher to the commonweale*, London: Printed for to undeceive the people, Aprill 5. 1652.
3. Gadbury, John: *Philastrogus knavery epitomized, with a vindication of Mr. Culpeper, Mr. Lilly, and the rest of the students in that noble art, from all the false aspersions (of the malicious antagonists) cast upon them, about the great eclipse of the Sunne. Whereunto is annexed an epistle to all moderate spirited men, shewing the peoples great mistakes, and misunderstanding of the honest and ingenious artists, who spake truly, as is averred by this ensuing tractate. / Written by J.G. a lover of all ingenious arts and artists* - Aprill the 5. 1652. London: Printed in the year, 1652.
4. Lilly, William: Merlini Anglici ephemeris or, astrologicall predictions for the year 1653, London: Printed for the Company of Stationers, and H. Blunden at the Castle in Cornhill, 1653.

---

[417]Gadbury: *Doctrine*, op. cit. p249 ff.

[418]Josten: op.cit and Curry: ODNB

5. Gataker, Thomas: *An answer to Mr. George Walkers vindication, or rather, fresh accusation wherein he chargeth Mr. Wotton, besides his former foul aspersions of heresie and blasphemy, with Arianism, Mr. Gataker with Socinianism, Dr. Gouge and Mr. Downham with a false attestation, Dr. Baylie and Mr. Stock with self-condemnation, all the eight ministers employed in the busines between himself and Mr. Wotton with partiality and unjust judgement : upon occasion of a relation concerning that busines / written by the said Thomas Gataker and by him now again avowed, wherein the said M. Walkers vindication is in many things shewed to be an untrue relation.* , London: Printed by E.G. for F. Clifton, 1642.
6. Gadbury, John: *Animal cornutum, or The horn'd beast: wherein is contained, 1 a brief method of the grounds of astrology, 2 a description of each planet and sign, 3 the way to erect a figure of heaven, 4 a narrative of what visible eclipses (both of sun and moon) will appear in our horizon, for these 15 years yet to come, with the month, day, and hour when they happen. Whereunto is annexed, an examination of a spurious pamphlet (intituled, Astrology proved to be the doctrine of daemons) laying open the antagonist's malice, and folly; with a refutation of his errors, by an astrological example, in figure, and judgement. / Composed for the benefit of all those that are desirous to exercise themselves herein, by J. Gadbury, a lover of the celestial sciences.* , London : Printed for William Larnar, and are to be sold at the Blackmores head neer Fleet-bridge, 1654.
7. Gataker, Thomas, 1574-1654 : *A discours apologetical; wherein Lilies lewd and lowd lies in his Merlin or Pasqil for the yeer 1654. are cleerly laid open; his shameful desertion of his own cause is further discovered; his shameless slanders fullie refuted; and his malicious and murtherous mind, inciting to a general massacre of Gods ministers, from his own pen, evidentlie evinced. Together with an advertisement concerning two allegations produced in the close of his postscript. And a postscript concerning an epistle dedicatorie of one J. Gadburie. By Tho. Gataker B.D. author of the annotations on Jer. 10.2 and of the vindication of them.* , London : Printed by R. Ibbitson for Thomas Newberry, at the three Lions in Cornhil, neer the Royal Exchange., 1654.
8. Gadbury, John: *Coelestis legatus: or, The coelestial ambassadour astrologically predicting the grand catastrophe that is probable to befall most of the kingdomes and countries of Europe. From the influences of those many planetary conjunctions celebrated in the month of September, 1656; but more especially from that eminent conjunction of Saturn and Mars in Virgo in the same month. Unto which is added a catalogue of all the conjunctions of those two planets since the year 1552 reaching to the year 1700. with chronologicall observations, of what hath succeeded those past, and a probable conjecture of what may succeed those yet to come. Together with some peeces of Haly in the English*

---

[419]Gadbury: *Collectio*, p127.

[420]Lilly: *The Life of…*, 421 ff. 178-223.

tongue. / By John Gadbury, Philomath. , London: Printed by E.B. and are to be sold by John Allen, at the Rising-Sun in Pauls Church-yard, 1656

9. Hartgill, George: *Astronomical tables shewing the declinations, right ascentions, and aspects of three hundred sixty five of the most principall fixed stars and the number of them in their constellations after Aratus : as also the true oblique ascentions and descentions of all the said stars upon the cusps of every of the twelve houses of heaven according to their latitude / first invented by George Hartgill ; and now reduced to this our age by John and Timothy Gadbury.* , London: Printed for the Company of Stationers, 1656
10. Gadbury, John: *Genethlialogia, or, The doctrine of nativities containing the whole art of directions and annual revolutions : whereby any man (even of an ordinary capacity) may be enabled to discover the most remarkable and occult accidents of his life ... : also tables for calculating the planets places for any time, either past, present or to come : together with the doctrine of horarie questions which (in the absence of a nativity) is sufficient to inform any one of all manner of contengencies neessary to be known* / by John Gadbury. , London : Printed by Ja. Cottrel for Giles Calverts, William Larnar, and Daniel White, 1658.

[421]Fiske, Nicholas: *An Astrological Discourse*, London 1650.

Chapter 5 The Development Plagiarism 1659-1664

Gadbury's *Doctrine* was published in 1658, the foreword is dated 21st April of that year, so we might assume that this work was being sold towards the end of 1658. We have already demonstrated that Lilly's active support had been obtained and thanks given to him in the foreword. The first attack on Lilly appears to be within the pages of *Merlinus Gallicus*; the imprint is for 1660, but a handwritten date of 10th October 1659 is found on the frontispiece and implies that that of 1660 was a second edition. Likewise, Gadbury's delineation of the King of Sweden's nativity has an imprint of 1659 with a handwritten date of 2nd May. It is clear from this pamphlet that it was written before Gadbury had decided that he no longer needed Lilly. Within the text is a fair quotation from Lilly's work, the only criticisms being within the epistle and on the cover. In its second edition it was bound with *The Spurious Prognosticator Unmasked*[451] which was printed in 1660. His delineation of the nativity of King Charles I was also printed twice, but the one to hand is that of 1659 with a handwritten date of August on the cover. This means that the earlier edition (without the attacks on Lilly) was later republished with the addition of an epistle and cover and coincides with Richard Cromwell's resignation on the 25th May 1659.

So within a few months of *Doctrine* being published, Gadbury was busy writing against Lilly and he appears to do this at every opportunity both in separate pamphlets and within his almanacs. The accusations became increasingly extreme and, in some cases, actually dangerous to Lilly where Gadbury draws attention to Lilly's writings relating to Charles I. But initially, Gadbury's primary purpose was to undermine Lilly's credibility and standing as an astrologer. A common criticism made by Gadbury is that Lilly had little or no knowledge of astronomy and was lacking in his calculations, so it is interesting to note Lilly's handwritten comments in *Doctrine* on this subject. Where Gadbury presents sexagenary tables, Lilly notes:

---

[422]Aubrey, John, *'Brief Lives', chiefly of contemporaries, set down by John Aubrey, between the Years 1669 & 1696*, edited from the author's MSS by Andrew Clark, Clarendon Press, Oxford 1898. In letters between Aubrey and Wood.

> These tables hee never understood, see the Nativity which is his owne about the proportional part of the 12. houses their Cuspes.

We see here and elsewhere Gadbury accusing Lilly of shortcomings which were his own and were shown to be so later[452]. Lilly's note suggests that either he had not been aware of these errors, which we find doubtful, or that he had advised corrections which were not done. This might have angered Gadbury enough to turn him against his master.

We estimate that Gadbury printed at least nine attacks on Lilly between 1659 and 1661. This was the period of political turmoil which occurred at the end of the Protectorship and the beginning of the Restoration, when Gadbury might have hoped for greater rewards with the Royalist party. However, we can find no direct reference or reply to these attacks in Lilly's writings. Indeed Gadbury was not the only one who criticised Lilly in savage terms and he did not reply to those, so there is no reason that we should find a reference to Gadbury. Neither can we find any replies from Lilly's supporters. We have discovered that Lilly responds to the political accusations in general terms, but there is no evidence to suggest that this was because of Gadbury alone.

The attacks increased when, in 1662, Gadbury's *Collectio Geniturarum* was published in which is a barely concealed accusation against Lilly of plagiarism. The accusation was that Lilly had used the unpublished work of Edward Gresham[453] in his first publication *Propheticall Merline* of 1644. There is no clear reason for Gadbury's waiting so long to make this accusation; according to him[454] he had known about this since his association with Nicholas Fiske who had died in 1659. We might speculate that having had no response from Lilly and having baited him for long enough, Gadbury felt that desperate measures were required. Certainly, he appears to have hit the mark, because Lilly breaks his silence and replies. Lilly may well have considered this to be a far more serious accusation than that of treason which had preceded it.

---

[423]Partridge: *Nebulo Anglicanus*, op. cit.

[424]For example: *Britain's Royal Star*, London 1661.

This particular example is important because it clearly shows the difference between Lilly and Gadbury in their respective positions in this contention and the moral code of each. Lilly writes[455]:

> …, we complain unto all Students in Astrology, of that slanderous aspersion cast upon us by J.G. in a late thing of his published, who being my Taylor from 1654 unto 1658 is not ashamed to commit to the press, this most egregious untruth, viz. That Richard Gresham was Author of the *Prophetical merline*, which was a Treatise of the effects of the last Conjunction of Saturn and Jupiter 1642 or 1643 and wrote by us in 1641. 1642. 1643. and published 1644. The truth is thus ----
>
> Richard Gresham died about the year 1616 left nothing to posterity in print but some Almanacks; if he wrote any thing of the *Prophetical Merlin*, he was the greatest Prophet ever lived. For we quote several books printed after his death, viz. *Keplers Epitome*, printed 1623. *Campanella* his Astrology printed 1630. *Aestedius* printed after that year: and relate unto the page in every book; we mention *W. Laud* Archbishop of Canterbury, The Lord Chief-Justice Finch, the Earl of Strafford, these men had no honour in Greshams time, we mention the death of King James not dead in Greshams time; we mention the Comet of 1618 which appeared not till Gresham was dead; we mention Dr. Bainbrig who wrote of it, and of its declination every day: we mention Longomontanus, the Death of Queen Ann, who died 2 years or more after Gresham, also several other persons; we take notice of the then present breach betwixt King and parliament, which was 25 or 26 years after Gresham's death: *Oportet mendacem esse memorem,* but we are not disposed to quarrel with our Quondam Taylor, the most Ingrateful person living.

This is a brief and straightforward reply not addressed to Gadbury, but to his readers. Lilly has been compelled to make a statement because a point of honour has to be made. Plagiarism is an expression of ingratitude and this, for Lilly, was far more important than any political points Gadbury had raised, even it seems when, potentially, it put him in danger of his life. It may be that

[425]Lilly's copy of Gadbury's *Doctrine of Nativities* includes this expression, written in Lilly's own hand.

Lilly took far less note of Gadbury's pamphlets which had a comparatively small readership than he did of the book.

Gadbury replies[456] in, what are for him, restrained terms:

> For Defending my self against the Sarcasms of that abusive person W.L. I suppose all Rational men will excuse me; he having fallen foul on me after a Truce was procured betwixt my self and him, by Captain G.W. which I kept inviolable, (I speak it in the presence of God, who is the onely Heart-Judger and Heart-Searcher) even in very words, for the very time I first thereunto consented: and not onely so, but have reproved others that (in hopes to please me) have reproachfully spoken of him; and of this, I have many Witnesses.

The epistle in this pamphlet, of which the above quotation forms a part, is dated 13th January 1664, which date is confusing. The pamphlet was licensed on 19th December 1663 and published in 1664, thus the date given by Gadbury should read, in Old Style, 13th January 1663/4. The point of these dates is that he speaks of a "truce" brokered by Wharton which he had "kept inviolable". The only hiatus in Gadbury's attacks that we can find follows the publication of *Collectio Geniturarum* in 1662; his epistle there is dated 8th August 1662. It is in this book that he accuses Lilly of plagiarism who replies in his almanac of 1664, which was completed in the Autumn of 1663. This is Lilly's earliest opportunity to reply without recourse to a separate pamphlet. As far as we know, the last time Gadbury attacked Lilly was in *Britains Royal Star* of 1661 (a date of 22nd November is written on the cover) and presumably the author was busy with his next book between times. So, Gadbury apparently published no further attacks between 1661 and 1662. If this is the period to which he refers as a "truce", then it was he who broke it with the plagiarism accusation. However, Gadbury also writes immediately afterwards, "And the matter concerning Mr. Gresham was written long before that time." If this is true, then the truce could have been in place only after that charge of 1662 and before Lilly's reply of August 1663, imprinted 1664.

---

[426]Neumeyer, Peter F: *Ingratitude Is Monstrous: An Approach to Coriolanus.* College English, Vol. 26, No. 3 (Dec., 1964), pp. 192-198. National Council of Teachers of English. Stable URL: http://www.jstor.org/stable/373589

Trying to make sense of Gadbury's versions of events is always difficult, but it is possible that Wharton approached Gadbury shortly before *Collectio* was published. They were on somewhat friendly terms (according to Gadbury), so this might have been an informal warning. Given what we know of Lilly, his status, reputation and circle of friends and supporters, it is highly unlikely that he would have made any kind of deal with Gadbury; in fact, it is incredible. Gadbury returns to his usual manner of expression at the end of *Dies Novissimus*[457] where he enters into eight pages of invective against Lilly. Since this is apparently the first time Lilly has responded to one of Gadbury's attacks and in reasonably measured terms, it is illuminating.

This chapter of insults is plainly an attempt to rid himself of the charge of ingratitude by aiming it at Lilly. He repeats that Fiske was his "honoured Friend and Tutor" which has been shown to be an exaggeration at the least, and given that his version of the so-called "truce" is faulty at best, is likely to be untrue. Gadbury is infuriated at the lack of attention his complaints and charges have received from Lilly:

> Well, but let Mr. L. play the Plagiarie still, and pilfer from whom he can; lisp and jabber, say and unsay as fast as oft as he please; he judges it wisdome it seems and honour enough to himself to raile upon my Person and Education, and that he thinks is satisfaction sufficient from him.

He goes on to accuse Lilly of ingratitude, lies, theft, of having been a tailor, a botcher, a "venomous… Sycophant", an impostor, and then goes on to repeat some of the troubles between Lilly and Gataker, and Lilly and Wharton. It is a catalogue of abuse, but there is one point he makes that is of interest:

> Mr. L. should have done well to have told me for what: for four years since he exhibited this charge against me, for which I questioned him before Mr. E. Carrent (now Adjutant-General of the honourable City of London) before whom he did not onely

[427] Seneca, *De Beneficiis* III, 1.

[428]Lilly: ibid

> deny the Expression [of ingratitude], and called a Learned Minister False Scot, for telling me of it, but pronounced me to him, The most Grateful Person living.

Thus, Gadbury casts back to 1660, or perhaps 1659, when Lilly is first supposed to have charged him with ingratitude. Gadbury says that he has brought the matter up before Carrent – presumably a lawyer of whom we have been unable to find any record. We have not found this matter to be raised anywhere else in any form even by Gadbury, so must conclude that Gadbury is being somewhat creative with the truth again. Furthermore, other evidence suggests that Lilly himself was preparing a legal suit against Gadbury for his accusations of plagiarism. Thus Gadbury's mention of some kind of legal case of his own would make sense.

Unusually, Lilly dedicates his *Anglicus* of 1664:

> Unto Elias Ashmole Esq; who in all changes and every Revolution of Time, since first acquaintance 1646. hath continued (Semper idem [always the same] this Annual Astrological discourse is dedicated, by W. Lilly Student in Astrology.

We suggest that the reason Lilly does this here is that Ashmole was working on his behalf in the matter of Gadbury. In Ashmole's *Notes*[458] for the 30th January 1663/4, which is a little over two weeks after Gadbury completed *Dies Novissimus*, he writes as follows:

> Mr. Gadbury in his Collectio Genituarum pag: 179 and 180 saith that Mr: Edward Gresham wrote this discourse of the conjunction of Jupiter & Saturn which Mr. Lilly hath printed under the Tile of Englands propheticall Merlyn.
>
> The discourse he here meanes, was written after the year 1618 for it gives an account of the Comet in that yeare: I having the originall in my hand, shewed it to Mr. Gadbury 30: Jan: 1663/4 who acknowledged to me that it was the very Booke Mr: Fiske shewed

[429]William Backhouse (1593-1662) well-known alchemist.

[430]Josten: op.cit.

> him for Mr: Greshams, & upon compairing it with this booke, found Mr: Lilly had made some, (but no Astrologicall) use of it, but very little. Beside it appears not to be the worke of Edw: Gresham, since it appears by the foll' Certificate he dyed many yeares before the yeare 1618.
>
> By the Register of the Parish of Allhallows the less London I doe finde that Edward Gresham Gent: was buried the fourteenth day of January In the yeare one Thousand six hundred & twelve.
>
> Examinatum per William Salusbury Notary Publick.

The certificate issued by Salusbury is preserved within Ashmole's papers and is another demonstration of how serious matters had become. We deduce from this that preparations were in hand to deal with Gadbury's accusations more formally with Ashmole acting as Lilly's attorney. However the matter was handled, and as far as we can ascertain, Gadbury's printed attacks and accusations ceased for about ten years.

---

[431]Partridge: *Nebulo Anglicanus*, op. cit.

[432]Ward, Susan: Beyond the Great Fire: Lilly and Ashmole.

Timeline

JG1 - 2.5.1659 (Epistle 29.1.1659)	2 editions – 2nd criticises Lilly Quotes WL p13	Gadbury: *Merlinus Verax*	1
JG2 - October 1659 10.10.1659	Missonne Philastrogus (Gadbury) questions Lilly's abilities	Philastrogus: *Merlinus Gallicus*	2
7.2.1659/60	**According to Gadbury, Nicholas Fiske dies (*Collectio*, p128)**		
JG3 - 23.2.1659/60 (Impr. 1660)	Gadbury refers to a previous attack of his, re. *Merlini Anglici*, 1660	Gadbury: *Novice Astrologer Instructed*	3
JG4 - 1660	Gadbury attacks Lilly	Gadbury: *A Declaration*	4
JG5 - 1660	Gadbury attacks Lilly. 2 editions – 2nd published with King of Sweden's nativity	Gadbury: *The Spurious Prognosticator* (Re: *Merlini Anglici, 1659*)	5
JG6 - 1660	Gadbury attacks Lilly	Gadbury: *Nuntius Astrologicus*	6
JG7 - 1660	James Blackwel publishes Lilly's "nativity". (In collaboration with Gadbury?)	Blackwel: *The Nativity of Mr. Lilly*	7
JG9 - 1661	Gadbury attacks Lilly	Gadbury: *Britains Royal Star*	8
1661	William Lilly' signature is still in place in Gadbury's 2nd edition of *Doctrine*	Gadbury: *The Doctrine of Nativities*	9
1661	Lilly writes re. Restoration and Scorpio	Lilly: *Merlini Anglici*	10
JG10 - 1662	Gadbury accuses Lilly of plagiarising Gresham	Gadbury: *Collectio Geniturarum*	11
WL1 - Published 1664 (written 16.9.1663)	Lilly replies to Gadbury's accusations of plagiarism and acknowledges Ashmole	Lilly: *Merlini Anglici*	12
JG11 - 1664 (Epistle 13.1.1663, licensed 19.12.1663; 1663/4?)	Gadbury replies to Lilly' *Merlini Anglici* of 1664, Wharton brokering truce.	Gadbury: *Dies Novissimus*	13
30.1.1663/64	**Ashmole acts for William Lilly (Ashmole's *Notes*)**		
Not before 1660	**Lilly's marginalia in Gadbury's *Doctrine***		

[433] Ibid, p8

[434] Ibid, p9

1. Gadbury, John: *The nativity of that most illustrious and magnanimous prince, Carolus Gustavus, King of Sweden, astrologically handled; and published for the honour of art, and the satisfaction of all sorts of persons generally, as well astrologers as others; and particularly for the better information of Mr. William Lilly.* Written by Merlinus Verax. , London: printed in the year 1659.
2. Gadbury, John: *Merlinus Gallicus: Or, A prediction for the year of grace, 1660. Representing the state and condition of all sorts of persons in Europe, from the crown to the clown. Deduced from the configurations of the luminaries, conjunctions and aspects of the planets, after a more certain manner then practised by English artists. Together with the nativity of the illustrious King of Denmark: proving it impossible (by the canons of astrology) for him to lose his kingdom, or for the Swede to become lord thereof, wherein Merlinus Anglicus may see his error. Also a question and answer in astrology, whether Copenhagen shall be taken or no: with many other things of profitable consequence. / By Monsieur Fr. Missonne Philastrogus. To which is added, an everlasting almanack; with an easie way to erect a figure, and give judgement of the weather, and tables of houses fitted for several latitudes.* , London: Printed by T.J. for Fr. Cossinet, and sold at his shop at the Anchor and Mariner in Tower-street, with other books of art; as, arithmetick, geometry, trigonometry, navigation, astronomy, and astrology., 1660 [i.e. 1659]
3. Gadbury, John: *Neophuto-astrologos. = The novice-astrologer instructed in a New-Years-gift to Mr. William Lilly; occasioned by the scurrility, scandal, ignorance, and flattery of his Merlin for the ensuing year. With two dedicatory epistles; the one to the learned divines, the other to the honest astrologers of this nation. / By G.J. or J.G. which Lilly the parasite pleaseth.* , London: Printed for E.C. and are to be sold at the Royal Exchange, Westminster-hall, and Paul's Church-yard, 1660.
4. Gadbury, John: *A Declaration of the several treasons, blasphemies and misdemeanors acted, spoken and published against God, the late King, his present Majesty, the nobility, clergy, city, commonalty, &c. by that grand wizard and impostor William Lilly of St. Clements Danes, other wise called Merlinus Anglicus presented to the right honourable the members of the House of Parliament : in order to secure him from acting any further villanies against His Majesty.* , London : Printed for Dan. White, 1660.
5. Gadbury, John: *Pseudo-astrologos, or, The spurious prognosticator unmasked. Being a short examen of the manifold errors and fallacies, falshoods and flatteries, published by Mr. W. Lilly in his Merlin 1659. Wherein his ignorance in astrology is explained and exploded; his scandalous girdings at the king of Denmark, duke of Brandenburgh, and the states of Holland, noted; his nefarious dealing with the late lord protector of*

[435]Ibid

[436]Ibid

England, and the king of Sweden, discovered; his impudent, arrogant and artless assertions, retorted and refuted. / By G.J. ... Merlini Anglici ephemeris. Merlini Anglici ephemeris. , London: Printed in the year 1660.

6. Gadbury, John: *Nuncius Astrologicus, or, The Astrological Legate: Demonstrating to the World the success there may probably (by the Influences of the Stars) be expected from the present , unhappy controverse, between the two Northern Kings: Deduced from the Nativity of His Royal Majesty of Denmark,* London: Printed by J. Cotrell, for F. Cossinet; and are to be sold at the Anchor and Mariner in Tower Street, 1660 [1659]
7. Blackwel, James: *The nativity of Mr. Will. Lilly astrologically performed shewing how he hath lived, and what death he may probably die. For the satisfaction of astrologers and others.* Published to the world by James Blackwel, student in astrology and physick. , London : printed by Tho. Johnson, at the White Cock in Rood-lane, 1660.
8. Gadbury, John: *Britains royal star: Or, An astrological demonstration of Englands future felicity; deduced from the position of the heavens as they beheld the earth in the meridian of London, at the first proclaiming of his Sacred Majesty King Charles the second, on May 8. 10h. 56m. A.M. 1660. And an enquiry made into the use and abuse of astrologie, resolving whether it be convenient to be continued or contemned. Also, an admirable observation of a conjunction of Jupiter and Mars made in the year 1170. by a learned monck of Canterbury, communicated to the learned in astronomy. Together with an exaination and refutation of that nest of sedition, published by Mr. H. Jessey, concerning frogs, dogs, &c. in his pamplet falsly intituled, The Lords Loud call to England, &c.* By John Gadbury, philomathematicus. Published by Mr. H. Jessey. , London : printed for Sam. Speed, at the signe of the Printing-Press in St. Paul's Church-yard, 1661. [i.e. 1660]
9. Gadbury, John: *Genethlialogia, or, The doctrine of nativities containing the whole art of directions and annual revolutions, whereby any man (even of an ordinary capacity) may be enabled to discover the most remarkable and occult accidents of his life ... : also tables for calculating the planets places for any time, either past, present, or to come : together with the doctrine of horarie questions, which (in the absence of a nativity) is sufficient to inform any one of all manner of contingencies necessary to be known /* by John Gadbury, London : Printed for William Miller, M.DC.LXI [1661]
10. Lilly, William: *Merlini Anglici ephemeris astrological predictions for the year 1661 /* by William Lilly, London: Printed for the Company of Stationers, 1661.

---

[437]Ibid, p12

[438]Gadbury, John, *ΕΦΗΜΕΡΙΣ.. Or, A Diary Astronomical, Astrological, Meteorological, For the Year of Our Lord, 1694*, London, 1694.

11. Gadbury, John: *Collectio geniturarum, or, A collection of nativities, in CL genitures, viz. princely, prelatical, causidical, physical, mercatorial, mathematical, of short life, of twins, &c. with many useful observations on them, both historical and astrological : being of practical concernment unto philosophers, physitians, astronomers, astrologers, and others that are friends unto Urania* / by John Gadbury, London: Printed by James Cottrel, 1662.
12. Lilly, William: *Merlini Anglici ephemeris, or, Astrological judgements for the year 1664* by William Lilly, London: Printed for the Company of Stationers, 1664 [1663].
13. Gadbury, John: *Dies novissimus, or, Dooms-day not so near as dreaded together with something touching the present invasion of the Turk into the German Empire and the probable success thereof* / by John Gadbury, London: Printed by James Cottrel, 1664.

Chapter 6 - The Conclusion

Scorpionist 1673-1677

In this last phase of Gadbury's battle against Lilly, the latter's health was deteriorating, to which he refers a number of times in his almanacs. During this period, Lilly writes little more than formerly, but on this occasion, others wrote on his behalf and we shall present parts of those responses.

Apparently, Gadbury was spurred into action by a short comment made by Lilly in his *Anglicus* of 1673 in which he refers to the Spring Ingress of that year:

> The sign ascending in this figure is Scorpio, a sign Stigmatized by all antient and modern practisers in Astrology to be of evil signification, whether it concern the manners of the Native in a Nativity, or is the ascendant in any horary question, or in the revolution of the World: it is *signam falsitatis,* a sign of falsity, denoting the person to be arrogant, ambitious, ingrateful, a great boaster, Lier, letcherous, perjured, given to all manner of vice and lewdness, revengeful, the worst sign of all the Zodiack;...

Most biographers and commentators, following Parker[459], take this as a deliberate insult to Gadbury, in whose nativity Scorpio ascends. We will not attempt to prove a negative and thus accept that this is possible; however, it was not the first time that Lilly writes so, "...Saturn in Scorpio, a most malapert and malicious sign,..."[460]. There are, of course, other examples of the same because what Lilly writes is a standard astrological principle. Gadbury had already complained about such remarks relating to Lilly's *Anglicus* of 1660. He printed these under the rather obvious pseudonym of "G.J. or J.G, which Lilly the Parasite pleaseth." in *The Novice Astrologer Instructed*[461], published just after that *Anglicus.* It is here that we see one of the earliest uses of the term "Scorpionist":

---

[439]Josten: op. cit. pp 1838 and 1846 give two examples of letters for Gadbury in 1687, both open with "Honoured Sir" and both close with "Your obliged humble servant". When compared to a letter from George Wharton, the differences are striking. A letter of 1651 is addressed to "his ever honoured friend..." and closes, "Yours usque ad Aras". Many of

> But why, I intreat you, Sir, is Scorpio grown so odious in your eyes? Is it because Saturn is therein, in your Nativity,... Or is it because you have an ignorant (undeserved) hatred to any, that have it Horoscopical at Birth? If so, were I a Scorpionist, I should tell you, You have foamed out your filth in scandalizing and abusing a noble, fixed, immovable Signe of the Zodiack as violent, &c.

In Lilly's copy of *Doctrine*, he uses the term, too, "...a bold impudent Scorpionist." It is not possible to tell who used the term first, but if it was Gadbury, we might then be able to place some of Lilly's marginalia at around 1660. However, Gadbury was not one to relinquish his grip on a subject of insult and he took up the matter again.

Aside from his almanacs, Gadbury responded with a long pamphlet[462] that, even by Gadbury's standards, was vitriolic. In it he attempts to prove that Lilly's comments were directed at himself particularly, and that they were unfounded in all ancient authorities. He produces twenty nativities of well known historical figures having Scorpio rising but who could not be accused of the qualities Lilly cites. He revisits all the old battlegrounds and makes numerous accusations, using what he knew of Lilly's nativity to support them. But Gadbury had done this on previous occasions, although perhaps not to this degree or at this length, which begs the question as to why he chose this particular time.

The political situation in England had quietened to some degree following King Charles II's accession, and the threat to Parliamentary supporters of the Interregnum had abated. The Third Dutch War had begun in the previous year (1672) and the King needed money to fight it which put him somewhat at the mercy of Parliament. In the same year he had introduced the Royal Declaration of Indulgence which required greater religious tolerance. Parliament took this as tolerance of, and thus danger from, Roman Catholics of which the King's brother, James the Duke of York, was one. In the following year the King was forced to withdraw it and it was replaced by the Test Act in which all those in or seeking public office had to receive the

---

Lilly's letters to Ashmole are preserved, and close with the word "friend" included.

[440]This is the period which followed the death of Charles I in 1649 which continued until the coronation of his son, Charles II, in 1660.

Communion of the Church of England. Thus, the Duke of York, as Lord High Admiral, had to resign. This demonstrates the increasing power of Parliament and the corresponding decrease in monarchical power.

With the threat of "Popery" on the rise and with open opposition to the King directed through his brother, James, Gadbury and his associates may well have felt uncertain about the future. When this last phase had reached its conclusion in 1677, it was only twelve years before Charles II had died, his brother, James, had abdicated and a Protestant king and queen (Mary Stuart and William of Orange) had taken the throne. But besides this broader political context, and after Gadbury's ten years' silence in respect of Lilly, the former may have wondered why Lilly's reputation and status remained intact, why Lilly was still king of his castle.

Whatever the cause for the renewal of hostilities, Gadbury was to be engaged in yet another battle but would lose the war. A reply of sorts from Lilly to *Obsequium Rationabile* was printed in his *Anglicus* of 1676:

> For the advertisement following, it is against our present health, & fully against any desire of ours to Contention, we were even inforced to say something in vindication of what we wrote in 1673 of the sign Scorpio, an illuminated conceited Scorpionist having contradicted all Antiquity about the signification of that sign, and abused with ignominious Epithets, all the younger sort of Astrologers, nay many of those who in the true fundamentalls of Art might be his Masters, viz. Mr. Saunders, Mr. Coley, Mr. Edlin, and many others, whose present names we remember not. ----- But we let pass all his invectives, and scandals, scorning to answer such an impertinent person, of whose ingratitude unto us, all studious persons in Art are well satisfied.

---

[441]Gadbury, Timothy & John, *Astronomicall Tables first invented by George Hartgill...*, London 1656.

ADVERTISEMENT

> Whereas there was lately published to the World a Pamphlet in Vindication of the Sign Scorpio, by an ungrateful Scorpionist J.G. a Pretender to Astrology, wherein he hath most unjustly and very unworthily abused our Person and Reputation; This is to signifie to the World, that we are altogether innocent of this impertinent Authors Egregious Calumniations, and look upon him far below us to respond to his malicious, vain, and ridiculous Forgeries, which is all the Answer he may expect from his Quondam Master.

This rather sparse reply, especially when compared to the 140 pages written by Gadbury, is still more than Lilly wants to say. His oath of over twenty years before still held sway, yet he felt compelled to defend himself. Gadbury had complained bitterly in the past when Lilly refused to be drawn into the fight, so we should expect nothing less from him this time.

---

[442]Partridge: *Opus Reformatum*, op.cit.

[443]Gadbury, T& J: op. cit., Preface.

Chapter 7 - A Just Reward for Unreasonable Service

Before Gadbury had time to respond to Lilly's rebuttal there was published another pamphlet, *A Just Reward for Unreasonable Service...*, under the pseudonym of Bentivolio Philo-Huff-Lash[463].

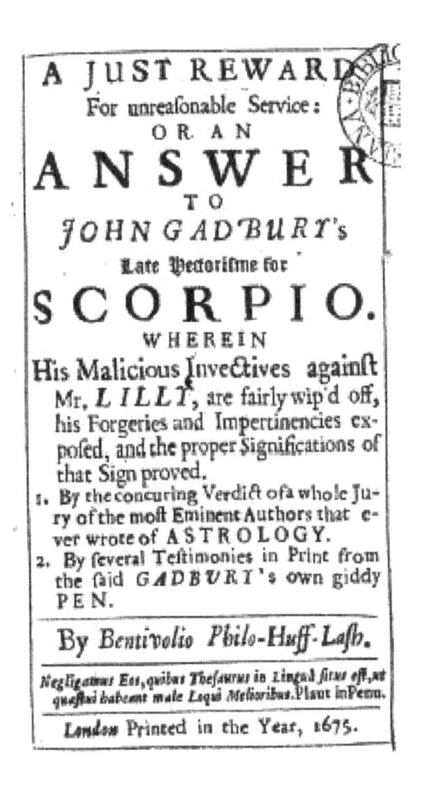

A JUST REWARD

For unreasonable Service:

OR AN

ANSWER

TO

JOHN GADBURY's

Late Pectorisme for

SCORPIO.

WHEREIN

His Malicious Invectives against Mr. *LILLY*, are fairly wip'd off, his Forgeries and Impertinencies exposed, and the proper Significations of that Sign proved.

1. By the concuring Verdict of a whole Jury of the most Eminent Authors that ever wrote of ASTROLOGY.
2. By several Testimonies in Print from the said *GADBURY*'s own giddy PEN.

By *Bentivolio Philo-Huff-Lash.*

Negligamus Eos, quibus Thesaurus in Lingua situs est, ut quaestui habeant male Loqui Melioribus. Plaut in Penu.

London Printed in the Year, 1675.

It is usually said that Lilly himself was the author[464], but this is most unlikely given the style, vocabulary and phrasing. It is printed following his *Anglicus* of 1676, but its imprint of 1675 suggests that it was printed at the very end of

---

[444]Gadbury, John: *Doctrine of Nativities*, London 1658, Lilly's copy is held in the Bodleian Library

[445]Partridge, John: *Nebulo Anglicanus* and *Opus Reformatum*, op.cit.

that year, which would have been the earliest that the almanac was available. The stated reason for writing is thus:

> And therefore finding by an Advertisement in Anglicus for 1676. that Mr. Lilly in a Generous scorn, would not condiscend to any particular answer of it, lest the vain man from thence boast hereafter, that his Trifle is unanswerable, I have bestowed these few sudden remarks thereupon,...

We see from the title that the charge of ingratitude still echoes, and by means of ridicule, sarcasm and scholarship, the author dismantles each of Gadbury's claims with obvious relish. Yet within all of this are serious points which must have caused Gadbury some discomfort, particularly those relating to his new religious practices of Roman Catholicism. There are many points of interest within these pages, however of note is that the author quotes many ancient authorities, indeed the very same Gadbury had referred to, to substantiate his arguments.

The structure of the pamphlet is logical and cuts a swathe through the tangle of words in *Obsequium Rationabile.* Particular points from the latter, in a numbered list, are chosen for attention. He mentions "the Gardiner's Daughter" to which we shall return a little later, Gadbury's accusation of plagiarism "to which J.G. would never yet return any answer." and that Gadbury had worked for Lilly as his tailor proved by "one or two of his Bills which I have accidentally by me under his own hand,...", he then reproduces these which he says are from Gadbury to Lilly, which in itself is interesting.

---

[446]Philo-Huff-Lash, Bentivolio: *A Just Reward For unreasonable Service: or an Answer to John Gadbury's Late Hectorisme for Scorpio...*, London 1675.

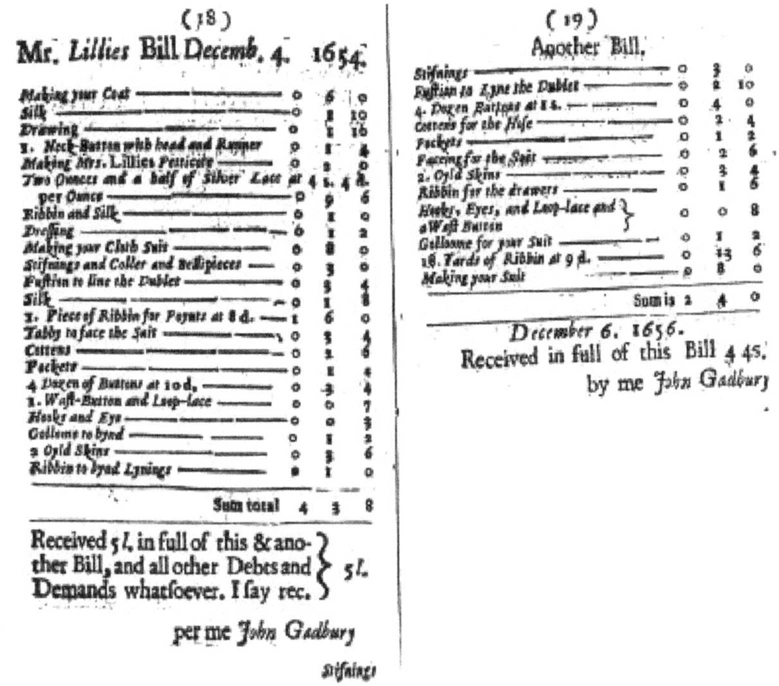

(18)

Mr. *Lillies* Bill Decemb. 4. 1654.

Making your Coat	0	6	0
Silk	0	1	10
Drawing	0	1	10
1. Neck-Button with head and Runner	0	1	4
Making Mrs. Lillies Petticote	0	2	0
Two Ounces and a half of Silver Lace at 4 s. 4 d. per Ounce	0	9	6
Ribbin and Silk	0	1	0
Dressing	0	1	2
Making your Cloth Suit	0	8	0
Stifnings and Coller and Bellipieces	0	3	0
Fustian to line the Dublet	0	3	4
Silk	0	1	8
1. Piece of Ribbin for Poynts at 8 d.	1	6	0
Tabby to face the Suit	0	3	4
Cottens	0	1	6
Pockets	0	1	4
4 Dozen of Buttons at 10 d.	0	3	4
1. Wast-Button and Loop-lace	0	0	7
Hooks and Eys	0	0	3
Gallome to bynd	0	1	2
2 Oyld Skins	0	3	6
Ribbin to bynd Lynings	0	1	0
Sum total	4	3	8

Received 5 *l*. in full of this & another Bill, and all other Debts and Demands whatsoever. I say rec. } 5 *l*.

per me *John Gadbury*

Stifnings

(19)

Another Bill.

Stifnings	0	3	0
Fustian to Lyne the Dublet	0	2	10
4. Dozen Buttons at 1 d.	0	4	0
Cottens for the Hose	0	2	4
Pockets	0	1	2
Facing for the Suit	0	2	6
2. Oyld Skins	0	3	4
Ribbin for the drawers	0	1	6
Hooks, Eyes, and Loop-lace and a Wast Button	0	0	8
Galloone for your Suit	0	1	2
18. Yards of Ribbin at 9 d.	0	13	6
Making your Suit	0	8	0
Sum is	2	4	0

December 6. 1656.

Received in full of this Bill 4 4s.

by me *John Gadbury*

They are provided to answer Gadbury's denial of having worked for Lilly or having ever been taught by him. In some of his attacks he states that he had written four books for Lilly and calculated numerous nativities and was never paid; clearly a response was necessary. As the image shows, there is much detail and the dates of 1654 and 1656 correspond with those given by Lilly.

Philo-Huff-Lash also repeats the story of Gadbury's private life where his lover had become pregnant and he had thrown her out, but the author then threatens to produce more evidence:

> …and was so hardhearted at last as to expose the poor Fool and avoid the keeping of his own natural Bantling by a Trick in Law, though I have by me a rare Copy of Verses Written by him to this Dulcina whiles he was yet battering the feeble Fortress of her Chastity,… which being a rarity and exquisitely written, is very fit to

[447]Curry, Patrick: *ODNB* op. cit.

> be Published for the benefit of young Inamourato's next Edition of Westminster Drollery.

After pointing out some major contradictions in Gadbury's writings which clearly demonstrate weaknesses in Gadbury's astrological and wider education, Philo-Huff-Lash sums the errors up with the sentence: "Now let any Oedipus come and help Gadbury reconcile these places". He may be referring to the fact that, according to the Greek tragedy, Oedipus blinded himself. One particular poem from the contemporary collection of pastoral poems, *Englands Helicon*, called *Amintas for his Phillis*, could have inspired him:

> Phillis is fled, and bides I wote not where
> Phillis (alas) the praise of woman-kinde:
> Phillis the Sunne of this our Hemisphere,
> Whose beames made me, and many others blinde.
> But blinded me (poore Swaine) aboue the rest
> That like olde Oedipus I liue in thrall;
> Still feele the woorst and neuer hope the best
> My mirth in moane and honey drown'd in gall.[465]

This is only the prelude to a brilliant character assassination which is summed up in the next sentence where Philo-Huff-Lash picks up the theme of unfaithfulness and betrayal with the sentence:

> *Et* Phillida *solus habebit.* He shall have his whole Reversion in the Gardiners Daughter for his pains.[466]

This clearly shows that the author of the pamphlet was well-educated as he uses quotations from literature to reveal John Gadbury's true nature. The reader of the pamphlet needed to be well-versed in this literature and theatre in order to have understood fully the implications of these lines. The sentence "*Et* Phillida *solus habebit*" is a quote from Vergil's *Ecloga Tertia*[467]. The conversation between two shepherds, Damoetas and Menalcas, is probably the earliest version of this story of love and betrayal.

---

[448]'The king did this on other occasions most notably to some of the English sailors involved in the naval battles against the Spanish. *Barlow's Journal of His Life at Sea in King's Ships...* (2 vols.) Transcriber Basil Lubbock, pub. Hurst & Blackett, London 1934.

Damoetas:
"Prithee, Iollas, for my birthday guest
Send me your Phyllis; when for the young crops
I slay my heifer, you yourself shall come."

Menalcas:
"I am all hers; she wept to see me go,
And, lingering on the word, 'farewell' she said,
'My beautiful Iollas, fare you well.'"
....
Menalcas:
"Say in what country grow such flowers as bear
The names of kings upon their petals writ,
And you shall have fair Phyllis for your own." [*Et* Phillida *solus habebit*]

In the 16th and 17th centuries pastoral poetry was very much in fashion and William Shakespeare drew on the same theme in *A Midsummer Night's Dream*:

Oberon:
"Am I not thy lord?"

Titania:
"Then I must be thy lady; but I know
When thou has stol'n away from fairyland
And in the shape of Corin sat all day,
Playing on pipes of corn, and versing love
To amorous Phillida."

Oberon's wife, Titania, accuses her husband, who is in the guise of the shepherd Corin, of being false to his marriage vows. And we can find another strand in the *English Helicon*, provided by another poem:

Phillida and Coridon

[449]Ward: op. cit. p76

In the merry moneth of May,
In a morne by breake of day,
Foorth I walked by the Wood side,
When as May was in his pride :
There I spied all alone,
Phillida and Coridon.
Much a-doo there was God wot,
He would loue, and she would not.
She sayd neuer man was true,
He sayd, none was false to you.
He sayd, he had lou'd her long.
She sayd, Loue should haue no wrong.
Coridon would kisse her then.
She said, Maides must kisse no men,
Till they did for good and all.
Then she made the Sheepheard call
All the heauens to witnesse truth:
Neuer lou'd a truer youth.
Thus with many a pretty oath,
Yea and nay, and faith and troth,
Such as silly Sheepheards use,
When they will not Loue abuse;
Loue, which had beene long deluded,
Was with kisses sweete concluded.
And Phillida with garlands gay:
Was made the Lady of the May.[468]

The pastoral theme and the characters used in the quoted poetry and by Shakespeare can be found as well in the tale of the *Gardiner's Daughter*, which must have been very popular throughout the 17th century. We have noted above that Philo-Huff-Lash wished on Gadbury that he "shall have his whole Reversion in the Gardiners Daughter for his pains" and 18 years later, in 1693, John Partridge is still reminded of the *Gardiner's Daughter* when writing about Gadbury's affair in *Nebulo Anglicanus*:

---

[450]As for example in *The nativity of ..., Carolus Gustavus, King of Sweden,* London, 1659, pA2, where Gadbury writes: "The Jews will sell good News for Gain, Of Silver, Pearl, or a Gold Chain"

> About the Year: 1667 he fell mightily in love with the *Gardiner's Daughter*, who was another Man's Wife at that time, who by Vocal Conversation, and Amorous letters, and Copies of Verse, he perswades her to leave her Husband Bed, and come and keep him and his Wife company; the silly woman complies, and was by this mountain Promises deluded, and by the help of *Don John*, under his Wife's Nose, she humbly conceived in a little time...[469]

A printed version of this tale was published as a novel with the title *The Triumph of Love over Fortune*[470]. In this novel Antonine is a foreign prince, disguised as a poor shepherd, who falls in love with Dorothy, the gardener's daughter. When the King meets Dorothy and also falls in love with her, he tries his utmost to separate her from Antonine and win her over. The Marchioness, wife to Don Augustin, a man close to the King, takes pity on Antonine. She tries to reunite the lovers but, suspecting he might be of higher status because of his manners, his education and his way of speaking, falls in love with him herself. Although Dorothy stays faithful to Antonine, the latter begins an affair with the Marchioness. After being found out and imprisoned, his true status as a prince becomes known to the King who frees him quickly. Antonine then marries Dorothy with the King's blessing.

In true satirical fashion, Philo-Huff-Lash compares Antonine's life with that of John Gadbury. Apart from the obvious allegation of being a cheat, the point being made here is, of course, of a complete role reversal. Diametrically opposed to Antonine, Gadbury came from a poor background and pretended to high status, education and gentlemanly manners. Both men pretended to be of incorruptible moral standards, but both proved to be deceitful: whilst professing true love for one they were engaged in an illicit affair with another mirroring Gadbury's betrayal of Lilly. The Marchioness recognises Antonine for what he truly is because of his manner of speech, refinement and education; this suggests that a reversal of this fact would have given away Gadbury's true status. With this in mind, it becomes clear what Philo-Huff-Lash meant when he wrote that Gadbury should "have the whole reversion in

---

[451]Gadbury, John: *The Spurious Prognosticator Unmasked…*, London 1660.

[452]Partridge: *Nebulo Anglicanus*, op. cit.

the Gardiners Daughter for his pains". As much as Antonine is discovered to be a prince, Philo-Huff-Lash reveals that Gadbury is the opposite – a knave.

Taking into consideration that Philo-Huff-Lash had a good knowledge of legal terms it is enlightening to read the definition of "reversion" in law:

> A reversion is a type of "remainder" interest created when incomplete ownership in property is alienated subject to a condition subsequent. Upon the fulfillment of the condition subsequent, the incomplete possessory rights cease to exist and exclusive ownership returns to the holder of the reversion interest by operation of law (or automatically).[471]

In other words, Philo-Huff-Lash thinks that Gadbury, after revealing his true position through his own actions and the incoherent, even contradictory statements in his pamphlets, should be discovered to be a knave. The main theme found in *The Gardiner's Daughter* is that of love, deceit and betrayal and is therefore a perfect choice to remind the reader of the Scorpionic theme, as well as of Gadbury's amorous adventures.

To appreciate the wit and satirical sense of humour of the person behind the pseudonym Philo-Huff-Lash, a closer look is needed at the choice of his first name, "Bentivolio". This forename was commonly used in Italy (ben ti voglio) and can be translated as "I love you", "I desire you" or as "good will" which paraphrases the main theme of the pamphlet perfectly and implies the possibility of an interpretation on many levels. It is a name of pretension and presumption, mimicking Gadbury's tendency towards histrionics and false displays of good manners. It expresses the exact opposite of the author's intentions towards Gadbury whilst simultaneously mocking him. But this is not the only reason that the author used this name. Between 1660 and 1664 Nathaniel Ingelo published his *Bentivolio and Urania*[472], a best-selling piece of religious and moral instruction in the form of a fictional narrative. Ingelo was an author and fellow of Queen's College in Cambridge; he accompanied Bulstrode Whitelocke on the Swedish embassy of 1653-4 as one of his

---

[453]Edward Gresham (1565-1612). Astrologer and author of almanacs for 1604, 1606 and 1607.

[454]Gadbury, John: *Dies Novissimus*, London 1664.

chaplains. The philosophy underlying Ingelo's work stems from the Cambridge Platonists who subscribed to a tolerant Protestantism, according to which humanity is capable of self-improvement through the exercise of reason and freewill. *Bentivolio and Urania* contains an outline of these views.

The Cambridge Platonists were Protestants; Ingelo was a friend of Bulstrode Whitelocke, the friend and patron of William Lilly. In fact Lilly played some part in this embassy by recommending Whitelocke to Claypool[473] strengthening these connections. When all are taken together they point out how antagonistic Philo-Huff-Lash would be towards Gadbury. Furthermore, having established the level of 'love' Gadbury was able to give, the name "Bentivolio" suggests that Philo-Huff-Lash's moral integrity, his views and his status were diametrically opposed to Gadbury's. A quotation from *Bentivolio and Urania* reveals the full depth of the satirical use of the name "Bentivolio":

> ....when Bentivolio appear'd to the astonishment of the degenerate world, which could not remember to have seen any Gentleman equall to him in Complexion or Stature. He was so perfectly made up, that one might easily perceive Wisdom, Goodness and Courage have done their utmost in his composure. The esteem of his Perfection did not rise by the measure of those disproportions in which the corrupt Age fell below him, but by such degrees as the exact rules of Vertue set up for an infallible standard.[474]

In so few words, the pseudonymous author brings the full weight of the intelligentsia to bear on Gadbury. Culture, education, moral standards, good manners, sophistication are clearly demonstrated, in fact, all the qualities to which Gadbury is said to have pretended – as well as the circle of influential literati to which Lilly belonged, but which was closed to him. In so doing, the author brought into sharp contrast the differences between Lilly and Gadbury, and with that, the latter's pretence as Lilly's rival was ended. And so it becomes clear that Gadbury had survived in his position partly by his attacks on Lilly which brought him into public view. Having been rejected by Lilly, he maintained the connection still through his pamphlets and almanacs.

---

[455]Lilly, William: *Merlini Anglici,* London 1664. The epistle is dated 16 September 1663.

[456]Gadbury: op. cit.

Yet Lilly ignored him and maintained his dignity and the respect of his peers. Indeed he had *never* perceived Gadbury as a rival hence Lilly's apparent aloofness.

As to the reason that Gadbury was engaged in battle at this point and not before cannot be explained, but we might speculate. Lilly's life was coming to an end, a fact to which his poor health alone would testify. Gadbury would simply not desist and Lilly was in no state to defend himself; his weariness is clear in his "Advertisement". His friends perhaps took up the cause on his behalf, as Philo-Huff-Lash says, to maintain the distance between the two men. Another distinct possibility is that Lilly's poor health would have precluded his attendance at court should he have wanted to instigate legal proceedings. If this were so, Gadbury would have been aware of it and may well have considered himself safe from litigation this time. The legalistic tone of Philo-Huff-Lash implies otherwise. However, by producing or offering to produce solid evidence in print (for example, the invoices sent by Gadbury to Lilly), the law courts may well have been beyond Lilly, but the 'courts' of the popular press were not. Gadbury had yet again gone beyond the pale, litigation was not now practicable given Lilly's health and age, thus perhaps another route had to be found.

Material evidence had been gathered against Gadbury regarding his accusation of plagiarism, about his immorality and against his accusations of slander. There seems to have been a strong case which may well have stood legal examination, but Lilly wanted peace and quiet and was probably not even mobile at this time. The evidence was made available instead to the reading public as 'jury' and would have circulated much more widely. Certainly it seems to have had the desired effect.

The Scurrilous Scribler

Gadbury replied within a few months at most with a single broadsheet and repeated yet again some of the accusations made against Lilly by Wharton and Gataker some twenty years before. However, amidst the insults and

---

[457]Ibid. p41ff

[458]Josten: op. cit. p980 ff.

repetitions, one comment stands out from the others and would have done so for the astrologers who read it:

> What if some Astrologers have called Scorpio a Sign of Falsity, &c. and others that have otherwise abused that glorious Sign, and together therewith contradicted themselves, as Bonatus, &c. as I.G. [J.G.] hath remembred the world of, and distinguish'd fairly upon such objections, tells them plainly, in p.11 of his Defence of Scorpio, that there have been Rebels against Heaven before W.L's days, and he doubts there will be so, when W.L. shall be no more. But I.G. denies that any of those Rebels against Heaven have proved ought of ill against Scorpio, ...

A ridiculous statement by any standard and one which betrays defeat. He goes on to criticise "Philo-Huff-Lash" calling him "W.L's lying Advocate" and so on. However, the most interesting point about this reply is that Lilly's own copy is extant and on that copy Lilly had made some notes, and was to be passed on to others – the phrasing makes this clear. *The Scurrilous Scribler Dissected*[475] is a large, single sheet with very narrow margins in which Lilly's comments are written. (Photocopying and damage to the edges make some words illegible.)

---

[459]Parker: op. cit.

[460]Lilly, William; *Merlinus Anglicus*, London 1661.

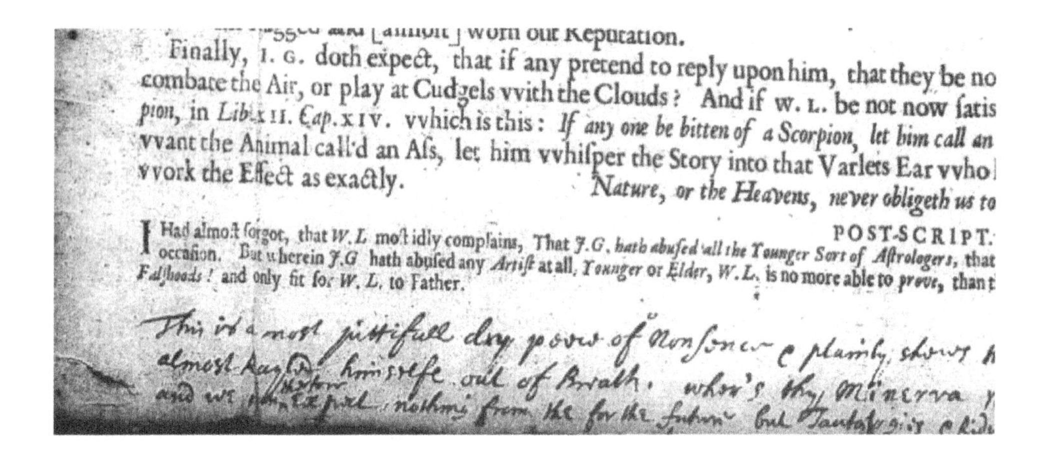

worn out Reputation.

Finally, I. G. doth expect, that if any pretend to reply upon him, that they be no
combate the Air, or play at Cudgels vvith the Clouds? And if W. L. be not now satis
pion, in *Lib.* XII. *Cap.* XIV. vvhich is this: *If any one be bitten of a Scorpion, let him call an*
vvant the Animal call'd an Ass, let him vvhisper the Story into that Varlets Ear vvho
vvork the Effect as exactly.

Nature, or the Heavens, never obligeth us to

POST-SCRIPT.

I Had almost forgot, that *W. L* most idly complains, That *J. G. hath abused all the Younger Sort of Astrologers*, that
occasion. But wherein *J. G* hath abused any *Artist* at all, *Younger* or *Elder*, *W. L.* is no more able to *prove*, than t
Falshoods! and only fit for *W. L.* to Father.

Across the top:

> This Paper was presented to me by one of Tory's Agents who pretended in Love to see me viz. on[e] Everand who has been in yr. [*illegible*] a long time, a sadd fellow indeed; An Apothecary gave him 3 of them he told me, & one was at my service; but I'm sure he had them of Tory with Directions to whom to del. [deliver] them, they were printed at Westm^{r}. [Westminster] at Gad: charg to present to his friends etc.

This note implies that Gadbury had no patronage in this instance, and raises the rather interesting question of whether or not others were behind Gadbury's previous pamphlets. It also shows that very few of these sheets were printed, so we might construe that this was nothing more than an open letter of sorts; something with which to 'save face' amongst his own circle of friends.

Along the right-hand edge and referring to a repeat of George Wharton's attack on Lilly in 1648:

> But in his Homeroscoprionis he recanted and gives him the Highest Charracter imaginable.

---

[461]Gadbury, John: *The Novice Astrologer Instructed:in a New-Years-Gift ot Mr. William Lilly*, London 1660 (handwritten date of Feb. 23. 1659, which refers to 1659/60.)

Lower down on that same border and referring to the "Gardiner's Daughter" which Gadbury denies:

> [a name] that all Westm^{r}. will witness.

On the left-hand border referring to a remark concerning Ashmole having possession of the manuscript which Gadbury believes proves Lilly to be a plagiarist:

> I hear Jack is displeased with E.Ash. but I know not for what & intends to visett him at Lambeth."

(This is why Josten gives a date for this broadsheet of not before 1675 because Ashmole moved to Lambeth in that year.)

Further along that border is the notation:

> La: Wh:

This is in relation to Gadbury's comment in response to the "Gardiner's Daughter" allegation. He says:

> For the Story of the Gardiners Daughter, which W.L's lying Advocate makes a scandalous noise withal, I.G. desires him to speak plainly, and not in Riddles: for he knoweth nothing that can countenance any such bold falshoods. Nor doth he remember that ever he had difference with any more than two women in all his life; the one was a Lady (so called) that having been Ruinous to many Families where she had lodged, he justly denied to entertain her into his House: …

This seems to refer to Lady Jane Whorwood, the same who had approached Lilly on behalf of Charles I a number of times, and who continued to consult

[462]Gadbury John, *Obsequium Rationabile, or A Reasonable Service performed for the Coelestial Sign Scorpio.* London 1675.

the astrologer for many years[476]. She had risked her life for the king on numerous occasions and was herself imprisoned in 1651. A violent, adulterous husband eventually led to their separating officially, and to her impoverishment. She died with an estate valued at only £40. It is this woman whom Gadbury, the Royalist, turned away.

At the bottom of the sheet, Lilly summarises thus:

> This is a most pittiful dry peece of nonsense & plainly shows that Tory's stock of Malice & Railery is neerly spent, or that he has almost Rayled himselfe out of Breath. wher's thy Minerva now Jack, certainly the world will Judge, tis strangly benighted and we can therefore expect nothing from the[e] for the future but Tautologies & Ridiculous Hodg-Podge.

And this indeed seems to have been true. We have not examined all of Gadbury's subsequent almanacs, but assume that he continued 'huffing' for a little longer. However, Henry Coley – by this time Lilly's amanuensis – had been adding to the weight of words written against Gadbury and he makes a number of comments in his almanacs relating to the 'Scorpio' contention.

Gadbury's last response was to publish a noisy defence of the sign of Scorpio by way of the nativity of Sir Matthew Hale (1609-1676), a famous judge of the period.[477] Gadbury uses this because he says that the rising sign is Scorpio, having given a time of "7h 08'" in the morning. However, in his *Brief Lives*, Aubrey offers the details as "in the evening, his father then being at his prayers", and:

> Sir Matthew Hales, Lord Chief Justice of the King's Bench, was borne at Alderley in com. Glouc., November 1st, 1609; christned the 5th. Quaere Mr. Edward Stephens horam, for he has it exactly. When his mother fell in labour, his father was offering up his evening sacrifice.[478]

---

[463]Philo-Huff-Lash, Bentivolio: *A Just Reward For unreasonable Service: or an Answer to John Gadbury's Late Hectorisme for Scorpio*..., London 1675.

[464]Parker, op.cit. p254

This, of course, places the birth at the other end of the day with a radical change of rising sign. It is possible that Gadbury mistook the time as before noon when it was after. He had chosen a good subject for his defence since Hale was recognised as one of the greatest judges of his time, and still is. However, Gadbury was also notorious for miscalculating charts, and still is.

Some Further Remarks

The third phase nears its conclusion with another pamphlet, *Some Further Remarks Upon Mr. Gadbury's Defence of Scorpio* printed under the pseudonym of "the Man in the Moon"[479]. Its motto and subtitle help us towards the content. The front-page motto of the pamphlet, "Bilem saepe, jocum vestri movere tumultus", shows that the Man in the Moon was as witty and as well versed in satire as the author of *A Just Reward for Unreasonable Service*, Philo-Huff-Lash. The educated reader of the time will have recognised the motto as a quote from Horace's *Epistles*:

> O imitatores, servum pecus, ut mihi saepe Bilem, saepe jocum vestri movere tumultus! [480]

This was quoted by Robert Burton in his *Anatomy of Melancholy*, first published in 1621:

> Bilem saepe, jocum vestri movere tumultus.
> Ye wretched mimics, whose fond heats have been,
> How oft! the objects of my mirth and spleen.
>
> I did sometime laugh and scoff with Lucian, and satirically tax with Menippus, lament with Heraclitus, sometimes again I was petulanti *splene chachinno*, and then again, *urere bilis jecur*, I was much moved to see that abuse which I could not mend.[481]

---

[465]*Englands Helicon*, printed for Iohn Flasket, London, 1600 p127

[466]Ibid, p13

The subtitle, "By way of addition, to a just Reward for unreasonable service", clearly indicates that this is a sequel to the pamphlet by Philo-Huff-Lash. It begins:

> To the Worshipful Mr. John Gadbury, Quondam Taylor in Ordinary to Mr. William Lilly; now Extraordinary Physician to Her majesty, and a Secretis to the Peerless Dulcinea, otherwise called the Gardiner's Daughter.

In just two pages and very few lines, the author repeats the charges against Gadbury, highlighting the worst of them. His stated purpose is to deal with the omissions in *A Just Reward* and addresses Gadbury's pamphlet in the same way, point by point, as did Philo-Huff-Lash. However, this author gives more attention to Gadbury's pretensions to knowledge of Latin and Greek and thus exposes Gadbury as a poseur and a fraud.

With the demolition of Gadbury's astrological arguments, the latter is left exposed and discredited through his own affectations. This would haunt Gadbury later in his contentions with John Partridge.

This pamphlet has much to recommend it, as does the previous one, raising many interesting points; the author confronts most of Gadbury's contradictions, and they are many. However, one point stands out among the others: this author confirms that Gadbury was Fiske's pupil in apparent contradiction to Lilly's account of the matter. In fact, this is simply another way of reflecting upon Gadbury's character, but may also suggest that the author was not aware of the fact and thus was not a very close associate of Lilly.

> I have nothing to say against Doctor Fisk, only Mr. Gadbury was his Pupil; and as he himself observes, *Qualis Dominus talis Servis*, Like Master like Man.

---

[467]Vergil: *Ecloga Tertia*, Rome, between 44 and 38BC.

[468]*Englands Helicon*, op. cit. p27

Obviously, the author did not have a high opinion of Fiske either, which echoes Lilly's words regarding Fiske's Ascendant being in Scorpio.[482]

For the first time in this whole affair, both pamphleteers deal with every one of Gadbury's accusations against Lilly going back to his first attack. They add their own analysis of Gadbury's character and make it known to an educated and influential readership. The tone is intellectual and patrician, dealing with Gadbury in unequivocal terms.

The Advocates

It is of some interest to this examination to try to discover who the authors of these pamphlets were, because it has been said so many times that Lilly himself wrote them[483]. Having knowledge of Lilly's writing style, his vocabulary and his phrasing, it is clear that Lilly wrote neither of these pamphlets. Another important factor is that at the time of their publishing, Lilly's health and eyesight were deteriorating and all existing contemporary records are unanimous in this. We have no definitive answer as to who wrote them, but we will present our suggestions according to the available evidence.

In *Scurrilous Scribler*, Gadbury refers to Lilly's "advocate" and it would seem that this was a deliberate choice of word and one which definitively excludes Lilly as the author of either pamphlet. The use of this term does not necessarily mean that 'Philo-Huff-Lash' was an advocate by profession, but it is possible. However, in his almanac for 1677[484], under his observations for March, Lilly adds:

> *I hope now the Huffing Scorpionist is satisfied with those two smart Answers lately emitted unto the world to his Railing vindication of the Sign Scorpio; written by two Learned and Ingenious persons (who ever they were ----) …

Using the word "learned" likewise does not necessarily mean that the authors were of the legal profession, but a closer scrutiny of the pamphlets, particularly the first, suggests the style of a case being prepared for the courts.

[469]Partridge: *Nebulo Anglicanus*, op. cit, p4.

Each point is laid down in the manner in which a barrister might as he presents a defence to the plaintiff's case. He uses phrases which would lead his readers to the same conclusion. On the cover (our emphases):

1. By the concurring **Verdict of a whole jury** of the most Eminent Authors that ever wrote of ASTROLOGY.
2. By several **Testimonies** in Print from the said GADBURY's own giddy PEN.

From the preface:

> If in other places the Language seem harsh (which I have Studied to avoid) tis only ***Lex Talionis***, …

Later:

> …for doubtless Mars is as good a Gentleman as Scorpio, and as ready to bring a *scandalum Magnatum*, or an **Action of Defamation**, and therefore let John look to his hits. *Incidit in Scyllam, cupiens vitare Charibdim.*

The threat of legal action is emphasised by the quotation from Homer's *Odyssey* which is rendered as "to be destroyed by falling into one evil while trying to avoid another" or we might say, "to be between the devil and the deep blue sea". Perhaps a warning that by trying to elude the charge of ingratitude, Gadbury was taking himself into a legal suit for defamation. "Lex Talionis" is an expression referring to compensation in kind (an eye for an eye, a tooth for a tooth), or simply, retaliation[485]. It is interesting to note that this is a term incorrectly given by Gadbury in one of his early attacks on Lilly[486]; its use here may be in direct reference to that. Then there is the quotation in Latin on the front cover:

> Negliamus Eos, quibus Thesaurus in Lingua situs est, ut quaestui habeant male Loqui Melioribus.

---

[470]Bremond, Gabriel de: *The Triumph of Love over Fortune, A Pleasant Novel*, translated into English by a person of quality, London 1678.

It is drawn from Plautus's comedy *Poenulus*, and, in the original, is translated as:

> That is a treasure hoarded in the tongues of fools, to deem it gainful to speak amiss to their superiors.

It is slightly altered for the author's purposes, but it is clear to what it refers, and the character who speaks this line is an advocate.

The Preface.

to ascertain them of such Truths *that their* Divinity *will never be able to reach unto. And, if it chance at any time to be put to the* Question, (*as who knows what* Question *may arise?*) Whether any Man, *&c.* born under Scorpio may be in hopes of Salvation? --- *Let them but go by* Mr Lilly *his black Character of such a Person, and it will most assuredly be carried in the* Negative.

Now, what Astrologer, *nay, what* Christian *man is there, that can with patience be contented to connive at Mr.* Lilly's *boldness herein, albeit he had not* Scorpio *ascending at his Nativity? Must this* Man *be thus suffered to* Rant *and* Rave *at his pleasure? tax Heaven and Earth as guilty? and confidently pronounce the sentence of* Evil, *upon that which God himself hath been pleased to own eminently as* Good? *And, shall any Man that hath a veneration for the* Truths *of* God and Nature, *be either* afraid *or* ashamed *to unmask him, and lay open those his* notorious Untruths, Scandals *and* Recriminations, *thus charged upon a most eminent part of Mankind?* Not *to take notice of this his dealing by* Heaven, *and by Men born under a glorious part thereof, and reprove him for it, is not only to be guilty of that his* black charge (*either in part or in the whole*) *but to partake deeply of the* Errour *he is tainted with in the* forging *it to a* wicked, *if not to a* murtherous *end. A* crime, *that not only a* Scorpionist, *but a sober* Rationalist (*though of a different Horoscope*) *ought zealously to* abhor.

Plato (as quoted by *Plutarch*) maketh Providence superiour to *Necessity*, or *Destiny*, Mr. Lilly, *if he*

The Preface.

he allow of Providence *at all, placeth it below them. If* Necessity *in Mr.* Lilly's *sence be thus powerful, and bear such* sway *in our* Actions, *&c. As that Men* born *under* Scorpio *must be such, (by vertue of their* Horoscope) *may we not bid a farewel to* Industry, Ingenuity, Reason, Order, Laws, *&c. There is then no use of these things; For* Men *are no other then a* brass Candlestick, *or* Joyned-stool; *predestinated to such and such* particular uses *for such a time:* Conduit pipes, *to conveigh some* trifling Message *or other, to the* World, *whether they will or not, and* Exit. *And according to this* Doctrine *Mr.* Lilly *hath not out of any wicked design, (may he say) --- but meerly by a* compulsive necessity (*a Law he could not avoid complying with*) railed *against* Scorpio, *and blasphemed God and* Heaven.

And, here by the way, I would fain know of what use is Mr. Lilly's Astrology, *if this his* Doctrine *of* Necessity *be true? at this rate,* he that encreaseth in knowledge, encreaseth sorrow in earnest. *And* Solomons Simpletons *in their foolish condition, are more happy then Mr.* Lilly *with all his impertinent and useless Science.* Many *things are* necessary *that are not of* necessity. And *thus was it necessary, that* Mr. Lilly, *for the undeceiving the World, should contradict himself in his* railing *against* Scorpio, *as the following discourse will plainly prove: but there was no* necessity *of it at all. It was in Mr.* L's *power to have prevented it. And this* freedom of will, Mr. L. *acknowledgeth in an* Epistle *to a thing of his called an* Introduct. *to* Astrology. *And indeed, if my reason did not be p*

---

[471]Wikipedia: http://en.wikipedia.org/wiki/Reversion_%28law%29 , accessed 17/07/2011

[472]Ingelo, Nathaniel: *Bentivolio and Urania,* in four books, London 1660

Having gone to some length to demonstrate the line of thought in this examination, the next piece of evidence is compelling: the copy of *Obsequium Rationabile* belonged at some point to Elias Ashmole himself as his signature is written on the front page. Throughout this copy are numerous underscores of words and passages among Gadbury's complaints. There are also two comments, but we cannot say whether or not they are in Ashmole's hand; one comment may be in Lilly's hand, but the second, longer note is not. These underscorings relate closely to the points raised by Philo-Huff-Lash, and far too often to be coincidental. Based on all of this, we suggest that Philo-Huff-Lash was Elias Ashmole, the lawyer. This is further supported by Lilly's comments on his copy of *The Scurrlious Scribler Dissected*, to repeat:

> I hear Jack is displeased with E: Ash: but I know not for what & intends to visit him at Lambeth.

Returning to the marginalia in Lilly's copy of *The Doctrine of Nativities*, we find that the points he comments upon have a striking resemblance to those in *Some Further Remarks*. Again, the writing style of 'The Man in the Moon' is very different from Lilly's and thus the evidence points towards another, but there is no evidence at the moment to suggest who this might have been. Had Lilly been preparing a legal challenge, he would have presented the evidence and a list of his objections. It might be that this is exactly what he did when Ashmole appears to have been preparing a case against Gadbury in 1664.

> The final note summarises the situation: Gadbury's attacks were nearly over – he was a spent force. The pamphlet campaign had ended and it had ended in Lilly's favour. It seems clear that Lilly, Ashmole and at least one other, working together, concluded Gadbury's war of words.

---

[473]Ward: op.cit. p80

[474]Ingelo, op.cit. p1

Timeline

1673	Lilly's Scorpio remark	Lilly: *Merlini Anglici*	1
1674	Henry Coley's (anti) Scorpionist poem	Coley: *Nuntius Coelestis*	2
1675	Gadbury's broadside re. Scorpio remark	Gadbury: *Obsequium Rationabile*	3
1675	Philo-Huff-Lash replies to Gadbury's broadside and supports Lilly	Philo-Huff-Lash's answer to Gadbury	4
1675 (Josten)	Gadbury replies to Philo-Huff-Lash	Gadbury: *Scurrilous Scribbler*	5
1676 (??) (epistle 1675)	Lilly gives reasons for Philo-Huff-Lash pamphlet (1675) health.	Lilly: *Merlini Anglici 1676*	6
1676	Coley writes about Gadbury, "Scorpio, Horned Beast"	Coley: *Nuntius Coelestis*	7
1676	Reply to broadside by the Man in the Moon, supporting Lilly	The Man in the Moon: *Some Further Remarks*	8
1677; Licensed Feb 21st 1676/7	Gadbury's defence of Scorpio.	Gadbury: *The Just and Pious Scorpionist*	9
1677	Lilly re. previous 2 supporter pamphlets and the end of the plagiarism dispute	Lilly: *Merlini Anglici 1677*	10
1677	Coley remarks against Gadbury	Coley: *Nuntius Coelestis*	11

1. Lilly, William: *Merlini Anglici ephemeris, or, Astrological judgments for the year 1673* by William Lilly. , London: Printed by J. Macock for the Company of Stationers, 1673.
2. Coley, Henry: *Nuncius coelestis, or, Urania's messenger being a brief description and survey of the year of humane redemption, 1674. Being the second after bissextile, or leap-year. Wherein is contained (besides the state of the year the solar ingresses, various configurations, aspects, conjunctions, and diurnal motion of the planets) also an account of such eclipses that shall happen this year, together with useful tables, and all other furniture that may condduce to the completing such a work. Accommodated to the meridian of London, To which is added a rational discourse of the nature and effects of transits of the planets in a nativity.* By Henry Coley Philomath. , London : printed by Samuel Simmons, for the Company of Stationers, 1674.

475 Gadbury, John: *The Scurrilous Scribler Dissected*, presumably printed in London in 1675 or 1676.

3. Gadbury, John: *Obsequium rationabile, or, A reasonable service performed for the celestial sign scorpio in xx remarkable genitures of that glorious but stigmatized horoscope : against the malitious and false attempts of that grand (but fortunate) imposter, Mr. William Lilly* / by John Gadbury, London: Printed for William Berry, 1675.
4. Philo-Huff-Lash, Bentivolio*: A just reward for unreasonable service, or, An answer to John Gadbury's late hectorisme for Scorpio : wherein his malicious invectives against Mr. Lilly, are fairly wip'd off,* London, 1675
5. Gadbury, John*: The scurrilous scribler dissected: or, A word in William Lilly's ear concerning his reputation, which he complains is injured by J.G. that ungrateful scorpionist, as he the said Lilly scurrilously terms him*, London: 1675
6. Lilly, William: *Merlini Anglici ephemeris: or, Astrological judgments for the year 1676.* By William Lilly, London: Printed by J. Macock for the Company of Stationers., 1676.
7. Coley, Henry: *Nuncius coelestis, or, Urania's messenger. Being a brief description and survey of the year of humane redemption. 1676. Unto which is numbred [sic] from years. The creation. [bracket] By the oriental and Greek Christians 7184 By the Jews, Hebrews, and later Rabins 5436 But according to Sacred Writ 5625 Being the bissextile, or leap-year. And from the constitution of the kalender by Julius Caesar. 1719 Reformation thereof by Gregorius --- 94 Wherein is contained (besides the state of the year) the solar ingresses, various configurations, aspects, conjunctions, and diurnal motions of the planets, with the southing of the moon, and rules to find her rising and setting thereby. Also an account of such ecclipses that shall happen this year, together with useful tables, and all other furniture that may conduce to the compleating such a work. Accommodated to the meridian of London, where the Pole Artick is elevated above the horizon 51 degr. 32 m. and without sensible error may serve for any part of Great Britain. To which is added a rational discourse of the several kinds of experience, and the manner how the respective natures of the planets, fixed stars, and signs may thereby be discovered.* / By Henry Coley philomathematicus. , London, : Printed by S.S. for the Company of Stationers, 1676.
8. The Man in the Moon: *Some further remarks upon Mr. Gadbury's defence of Scorpio by way of addition, to a just reward for unreasonable service. Wherein not only Mr. Gadbury's pretentions to astrology are dissipated; but even his title to learning and right reason (which by virtue of his horoscope he challenges) is shaken*. By the Man in the Moon. , [London : s.n.], Printed in the year MDCLXXVI. [1676]

[476]Fox, John: *'Whorwood , Jane (bap. 1612, d. 1684)', ODNB*, online edn, OUP, May 2009. The author states that Lady Whorwood "... consulted the astrologer William Lilly on Charles's behalf. Lilly's incomplete papers show appointments with Jane ranging from May 1647 to June 1659."

9. Gadbury, John: *The just and pious scorpionist, or, The nativity of that thrice excellent man, Sir Matthew Hales, late Lord Chief Justice of England who was born in the year of our Lord 1609, on Wednesday Novemb. the first 7h 8' manè, under the coelestial scorpion, astrologically consider'd* / by John Gadbury. , London : Printed by J.D. for Robert Boulter, 1677.
10. Lilly, William*: Merlini Anglici ephemeris, or, Astrological judgments for the year 1677* by William Lilly , London : Printed by J. Macock for the Company of Stationers, 1677
11. Coley, Henry*: Nuncius coelestis, or, Urania's messenger being a brief description and survey of the year of humane redemption 1677 : unto which is numbered ... : accomodated to the meridian of London ...* / by Henry Coley, London : Printed by S.S. for the Company of Stationers, 1677.

---

[477]Gadbury, John: *The just and pious scorpionist, or, The nativity of that thrice excellent man, Sir Matthew Hales, late Lord Chief Justice of England* ... London , 1677.

Chapter 8 - Annexed unto my Name for ever

In 1693, the astrologer John Partridge published *Nebulo Anglicanus*[487]. The frontispiece shows John Gadbury with the name "Merlinus Verax"[488] (the "Truthful Merlin") written above his head. Partridge is reminding the reader of the pseudonym Gadbury used in 1659 in his pamphlet *Nativity of that most Illustrious King of Sweden,*[489] in which he first attacked Lilly. ("Nebulo Anglicanus" is a pun referring to the title of Lilly's *Merlinus Anglicus* and to Gadbury's *Merlinus Verax*; "nebulo anglicanus" means "the Anglican scoundrel".) And so we return to where it all began.

In Gadbury's pamphlet regarding the King of Sweden's nativity, the subtitle immediately informs us of its nature and the reason it was published, "particularly for the better Information of Mr. William Lily"[490]. Partridge, reminds the reader that this was the first publication wherein Gadbury turned against his master, and leaves no doubt that even twelve years after Lilly's death the crime of ingratitude is far from forgotten. In the "Epistle Dedicatory" of *Nebulo Anglicanus* he writes:

> To the Most Exquisitly Acomplish'd in Plotting, Tricking, and Ingratitude, My Honoured Friend, Mr John Thimble, of Brick-Court.[491]

In the following he gives a summary of Gadbury's behaviour towards Lilly and towards Partridge himself later on:

> I humbly desire you to remember how grateful you were to Mr Lilly, your Kind and Generous Master, that rescued you from the Thimble-Dispensation, and taught you how to get meat to your Bread, that being (you know) the First and Second Course, when you lived within less than a Mile of Strand-Bridge; and after this abundance more of Kindness, which you have acknowledged in Print, the worst Word in your Budget was too good for him; and you have abused him who was your Master, as much as you have

---

[478]Aubrey, John: *Brief Lives, chiefly of contemporaries, set down by John Aubrey, between the Years 1669 & 1696.* Edited from the Author's MSS. Vol. I by Andrew Clark. Clarendon Press. 1898. p278.

done Me, that You say was your Pupil Hah Jack, Gratitude, Gratitude! Master and Pupil both suffer alike, no Mercy in Brick-Court.[492]

In 1693 John Partridge published *Opus Reformatum*[493], wherein he, in his own opinion, attempted to expose and reject the common errors of the art.[494] In the second part of this book Partridge delivers a detailed criticism of Gadbury's *Cardines Coeli*[495]. He reminds the reader of how the latter created his "100 Choice Aphorisms" and of the source of the inspiration for his book:

> For in the year of our Lord, 1660 and 1661, he made a Collection of Nativities, and most of them false ones, as shall ere long appear. From these Nativities thus made, he form'd a hundred Aphorisms, and most of them as false as his Nativities. I say from these false Nativities, he form'd those choice Aphorisms, a quarter of which, I am confident, to this day he never prov'd to be true. And from two of these Nativities (and I am certain they are both false for I have made one appear so already, and will do so by the other before I conclude this Treatise) namely *Charles Gustavus*, King of *Sweden*, and *Oliver Cromwell*, he formed the Eighteenth Aphorism, which was this, *Cardinal Signs possessing the Angles of a Nativity, makes the Native* [of any Condition or Capacity*] most Eminent and Famous in his Generation, and to do such Acts as After –ages shall admire him*. And from this Aphorism made in the Year 1661. he writes a Book in the Year 1684. to justify and promote the thing which he calls *Cardines Coeli*, which is my present business to inquire into.[496]

Partridge continues to point out Gadbury's errors, dealing with each paragraph of *Cardines Coeli*, until he arrives at paragraph 28:

> …in which he hath really out-done himself, and not only shewed the World the Authority of his groundless Foundation, but his unskilfulness in Grammar and his confidence (I had like to have say

[479]Man in the Moon, *some Further Remarks Upon Mr. Gadbury's Defence of Scorpio…*, 1676.

[480]Horace: *Epistolae,* I., 19, 19.

> something else) in affirming a thing without the least pretence and shew of Authority in the very Aphorism itself.
>
> He quotes only four words of the Aphorism, i.e. Cometae in Cardinibus, Regum mortes, &c. *Comets* (says he) *whenever they appear in Cardinal Signs, they betoken the Death of Emperors, Princes, Potentates, &c. Cardinal Signs you see, do still carry a Signal of Wonder and Amazement in them.* By which you may see he renders the stress of the whole Aphorism on the word *Cardinibus*, which he renders for Cardinal Signs, and therefore pray take the whole Aphorism together, that you may see the Impertinence and Ignorance of the man.[497]

Partridge then gives the original passage from Cardan, the basis of Gadbury's quotation:

> *Man. Seg. 3 Aph. 117. Cardan. Comet immobiles Seditiones, mobiles autem Bella indicant ab Externis. In Cardinibus Regum Mortes in nono loco Religionis Jacturam, in Octavo vel Duodecimo loco Pestilentiam, aus Jacturam segetum, in undecimo Nobilium Mortes.* Which is thus in English: Immovable Comets give Seditions; but movable Comets shew Wars between Nations, in the Angles, Death of Kings; in the Ninth House, injury to Religion; in the Eight and Twelfth Houses, pestilence and damage to the standing Corn; in the Eleventh House , the Death of Noblemen. And now where, and by what word of all these shall we get power and room enough to lug in Cardinal Signs, I vow it seems to me impossible, unless we were animated with such Souls as honest J.G. was, when he wrote it. Oh my dear Joy! That ever thou shouldst translate Cardinibus for Cardinal Signs, and mistake *Cardinibus* for *Cardinalibus.*
>
> Now, if John can but tell us, by what rule in Grammar, by what Figure in Writing, or Construction, this word is to be thus understood in favour of his new-invented Principle, alias, whim of Cardinal Signs or Angles, I shall be ready to recant what I have written,....[498]

---

[481]Burton, Robert: *The Anatomy of Melancholy*, London 1854, p4

[482]Lilly: *Life and Times of*.... op. cit.

We can see from these quotations that Gadbury's education, contrary to his own claims, was not of a high standard and this lack of basic understanding led him to make a serious mistake. He mistranslated, and therefore misunderstood, Cardan's aphorism concerning comets which error formed the basis not only of one of his own aphorisms, but also, many years later, of a whole book: *Cardines Coeli*. Reading Cardan's original aphorism it becomes obvious that "Cardinibus" has to be translated as "Angle", because it is mentioned in context with the 8th, 9th, 11th and 12th houses, the other four houses above the Earth, as Partridge recognised correctly[499]. This mistake had far-reaching consequences as Partridge demonstrates mercilessly:

> Why then perhaps upon the Presumption you undertook this mighty work, to unhinge the principles of Astrology with your *Cardines Coeli*, and throw Heaven out at Windows, by help of a New Invention from Brick-Court; or perhaps he hath got the *Circulatum majus Paracelsi*, which they say dissolves all Metals, and may, being used and improved by so great a *Virtuoso* as this is, easily dissolve the *Angles* of a Figure into their *first Matter*; and from thence to make *Cardinal Signs* at pleasure.[500]

To understand this accusation we have to look at Partridge's criticism of the 29th Paragraph in *Cardines Coeli*, wherein Gadbury quotes Cardan for a second time, claiming to prove the validity of his theory through this aphorism, postulating that:

> he, who is born at Noon, when the Sun enters the Vernal Equinox, will be great and famous, without other Testimonies. Nor need we fear to believe him, since at such a time all the Angles of the Celestial Figure will be adorned with a Cardinal Sign. This is the most convincing Proof that can be of the *Truth* of the matter in Question.[501]

Partridge makes it absolutely clear that, even if such an aphorism of Cardan ever existed, this rule would account for a latitude of 54 degrees only, ruling out Scotland, Denmark, Sweden and so forth:

---

[483]Plant, David: 'John Gadbury, Politics and the Decline of Astrology', *The Traditional Astrologer Magazine*, issue 11, Winter 1996

[484]Lilly, William: *Merlinus Anglicus*, London, 1677.

> this is plain, because in the Latitude of 55 degr. when the first Scruple of Aries is on the Cusp of the 10th House, the first degree of Leo ascends on the Ascendant, which puts the Aphorism quite out of doors, to all them People in that Latitude.[502]

The accusations made against Gadbury in earlier years are not only repeated by Partridge, but also supported in fact. Partridge adds substance to the handwritten comments by Lilly in his copy of *Doctrine,* made over thirty years earlier, that Gadbury's grasp of mathematics, Latin and astrology fell far below his own claims; that, in fact, Gadbury was a charlatan.

The End

We have gone to great lengths to demonstrate how necessary detailed research is and how a very different result can be obtained. We hope that by offering our sources others will be inclined to follow this line of investigation, because there is still a great deal to be discovered. It is difficult to maintain a neutral position because the balance of opinion has swung so far in Gadbury's favour. Whether or not the opinions we have drawn from the evidence available to us are correct, having given detailed references, an informed discussion may continue.

The backgrounds of the two men have been shown to be fairly similar; neither had the benefit of wealthy parents and the education which would have followed, but it is in their characters that the dissimilarities are found. Lilly made a large number of friends and close associates and this he appears to have done largely through merit. He gained the respect of very clever and influential men. Gadbury, on the other hand, and on a number of occasions, seems to have alienated the very people who might have helped him. Lilly worked hard and broadened his knowledge and education, Gadbury did only what needed to be done to further his own ends and pretended to the rest. Lilly never forgot his early impoverished circumstances and tried to ease the way of those who wanted to study astrology. Gadbury, on the other hand,

---

[485] *Shorter Oxford English Dictionary,* Clarendon Press, Oxford, 1971

[486] Gadbury: *Novice Astrologer* op. cit. p29

spent most of his life trying to disguise his humble beginnings, affecting a higher social position than was ever his.

Gadbury wanted the very qualities in Lilly that he attacked the most violently. He wanted Lilly's social and professional status, he wanted Lilly's knowledge, and wanted Lilly's astrological adeptness; in short, he wanted to be Lilly. He wanted possession of Lilly's 'mountain' or, if that could not be achieved, its destruction. However, he did not have Lilly's capacity to make astrological thinking the main focus of his life. Lilly's astrology was the mundane expression of his beliefs and the practical application of the hermetic arts he had studied – the core of his being. This ability enabled him to put astrology first and to overcome the political and religious differences between himself and his friends. John Gadbury, who only used astrology as a means to a material end, never approached Lilly's depth of knowledge.

Our research demonstrates very clearly that there was no rivalry between Lilly and Gadbury; Lilly was almost completely unaffected by Gadbury's attacks. Except in the instances we have pointed out, Lilly ignored him, and when he stopped ignoring him, Gadbury was defeated utterly by intelligence, education, sophistication and a morality which was alien to him. Gadbury was of no consequence to Lilly or to any of Lilly's friends and associates and the more Lilly ignored him, the more belligerent and insulting Gadbury became.

Had he been of a quieter, less antagonistic disposition, Gadbury may well have escaped ridicule. However, he demanded to be taken seriously; he demanded respect as an astrologer, but he was largely ignored by his better qualified contemporaries. It was only in his later life, having again attacked a man who had been his friend, that the final blow was struck. John Partridge made his thoughts on Gadbury's astrological abilities public[503] and completely destroyed his reputation as a 'scientific' astrologer. Gadbury would not recover from this devastating blow. Apart from his almanacs, he would not publish anymore attacking pamphlets on astrology.

---

[487]Partridge: *Nebulo Anglicanus* op.cit.

Gadbury's assault on what he perceived as Lilly's stronghold was doomed to failure from the beginning, but it would seem that he had to try to clear his name no matter how long it took. No-one of any account took notice of his furious outbursts at that time, so it is a strange phenomenon that astrologers and historians of modern times do give credence to Gadbury's nonsense. We are not optimistic that change will occur because so many modern biographies have depended for so long on this flawed research.

Historians repeatedly state that the contention between Lilly and Gadbury was one of professional and political rivalry. While these matters may well have entered into it, its source lay in Gadbury's ingratitude, his betrayal of Lilly's friendship and trust. We have demonstrated that John Gadbury is wholly unreliable as a source for historical research and we hope that historians will desist from referring to him in this way simply because he was a prolific writer. Indeed, our research has shown us that most of what Gadbury wrote is unsafe to the point of worthlessness.

---

[488]Gadbury seems to be the first astrologer to use the name of Merlinus Verax. The astrologer Robert Neve who published almanacs from at least 1662 onwards did not use the name Merlinus Verax before 1668 and there does not seem to be any publication of his after 1672. In 1687 an almanac with the title Merlinus Verax was published. The author called himself 'A

Timeline

1684	Gadbury uses nativities from *Collectio,* mentions WL	Gadbury*: Cardines Coeli*	1
1687	Gadbury attacks John Partridge's almanac	Gadbury: *A reply*	2
1687	John Partridge replies to the former	Partridge: *A short Answer*	3
23.5.1689	Partridge denies having been a student of Gadbury	Partridge: *Mene Tekel*	4
1693	Partridge attacks Gadbury	Partridge: *Nebulo Anglicanus*	5
1693	Gadbury, as 1675	Gadbury: *Scurrilous Scribler*, reprinted	6
1693	Partridge criticises Gadbury's *Collectio* and *Cardines Coeli*	Partridge: *Opus Reformatum*	7
1697	Partridge criticises Gadbury's *Collectio*	Partridge*: Defectio Geniturarum*	8

1. Gadbury, John: *Cardines coeli, or, An appeal to the learned and experienced observers of sublunars and their vicissitudes whether the cardinal signes of heaven are not most influential upon men and things proved by X. remarkable genitures, &c. in a reply to the learned author of Cometomantia wherein the character of Gassendus is defended and sundry other starry truths are justified* / by John Gadbury, London printed: MDCLXXXIV [1684]
2. This pamphlet seems to be lost, but is mentioned in Partridge, *A short answer* (see fn 36)
3. Partridge, John: *A short answer to a malicious pamphlet called, A reply written by John Gadbury, the King of England's juggler, and astrologer in ordinary to the Pope, to help on the work.*, [London: 168-]
4. Partridge, John: *Mene mene, tekel upharsin. The second part of Mene tekel, treating of the year MDCLXXXIX. , And modestly shewing what may probably be conjectured to succeed in the affairs of Europe in general, and of England, Holland, Scotland, and France in particular; with something also about the affairs of Ireland, and the French King's forces there. : To which is added a treasonable paper dispersed among the papists, by J. Gadbury, with some reflections thereon, and also on his almanack for 1689. /* By John Partridge. , London, : Printed for Awnsham Churchil, MDCLXXXIX [1689]

Lover of Loyalty, and an abhorrer of all wicked Plots and Conspiracies'. It mentions John Gadbury frequently in the text and there is an advert for *Cardines Coeli* included, mentioning the 'Refutation of the Idle and Ridiculous Story of Pope Joan against the Author of Cometomantia and his unjust Recrimination against J.G. …'

5. Partridge, John: *Nebulo Anglicanus, or, The first part of the black life of John Gadbury it is the same John Gadbury that was in the Popish Plot to murther Charles II in the year 1678 : it is the same John Gadbury that was accused of being in another plot, to dethrone and destroy King William, in the year 1690 : it is the same John Gadbury that at this time is so strait-lac'd in conscience that he cannot take the oaths to their majesties : together with an answer to a late pamphlet of his /* by J. Partridge. , London : Printed, and are to be sold by the booksellers of London and Westminster, 1693.
6. Gadbury, John: *The scurrilous scribler dissected: or, A word in William Lilly's ear concerning his reputation, which he complains is injured by J.G. that ungrateful scorpionist, as he the said Lilly scurrilously terms him.* , [London: 1693]
7. Partridge, John: *Opus reformatum, or, A treatise of astrology in which the common errors of that art are modestly exposed and rejected: with an essay towards the reviving the true and ancient method laid down for our direction by the great Ptolomy, and more agreeable to the principles of motion and nature than that commonly practised and taught : in two parts /* by John Partridge. , London: Printed for Awnsham and John Churchill, 1693.
8. Partridge, John: *Defectio geniturarum being an essay toward the reviving and proving the true old principles of astrology hitherto neglected or at leastwise not observed or understood: wherein many things relating to this science are handled and discoursed /* by John Partridge. , London: Printed for Benj. Tooke, 1697.

[489]Verax, Merlinus: *The Nativity of that most Illustrious and Magnanimous Prince, Carolus Gustavus, King of Sweden,* London 1659

APPENDIX – John Partridge: Nebulo Anglicanus

[490]Ibid, frontpage

[491]Partridge, John: *Nebulo Anglicanus*, London 1693, pA3f

Good people pity me, for I'm half mad,
Both Fool *and* Knave, *and every thing that's bad:*
Beget by Chance, my Stars *with Loves soft arm*
(No Priest concern'd) gave *Figure to the Sperm.*
My Furious Form *thus laid, her sullen Womb,*
Preserv'd the wonder *of the Age to come;*
I've Liv'd in Vice and Tricking all my days,
And I'll be any thing to live in Ease;
I'll be a Heathen, Protestant, *or* Jew,
A Turk, *a* Papist, *any thing that's new;*
Let but the Priests *of my Religion say it,*
Go Swear, *or* Kill. *I'll certainly obey it;*
My Crimes (Pox take my Fate) I can't disown,
There's nothing vexeth me, but that they're known;
Nay, many Vices *more infect my Will;*
But my Discretion keeps them secret still;
Well, pray for me (Romes Saints) *'tis that I crave,*
A poor fall'n Brother, *but all over* Slave*;*
And in my good old Shape too, I'll appear,
Your Thimble Prophet, *and your* Bodkin Seer.

[492]Ibid

[493]Partridge, John: *Opus Reformatum: or, A Treatise of Astrology*, London 1693

NEBULO ANGLICANUS

Or, The First Part of the

BLACK LIFE

OF

John Gadbury

It is the Same

JOHN GADBURY

That was in the Popish Plot to murther Charles II. In the Year 1678.

It is the Same

JOHN GADBURY

That was accused of being in another plot, to dethrone and destroy King William, in the Year 1690.

It is the Same

JOHN GADBURY

That at this Time is so strait-lac''d in Conscience that he cannot take the Oaths to their Present Majesties.

Together with an Answer to a Late Pamphlet of His.

By J. PARTRIDGE.

I have fought with Beasts after the manner of Men, &c.

London : Printed, and are to be sold by the Booksellers of London and Westminster, 1693.

[494]Ibid. titlepage

[495]Gadbury, John: *Cardines Coeli*, London 1685

[496]Partridge: *Opus Reformatum*, op. cit. p70

[497]Ibid. p81

TO THE

Most Exquisitly Accomplish’'d

IN

Plotting, Tricking,

AND

INGRATITUDE,

My Honoured Friend,

Mr. John Thimble, of Brick-Court.

[498]Loc. cit.

[499]Ibid. p82

May it please Your Insolency,

Out of a horrible respect to Your Ignorance, and want of Merit, as well as Vertue and Honesty, I have made bold to borrow a Grain from your vast Treasury of Impudence, to qualifie and render me more acceptable to your superbious Tutorship; and that by the help of your Frowns I may more carelessly approach your Imperious Carkass, to kiss your Fist of Violence with this small bundle of Gratitude, and with a great deal of Submission (for I know you expect Surreverence;) I humbly desire you to remember how grateful you were to Mr. Lilly, your Kind and Generous Master, that rescued you from the Thimble-dispensation, and taught you how to get meat to your Bread, that being (you know) the First and Second Course, when you lived within lesse than a Mile of Strand-Bridge; and after this and abundance more of Kindness, which you have acknowledged in Print, the worst Word in your Budget was too good for him and you have abused him who was your Master, as much as you have done Me, that You say was your Pupil. Hah Jack, Gratitude, Gratitude! Master and Pupil both suffer alike, no Money in Brick Court. And so I take my Leave of my Confoundedly Learned Pythagor-Ass, and both with Goad and Awl I shall attend your Thimble and Bodkin, and am ready to serve You, while I am

J. P.

---

[500]Loc. cit.

[501]Gadbury: op. cit. p13

To the Impartial

R E A D E R.

Friend, or no Friend,

I have lately met with a Scandalous Invidious Pamphlet, sent into the World without a Name (called *Merlini Liberati Errata*) as if the Author of it, either for Scandalous Crimes, or other Villanies, were asham'd to let the World know from whence it came, and also would very fain have the World believe it was done by some Friend to *J. G.* one that is willing to defend him, that is either unable, or asham'd to defend himself: But whosoever hath had any Conversation with Mr. *John Thimble*, will easily guess who spawn'd this spurious Brat, for it is as like its *Dad*, as if it had been digg'd out of his A____ with a Pick-Axe: In a word, it came from our *Popish-Protestant Conjurer* in *Brick Court.*

And therefore, good Reader, pardon the Entertainment I must here give you of such a Fulsome and Nauseous Subject; and pray pity me that must endure the Stench of raking into the Vicious Actions, and worse Conversation of a *Dung-hill Fellow*, that stinks in the Nostrils of all good and sober people: A *Fellow* that is a Scandal to Humanity, a *Satyr* upon Vertue, a *Hater* of Truth, a *Promoter* of Slavery, a *Protestant* in Masquerade, a *Renegado* in Religion; *unkind* to those that have served him, *unjust* to his Wife, *unchaste* in his Conversation, *unfaithful* to his Friend, *treacherous* to his Prince, and a *Sworn Enemy* to the Religion and Liberties of *England.*

I know very well that Contention of this nature is never welcome in *Print* to Mankind in general; nor had I took the pains of writing, or given you the trouble of reading these *Sheets* of *Controversie*, had it not been to justifie my self from the Aspersion of my Adversary, who hath bespattered me with Falshood; and to tell you the Truth, he is a Common Lyar.

If you meet with any Rough *Words*, or *Personal* and *Mechanical Reflections* in the Pages following, I desire you to read them over with a charitable and friendly Censure; for I do assure you there is not any thing of that nature but what falls from my Pen unwillingly, and was forcibly drawn from me by his foul and scurrilous Language; and in reference to Mechanical Reflections, as my Pen never quarrelled till his threw down the Gantlet, so I never touch'd upon those till he broke the Ice: So that you see he is still the Aggressor in all things of this Nature.

---

[502]Partridge: *Opus Reformatum*, op. cit. p83f

[503]Partridge: *Nebulo Anglicanus* and *Opus Reformatum*, op.cit.

As to his *Unskillfulness* in his *Profession*, his *Self-contradiction*, *False* and *Ignorant Assertions* in *Astrology*, and *Confused Rules* and *Aphorisms, stolen, asserted,* and *applied,* I do not think fit to publish them in such a treatise as this is, but in one where they shall remain not for a Year, but for an Age, and to be read by such persons as will be competent Judges in the Matter, whether I speak Truth, or not.

But I will here take the Liberty to remind him and the World of one thing, since he hath endeavoured to make me appear so ignorant and silly a Fellow as he doth; and that is in his Epistle to my *Vade Mecum*; where he says, "This Learned Epitome of Astrology, here presented unto thee (Worthy Reader) is a most Exact and genuine a Piece of Art, free from Impurity and Falshood; Thou hast here the Oar of Science without the Dross; the True Wine without the Dregs; and all the Parts of this Most Excellent and Useful Learning so well and judiciously methodised, and so nearly and curiously handled by our Author, in a Vein so modest and taking, without perplexing his Matter with any thing impertinent and useless, that this Book alone is sufficient to make thee a Competent Artist in every part of Astrology — In a word, there is nothing wanting but our Thanks to the Author for his *Great Care* and *Pains* taken therein." Now I suppose no man will doubt but he meant what he said at that time; if so, it is a wonder I should be so much altered (as he seems to infer and prove in his late Libel) and grown less skilful. If I did deserve that Commendation then, he is an ill man to endeavour to prove the contrary now; if I did not deserve it then, he was a Fool or a Knave to give it.

But in a short time you will have a full and a fair Account of our *Brick Court Astrologer*, where he shall appear the most ignorant man that ever pretended to the Art in Print.

By Your Friend. J. P.

A

Short A C C O U N T

Of a Few

REMARKABLE PASSAGES

IN THE

EDUCATION and LIFE

Of Honest J. G.

We see plainly that nature hath not bound her self to a particular Method in the Order and Way of Generation in all Creatures, but sports her self in the Variety and order both as to Time, and method, just as she doth in the Colours of Herbs and Flowers: A *Fly-blow* on a *Cabbage* turns to a *Maggot*, and afterwards to a *Butterfly* with curious Colours. Serpents lay their Eggs, and they are hatch'd by the heat of the Dung, or some other hot Soyl; They tell us of a sort of Creature in *India*, that when they conceive, the Female bites off the Male's Head; and when the young ones are ripe for Production, they are not brought forth like other Creatures, but gnaw their way through the Damm's Belly. *Cats* are very modest in Coition, and always do it privately; but *Dogs* and their Kind generate openly in the Streets with a sort of Impudence, as some other Creatures do. Hence the *Poet*

> Vipers bring Vipers forth, by this I find
> Bitches *get* Puppies *to supply their Kind.*

It is no Scandal for any of the *Divine Urania's* Servants either to be a *By-blow*, or *got*, or *born* at a venture, without the consent either of Priest or Parish; nor is every one bound to wait for the Conveniency of Chamber-Furniture, or the Invitations of the Kindred; Sometimes a *Tayler* waiting to try the *Lady's Stays*, lets fly at the Game, and receives the Fertile Product of his Labour at Nine Months end. They say an ill *Bird* lays an ill *Egg*: If so, the *Brood* must be of the same Nature that is thence produced. You see Children born of dull heavy Parents, how stupid and blockish they naturally are; and that *Bastards* are generally brisk and airy, and also promoters of the same way that gave them their Being. I know a *Hero* born of an *Illustrious Dam*, who had a peculiar way to consecrate Nosegays to borrow money with; you'll wonder how, I'll warrant you; and indeed so you may very well; ------ and so let's enter *Don Phylo Mathematicus, Secretary* and *Buffoon* to the *Divine Urania*, who was born *December* 31st. between the Old Year and the New, as if Nature had form'd him for a Squint-ey'd Proselite, always looking two ways; or like a Waterman, that looks one way, and rows another; one that was doom'd by his Stars to draw his Religion once a year, as people do Valentines by lot; and also defends the Faith he hath drawn, till the Season comes again for him to draw a new one.

This Little *Furioso*, while in Swadling Cloaths, gave early Demonstrations of his respect to Religion; for where-ever he saw a *Cross* (especially a gilded one) he would always make a *Reverend Bow* to it, which have his Mother (who was a Papist) mighty hopes of his future Perfection in the Old Faith; nor did there want early Arguments of his *Fertile Fancy*, and *Quick Parts*, for they say he would often B------ two or three Clouts before his Nurse could wash one. Likewise when he did arrive at the growth of a *Standing-Stool*, he was immediately hammering at the crabbed Expressions of *Silly-gisms, Dilemma's, Arks* and *Semediameters*; so that his indulgent Parents began to think of sending this little Elf to the University of *Oxford*, before he was corrupted with the Education of his Hornbook.

And indeed this was soon put in practice afterwards, and away they sent him to *St. Nichols's* Colledge, where by the help of a good *Tutor*, and a *whetting Diet*, this little Thief grew as sharp as a Needle, to the admiration of all the Fellows of that House, and the circumadjacent Colledges, who spent their time in that kind of *Study*; so that it was generally agreed on as a Gratitude to his Merit, and for the Reputation of his parts, to confer on him that Honourable Title of *Lousy Jack*; and under this Reputation he was for some time made *Runner General* for the whole Society, where he spent a few years to make him fit to make his Degrees at *London*; to which place he came at a good suitable Age, as you shall suddenly hear more at large.

To compleat his Crimes in the future part of his Life, to *London* comes our *Academian*, and put himself a *Club* (he knows the Term which is common among

Philosophers of that Sect) to a *Merchant Adventurer*, whose Name was *Thorn*, living near *Strand-Bridge*: these Merchants do generally use a Sparing Diet about *July* and *August*, walk with their *Hands in their Pockets*, and suddenly after go a Nutting: With this Master he continued for some time, and in conclusion (being moved by a pious Inclination) entered into the Holy State of Matrimony: But under what Circumstances he was afterwards, I shall forbear to mention, as being unwilling to reflect on those Accidents that naturally attend the Order of Nature, and the Fate of Mankind, Poverty and Necessity being liable to every man at one time or other of his Life, and he that never feels the smart of it, may be reckoned among the happiest sort of men in this World: And indeed here must I put an end to the more innocent part of his Life, and also make a bar between the former and the latter; for now he puts on the *Armour* of a bad *conscience*, to justifie and defend his *worse Crimes*, and also a Vail of Piety, *alias* Hypocrisie, to be thought a man of great Religion and Vertue in his new Undertakings; For now he resolves (as his Actions prove) to be *aut Caesar, aut Nullus*, and to want no Preferment that Crimes can procure.

And to qualifie him for the Excellence of such Undertakings, he falls in with the then *Presbyterian congregations* in *London*, and afterwards with the *Independants*, as himself says in his Doctrine of *Nativities*, pag. 262. "About the 22d year of Age (he says) he was almost mad about the Doctrine of Predestination, because he could not find in himself those signs of God's Love and Favour which they told him of; and therefore sometimes concluded that he was in a state of Damnation." But this Religious Strain did not hold long, for indeed it was too hot to hold; and if you do but observe, you will for the most part find such *Young Zealots* as he was, are generally more *Whoremongers* than *Divines*; he suddenly thinks of hunting for a new Religion, and it must be such a one too that must secure him from the fears of Damnation under his greatest Crimes and Villanies; and the first he met with, and most suitable to his Humour was the *Family of Love, Ranters,* or *Sweet-finger* of *Israel; Coppe* at that time being the Head of them, and my Friend *John's, Spiritual Father*; and as the Cant then run, *He begot him in the Lord*; which was as much as to say, He converted him: This was the only fit Faith and Religion that ever my Friend found, for never was *Halter* and *Thief* better matched, than *John* and this *Family* of *Love*; for Lewdness, Whoredom and all Vice, were the Principles and Practice of this Zealous Crew, they holding all things in common, from the Purse to the Placket; now our Friend begins to put himself forward, and shew his Parts by instructing the rest of the Crew; and to that end, being more than half drunk, at *London-Wall* he undertook to preach from that Passage in the 11th of *Judges*, and the 1st. *ver. And Jephthah was the Son of a Harlot*; a very proper Text for Mr. *John* to discourse to the people, and especially if he doth but consider how plaguy doubtful his own Birth was (he knows the meaning of it) and recollects the Passages that then occur'd.

This sort of *Faith-jobbing* did not content him long, and therefore some new thing was to be again found out; and to that end, when *Cromwell* came to be *Protector*, he begins to insinuate at *Whitehall*, in order to make an Interest, to dedicate his Book, called the *Doctrine of Nativities* to *Oliver*, to which end he tells how he had been a Sufferer, and lost his Fortune and Estate by the *Royal Party*; and that he was ready to ingage all that he had left to serve that Interest; but somebody cut the Grass under *John's* Feet, and no Butter stuck upon his Bread at that time, so that then he thought it most convenient to turn *Book-wright* for a *Spiritual Livelihood.*

The *Protector* going off the Stage, and *Charles* II coming in, *John* then falls in Hand and heart, with that Government; *Turns* Church of England *Man*, and it was *Charles* the *Martyr* at every Word; then he call'd the *Nonconformists, Rebels* and *Rascals*, and rail'd like a Butter-whore at them in defence of the Church; and by this way of Insinuation he was at last taken notice of by some of those then Red- hot Saints, and from *Jewin Street* in 1666. he comes to *Westminster*, where he did generally appear at the *Abby* once every *Sunday*, to cheat Mankind into a good Opinion of his Sanctity; when to say the Truth, it was no more but a *Hypocritical* Paroxism, as you will see hereafter.

About the Year: 1667 he fell mightily in love with the *Gardiner's Daughter*, who was another Man's Wife at that time, who by Vocal Conversation, and Amorous letters, and Copies of Verse, he perswades her to leave her Husband Bed, and come and keep him and his Wife company; the silly woman complies, and was by this mountain Promises deluded, and by the help of *Don John*, under his Wife's Nose, she humbly conceived in a little time; then he decoy'd her to Mrs. *W's*. with great Promises to take care of her, and visit her often, but after he had got her out of his own house, he never went near her: this put her into a deep Melancholy which made Mrs. *W*. ask the reason, which when she knew, went to *John*, and acquainted him with the Matter: *Ay*, says he, *hath she told it? Then let her go like a Whore as she is*; a true *Scorpionist*. The poor Woman made hard shift to subsist, and at last was brought to Bed; and when she was up again, three Whores (you may guess by whom employed) met her in the Evening, and had like to have killed her: After this her *Husband* indicted this Friend of Mine at the Sessions, for debauching his Wife, and a few days before it was to come to Tryal, he was murdered privately, and 'tis forty to one but you will guess who did it, or at least had a hand in it: *A True Blew Catholick Saint*, and all this time one of our *Church*, and at the *Abby* almost every *Sunday. Monstrum horendum*! Can any man sleep in peace that has the gashly Ghost of a murdered man in his mind? or appearing before the Eyes of his wretched restless Conscience: It is no wonder to me, to see men run and rush into the most flagitious Crimes in Nature, that have been once flusht in the *Blood of Mankind*, and what is a leader to it, *Subornation of Perjury*; two such Crimes, that all Christian Governments have provided the severest of Laws for their severe punishments.

From this time forward for some years together, he was ruffling all Mankind, vindicating *Scorpio*, and promising us his *Body of Tautology*: Not to mention any thing of the Two *By-blows* that were at Nurse in *Tuttle-fields*, where his Friend *Baxter* told me he had been with him divers times; nor the Friendship and Intimacy he then contracted with the Trayterous *Popish Priests*, from whom he learned the Murdering Principles afterward discovered in the *Popish* Plot, as you may see by Mr. *Dangerfield's* own Words, in his Animadversions on *Gadbury's* Almanack for 1682 his words are these, speaking to *John Gadbury*.

"That you and I, upon, or about the 2*d* of *September* 1689, entring into Discourse, I perceived your countenance to change; when looking very angrily on me, that you wondered that I would offer to displease the Lords of the *Tower*, especially the Lord *Castlemain* (then out upon Bail) who design'd to advance me in the World, and help me to make my Fortune. To which I replied, That I was not a little surprized to hear such words from *you*, and asked *you* if *you* knew the ground of their displeasure, *you* Then replied yes, yes, *you* did; and then falling into a great Passion, said, It was because I would not *kill* the King; said *you* to me, I admire at your Ingratitude, that when you could not propose to your self any possible way of getting out of Prison, &*c*. that you should offer to refuse it; Nay, said *you* to me, I might have done it with all the ease in the world, for no manner of hurt could have befallen me: Why , said I, would not Death unavoidably have been the consequence of it? No, said *you*, for before I was released out of the *King's Bench*, *you* had an exact account from Mrs. *Cellier*, of the Year, Month, Week, Day and Hour I was born in, and the Countess of *P*. ordered you to calculate my Nativity; And it is so clear, said *you* to me, that you are by all adjudged the Person allotted for that bold and daring Enterprize." This is the Attestation left by Mr. *Dangerfield*; So that you see he is not content to be paddling in Blood himself, but for perswading others to engage in those Black Crimes also; for which he was taken into custody the 2*d* of *November*, *Anno* 1679. And this is the first notorious Plot that we find him engaged in against the *King, Religion* and *Government* of *England*, at which time he was certainly a *Papist*, he having at, or about that time told a Friend of mine, That under this last Conjunction in *Leo*, and its Effects, all *Europe* would be subjugated to the *Romish See*, and that it was good policy in all wise men to turn betimes, and so advised him. Hence you may be certain, that he who advised others, was without doubt of that Perswasion himself. Yet for all this, he denied it before the *King* and *Counsel*, and forswore it upon the Sacrament, in his *Magna Verstas*; and yet in 1685 I heard him own it; and afterwards he openly profest himself a *Papist*. And after all this *Hypocritical Faith-jobbing*, I hear he is turn'd *Protestant* again, and a special one too, no doubt, and it is indeed, the fifth or sixth time he hath found it convenient to change his Religion, if ever he had any.

While he was in Prison, he sent his Maid with a Present of Plate to Sir *T. D.* to get his pardon, but he finding the Case so foul, refused to be concerned in it; however he trebled the value of his Present, and sent it to another (now dead) by whose means, and some *Popish* Interest, his Pardon was produced: Yet during his Confinement he had accused *Dame Cellier* of some foul Treasonable Crimes before the King and Council, which he gave under his Hand; but when she came to be tried the *Summer* following, in *Westminster-Hall*, and he called to justifie what he had before sworn against her; He told the *Judge, He did not remember any such thing;* he own'd it was his Hand, but his Memory was bruised by being in Prison, and he could not say any thing to the Matter: *A very honest Fellow*! For this and some other *Popish Services* he received 200*l.* In the Year 1681 a certain Member of the *Church of Laodicea*, that liv'd within a mile and a half of *Strand Bridge*, and well known to my Friend *J. Gadbury* and my self, for many virtuous Qualifications, drew up in a Paper certain *Articles*, of several high and Treasonable Crimes against Sir *T. D.* and then brought these to Mr. *Sprigg* in *King-street*, *Westminster*, and desired him to go before a Justice of Peace, and make Affidavit of its Truth, but Mr. *Sprigg* desired a little time to consider of it; which being granted, away he came to me, and asked my Opinion what he should do in it? I asked him if it was true? He said, No; Why, then said I, do not you by any means oblige a Villain with a False Oath, to ruin any Gentleman's Reputation and Estate, and perhaps life too. But, said he, I owe him Money, and am afraid, if I do deny this thing, he will arrest me. No, said I, never fear that, for this thing of *Subornation* will keep him in awe I dare ingage; and from that time this *Laodicean* did differ with Mr. *Sprigg* for refusing this horrid thing, and *Knave* and *Villain* were the best Words he could give him; and there are several yet living, that know this Villanous thing from Mr. *Sprigg's* Relation, &*c.*

In the Year 1681 and 1682 his *Maid* took an occasion to leave her Master (he then being a Widower) I think twice, *Ay*, says he to his Kinswoman, *let her go, she will be glad to come again, when she finds she cannot mend her self*. And truly just as he said, so it fell out; for after she had been gone about three Months, she returned much slenderer than she was when she went away, for I supposes she had been cured of a *Timpany*, or some other disease of the *Bowels*; perhaps some *Tumor* or *Excrescence* in her *Womb*, of which she did very well, and was fit to follow her former Employment again. Now what man of Sense can doubt his being a *Conjurer*, for how should he know else she would come again? he must have this from some plaguy cunning Star, such a one, I suppose, as he predicted the Prince of *Wales* by, in 1686. Ah *John*, did you ever know an *Owl* and a *Sparrowhawk* build both in a Hole? Pray where was your *Handmaid church'd* after the cure of the *Timpany* that you infused into her?

In the Year 1684 he was frequently conversant with the *Popish Priests*, and no doubt but he could have given us an account of the fatal Stroke that was given the 2*d* of

February following, if he had thought it convenient; *Popery* was his *Darling*, and it must be brought in, though the Nation was wash'd in Blood for its Entertainment.

In the Year 1685 he was extremely full of Business, the Nation being then a Sacrifice to *Popery*, and he as a Servant to the *Idol Priests*, did expect a share in the Offerings; it was now time for him to shew his early Complyane with the enemies of *England*, and shew early Signs of his conversion; for it was his *Maxim* to several at that time, *That none should be preferr'd but* Roman Catholicks, *and such as would be so when the King pleased*, Ergo, &*c*. Now it was that he told Mr. *B. that the first time he went to Mass, there were twelve* English Peers *there at Mass at the same time, and now was the time for him to make his Calling and Election sure. A pious hopeful Christian!* And the better to pave his way to Preferment he now undertook the Office of a *Runner*, and an *Informer*, in order to ruine five or six Gentlemen in *London*, by a *Scandalum Mag.* for publishing Mr. *Dangerfield's Narrative*; this was a blessed time. But to say the truth, *John* got 20 *per Cent.* by it. And who of *John's* Perswasion would not be a Villain for that Wages? when, for ought he knew, there were half a dozen men to be ruined for it. But no matter for that; were his Father now living, and a *Protestant*, he would betray him too, rather than miss getting the Money; I know his Principle so well.

In 1686 and 1687 Mr. *Bounce* went about like a roaring Lyon to make Converts for his old *Granny* the *Whore* of *Babylon*; now it was that the told Mr. *B. He must be forced to have him to Father* Petre, *and Father* Ellis; those two who he had brought him to before, being not able to convert him. Now it was that he impudently said, *It would never be well till that King laid by Parliaments, and rul'd by his Absolute Power.* Now it was he said, *The Kings of* England *were not obliged by Law, to take the Coronation Oath*, Reply, *pag.* 8. Now it was he promised the *Papists*, *An Eternal Settlement in* England, *and that their Cause and Power would be as durable as the Sun*, Epistle to his *Almanack* 1686. But alas, they had nothing to say for it, but *Honest Jack's* Word: His Word, What's that worth, when the Nation knows he is a ---- Now it was that he told us, *There never was any such thing as a Plot by the Papists in King* James *the First's Time*, Reply *pag.* 3. which I suppose implies a Reason why he always omitted it in his *Almanack* every Year. Now what think you of my Dark Lanthorn conjurer, is he not a Seraphick Youth? at this time I can assure you he was an *Impudent, Insolent, openly-professed Papist*, and talk'd both like Knave and Fool. Now it was that he rail'd and rav'd against the *Church of England* in defence of *Popery*, as he used to do against the *Nonconformists* and *Fanaticks*, in defence of the *Church of England*, after *Charles* the Second came in: Now it was that all were Villains and Traytors (in *John's* Opinion) that would not submit against the Laws to a *Popish King*, and give up their Liberties, Estates, &*c.* to Old *Granne Church* again, to maintain Abby Lubbers, and Whorish Nuns, *John's* peculiar Saints; and now it was he wanted to be a Justice of Peace.

In 1688 when the Party began to apprehend a Storm, *Jack's* Business was to support them with Promises, and apply warm Clouts to their Capacities, while his own trembled like an Aspen-leaf; see his fulsome *Almanack* for that Year. Now it was he gave a written Paper out among the *Papists*, wherein were Words to this purport, the Prince being then coming; *He hoped to see him, and his Great men with him, brought to make Speeches at* Tower-hill *and* Tyburn: you see Honest *John* was then for making thorough Work; whoever affronted him, or *Granne Church* at that time, he scorn'd to give himself the trouble to contend, or talk out his Thoughts to them, or convert them, but throw a *Halter*, a *Hatchet*, or a *Gallows* at them, and then their Work was done, and they were certainly dead in Law; What! Affront *Jack*, or his Church!

In 1689 *John* was come to his *Ne plus Ultra* in *Popery*, and for a long time never said his Prayers, because he did not know what sort of them he should take up with next; for he resolves to go to Heaven by no other Religion than that which is in fashion; no matter if it be *Mahumetism,* that will do according to *John's* Notion in his *Epistle* to his A*lmanack*, 1682 where he says, *That God always sends Kings of that Religion which he expects those Nations to be of, where they govern*: This is a very honest Fellow, he came *raw* into the World, and will never go roasted out for *religion*, I will pass my word for him.

In 1690 about *June*, *John* was catch'd at the *Post-Office*, in sending a Bundle of Treason to some of his *Popish* Friends, in which was one of King *James's Declarations*, a *Treasonable Copy of Verses* against the King and Queen, which he promised his Friend should be printed in a short time; but above all, a most *Villainous Letter* against the *Government*, in which he assured his Friend, that King *J's Declarations* were set up on all the *Church Doors* in *Devonshire* and *Cornwall*, and that they had agreed with the *French* King to take off all their *Tin* at a certain rate, and they had all declared for King *James*; and to use his own Words for it, he said, *King J's Interest was like a Cart overthrowed, and therefore they must get a considerable help to set it upright on its Wheels again, and then drive on as before.*

Now I would ask him if this Rebellious Principle is agreeable to his old *Noisy Doctrine of Non-resistance*, when he asks, what is *Passive Obedience* turned into, *bearding*, *upbraiding*, and *dethroning* of Kings, *Rep*. pag. 21. But at that time *John* was a *Popish* Casuist to defend a base and Villainous Cause, the shaven Crowns, and their Dow-baked Gods; the very Treason that he was taken in that Year, in the *late bloody Reigns* would have hang'd any man: The D. of *Monmouths* Declaration took away *Will. Disney's* Life; and Collonel *Sidney* died for *publishing a Book in his Study;* Mr. *Colledge* for carrying a Regiment of men in a Portmanteau to seise the King at *Oxford*; but *John* met with a more merciful Government, and a better Fate, but how he deserved it, I will leave you to judge.

In 1691 his time was employed in supporting the Party, and giving them assurances of their old Master's Return, and this by the power of the Stars. In the end of 1688 he did assure them he would be here again by *Christmas*, or to use his own words for it, For a *New-years-Gift*; that failing, he engaged he would be here at farthest, by *Easter*, in 1689 but that also failing; and then he was certain he would not fail of being here by *Michaelmas*, and then he put them off till *Easter* 1690 and because he would be sure of it then, he was in a Plot himself to restore him; just like Young *Nostradamus*, they tell of, who predicted the burning of a City, and rather than have his Prophecy want success, he fired it himself, for which he was hang'd.

In 1692 he had a fresh Ferment in his Conscience about Religion, and having not confidence to go to the Abby where he used to go, when he was a supposed *Protestant* before, I hear he comes now to St. *Margaret's* Church as a Protestant, and with abundance of Devotion, you may be sure; where he certainly lies *purdue*, to watch for another Opportunity to change his Religion, or rather to shape his Conscience according to the next New Cut of Faith that he finds suitable to his Advantage and Interest, they being the two main Arguments of his Religion and Piety; and notwithstanding he is again turned a *Mungrel protestant of the* Church *of* England. I have heard very lately, that he hath trumpt up a New Argument, to encourage the Papists, and their Accomplices to expect their Old Master next Year 1694 and that is from the MC *ad* m6 : but the Lord help his Ignorance and his Folly, and pity those that are deluded by him, for that Direction will not come up before he is almost 69 years of Age, in the year 1702 and for the MC *ad* p 1 that comes up not till 1709 so great is his Ignorance and Confidence, to comfort the Party with Lies and Juggles.

Thus I have brought this worthy Gentleman to the 65th Year of his Age, and very fairly given you the Account of his Life, as to those things I treat of, and do really think I have not done him any Injury in relating Matter of Fact; if I am any ways out, or amiss, it is only in being short, and not relating his Crimes to the height they were acted by their Author; and therefore I had rather modestly screen his Villainies with a deficiency in relation of them, than to abound in their History at this time; and this the rather, because the very Glimpse of them in this short Account, will give him so foul, and so black a character, that all men of Honesty and Honour will detest his Principles, and conclude him to be the greatest ----- ----- in the world. What will you say to him that enticeth away and steals his Neighbour's Dog? Why, you cannot call him less than Thief; but then what will you judge him to be, that by *Amorous Letters, Copies of Verses,* and *Vocal Perswasions*, enticeth away his *Neighbour's Wife*, takes her to his House, gets her with Child, and then kicks her out of Doors again, to the mercy of the wide world, and the fury of her Husband, not to speak a word of the Murther of Mr. *G.* and these are so well known, that there are many in Town acquainted with each Particular; and indeed I know something of the matter my self, having had the honour to see her at his house at that time.

What will you think of him that hunts for a New *Faith*, sometimes once a year, but for the most part, once *every Seven Years*? What will you think of him that was in a Plot to *murther* the *King* he always pretended to support? What think you of him that as in another Plot, to *murther* and *dethrone* that *King* that had before pardoned him, and forgave all his Villanies and Treasons against him?

What will you think of him that railed and raved at the *Royal Party* in 1657 that railed at the *Fanaticks* from 1660 forwards; that railed at the Church if *England* in defence of Popery, in the Year 1687 and now curseth his own *Stars* that he wants power to be a greater ----- than he is.

What think you of him that would have suborned a man to have sworn Crimes against a *Gentleman*, even to *Life, Liberty* and *Estate*? This is such a *Villany*, that none but such who are perjured themselves, would ever attempt; *Suborners* of *perjury*! Why they are worse than *Highway-men* and *House-breakers*; for we may be safe from one sort by strong Doors and Walls, and from the other by staying at home; But who can be safe against false *Oaths*? who can be safe when two or three conspire together, and are willing to take a False *Oath* at the price of their own Damnation and Eternal Ruin: What shall we say: when a Man hath his Life snatched from him, by the False *Oaths* of two *perjured Villains,* and dies an Ignominious Death, for a Base and Scandalous Crime that he was never guilty of! (The Lord remember the sufferings of the people in the *Late Bloody Reigns.*) Perjury is such a Crime, that next to Murther, our *Lawgivers* have thought fit to make a severe Act for the punishment of such Offenders; and yet you see when Malice rides abroad *Rampant*, and *Conscience* stays at home, it is no hard thing to find a certain Saint, that used to go with abundance of Devotion to the *Abby*, who is willing to undergo not only *Drudgery* of *Swearing*, but Swearing falsly, or at leastwise to perswade others to do it, which if there is any difference is the worst Crime of the two; and I doubt not but every one who is willing to perswade others to such Offences are ready to do it themselves, or else have been guilty of the same Crimes formerly. Who can have the impudence to look God or man in the Face, without blushing, or a dejected Countenance, when he knows his soul is loaded with such a horrid Villany, and his Conscience tells him every moment, that he deserves the punishment due to so heinous a thing; or else on his Knees he ought to confess it, and beg the *Gentleman's* Pardon, if he is not past Grace and Repentance.

And so I come to consider a *Pamphlet* lately sent forth into the World without a Name, as if the Author of it was either afraid or asham'd to own what he had done; or else by reason of other Crimes, he thought his Name instead of making his Book sell, might have damn'd it to a perpetual oblivion and have saved us the labour of reading it; *Ex pede Hercules*, by the man you may know the Matter; and you may be certain that *J. G.* can as soon eat that Paper, as write a treatise without his Two *Martyrs* in it; just like *Roger* wedded to *Forty One*. And tho it comes without the Author's Name in the Title Page, yet I can without the help of the Stars, tell it came out of *Brick-Court*, and that *John Gadbury* is the Author if it; which he calls *Merlini Liberati Errata*; which I will consider, and give an Answer to his material Objections therein alledged against me; and do assure him, that as I have already made him appear a *Knave*, so I will shew the World he is also a *Fool*, especially in that *Profession* he pretends to, which is the *Art* of *Astrology*; and likewise how silly, as well as false, the most part of his Objections are, passing by his witticisms, as well as his Reflections, being sensible that the best of Authors, nay, the Word of God too, hath been defamed and abused by the Witty *Jests*, *&c* of Debauched Men; and by some in particular, of *J. G's* Acquaintance that I could name.

A N

ANSWER

T O H I S

Idle P A M P H L E T.

In his Title Page I perceive he is an earnest Honourer of his *King*, *&c.* I am glad to hear of such a Reformation, for it is not three years since he was accus'd of being in a Plot to *dethrone* and *murther* the *King*; and to this day he cannot in conscience take the Oaths to Their *Majesties*, and yet an earnest Honourer of the King, *&c.* It would be convenient, I think, to ask him, *What King?* For I am sure our King is not his, if he cannot take an Oath to be true to Him.

In his Epistle to the Reader, he complains of my *Brutish Bawling*, and *Beastly Language*, which is needless (if true) seeing he pretends to be my Master; having taught me one by his *Bouncing Empty Writings*, and the other by his *Debauched* and *Beast-like Life* and *conversation.* In the very next Words he takes care of the *Church* and *State*; meaning, I judge, that of *France*; for a *Papist* can never intend the *Church of England*; if he doth, and designs what he says, he is damn'd by his own Principles; but you may see he hath undertaken to patch up the Cause, and therefore let it be so; and for his two Martyrs, I refer my Reader to *M. G. Ludlow's* Letter for the one, and to the *Cruelties* of the *Star-Chamber* (especially Dr. *Layton's* Case) for the other; for I have something else to do, than to spend my precious Time about such things as are not to my present Purpose. And at last of all, he calls out to the *Church of England* for help; one would think he might call to his own *Church*, if he knew which it was, which I doubt he doth not, after all this chopping and changing of his Religions; for he always serves his God in the newest Fashion; and so I come to the Matter it self.

Pag. 6. The first thing he falls foul on shews the Fellow to be *top-full of malice*; and what little things must serve him to make a noise with in my *Epistle*; I said, *This little Book will run the Nation thorough*; but that way did not please him, it seems, to express it; and therefore after a great deal of noisey stuff, he puts me, as he thinks, in a better way, to say this little Book shall run thorough the Nation; a very Learned Distinction, and after his usual Banter, he adviseth the Nation to be provided of good *Surgeons*, I suppose he means *Cloath-Surgeons*, alias, *Strand-lane Garret-men*: As for the Cause of our *Difference* mentioned in that Page, I shall take notice in another Place, more proper than this, and also set the *Goad* and the *Awl* he mentions there against his *Bodkin* and *Needle*, and let his Sixfooted-straglers take which they please to contend for their Master's Honesty, when he was saving the Remnant; in the same Page he quarrels because I say, here were no material *Rays* and *Positions*, &c. and then the *Blockhead* with his *Rumbling Nonsense*, draws an Inference, as if I said there were no *Rays* and *Positions.* I said there were no *Rays* material, to give any kind of remarkable things in the *Air*, or *Mundane Affairs*; but our *Popish-Jugler* is for any thing, so he can but make a noise: *Oh the Impudence of the Fellow!*

Pag. 7th. In *February*. I wonder he should be so impudent to deny there was a *Popish Plot* going on in *February*, according as I predicted it, from the preceeding Conjunction of *Mars* and *Saturn*, in the *Gadburian Sign*; when he knows he himself (like an ill man) was taken a few Months afterwards, as he was sending *Treasonable Letters, Popish Declarations*, &c. to his *Popish conspirators*, to embroil the King and

Government; here it is plain the Design was then going on, or else I must conclude *John* made a *Plot* himself, on purpose to verifie my Prediction, and now takes this Opportunity to let the World know how kind he was to me; 'tis strange that *Nature*, his *Stars*, his *Parents*, and his *Profession*, should all conspire to compleat this Monster of *Mankind*; he was *doubtfully begot, painfully born, thievishly bred, whorishly vicious, impudently lives,* and doubtless will as *knavishly die*; And then for the Story of the *Stars* giving, I will talk with him by and by. *Pag.* 7. In *March* he tells me, *I mention a great Congress of the Planets in Pisces*, which is a most *notorious Falshood*: My words are these, *We here find no less than six of the Seven Planets in Watery Signs,* &c. and at the time they were all in *Watery Signs*, except *Mars*, and no one Word of a *Congress* there, till you come to the next *Paragraph*, where the word *Congress* is used, and I suppose not improperly, when there are *Five Planets* in one *Sign*; *Ah my* Popish *Apostate*! *thou hast been always gifted with Lying and Treason, ever since you gave over going to the* Abby Church.

Pag. 8. *April.* He makes a great noise about the Word *give*; I having said, *The* Planets *give such, and such things*; methinks the Word may do well enough, tho the *Stars* have no hands: What think you *John*? We give a man a good Word, Why hath the tongue Hands? You gave the Wench a *clap*, what hath your Belly Hands? I *give* my consent, Prethe how shall this be done? Perhaps I go to do it, Hath my Feet Hands? My Brain contrives it, Hath that Hands? at last my Tongue actually doth it, and yet no Hands; so that we shall set the Members together by the ears, who it is that gives this Consent, and this may be done by a man that hath no Hands: Well, but I am condemned for a *Fool* and *Blockhead*, to use it and that it is a very improper word: Let it be so, I will find a Companion presently: There was a *Sorry empty Treatise* a few years since, writ by an *Impudent Fellow* in *Brick-Court*, and called a *Collection of Nativities*, in which he printed a hundred *Aphorisms*; no less than seven of those *Aphorisms* have the very same word, and just so applied; as it is by me, as in *Aphor.* 13. *Fixed Stars on the Angles of a Nativity,* Give *the Native eminent honour* &c. *Apho.* 22. again gives the *Native*, &c. *Apho.* 50 ♄ and the ☉ in the Second, *give* the *Native* and *Estate. Apho.* 67. ☿ in the Houses of ♄ *gives* an Excellent Understanding; and so in the 68 and 82 *Aph.* It seems when that *Fellow* writ these *Aphorisms*, this was a very good and proper way to express things, but now *Jack*, and the way of expressing things are changed. *Well, what say you; are you and I Brother-blockheads or not*? Remember the old Adage, *Turpe est Doctore cum culpe redarguit ipsum;* what! correct me, *Jack*, and guilty thy self of the very same Crime? And indeed it is so in most of the rest, if I had but time to examine all thy old Nonsense; thou hast lay so long by *Inops mentis*, that thou art really mad thy self, and I fear thou must be sent to the Colledge in *Moor-fields*, to have thy Senses restored, and thy Memory too, if possible: St. *Paul* and you, seem to be parallel in your Cases, but differ in the Terms; for *Festus* told him, *that much Learning had made him mad*; but that is none of your Crime; a great deal of *Knavery* and *Impudence* makes you so, with the want of the other.

Pag. 8. *May. Indeed* John *you fib*, for when that *Almanack* was writ, there was no War in *Ireland*, for your Master had not been long landed then, *but there were Wars and Confusions too*; yes 'tis no matter, I must allow my Friend the use of his Talent, Lying, *&c.* It seems *Mercury* hath affronted him, or else I have, for using the young Gentleman's Name; for he says, *That* Merlin *is constrain'd by the power of* Mercury, *to utter Lies, as Honest* J. G. *was to go to Mass in* 1686. *or to get his Maid with Child in* 1681. And now I must shew my Parts in teaching my Master, for here he asks me a Learned Question, *How* ☿ *in* Taurus *comes to concern* Ireland *and* France? Why I will tell you *John*, because you are a *Friend*, and because I would willingly keep your Friendship; *All Countries do suffer, and are concern'd for Good or Ill, according as the Princes* Nativities *are affected or afflicted*, *not that I reject the Radical Figure of that Country, if it can be had:* and now I think on't, *Pray what* Direction *had* Jamaica *at the time of its* Earthquake, *by the Nonsensical* Table *of* Directions *that you bubbled those Gentlemen into a belief of? what must we say, was its* Nativity *false, or the* Directions *false? or did not* J. G. *know how to work them true? which is most likely, for he is a very Ignorant Fellow, and also very Impudent, or else he would be asham'd of this, as well as of his* Prediction. That Dr. *Oats* should stand in the Pillory every year on certain days, and this as long as he liv'd; *but he hath liv'd to see himself prov'd* Fool *and* Lyar.

Pag. 9. *June*. Here our *Popish Juggler* would be nibbling at something, if he knew what, but it is not a rush matter, so it makes a noise, whether it is to the purpose or not; his *Noisie Objections* are so silly, that I do not think it worth my answer, for every Reader may easily see both his Folly, and his Malice: But for a Confirmation of his Skill in *Astrology*, I will here relate a short Story of his Confidence in one of his groundless *Predictions*, about his Friend Mr. *Lloyd* of *Wales*; *The poor Gentleman having lain some time ill of a* Hectick, *was at last given over by his Doctors, but he was unwilling to take the* Sentence of Death *from them contentedly, till he had acquainted his Friend* Gadbury *with what they said, and to request his Opinion about his* Life *or* Death, *and so writes him a Letter, and sent it to him by the Post; which being done, his Friends prevailed with him to make his Will, which he did, in which he gave* J. G. 40 *Shillings for his Judgment on his Case; so Mr.* G. *writes his Answer, and told him, That his Doctors where Fools, and did not understand either his* Case, *or their own* Business; *and also assur'd him upon the* Reputation *of a* Brick-Court Juggler, *that he would live two years, and some few Months, and of this he was certain; so away went the* Epistle; *but before it came to hand, his Friend was dead; and the Copy of his Letter is now in Town, in a* Physician's *hand, who told me the Story, and perhaps it may be printed for the use of him and his* Friends. Now pray tell me what is *J. G's Credit* and *Reputation* worth in *Astrology*? for he assured him on his *Reputation*, &c. but I can tell him, he is far better at *Faith-Hunting*, than at reading a Lecture on the *Effects* of the *Stars*.

Pag.9. On *July*. Here our *Paraphrastical Coxcomb* would be writing a Comment on he knows not what, and repeats my words about the *two Lights being in a Mundane Parallel with* Jupiter, and tells his Reader the Reason why it cannot be so, and that is because the *Lunation* did not fall in *Cancer*, but *Leo*; Ha, ha, he! Did ever Soul hear such Ignorance and Nonsense, set off with so impudent a Flourish; and I am certain he knows not what a Mundane Parallel is, nor how to work it; ad yet this is the Fellow that sets up for my Master; but ignorance seldom goes without Confidence and Lying; and this being proved false, all the rest he says on that Month is of the same Stamp, which he had by the help of his old Friend, the Father of Lies.

Pag. 10. In *September*. Here he chargeth me with Lying; he might indeed with a Mistake; for the Moon did apply first to the *Sextile* of *Saturn*; I own that, but it was a mistake, and no design to do it; but I shall be even with him by and by, and I suppose he knows I will.

Pag. 9. In *October*. He quarrels with something, but what he cannot tell: I do say, *That there were five violent Lunations, and most of them in* Libra*:* It is true, What would my Popish Prophet be at, I wonder? There was one on *September* 15. and on *Septem.* 22. a third on *Septem.* 30th. and a Fourth on *October* the 8th. and all these were in *Libra*! And all of them violent; therefore the most of them were there, as I said before, which is the very thing he carps at; but any thing to make a noise with; be sure the empty Cask makes the greatest sound; Why doth not he clear that thing to the world, that I have charg'd upon him, about the MC. to the *Body of Saturn* in his own *Nativity*, that came up, as he affirms, in the Year 1670. and is a most ruinous Direction, according to his own Rule, pag. 189. in *Doc.* of *Nativ.* And yet gave him nothing but Grandeur, contrary to its Nature, and his Rule; then it was *every one pull'd his horns at the dash of his Pen, not daring to peep out in their own vindication*: Is it so now too? I think not.

Pag. 9th. In *Novem.* Here the word *Wretched* affects him; I suppose it is because the word best suits his Inclinations, for he is a *Wretched Fellow*, as you may see by the *Actions of his wretched Life*, that precede this Part.

Pag. 11. *December*. In his witty harangue on this Month, he first makes a Puppet of his own, and then sets it up and laughs at it; it is he indeed that makes the Nonsense; I do quote these words, *Significat bellum, effisionem sanguinis ac multitudinem Febrium*, and do say the *French* King would feel its Effects; for a Prince may suffer by the loss and destruction of his People, as well as in his own Person; so after he hath in his way ridicul'd, these things, he condemns our poor *Merlin* for a very silly ignorant Fellow, and gives the Chair to our Blackthumb'd *Merlin*, and then I am sure he will chuse a couple of Lowsy *Strand lane* Centinels with Bodkins in their hands, and a Case of Needles by their sides to be his Guard, and *Verax* in *Brick court* is to be the Right-hand man; so now I think we are all fitted with Places, and being provided, I hope we shall be contented, and live lovingly as we used to do; and so I come to the end of his Opinion on my Twelve Months; and now to shew you he is a very silly ignorant impudent Fellow, I will give him a home-thrust at once, and expose him to the world, tho I think I cannot make him more notorious than he is; yet I will give my Bodkin-Prophet a Glimps of his Skill, which I am sure he cares not to hear. In his *Epistle* to that *Ephemerides* that he stole from [__]cker, he tells Sir *Frech. Holles*; he should live some Decades of years; First here's his Impudence, he affirms he should live some years; secondly his ignorance, the Gentleman died within Six Months after: Is not this a very fine *Astrologer*, and fit to be a Corrector of others? In his own *Nativity* he tells us he passed the *MC.* to the Body of *Saturn* 1670. and gave him nothing according to its Nature. In the *Nativity* of the Princess Royal *Collect. Genitur.* Page. 20. he says she married on the *Midheaven* to the Body of *Mars*, and yet he sends Bishop *Laud* to the Tower on the very same Direction, *pag.* 90. of the Collect: And he kills *Charles Gustavus*, King of *Sweden* on the *MC.* to the Body of *Saturn*, which in his own gave nothing at all. Certainly whoever reads these Contradictions, must judge *Astrology* a very idle Study, or else our supposedly Learned *Thimble Conjurer* to be a very *Ignorant Fellow.* How *John*! You my Master, and guilty of this Nonsense! My Master was no *Faith-hunter*, but a Man of a steady Reputation, one that understood *Astrology* better than this, and how to teach it better than you do: Before you quarrel with me in point of *Art*, I challenge you to make these Things clear to the World, in an *Astrological* way, which if you do not, you must expect to hear from me about them another time. You the *Top-man* and *Bell-weather* of the whole *Society* of *Astrologers*! Are not you a fine Reputation to your *Profession*? you shall have the Chair, but it shall be to sh----- in, not to read *Astrology*, unless it is a Nonsensical one.

Pag. 12th. On the *Winter-Quarter.* Here he shews himself in his True Colours, and to any one that understands what a Mundane Parallel is, he will soon appear to be what he really is, a Malicious silly Fellow; and therefore I will not spend time about this, for it answers it self, and doth not want mine.

Pag. 12. On the *Spring-Quarter.* Here my *Thimbletonian* doth charge a notorious lie upon me; for he says that 24 of ♐ ascends &c. when I say 19 of ♑ doth; pray you that understand how to set a Figure, enter the Column of Time from Noon, with 15h. 25m. and see if the 25th *Degree* of ♏ will not be on the Tenth House, and 19 of *Capricorn* ascending; if so, What doth the *Fellow* make a noise about? You see he sticks a Feather in his own Cap, and laughs at his own Folly; for he says himself, that I give the Ingress at 15h. 25m. *PM.* And for my saying there may be a mistake of a Sign, two or three in the Ascendant, when Signs of short Ascension rise in the *East*, is no strange thing; for Operations of that nature being wrought by divers Tables, will differ one or two Hours in time, perhaps more; and it is well known to all Pretenders to *Astrology*, that ♒ ♓ ♈ and ♉ are but 4 hours ascending, and two of those Signs but 50 Minutes a piece, which proves what I say; and so he goes on to ridicule me for *Mundane Aspects* and *Parallels*, which I am sure he does not understand: And now pray do but observe the *Ignorance* and *Impudence* of this *Fellow* that pretends to correct me, that am more true and exact than himself.

In his own *Popish Almanack*, pag. 4th. He says that the ☉ enters ♈, on *March* the 9th at 6 Hours, 42 Min. after-noon 1693. and how he will prove this, seems strange to me, without some *Popish* Miracle; for in his *Almanack* the *Sun* at Noon, wants 16 Min. to enter *Aries*, which gives in time 6 Hours and 30 Min. which falls short of 6. 42. and therefore if you examine *Shakerly's* Tables, the Sun by them enters ♈ at 7 hours 10m. *PM.* And these are the Tables which he pretends to go by. Hence it is plain he hath imprudently impos'd a time upon us, not agreeable to his own *Almanack*, nor the Tables he pretends to, which shews him both ignorant and confident. He understand the *Stars*! he knows better how to cuckcold his Wife, and lie with his Maid (as he call'd her) than to work any *Mathematical Operation*: The *Fellow* is certainly mad, and how it came to pass I am not certain, unless his *Priests* made him so when he was a *Papist*, or that he hath taken a *Frenzy* by Contaction, in lying by his Mad Wife; for in 1686. or 87. for the lucre of a little Money, he married a Woman that was really mad, and so she is still, and a *Papist.*

Pag. 14. On the *Summer Quarter*, he here carries on the Rattle as before, and the principal thing is to prove my Figure false, and wittily objects at my Saying, *where Armies are in the Field*; and asks me, *If ever I knew Armies in a House*? a very wise Question; but I shall answer my *Popish Laplander*, with an Examen of his most erroneous Calculation, for the *Summer* Ingress, 1693. which he tells us, *Is at* 8 *hours* 48 *Min.* PM. June 10th. Now if you will but work that Ingress by *Shakerly's* Tables, you shall find that it is at 43 Min. past 9. differing almost an hour in time from his, and this from them Tables that he pretends to work by: and I hope his Worship will allow that an hour in time, makes a great alteration in a Figure of the Twelve Houses. What think you now of my Corrector, is he ignorant or impudent? I judge it was from such Rules and Grounds he promises the *Papists, That* Popery *should continue in* England *for ever.*

Pag. 14. In the *Autumn Quarter*, that is to say, in his Dialect, *Cucumber-Time*, here he is upon the old Rumble again, and as true as the former: *But prithee* John, *Why shall I not be true to my Wife, if I marry*? Here you might have forborn that especially, when you consider how you used your first Wife; Take one into the House, and get her with Child under her Nose; *What do you mean by being just? It is not in your Nature; you were never just to God nor man,* Ergo *not to your Wife.* And for my coining of false Books, that charge lieth at your Door, not mine: And let me tell you, I have begun to publish a

Doctrine that shall stand when you and I are gone; but I will take care to give the World an account of what you have writ, and that very speedily too. But you, Mr. *John*, would do well to have your Calculations done better next year, for at the *Winter* Ingress, by the Suns place, it is at three quarters past 12 at Night; and *Shakerly* at half an hour past one; but an hour is a small matter in *John's* Calculations.

Pag. 15. Of the Eclipses. I will answer the first in your own *Almanack* for 1693. pag. 4. You say the ☽ will be eclipsed near [ab]out 4 in the Morning; in the same page you say the Sun will be eclipsed on 16th of *December*, at our Midnight; and yet in *Dec.* you say it is at one in the Morning; what! is there the difference of an hour between the Full Moon and her Eclipse, and between the New Moon, and the Sun's Eclipse? For shame do not be guilty of these fulsome Contradictions; prithee forbear correcting others, till you mend your own Faults, and understand better, or else you and your Family must get to the Colledge in *Moor-fields*: With these fulsome Errors, remember you tell us in your lying *Ephemerides, That the Sun's Eclipse in* June *will be almost total*: And in your *Popish Almanack* for 1693. you say, *it will be but half a Digit*: What Stuff this is to come from *John Gadbury*? *fie* John *fie*, are not you asham'd of this? I am sure you may, only I think you are past shame.

And for the Quotation *Jack* carps at, I do assure him he is mistaken; and whosoever will look into *Ptolomy, Lib.*6 *Quadripar.* They will find the same Words, only in another Language; but for that Book I am sure, *John* understands it not, nor never will; and therefore *Proclus* and *Ptolomy* are indeed all one to him.

And as to the Second Eclipse I mentioned, I did not take it from the patch'd-up 20 years *Ephemeridies* that he falsly calls his, but from *Mezzavachis*, who doth assure me it was almost 7 Digits and a half, and said, *almost three Parts of the Moon's Body would be darkened*: Pray then where is the Error that this foolish Fellow makes a noise about? In the two other *Eclipses* he shews his malice and his Ignorance in carping at my Quotation of *Junctine*; for the Texts there alledged, he knows very well they are printed by *Junctine* in his *Speculum*; and if so, Where is the cause for this silly rattle-headed Fellow's Noise and Clamour? I am afraid really the Fellow must to *Bedlam*, and his Family too, if the Mad-Moon doth not prove the more kind to him; and so I come to the *NB.*

Pag. 17. Here he wriggles about, and I cannot tell well what he would be at, but at last he quarrels with my false *Grammar*; pray see his Ability to correct me, in *pag.* 81 and 82 *opus Reformat*; but at last he concludes my measure of Time is mortal, because I use the word Expire: Pray *Jack* tell me if your Measure of Time doth not expire, how do you know when your Direction begins to operate? For according as I understand it, when the measure of an Ark of Direction is out, or the Years, Months, and Days, are expired, allowed by that Measure, then the Direction begins to shew its Effects; if so, I am right in the Word *Expire*; and again, if your Measure is as you say, Immortal, and hath no End, how is it a Measure? For Time it self, that is to be measured, is not immortal, then how can your Measure be so? And every Measure is extremely less in length, than the thing measured; but this Objection is one of the exquisite Points of your Nonsence; and besides, thou art one of the impudentest Fellows in nature; for I say, at the □ of ☉ ♄, the same is on the Moon's radical place, she at his Birth being near 6 degs. in ♌ , and when the Sun came to six in ♌, he was applying to the Square of *Saturn*, within about five Degrees: What! doth such silly Cavils as these become the Great man in *Brick-court*? *Fie for shame, learn more with, or else more modesty.*

Pag. 18. I do confess the *French* King's *Nativity* is as certainly mine as the *Merlini Liberati Errata* was *Jack Gadbury's*; nor do I disown any of it, tho I confess it was done by the approbation as well as the instigation of *J. G.* nor do I deny his *nativity* to be a great one; but this doth not hinder him from being a *Tyrant* and an *Oppressor*, and I was deluded by *Jack* at that time, to print that *Tyrant's Nativity* and it was he that provided me a Bookseller, with whom I suppose he agreed to bubble both the Printer and the Author, for I never had a penny for my Copy, tho perhaps he had; *Remember* Stow's *Chronicle*, Jack.

At the same time that he encouraged, and put me upon doing this thing, he then also gave me a Copy written by himself, called *Utrum Lorum*; Rome *or* Geneva, *Never a Barrel better Herring*; designed against all *Religions*, but most chiefly against the Reformed *Protestant Profession*; this he bid me carry to one Mr. *Reynolds* a *Bookseller* (which I did) and desire him to print it with my Name to it: but he refused to do it (asking me: *If I knew what it was*?) I told him, *I knew nothing but the Title* (believing my *Friend J. G.* would not have put an ill thing upon me); he said, *It was an ill thing, and against Religion, and therefore he would not print it*; and the *Copy* I believe I have by me still; and had this *Villainous Book* been also done in print, I doubt not but he would abuse me for it, as well as he doth for the other; and to say the truth, it is his Doctrine and Method, but both false; yet it was my Labour and Pains taken in the compiling of it; all which I do at present disown in this my Practice, having a Method more agreeable to nature, and the real Motion that we all contend for; and let this Fellow if he can shew what I have said in any Predictions about him, that is opposite to the very matter he relates.------- But at the bottom of that page, he says *He owns it his duty to serve the king and Country in Purse and Person, and this he resolves to do cordially*: You serve the King both with Purse and Person! Yes, so you did in 1690. with your *Popish Declaration*, and your *Treasonable Letter*. You boast of your Loyalty! I suppose you mean to your *Popish King*: Do you think *Non-resistance* is not a Duty now, as well as it was six or seven years ago? leave off your canting and lying, and learn your Duty to God and our King, without *Popish* and *Knavish Equivocations.*

Pag. 19. If there were nothing else to prove that *Pamphlet* writ by *J. Gadbury*, this Page of it self is sufficient; for I think no man but him hath a Face so qualified, to put such a Falshood upon the World, and to entertain his Reader with the relation of a Story, that gives the lie to his own knowledge, at the same moment; and therefore I do refer it to every, or any Reader for judgment, provided he hath not been of too many Religions. He chargeth me with saying, *That I knew no ground of a difference in the Year 1690.* and now in 1693. *I pretend to find one*: I stand amazed to think any man should have such a Stock of Impudence to tell such a notorious Lie with so much Confidence, and therefore pray hear the Story fairly. In the *Epistle* to my *Almanack* 1690. I have these Words, *The Ground of our Difference I know not, and would desire him to tell that; but when I was beyond Sea, and he thought he should never see me more, he wrote a Book against me, called a* Reply, *so full of malice, Ill Language, Lies, and malicious Expressions, almost impossible to be believed, or that a Villain should be so ungenteel to a man in Tribulation, that never gave him the least occasion imaginable; if I did, let him speak,* &c. Now it appears that he takes the first six or seven words of the *Paragraph* and from thence says I tell the world, *I know no cause of difference*: 'Tis true, I say so still, *I know of no cause he had to begin that Quarrel with me*; and he knows he began, for he printed first, and abused me basely, and that was the Cause on my side; but the Cause on his, and the reason why he writ that villainous *Reply* in 1687. I know not, and therefore would desire him to tell it, for it is not his Impudence, and *Popish* way of lying shall silence me, so long as I have Justice on my side: The first occasion of our difference did indeed appear to me, in the end of *September* 1680. he and I then being in company, I called his *cousin Cellier* (so he then own'd her) a hard Name, for which I thought he would have beaten me, but that I was not willing to it: There was also another Reason about that time; for one day he told me in some Anger, *That I had spoil'd my Fortune by writing against Popery in my Prodromus*, a little thing that was published about the time he was in *Gaol*; these things might broil in his Stomach all this while, as indeed I know they did; and tho I have heard by others of his scurrilous Reflections on me, I always spoke of him with respect, and gave him a good Report; and however these might be the occasion of difference on his side, I did not take notice of any thing till he printed in 1687. and that was the cause I contend with him; but what cause and reason he had to write that I know not, and desire him to tell me; for the cause of that Book must be the cause of our difference.

But at last he quarrels with *Merlin's Black-Thumb*! Alas, poor *John*! set *Merlin's Black Thumb* against *Jack Thimble's Black Life*; What! meddle with my Trade, when you know what a Broadside I have at you? Indeed *John* I thought you had been better furnished with Sense, than I find you are; remember from whence you came, you are indeed hot and heavy, like a *Taylor's Goose*; and therefore have at you in your own Way, and your old Trade.

'Tis a Champion great,
My Muse doth relate
With St. George *and the rest of the Fighters*
How with Finger in Neck
He did boldly attack
His Bosom Friends, and his Backbiters.

Cross-Legg'd on his Throne,
He govern'd alone,
Notwithstanding his Hell was so near,
He call'd for his Bodkin,
And Thimble, *that odd thing*
And obediently both did appear.

And because he shall not think I am grown dull and barren in Anagrams, I'll give him one in answer to his, tho not so Gallows high.

John Gadbury

She got the Swine, Hell form'd this
Bury'd in a Hog.

At Hell of old did to the Swine retire,
So the old Sow *did the* young Boar *inspire.*

(*vicious* Bog,
And all her Pains was bury'd in
(*a* Hog.

Pag. 20. As to the Book he here rails at, and reviles, there are more Astrological Truths in that contemptible Treatise, than ever he knew, or was able to inform the World of; and for his calling it a railing beastly Treatise, I shall only say this, *That I have a Nasty beast-like Fellow to deal with*; and let him, if he thinks fit, answer the Astrologick part, and let that which he calls railing alone; and I do assure him, I shall kiss his hand in Print again very speedily.

At last he asketh me, if *J. G.* is so bad a man as I represent him to be, how doth he keep clear of the Law, *&c.* Why *John*! were not you indicted by Mr. *Godden* for debauching his *Wife*? Were not you taken up in *Charles* the Second's Time, and kept in Prison 8 or 10 Weeks? Were you not taken up in the *Summer* 1690. and in custody 8 or 9 Weeks, and both these for Crimes against the Government; and do you call this escaping the law all this while? Take your self by the Memory again, and consider. And whosoever will but consider the number of men destroyed in 1685. Blood being then spilt in Pastime; and the Blood-hunting then, and in some Years before, he will soon be able to tell whether they were Bloody Reigns or not?

I find in the conclusion that Mr. *J. G.* is going to publish a *Book* called the *Ungrateful Daemon dispossess'd*, I believe it will be a mighty ingenious thing, because it is founded upon *Conjuring*; for whoever goeth to dispossess a *Daemon*, in *English* a *Devil*, must do it by *Prayers*, or by *Conjuring*; by *Prayer* he cannot, his Life and Conversation too wicked to effect such a thing; but by *Conjuring* I cannot tell what to say to it, because it is a new Trade he hath taken up, and that he learn'd it of his *Priest*, with their *Hoc est Corpus*: But methinks if he could do it by *Conjuring*, he might have cast the *Devil* out of his *Wife* by this time, she being mad, and he having had her about six years, long enough to have done that, which to this day he hath not done; I am afraid he is a meer *Juggler*, and cannot conjure: however I will at the End of my Book, give him a *Copy* of *Verses* to put at the beginning of his; And they are as followeth:

In Commendation of J. Gad. and his

New Conjuring Book.

Call good Assistance in, the Men of Note,
Go fetch the Tapers, Rod and Conjuring-Coat;
Now draw a Circle, draw it plain and fair,
And in the middle place our Conjurer;
Make all the horrid signs and characters,
To raise in the spectators dreadful Fears;
Write all the Thundring, Frightful Names thereon,
Of Anael, Raphael, Zadkiel, Metroton,
Pauiel, Cassiel, Tetragrammaton:
With Rod and Book in hand, let him appear,
Arm'd with the Cross, that makes his Devils fear:
Now is he safe, now let the Work begin,
Now let him call his Captain Devil in,
With all this Rake-hell Tribe, Old Satan by,
And bring with them Hell's Grand Artillery.
His Joyful Fiends thus met, with fury hurl'd,
We'll leave them now to dispossess the World;
Go call Queen Mab, and Great King Oberon,
And ask them what the Devil they have done?
To send a Fool, a Fool that prides himself,
Of being Chief, nay the Chief Sovereign Elf;
Satan's Successive Heir, the Errant Fairie,
That pinch'd by Night the Thighs of Joan and Mary;
This Prince of Daemons, that commands each Elf,
What! cast them out of others, not thy self?
The Reason's plain, he to himself is civil,
He is a Compound, and the most part Devil:
Then who can think the Elf from's self will run,
That Satan e're will dispossess his own.
What! cast out Daemons now, is Trade grown slack,
True Juggler still, here's honest Conjuring Jack.
Your Wife is mad, pray let your Skill appear.
Begin at home, cast out the Devil there.
But hold, to give Advice in that I'm loth,

You Two being one, one Devil serves you both:
Nay, 'tis a frugal way, can you agree,
One single Devil serves a whole family.
But what's one Devil to the mighty Host,
When Jack himself can of his Legions boast.
Well, by these Titles now may'st thou prefer,
Thy Prince's slave, and Hell-born Conjurer.
Go Curse and Conjure with your Popish-Crew,
Your Cross, your Dagon-Deity and You.

FINIS.

Lightning Source UK Ltd.
Milton Keynes UK
UKOW06f2309110814

236775UK00013B/299/P